Thirteen Ways of Looking At a Bureaucrat:

Writing on Governing

JEFF RICH

Copyright © 2023 by Jeff Rich

The moral right of the author has been asserted.

First paperback edition: July 2023

ISBN: 978-0-6451592-4-0 (Print)

ISBN: 978-0-6451592-4-0 (E-Book)

www.theburningarchive.com

Melbourne, Australia

Yet, Warwick, in despite of all mischance,
Of thee thyself and all thy complices,
Edward will always bear himself as king:
Though Fortune's malice overthrow my state,
My mind exceeds the compass of her wheel.

(Shakespeare, *King Henry IV*, IV 3)

The only way to be in agreement with life is to disagree with ourselves.

(Bernardo Soares, heteronym of Fernando Pessoa)

Table of Contents

Chapter One Entering the Maze of Power..........................2
 Entering the maze of power..3
Chapter Two Silenced Voice of the Bureaucrat..................26
 On writing speeches..27
 An interlude on disaffection and truth..31
 Free speech and the public service..32
 Cultural decay and political institutions.....................................37
 On the traumatic origin of Machiavelli, *The Prince*...................41
 On the renunciation of the political world..................................43
 Free speech for public servants and Mandelstam......................46
 Oh Henry, what have you done?..49
 Writing between the lines...50
Chapter Three Thirteen Ways of Looking at a Bureaucrat.54
 Thirteen ways of looking at a bureaucrat...................................55
 I Vigilance among stillness...58
 II The three-eyed raven..61
 III The craft of the cameo actor..64
 IV In unity is death..66
 V The beauty of the bureaucrat..70
 VI Through barbaric glass darkly...73
 VII At the feet of thin men...76
 VIII Involved in what I know..77
 IX Servants of Utopia...78
 X Flight in green light..83
 XI People who live in glass coaches...86
 XII The thaw, the flight..87
 XIII The long waits of winter...88
Chapter Four Governing the Drunken Commons................90
 Governing the drunken commons...91
Chapter Five From Flashbacks to Testimony....................122
 Reflections on the Child Abuse Royal Commission...................123
 The remembered child who speaks of trauma..........................124
 Notes on history of child sexual abuse in Victoria....................137
Chapter Six Ordinary Virtues of Governing Well.............152
 Good government starts today..153
 From political decay to ordinary virtues of governing well......159
 On humility..161

Republics in distress...165
To repair republics with big ideas or ordinary virtues?...........169
On human frailty in governing...174
Able Archer, virtue and human decision-making...................178
On the virtue of not knowing..180
To govern does not equal to change....................................186
The ordinary virtues of governing well................................189

Chapter Seven The Crisis in Australian Politics...............206
Three dilemmas of government..207
The crisis in Australian politics 2010-2013..........................211
Untimely thoughts on the parliamentary crisis.....................230
Time for a real debate on debates.......................................233

Chapter Eight Journal of Some Plague Years..................236
The Plague Year...237
The Great Seclusion..239
Plague notes..242
Thucydides' tower..245
Public health rules, OK?...246
Reflections on the current unrest..251
Captain Ahab and lockdown in Melbourne...........................253
From here to immunity: from pandemic to endemic..............255
Report from a besieged city..259
Dr Cogito endures Melbourne's fifth lockdown.....................261
Cease the endless war against the virus..............................264

Chapter Nine Political Disorder..270
Political disorder and decay in Australia..............................271
Citizenship is a spiritual experience....................................274
Myths of power: merchant, soldier, sage...?.........................276
Perestroika..278
The Meaning of a coup...281
The political ghosts of literature...285
Identity crisis: some theses on identity politics....................290
Frankenstein's children..294
The impeachment of the republic..296
Notes on my reading in 2019..302
Six asides on the USA 2020 election....................................306
The Time of Troubles to come in America............................320
Doom, disaster and decay..323

Chapter Ten On the institutions of government...............340

On metaphors and machinery of government..........................341
　　Structure of government paper..351
　　Treasury's Red Book - seven reflections...................................376
　　Behavioural Anecdotes Team...378
　　The collapsing new buildings of government..........................382
　　Bureaucratic Utopianism...388
　　The failure of institutions in the pandemic crisis....................393
　　The true history of the bureaucracy gang................................396
　　Politicisation of the public service...413
Chapter Eleven Beware of Staring into the Abyss............*428*
　　Governing through disasters..429
　　The tragedy of the modern university......................................430
　　On suicide..433
　　Mental illness and government failure.....................................436
Chapter Twelve Towards Life After Democracy...............*448*
　　Cultural fragmentation and authority collapse.......................449
　　The post-democratic society is here..452
　　Our barren, deformed political society.....................................455
　　How democracies really die...459
　　Democracy's discontents..463
　　Letter from Melbourne, mirror to the post-democratic world.468
Chapter Thirteen On Leaving the Maze of Power..............*486*

13 Ways of Looking at a Bureaucrat

Chapter One   Entering the Maze of Power

Entering the maze of power

1. The Maze of Power

When I look back now on my life as a bureaucrat, I see a man lost in a maze. The man imagined himself into this maze. His imagination threw him into this maze. The maze was made from images and mirrors of power, and at the centre of the maze, so the story was told, was the Minotaur of Power itself.

This lost man, who called himself alternately writer and bureaucrat, both with blends of pride and shame, wandered lost in this maze for thirty-three years. The maze of power was not a diversion from life. It was the necessary adventure of my life. Few who called themselves both writer and bureaucrat have walked so deeply into the maze and left to write the tales.

There is no solution to this maze. The maze cannot be abolished or solved. It is like Kafka's fable of the law. No one else could ever have been admitted to this powerful maze. This maze was made only for me. Some unknown beast who prowled the maze shut all its exits to any other entrants. Then the beast left and laughed at the darkest secret of the maze. There was no Minotaur at its centre, or so I believe now, after 33 years searching to find it. There were monsters in that maze, but no central Minotaur, and the monsters who did prowl the ways of power were made by my own mad mind.

Perhaps you will believe my parable of the maze after reading my fragmentary tales of search, adventure and illusion, which I have documented in this book. Perhaps you also are lost in a maze of power, a maze invented by your imagination. You may have been lured into that maze by tradition or ambition or progress or social justice or a love of political combat. But, you will never see the maze whole. You will only ever see fragments, glimpses around corners. There is no big picture in the maze. There is a kaleidoscope of fragments. There is no solution. There are only stories to share with survivors.

Ultimately, I wrote myself out of the maze. Or rather, I was writing when the floor of the maze gave way, and I fell into an underworld where I could no longer say I was a bureaucrat, where I could only say I was a writer. There was no lord of this underworld. There was no prohibition on looking back. So I did look back, and, in these fragments, shards, essays and notes, I reported all thirteen ways of looking at a bureaucrat.

2. My story from the outside

Viewed from the outside, like some newspaper article, if newspapers wrote articles about real bureaucrats, my story is simpler. There are no parables. There is no drama. It is a simple, dull story of career failure, concealed beneath an overcoat.

I was born in 1963 and grew up in Brisbane and Melbourne, in that outer reach of the Global American Empire, known by some as Australia. I was old enough to know the last decade of quality university education, when it was still free, in more ways than one. I studied history at both the University of Melbourne and Australian National University, where I met most of the greats of post-war Australian history. I briefly engaged in student politics, before I realised I was not a political animal. I dedicated myself to curiosity and culture, and read widely in the humanities. I began to form a view, or many views, of the world. I sensed even then that my views would never fit into any school. Yet I followed the PhD path to become an academic; but I was born too late to belong to the boomer generation that enjoyed the post-war booms of the economy and higher education, and the years of easy appointments to tenured posts. The songs of my youth were about unemployment, recession, social alienation, and the restructuring of education to drive the economy forward. I had no powerful friends, no supportive patrons, and no confidence there was a market that would buy my dream to write for life. By the last year of my university days, 1989, there was no prospect of a career for me in the academy. So I turned back to a safer form of political adventure and a securer form of stable employment, and sought a job in the public service.

My last year at university was also the final year of the declared Cold War. The Berlin Wall fell. Tears were spilled in Canberra for the fate of protesters at Tiananmen Square. While my career as an academic historian fizzled, Francis Fukuyama declared the End of History. Mikhail Gorbachev sought to revive democratic socialism in the Soviet Union when it was dying in the West, infested with the cancer of financial markets. Socialist politics had already died in Australia. Since 1983 the nominally leftist Hawke Government had implemented the 'Third Way' or 'triangulated' politics that would later be claimed as the invention, in Britain, of Blair and Anthony Giddens, whose works I knew in detail, and in the USA of Clinton (Bill) and his pretend Machiavelli, Morris (Dick). Economic restructuring, market liberalism and American globalism ruled the air waves. There were still pockets of resistance in Australia, including in the state to which I was returning, Victoria. There, the philosopher-economist-bureaucrat, Peter Sheehan, still dreamed grand plans for socialism in one province. The Government of John Cain energetically pursued industry policies and social justice strategies, and even declared gestures of defiance to America, such as making Melbourne a nuclear-free port. But the progressives of the South had misread the times, laid some bad bets, and found they could not pay the bills. As the economy turned, the State Bank collapsed and the unions revolted. This last democratic socialist government of the South, snared by history's crooks and turns, however, was the same government that I would join as a trainee public servant in January 1990.

The collapse of Victorian social justice dreams gave me many lessons in history, power and the real world. Indeed, my choice of the Victorian bureaucracy as the arena of my new career was not wholly without luck. My writing skills were more admired and appreciated here than by the saturnine academics of ANU. I had entered the maze of power, but, at that time, I did not understand that it was actually a maze, nor that there were monsters that prowled its halls. I believed I was in the playground of power, and sat at the shoulders of the commanders of government, the masters of bureaucracy. I met some extraordinary people, some of whom you will encounter later in this book, and for a decade enjoyed what seemed initially like the rise of a talented, senior bureaucrat of the future. After my trainee year, I spent three years in the education and training bureaucracy where I advised on glamorous strategies and councils of state and federal powers. I moved in 1993 into the Department of Premier and Cabinet, and witnessed up close the mobilisation of the institutions of the bureaucracy under the Kennett Government. In 1995, I moved sideways to RMIT, the technical college promoted to university in the 1980s, with a former mentor from those days of public sector reform, but stayed only briefly before I returned to the core public service in 1998. Then I pulled an oar on the transformation of the economy, society, culture, and government itself by the new wide world of the web, e-commerce and information technology. In 2000, I moved back to the Department of Premier and Cabinet to manage Commonwealth-State relations, write keynote speeches, and practise rare, arcane arts to fire all the synapses of government. In 2004, I joined a new Department for Victorian Communities to support social enterprises, business philanthropy and the not-for-profit sector. In 2006, I joined the strangely named Department of Human Services, in which I would stay until the end of my career in November 2022, through this Department's happy divorces and forced remarriages of the health and welfare functions of my provincial home. The Department was renamed Health in 2009, Health and Human Services in 2014, and back to Health in 2021. In those last sixteen years in the Health Department, I lost the early sheen of a successful career. I did good, but I did not do well. Over time, I would make hidden, silent contributions to the way of my life in my minor province of South Eastern Australia. I sought insight, judged with prudence, and listened for compromise on many vexing social problems: alcohol, drugs, child sexual abuse, infertility, IVF, ageing, surrogacy, mental illness, trauma, violence, terrorism, health budgets, health technology, the COVID pandemic, child health, adolescence, grief, remembrance, redress, and, in general, the whole range of human suffering. Yet the outward signs of success did not come. There were no prizes, no honours, no celebrations. I was never promoted above the rank, or job classification level to use the bureaucratic language of human resources, that I had attained by the mid-1990s. More junior, ambitious, favoured colleagues climbed to the top of the public service, while I was left to brood on my constant failure to join the decorated ranks of the executive class. I made dozens and dozens of applications, and received more rejections than was good for my soul. I secured no real patrons. My mentors retired, grew old and drifted away. My independent mind and poetic soul no doubt estranged me from managers and rivals. Rejection harvested shame. Shame bred resentment. I came to believe I was blacklisted, not without some intuited and observed evidence. The balance of my identity shifted. I was no longer a bureaucrat who wrote at night for the drawer. I became a writer who drew on his dark night as a bureaucrat to support the life of the mind.

Despite the pain of my final decade in the public service, I remain proud of what I did with so many colleagues and fallen comrades over those 33 years. Much of what I did found its way into writing, letters, emails, briefs, submissions, presentations and reports. A few pieces of that writing can still be found on the internet or in the State Library of Victoria, such as the policies I co-wrote (since all writing in government is a compromise of authors) on alcohol and drugs, and on assisted reproductive treatment. But most of the writing is locked away, lost or concealed in the Public Record Office; or destroyed as the transient ravings of a disowned minor government official. I no longer have access to it, and I cannot share those texts with you. I remember some of those texts fondly. One of the good things I did in my 33 years of public service was to strive to write, even when lost in the maze of power, meaningful words of truth, beauty and compassion.

13 Ways of Looking at a Bureaucrat

3. My strange inner life as an outcast bureaucrat

But throughout those 33 years I did write on government, power and bureaucracy outside of the office. I wrote in diaries. I wrote in conference papers. I wrote in private letters, blogs, and essays. By the end of my career in 2022, I had accumulated enough writing on government to make a book; a book that might redeem the pain of my many career disappointments and failures; that might show other searchers in the maze of power some tricks to dispel illusions; that would speak honestly at last of that profession damned to silence, the bureaucrat; and that might offer songs of innocence and songs of experience that commemorate the true history of the bureaucracy. These writings appear through this book, culled from the many notebooks in which I recorded my torments, and conceived from the many perspectives with which you may glimpse a bureaucrat.

These writings were driven by an inner torment, an unanswered question, and the shame of being an outcast in the vocation I had chosen. The inner torment was my doubts over whether I could write, and whether by sacrificing my time to serve governments in an office I was not destroying my spirit, and any potential I had to write a text that might be taken up in the infinite conversation of culture. Was I a writer or was I merely a that despised character, a bureaucrat? And if I was a bureaucrat, was there any way to confer some nobility of spirit to this lowly caste that fate had assigned me to? The unanswered question arose from that search for some nobility work. Today, I think the question is: how do we govern our shared lives? But for years that question was concealed by a mirage question. What is power? I realise now that for three decades, when I looked for the Minotaur of Power, I was also asking: how can power be used for virtuous government, and was I capable of defeating the monsters required to govern with virtue? Could I be the hero who confronts the monster in the labyrinth? The shame was caused by my manifest failure to be that hero of art or power. All outward signs pointed to failure. I was neither the writer nor the bureaucrat that I wanted to be.

Entering the Maze of Power

Over 33 years I wandered through the maze of power seeking relief from the torment, the words for my unvoiced question, and acceptance to cure my shame. But I could not find them. So I also searched the libraries of the world for some scholarly, philosophical or literary map to allow me to escape the maze. I looked for books on bureaucracy.

4. Books on Bureaucracy

I tried hard to find the best books of bureaucracy or on the form of conduct that I began to call governing. There are many books on politics, and many manuals for princes; but there are few good books on governing and no good books on the bureaucracy. Weber laid out axioms but did not animate them. Kafka presented a nightmare of bureaucracy, but did not speak of his daytime experience. Hannah Arendt projected from her philosophical cave the banality of evil onto pitiless bureaucrats, and, following her model, the entire academic apparatus of America piled on the banality of bureaucracy. The discipline of the oxymoron, political science, has produced almost nothing with insight, despite reams of petty resentment about the people who organise the affairs of their comfortable lives. Public choice theory turned bureaucracy into a rent-seekers' cartoon. Political memoirs rarely disclose the work of the servants and stage-hands who work away from the cameras. Journalism is one large puff of smoke, and all the news reporters, commentators and talking heads of modern media dare not admit they are mostly stenographers who serve communications bureaucrats. They have observed nothing. They have learned nothing. A few novels, such as *Wolf Hall*, may offer glimpses. But television and film has been corrupted by the rise of the political mercenary and spin doctor, by monotonous marketing, and American fantasies of the *West Wing*. As a result of this cultural silence, the public imagination has next to no way to look at authentic, complex, real bureaucrats.

So, I decided to write a good book on the bureaucracy. For a long time, I thought this book had to conform to outsiders' expectations. It would have to persuade the academics, the publishers and the senior officials. It would have to provide a solution, and not only analyse problems. It would have to be sound and unimpeachable for its consistent, coherent political opinions. But all these expectations silenced me. I realised instead towards of my career as a bureaucrat that I had been writing this good book on bureaucracy all my life in my notebooks, briefings, essays, diaries and fragments. I realised this writing arose from conditions that all the bad books on bureaucracy did not share. I had lived and lost my way in the labyrinth. I had struggled in my notebooks to describe the enigmatic *habitus* that housed this way of life. I had struggled to give testimony on this despised profession that knows power more intimately than any other.

So I came, at the end, to view differently all my shameful failures to write and to voice the unknown question of how to govern. These texts and fragments were not shameful confessions to be hidden and burned on my death. They were the fabric of the book that might show a handful of readers some new ways to look at a bureaucrat. I decided to use them first in open public writing on governing, and then in 2023 to sew them into this book. Here are two fragments from my notebooks that recorded both my failed attempts to master the maze of power, and the early steps I took to leave the maze.

In an undated, untitled *Notebook,* which I think I wrote in 2000, I first intuited the metaphor of the maze to evoke the paradox of power. *Governing, it is a strange action, a strange way of being. Few ever approach it. It is subject to so many myths. Its essential unapproachability is the enigma at the heart of the castle. We want to grasp power, to see the room, the person, the act in which it is done. We want to seize power like the vital essence. But there is never such a moment. This power is always elsewhere. As we move closer and closer to the rooms of power, we find again and again, it slips away.*

In a *Notebook* from 2003, which I named, *The Angel of History*, I used the metaphor of the labyrinth and expressed the frustration with

Entering the Maze of Power

bad books on bureaucracy. *Few men have written about power from power's centre. By contrast, there are many unreliable fantasies. Sanctimonious jeremiads who blunder 'J'accuse' on their return, to be fêted in New York. Flattered egotists who are carried away by conversing on a first-name basis with the masters of the universe at cocktail parties. But I have crawled through the maze of the Minotaur, felt the beast's hot breath, and crawled back to contemplative silence, where with every attempt at fidelity, I piece together the perceptions, the emotions I felt there. And now I am not even certain that there was a real centre. Was the beast in the centre? Was there a centre? Was its breath an illusion? Was it following me? The centre always receding from itself, like some non-Euclidean geometry.*

I am a refugee from this many-dimensional maze, and do not even know if I can write a good book on the bureaucracy. All I can do is to give my testimony. My writings on bureaucracy might illuminate a form of conduct, governing. To appreciate how governing is different to politics, you need to have been in government; but, after all, many of us have. A good book on bureaucracy can change minds about governing, politics, and democracy. It can open minds to ways that the governed and governing can live well with each other. No utopias. No grand plans. But some modest improvements and accommodations of our crooked timber. My book has this modest goal, however strange or monstrous its shape.

5. Machiavelli

If I could find no good books on bureaucracy, I still was able to find four writers who could guide me out of the maze. Niccolo Machiavelli is the first of those guides through this maze. You might think of him as a master of political philosophy, or the inventor of modern realism about politics, or the Renaissance genius of political chicanery. There have been many Machiavellis. I think of Machiavelli as rather like me: a humble, failed bureaucrat, who turned to writing and to conversation with the ghosts of power to overcome the trauma of his dismissal from office. In the 'Dedication' to *The Prince* he wrote with pride about his book on princes, and how princes are best observed from the perspective of an outcast citizen with no power.

> Nor I hope will it be considered presumptuous for a man of low and humble status to dare discuss and lay down the law about how princes should rule; because, just as men who are sketching the landscape put themselves down in the plain to study the nature of mountains and the highlands, and to study the low-lying land they put themselves high on the mountains, so, to comprehend fully the nature of the people, one must be a prince, and to comprehend fully the nature of princes one must be an ordinary citizen.

Machiavelli wrote in a tradition known as the mirror of princes. His most famous work, *The Prince*, which earned him enduring fame, was an attempt to advise the new Medici rulers of Florence how to govern the city. Machiavelli was the former Secretary to this small but influential city government in a divided Renaissance Italy. But his book was not the work of an acclaimed, esteemed, honoured bureaucrat. Machiavelli wrote *The Prince* at his farmhouse retreat after being dismissed from office, tortured by the new powers, and exiled from his city. His preferred form of government, the self-governing city republic, was destroyed. His one big idea, a civil militia to defend the republic and to protect an independent Italy, lay in ruins. His skills and wisdom were unwanted. His mind was scarred by his humiliation and torture. So Machiavelli wrote *The Prince* to restore his dignity, and to find himself a role as a counsellor to the newly powerful court.

We might imagine, on the basis of his mythic reputation as the most ruthless of schemers, that Machiavelli succeeded in his aim, and realised his ambition so that he could practise what he preached. But his plaintive pleas were ignored. His books on power were never published in his lifetime. Only after decades did the Medici indulge the pleading Machiavelli with a patronage project to write a history of

Entering the Maze of Power

Florence. His schemes remained imaginary only. He died a banished, humbled, impotent outsider and failed bureaucrat. But his writings outlived him, and became part of the infinite conversation about power, history and statecraft. He left a legacy because he searched the maze of power for insight, not appearances. He searched for effect, not position. In the Dedication to *The Discourses,* he wrote

> For to judge aright, one should esteem men because they are generous, not because they have the power to be generous; and, in like manner, should admire those who know how to govern a kingdom, not those who, without knowing how, actually govern one.

There have been times over the last two decades when I have identified with this story of Machiavelli as an outcast official who redeems himself through writing on history and government. But I have not written a mirror of princes. Rather I have taken secret snaphots to a hidden experience: the bureaucrat who governs.

6. Havel

The second inspiration for this guidebook to the maze of power is Vaclav Havel. Havel was no bureaucrat. He might even be considered the antithesis of bureaucracy. The Czech playwright, essayist and dissident celebrated the strange, eccentric and vital, not the regulated, standard and conformist. But he did propose a virtuous politics that lived in truth, and he did find himself lost in the maze of power in 1990 when, after years of surveillance and imprisonment by his government, Havel became the first President of post-communist Czechoslovakia.

Havel will appear many times in this book, and he has long inspired both sides of my double life. I will only say here that Havel gave me the idea and the design to sew the shreds of my life in government into this book's tapestry of fragments. His memoir *To the Castle and Back* is the best literary memoir of a political leader. It is composed of fragments, including notes from his work diary as President, later reflections, his instructions to officials, and brief notes on politics and power, which never quite rise to the status of essays. It needs to be read not as a linear narrative or a coherent argument or a preening piece of reputation management, like most memoirs of politicians. It is a text informed by the literary experiments of the twentieth century. It is also a text informed by Havel's conscience, humility, and awareness of his many failures. I have used his text as a model for my own book about my journey to the maze and back.

7. Kafka

My third guide is Franz Kafka. Kafkaesque is a term for bureaucracy that is passing out of usage with our declining cultural literacy, and the passage of time. *Game of Thrones* or *Utopia* or *House of Cards* or some other Netflix show has supplanted the master of Prague, who wrote and lived in the shadow of the great Castle . Kafka's great unfinished *Das Schloss* (*The Castle,* although *schloss* can also mean 'lock') described the same castle that Havel inhabited. I suppose it is rarely read these days, however common the term, Kafkaesque. But for nearly a century, Kafka was considered the greatest literary guide to bureaucracy.

Kafka could even make a claim to be a bureaucrat. He worked as a lawyer in the workers health insurance authority. I can only imagine he would have been a difficult employee to manage, perhaps not unlike myself. His perceptions of reality were the very opposite of the recipe for leadership trucked in some schools of government: uncommon abilities matched to common beliefs, and constant adaptation to the demands from above.

His novel *The Castle* represented an early version of the symbol of the maze of power. Its protagonist, a land surveyor known only as 'K.', arrives in a village, located beneath a great and mysterious castle. Kafka recounts the futile attempts by K. to enter the Castle, and to master the strange rules that control access to the masters of that universe. He never gains access to the corridors of power. He never even confirms for certain that the Count he assumed controlled the castle even exists. The Count is another version of my Minotaur of Power. There are times throughout this book that I refer to myself as a lowly under-castellan of a minor provincial government. I imagined myself as a character like K. searching for the mysterious authorities of *The Castle*.

8. Stevens

The fourth and final guide to my ways of looking at a bureaucrat is the American poet, Wallace Stevens. This whole book is the final realisation of an idea that I many years ago to respond to all the bad books and lazy journalism on bureaucracy, which locked perceptions of the bureaucrat in narrow confines, by writing an essay variation on Wallace Stevens' poem, *Thirteen Ways of Looking at a Blackbird*.

Stevens poem is one of perspective. Each segment of the poem, way of looking at a blackbird, evoked sensations that are fragmentary, incomplete, partial, particular to the viewer, but not restricted to the viewer. The reader of the poem discovers, within the simple reality of the humble blackbird, connections to the enigmas of the universe. I wanted to show how the plain, despised, ordinary life of a bureaucrat, made invisible by the perceptions of outsiders, could be perceived poetically with the insights of an ostracised insider.

Stevens is also a guide in other ways. Stevens is a great modernist poet. I have read him for my whole adult life, and have written minor, late modernist poems in his shadow. Stevens also combined, like Kafka, Machiavelli and even Havel, the life of a writer and a bureaucrat of sorts. He pursued a successful career as an insurance executive. He published late, after a long silence. He believed ultimately, and for little reason, that the imagination is the greatest good. He celebrated the nobility of the quiet, ordinary suburban life.

Ultimately I realised my idea to rewrite Stevens' poem as an essay on bureaucracy through a series of long blog posts, screamed to a silent internet, in 2016. Those posts, now edited, form the third part of this book and its spiritual core.

9. Ambivalence from the beginning

Unlike Stevens I never really succeeded as an executive in my company. I never had a secretary to write out the poems I composed on my commuter ride. I never became a bountiful emperor of ice-cream. Instead, I recorded my gnashing ambivalence in diaries, journals, notebooks, and slips of quotations. I did this for decades, until finally in 2015, the long suppressed voice moved into the symbol of the burning archive, the blog from which are drawn the essays of this book and my earlier essays on culture, history and literature, *From The Burning Archive: essays and fragments 2015-2022*.

Many of the earliest notebooks are lost, although I remember almost from the start of my career this terrible ambivalence. Was I a writer? Was I a bureaucrat? Do I follow the path of invention or the tracks of necessity? And is there another path, the life of the thoughtful bureaucrat who also writes? Could I make that path my own, without precedent, without patrons, and with very few models?

Today, as I sample these old notebooks, I see the recurring images of my imagination of power. Here are some samples.

Notebook, January 1995. I want to be a sage, to write like a sage; but when I write I feel like a confused, cliche ridden fool. But I can change my thinking. I can write like a humble pilgrim, one not granted with great gifts, but with an insatiable passion of the spirit.

Notebook, March 1995. A dream. The evil king is seated on the throne, at the end of the carriage, beckoning me to join him. His crown of thorns, twisted inwards, makes me think him evil. Two attendants prepare a declaration, which concerns my work, the Department of Premier and Cabinet. They prepare a parchment for my signature, which has my name on top, and is written in archaic, formal calligraphy. I snatch the parchment from their hands and set

Entering the Maze of Power

fire to it. As I burn it, holding it up for display, I retreat and escape from the king and attendants.

Notebook, March 1996. In doing my current work there is a vileness to it. I know I am pretending, being an agent of others' powers. This pretending is deeply distressing. I keep at it for the money, not the satisfaction of the task. Is the writing a way to avoid my being? Hard thoughts on demoralisation and depersonalisation at work. The games of work let the psyche disintegrate. That is the power of Bliss for me: the rebirth of the soul after its death in work.

Notebook, April 1997. Where is civility in intellectual discussion about the Prime Minister? We are talking speech acts here. There is a disavowal of personal responsibility – one's own and others – for what is said. And, of course, lots of cheap and stupid rhetoric about politics, most of which is no more than dumb opinion, petty, sniping gossip. Where to find and put a voice in this craziness? How to avoid being choked in this stupidity? Maybe a book of essays arguing for a different tone in public discussion, a style of responding to concerns and views of others.

Notebook, 1998. I discovered a rhythm and a metier more true than the consuming nonsense of my government, my suit and tie self. This time I know that I cannot lure myself on with one more deception about ambition. This time I know that I must imagine my life differently.

Notebook, 2000. We all would rather be at home with our children enjoying the garden or a sunny lunch with friends than here discussing the laws of State. The bureaucrat is a troubled witness of power's dismays. The bureaucrat's deceptions begin with himself. He is a liar for his country who conceals even from himself the truth. He is a coward who cowers from his mirror and jumps at his own shadow. The archetypal story of the bureaucrat is the survivor of the purge.

13 Ways of Looking at a Bureaucrat

Notebook, August 2015. Here I am listening to the Premier, feeling alienated from government, the department, political rhetoric. I feel my own path must be to write, but do not believe I have any secure likelihood of success. Here the Premier says determining priorities is about changing KUL-CHA ... I wonder if I can find my way back to any real job. Nothing will ever happen for me as long as my nemesis is around. I want to find a way to produce a meaningful contribution, but I have lost the thread of the value of my working life.

10. My prison as a private intellectual

In 1997 I wrote down in my diary a text from the *Bhagavad Gita*,

> The man who in his work finds silence, and who sees that silence is work, this man in truth sees the Light and in all his work finds peace.

Notebook, June 1997. Too long with no writing, but then the noise of caring and action, deepens in contrast the silence of this contemplation. The temptation of silence is made alluring by the idiocy of solipsism. To write is to flee conversation; but conversation may be the only time when words matter. Inventing thoughts and sentences which to float them beyond my death, I repeat the ceremonies of many past times, the floating biers of the Celts. I can find in the words of a few writers a place to dream myself into active thought; but these writers are uncommon, and mostly now, old men, who were disciplined in a style of thought, a manner of dispute, which I admire and aspire to even though I rarely experience. It is not the clubby identifications of today's academics, hence my appeal for my private intellectuals. Our marketplaces of ideas are crowded with rubbish. I would like a thinker to come to my room and converse with me intimately, and in the private concerns and communion, a true growth in thought might occur, as in a Zen retreat or well-practised psychotherapy. There are more paths to wisdom than the prolix chest-beating on subjects indirectly known by journalists and

Entering the Maze of Power

academics. So give me private intellectuals: how little is gained by public wrestles over words and phrases. It is comic, futile sport that some lucky talents profit from. Does anyone imagine success or failure in a sporting match affects the fate of the world? In the stands there may be conversations of moment, but the field stages a performance of sound and fury. The partisans of thought fall for the illusion that this performance mimics the world. Alas, no!

Give me more private intellectuals. We hear too much about public intellectuals. They alone will improve out culture, We do not have enough of them. They do not receive enough support. They bear the responsibility to speak for the lives of others, to act as a voice for the voiceless, even though we all know where ventriloquism takes us. But they provide whitewashed solemn tones. Political views rinsed in the same bleach, almost always insulated from responsibility for actual decisions. I want to see more of their opposite number, the private intellectual. Private does not mean silent. It does not seek a voice on some issues. It implies modesty and limitation of voice. It is Montaigne writing to his friends. It is an adviser speaking truth to power. They do not speak from a soap box or in a raggy magazine full of pompous ignorance or another newspaper elaborating information fictions from unreliable sources.

Notebook, April 1997. We expect too much of the wrong standards of our politicians, and do not acknowledge the hard, dirty task they do. That is the part we do not want to see.

For years I meditated on the words of George Steiner ("Silence and the Poet") in my prison of silence: "When the words in the city are full of savagery and lies, nothing speaks louder than the unwritten poem." And the nighttime torments of my fellow bureaucrat, Kafka ("The Silence of the Sirens") enchanted me:

> Now the sirens have a still more fatal weapon than their song, namely their silence. And though admittedly, such a thing has never happened, still it is conceivable that

someone might possibly have escaped from their singing; but from their silence certainly never-ending.

The idea of being a private intellectual, a loyal and invisible servant of power, silenced me for a long time. I did not want to mix my life of the mind and my life as a bureaucrat. I imagined a *vita nuova* of the spirit that would refuse to contemplate the banality of the office. But, from about 2010, I began to release myself from this prison. I began to give speeches in my name. I began to write a blog, *The Happy Pessimist*, under the cloak of a pseudonym. I began to write and talk to selected outsiders. I wrote what I observed when looking at the peculiar bureaucrat that I had become. I released slowly and painfully the shackles of conventional ambition. I relinquished predictable desires for promotion to executive office. I became more writer than bureaucrat. Then, in 2015, I began the *Burning Archive* blog. My writing on government became more common, more forceful, and more open. Sometimes I even broke the old mental patterns that kept me lost in the maze. Many of the pieces in this collection are edited from pieces that appeared originally as those blog posts.

12. *The Year of Governing Dangerously*

In the last year of my career in the bureaucracy, I began a journal of my observations on the failed government institutions in Victoria. I thought I would record some of the malfeasance and stupidity that I saw around me. I subtitled this journal, melodramatically, "a journal of my adventures in 2021 and 2022 to restore decent public institutions in Victoria and save my state from the new authoritarian threat to democracy."

The journal was a response to a specific threat to democracy. It began with me writing,

> On my birthday the Premier declared war against democracy and decency in Victoria through the *Public Health and Wellbeing Amendment (Pandemic Management Bill 2021*. It creates dictatorial powers, but

crucially puts no constraints on the decision-making on pandemics. It even allows for discrimination on grounds of 'attributes and characteristics', including political beliefs or activities.

Victoria's descent into a post-democratic state during the years of the pandemic created the final storm in my mind about my life as a bureaucrat. The journal had mixed motives, as any piece of writing does. At times, I wanted to observe, to document and to interpret what was going on, and my unique insider perspective on the death of a democracy. At other times, I wanted to build on an interpretation of modern politics that was slowly emerging for me, especially after reading John Dunn, *Breaking the Spell of Democracy*, Stein Ringen on power and democracy, and Fukuyama on political disorder. I responded to deep disappointments with governments over decades, and kept alight hope that I could resist the post-democratic state. I harboured, at times, the belief that I could advise an incoming government, or an opposed elite, on how to unwind this disaster, and how to restore decency to modern government. But even then, I wondered whether my thoughts were in any way practical; whether I was driven mostly by a desire for revenge; whether I longed for acceptance and forgiveness by some good lord after so many years experienced as being outcast, unrecognised, and unvalued. I wanted to do more than just be a silent bystander at this tragedy. I wrote, "I realise this morning that I have watched the slow degeneration of the Labor regime for my whole adult life." But the journal was also a way of letting go. I wrote in late October 2021, "I find a kind of peace in just allowing work to follow its course – I am calmed in the morning by the Taoist concept of riding the wind – I see myself as preparing myself for the fall of the regime or indeed its survival."

I wrote that I was forced again into a problem. I was stuck as the inner critic, who had made the socially inconvenient mistake of pointing to the gap between values and practices in the institution that I still believed, falsely, that I had belonged to. In that false belief, I still took some responsibility for this institution, rather than my own life. I knew I was impotent and excluded. Yet I still wanted to find a small, safe, quiet niche, where the collapsing buildings of this broken regime would not fall upon me; and where I could make small improvements to the virtues, culture, bonds that I cared for.

But this wish was stymied, at every turn, by what the bureaucracy and the government had become. I am the despised, accursed share, I wrote. Is exile an option? Is defeating the regime by hiding my capabilities and biding my time a possibility? I began to feel, from pressures of ostracism in the institution and propaganda in the society, like an ostracised Cassandra. I began to wonder whether it would be better to let it all go.

I wrote down from Jordan Peterson, *Beyond Order:*

> How much of my old map do I have to let crumble and burn – with all the pain dying tissue produces – before I can change enough to take my full range of experience into account? Do I have the faith to step beyond what should and must die, and let my new and wiser personality emerge?

I was faced with the dilemma of exit, loyalty, or voice. I chose exit ultimately, but only after the same cycle of thoughts had recurred over thirty-three years. This book was the slow revelation over many painful years of the path for that exit. But I am getting ahead of my story.

13. The maze of this book

My first manager when I joined the public service was weirdly also a poet. She was a member of the Collected Works collective, that was fortunately just around the corner from the office near Flinders Lane where I began as an administrative trainee in 1990. She was a protege of Vincent Buckley. She ultimately returned to the infinite conversation and the teaching profession, but, when supervising me, she complained how the compulsion of managed organisations to write in dot points was destroying her literary style. After 33 years of writing briefs and submissions and talking points, all sorts of texts that had to conform to the hasty reader, I have produced a book of compilations that is encoded against an enigmatic and inexplicable poem.

There are thirteen chapters, of course.

This first chapter is a kind of overture, containing themes and premonitions of my path out of the maze. As you would surely have noticed by now, it is composed of 13 segments, 13 fragments from my burning archive, 13 ways of looking at my life as a bureaucrat.

The second chapter is 'The Silenced Voice of the Bureaucrat'. It contains blog posts on the topic of public servants who write in public, which arguably they are forbidden to do. I felt this interdiction, and the fear of damnation for my transgressions. This chapter includes posts from my first and earliest blog, the *Happy Pessimist*, which can no longer be read online, except if you strike it lucky on the wayback machine.

The third chapter is 'Thirteen Ways of Looking at the Bureaucrat'. I have made small revisions to this essay since its first posting. I have already explained the origins and aims of this chapter.

The fourth chapter is 'Governing the Drunken Commons'. This chapter includes a conference paper that I wrote in 2013/14. It was my first open attempt, while still secretly writing my pseudonymous blog, to step out of my shackled voice as a bureaucrat, and to reflect on the challenges of government. I spoke as a still ambivalent bureaucrat who believed there was a career ahead in that profession, and yet already felt banished to the role of the dissident sage. In this paper, I articulated a kind of ethic of governing, that later found expression in ideas about the ordinary virtues.

The fifth chapter is 'From Flashbacks to Testimony'. This chapter reflects on the intense period in which I combined a life as a private intellectual, historian and bureaucrat. I worked on the Victorian Government's response to the Royal Commission into Institutional

Responses to Child Sexual Abuse. I wrote the paper here during a period of long service leave, when I hoped to make life as a late career academic, only to discover that the universities of today do not have such imagination. It was another major step away from the shackles of the silenced bureaucrat.

The sixth chapter is 'The Ordinary Virtues of Governing Well'. This phrase was for a long time my inspiration, and how I screwed my courage to the sticking place each morning. It was the positive vision that kept me going through all the disillusions and darkness that follows. This chapter includes the transcript of a podcast I did on this topic in 2021.

The seventh chapter is 'The Crisis in Australian Politics'. This was a long piece that appeared on the *Happy Pessimist* blog. It responded to the political crisis that arose in Australia during the leadership crises in the Government in 2009-2013. At the time, I believed the political party system might collapse. I was wrong, but I have not tried to hide my mistakes in these essays. Needless to say, my writing on political matters under a pseudonym was then a risky thing to do. I felt confident, however, that my focus was on institutions and culture, not the horse race of electoral party politics.

The eight chapter is 'Journal of Some Plague Years'. This chapter includes the edited posts on my evolving response to the COVID pandemic. I wrote several posts when working as a very small cog in an out-of-control Catherine Wheel on the Victorian Government response to the pandemic. These texts are written between the lines, to some degree. No inappropriate secrets are revealed. Some scandalous truths are told.

The ninth chapter is 'Political Disorder'. This chapter includes my blog posts on political decay, and the transcript of a podcast I did on this topic in 2021. The podcast also reflects on government responses to the pandemic, as a more general phenomenon of decay in political institutions.

Entering the Maze of Power

The tenth chapter is 'On the Institutions of Government'. This includes blog posts from the *Happy Pessimist* and *Burning Archive* on government culture and institutions. I have included my podcast on the history of bureaucracy, set against the argument of Francis Fukuyama on political disorder. I referred to this argument also in my submission to the Ombudsman on Politicisation of the Public Service that I have included here.

The eleventh chapter is 'Beware of Staring into the Abyss'. It contains my reflections on some of the most ethically and intellectually challenging social policy issues that I dealt with as a bureaucrat, principally in the field of mental health.

The twelfth chapter is 'Towards Life After Democracy'. I have gathered here the essays and fragments that I wrote in the last years of my career in government when I had lost my illusions not only about my career, bureaucracy or the governments which I had served, but I had lost my illusions about our democracy itself.

The thirteenth and final way of looking at a bureaucrat, 'On Leaving the Maze of Power', follows my final days in government. It concludes the story I have begun in this introduction to my imaginary labyrinth.

Chapter Two   Silenced Voice of the Bureaucrat

On writing speeches

(First published on *The Happy Pessimist* blog, July-November 2010, under the pseudonym, Antonio Possevino.)

The embarrassed cliche – calling Julia's rhetoric

"Moving forward" has hit the airwaves, and already the press are wincing in embarrassment when reporting the phrase. Was this reception expected? Maybe, but I doubt it. This was a slogan born of an insular machine. Within a few days of its launch, its use became the story, not the vision that it claims to point towards. Editorials have appeared in the papers saying that surely voters are entitled to something better than trite cliches. A bit of substance, please? Three cheers for the journalists and the commentariat who refuse to swallow and repeat this banal con.

But I expect that Aunt Julia will stubbornly go on and on with the phrase, egged on by the advisers who will tell her it means something important to the focus groups, and that political vision cannot soar above the limited thinking of the ALP's factional hacks. You cannot expect otherwise from this group of professional political operatives, who have made and fabricated the political culture that we live in, by their modern, professional campaign techniques. This slogan is just one such technique: the tie-in phrase, empty enough of meaning that it can serve as a tag line for every ad, every policy, every image. Aunt Julia's rise is nothing if not the return to ascendancy of these hacks, and we can expect them to fill our media with their banal expressions for the next five weeks.

It is unfair, of course, to single out Julia for this weakness - she is but doing what must be done, moving her party forward, not expecting lines delivered in the media to have the value of direct conversations, or acute observations. Tony Abbott's rhetoric I have not yet even looked at, except to see the image of 'action'. Did I really see an image of an 'action contract'? But I am curious whether the mockery of the slogan will crack the shell under which our political leaders defend their inauthenticity. This morning, Jon Faine, the Melbourne radio host, began an interview with Lindsay Tanner, the Government Finance Minister, on this very point. 'Why do you continue to use this meaningless phrase that has already worn out its welcome?' Lindsay Tanner replied, 'Well, it's just a campaign phrase, you can't expect much of it.' Yet only last week we were being told 'moving forward' was a national value.

Speech Writer Review

David Uren reports in the *Australian* on who is penning Aunt Julia's fine phrases, Denis Glover. It is part of a gushing story on the influence of the Per Capita think tank on Julia Gillard's policy thinking, and the nested influence of a bunch of boffins, who are close to the head of the Prime Minister's Department for most of Kevin Rudd's reign, Terry Moran. The story includes praise for two bureaucrats linked to Per Capita who are in charge of the Prime Minister's Department's Strategy and Implementation Division. Nice job they've done in the last two years!

Denis Glover has been plying the vexing trade of political speech writer for some years, working in this role for former Labor leader, Mark Latham, and others. He has freelanced to Labor Governments around the country. Julia Gillard must be a dream to write for. Her delivery is slow and measured. She clearly wants to communicate with others simply and well, and this friendliness helps to warm the dullest speech. She can speak both of simple experience and difficult concepts with a generous and authentic voice. How much of this success is Julia's native political skill, and how much Denis Glover's speech writing skill? I'd say mostly it's Julia's skill. For all his years writing

Labor political speeches, there have been few memorable Labor speeches since Don Watson's demise, and much dull repetition of orthodox thought.

David Uren's story makes much of Julia Gillard's speech to the Per Capita think tank, which failed to be posted on the PM's website. Uren celebrates how it focused on the idea of market design, a telling concept that, according to Uren, is the creative product of the Per Capita think tank. Uren writes, "Per Capita argues that with due government guidance, markets can perform a powerful role in delivering human services, such as the jobs network." Wow! - sounds like Per Capita has caught up with the OECD circa 1979 to me. Let's hope Julia's better side wins out over this kind of influence in the future battle over what "moving forward" means. Maybe, Julia should reread the judgement on Glover in Mark Latham's diaries, and move forward here too. And by the way, the last great Labor speechwriter, Don Watson, is not impressed with Denis's work so far. The *Herald-Sun* reports him saying, "People think the only way you can make a political point or persuade people of an argument is to treat them like imbeciles. It's like training a dog."

Aunt Julia's vulnerability with verbs

Julia Gillard's speeches are often marked by the use of sentence fragments or single nouns or gerunds with no predication and no subject. The speaking style is a habit of conversational tones of talk-back radio. The snatches and grabs of talkback are repackaged for speech making. They help the speech writers pull together unsorted and unordered ideas, without the bother of clarifying their relationship, or their meaning. Taken away from the immediacy of personal delivery, where tone of voice and body language can convey the inflection and emotion attached to the hanging fragment, this speech habit loses persuasive power and becomes vulnerable to misinterpretation. The delivery of real speeches uses a more dynamic and forceful rhetoric, that connects ideas together in real sentences. It does not just read them out in a supposedly self-evident list. One clear example from today is the way she characterised the year ahead as one of delivery and decision:

> I intend for 2011 to be defined less by politics and more by government. Australians do not face a Federal election next year – or the year after. Australians do not want their Government to campaign. Australians want their Government to govern. We are and we will. So 2011 will be a year of delivery - and decision. Methodical. Making steady progress on our plans, day by day, week by week. Working hard for all Australians, wherever they live. Modernising. Preparing Australia for the long-term with modern market-based solutions. Carefully weighing the hard decisions, at the right time, for the right reasons. Driven by our values and our vision. Hard work, a fair go through education, respect. Opportunity for all, and keeping our economy strong.

Tony Abbott spotted the weakness of this rhetoric instinctively. Whatever else you think of his political judgement and thought, Abbott has a flair for more direct and active language. His rejoinder to Gillard's speech was: "People expect their Governments to decide and to deliver every year, and if this Government did not decide and deliver in 2007, 2008, 2009, 2010, why would anyone believe it will in 2011?"

Abbot's sentences are longer, but form a more powerful story and a more powerful argument. The concepts are tied together with the structure of verbs. It really is time for Aunt Julia and her scriptwriters to find their way to speak – and, more decisively yet, to think - in language other than the hollowed-out bullet points that consultants transcribe from subject analysis sheets of focus-groups. Thought in action requires verbs.

Silenced Voice of the Bureaucrat

An interlude on disaffection and truth

(From *The Burning Archive* blog, 8 October 2015.)

Yet again today I had the experience of feeling like I belonged nowhere and with no one when stranded in a room discussing political ideas. Yet again I felt disaffected from all political institutions, homeless among political ideas, cast out and made to appear a madman when I expressed political thoughts. In the city where everyone appeals to networks and reputation, I am an outcast, who has no audience, no followers, and who is never asked for his thoughts on any matters. Yet, in my heart, I believe I respond to the world with all of my humanity, and devotedly seek to live with truthful and caring concern that can realise better lives for more people.

So tonight I have turned to Vaclav Havel for courage and consolation. In 'Politics and Conscience', he wrote that he practised:

> Politics as one of the ways of seeking and achieving meaningful lives, of protecting them and serving them. I favour politics as practical morality, as service to the truth, as essentially human and humanly measured care for our fellow humans. It is, I presume, an approach which, in this world, is extremely impractical and difficult to apply in daily life. Still, I know no better alternative.

Let those words never die.

Free speech and the public service

(From *The Burning Archive* blog, 13 August 2017.)

A minor controversy has broken out in Australia over restrictions on the free speech of public servants. The controversy began when the Australian Public Service Commission issued revised guidelines on the use of social media by public servants. The guidelines state that 'criticising the work, or the administration, of your agency is almost always going to be seen as a breach of the Code'. So, such criticisms invite dismissal.

The Public Service Commissioner, John Lloyd, who I worked beside many years ago when he ran public sector industrial relations under the Kennett Government (1992-99), which was guided by free market ideas, made the already provocative guidelines worse when he commented that public servants may, subject to the discretion and judgement of their employer, be 'in trouble' if they liked a Facebook post of a family member on the issue of gay marriage. The current Government has a policy on gay marriage, which even some of its own parliamentary members criticise; but if a public servant were, however faintly, to express a differing view, then according to Mr Lloyd's code of convenience, they would imperil the reputation and capacity of the public service to serve the government of the day impartially and professionally. They could be dismissed for a simple social impulse that takes one second to act on and that in no way affects anything they do at work.

These guidelines are deeply wrong. They breach the right to free speech of public servants, and breach other rights under the International Covenant on Civil and Political Rights. Let's look at some of the articles of the Covenant.

> *Article 17 1.* No one shall be subjected to arbitrary or unlawful interference with his privacy, family, home or correspondence , nor to unlawful attacks on his honour and reputation.
>
> *Article 17.2.* Everyone has the right to the protection of the law against such interference or attacks.

The Australian Public Service Commission's social media guidelines expose people's private correspondence on social media to the discretionary judgement of an agency, or rather the discretionary action of an agency's most powerful executives who may decide certain comments hurt the agency's reputation. The consequence is to attack a public servant's ability to perform their job professionally, and hence, in breach of the Covenant, to make unlawful attacks on their honour and reputation. To task the executive management of public sector agencies with patrolling the social media posts of their staff is no better than Stalin and his loyal party comrades monitoring the correspondence of the dissident poets of the Soviet Union. Must we be like Akhmatova and burn our opinions after speaking them to another so that no evidence is left behind?

> *Article 18.1.* Everyone shall have the *right to freedom of thought* [my emphasis], conscience and religion. This right shall include freedom to have or to adopt a religion or belief of his choice, and freedom, either individually or in community with others and in public or private, to manifest his religion or belief in worship, observance, practice and teaching.
>
> *Article 18.2.* No one shall be subject to coercion which would impair his freedom to have or to adopt a religion or belief of his choice.
>
> *Article 18.3.* Freedom to manifest one's religion or beliefs may be subject only to such limitations as are prescribed by law and are necessary to protect public safety, order, health, or morals or the fundamental rights and freedoms of others.

13 Ways of Looking at a Bureaucrat

If I manifest my beliefs in a vocation of public service on this blog, and I criticise the leadership of the public service for failing to live up to those ethical beliefs, the ordinary virtues of governing well, which I espouse and derive from traditions of virtue ethics and political philosophy, then, according to Mr Lloyd, I should be sacked. In threatening such action, the new guidelines restrict my freedom of thought. While commonly referred to as the article that secures freedom of religion, this right applies more broadly to thought and conscience. The public service guidelines and threats of executives restrict my ability to manifest my beliefs, as stated in part 3 of this article.

There are two common defences of such restrictions: that it is necessary to protect the reputation of the public service as impartial and professional; and that it is a right that I waive by signing an employment contract. The second of these defences may go to an interpretation of the rights and freedoms of others, such as employers, as shown in several industrial cases. However, properly understood these defences protect the current interests of these others, not their fundamental rights and freedoms. Should their interests prevail over my rights and freedoms, as set out in the covenant?

The primary defence of the restriction relates to the protection of public order, in the language of the covenant. How can public order be maintained if the servants of the government of the day can criticise willy-nilly Ministers and agencies, and lead the public to believe that government acts without a single voice, without a common body of authority? There is clearly a threshold issue here. No-one has the right to falsely scream fire in a cinema. However, none of the illustrative examples of breaches of social media imperil public order so gravely. They tend rather to expose senior managers who are hypersensitive to criticism, and unable to project legitimate authority.

> *Article 19.1.* Everyone shall have the right to hold opinions without interference.

> *Article 19.2.* Everyone shall have the right to freedom of expression; this right shall include freedom to seek, receive and impart information and ideas of all kinds, regardless of frontiers, either orally, in writing or in print, in the form of art, or through any other media of his choice.
>
> *Article 19.3.* The exercise of the rights provided for in paragraph 2 of this article carries with it special duties and responsibilities. It may therefore be subject to certain restrictions, but these shall only be such as are provided by law and are necessary: (a) For respect of the rights or reputations of others; (b) For the protection of national security or of public order, or of public health or morals.

You do not have the right to hold opinions without interference if you are threatened with dismissal for shaping your thoughts on a blog that may be followed, such as this one, by less than fifty people. You do not have the freedom to choose the media of your choice if you are told you can say some things in private, but not by liking Facebook posts.

As with article 18 there is a balance of right and responsibility in article 19. But Mr Lloyd's *diktats* restrict many more acts of free speech than the very few that genuinely breach the rights and reputations of others. Criticism, after all, is neither sedition nor defamation.

These social media guidelines are not the work of only one side of politics. They are part of a general regime of control and impoverishment of public debate by managerial elites. They reflect a general practice that ushers public servants, who often are well informed and capable of meaningful contributions to public dialogue, into a dark, silent corner, while political advisers and communications consultants dominate the airwaves with inane talking points.

I believe these guidelines, moreover, are a form of intimidation of critics by a managerial elite who are incapable of conducting respectful dialogue with the employees of their own institution. I am considering making a complaint on the matter to the Australian Human Rights

Commission – but think that my energies are better spent looking at ways of sheltering, protecting and renewing the genuine ethos of public service that I espouse.

The irony, of course, is that this managerial elite has done far more damage to the reputation of the public service than a few grumbles on social media. They have stripped the capacity to serve both the government of the day and the broader public with impartiality, professional ethos and pride, as I say, in the ordinary virtues of governing well. I look around my own institution and see dozens of senior executives who have made their way through patronage, partisan service in political adviser roles, or mercenary service in management consulting.

Indeed, Mr Lloyd himself does not have a distinguished career of serving both sides of politics. He has migrated from one conservative government to another, and long been a member of the right wing industrial relations club at the Institute of Public Affairs. His appointment as Public Service Commissioner, in my opinion, dishonoured the service.

There are, indeed, much greater threats to the reputation, impartiality and professional ethos of the public service than the occasional impulsive social media post. We would do well to act on them, rather than to persecute people for opinions. Recently, a distinguished Commonwealth public servant, Dennis Richardson, called for a Royal Commission into the institution. He was quoted as saying:

> We had a Royal Commission into the public service in the 1970s and I think every so often institutions need to go back to their philosophical foundations. And I sometimes wonder whether the time has not come for a second Royal Commission, because community attitudes and standards have changed; the way in which ministers, ministerial advisers and public servants work together has completely changed; and I wonder whether we should not be

revisiting the philosophical foundations of that.[1]

I agree with this call. I would also support such a Commission or Inquiry into the public service of the Victorian Government, which is very much rotting from the head down, led by a man who espouses a mercenary belief in something called the 'public purpose sector'. Such a Commission or Inquiry should be able to look at the broader foundations of democratic institutions, that is, parliament, parties, public universities, and public dialogue across many media. Such a Commission or Inquiry would better preserve and improve the reputation and integrity of the public service than these contemptible guidelines on social media use.

Cultural decay and political institutions

(From *The Burning Archive* blog, 24 December 2017.)

In reviewing my notes for the year – diligently if effortlessly recorded in Evernote – I came across my discovery of an essay from the late 1970s by Leszek Kolakowski, 'How to be a Conservative-Liberal-Socialist'. I do not recall how I discovered this gem, as apposite to our times as Kolakowski's exile from Poland in the 1970s. Perhaps it was a book review by another politically ambidextrous thinker, John Gray? In any case, the recommendation fell on prepared ground; and spoke to some universal themes in this year's political chronicle.

Kolakowski was a philosopher and former Communist from Poland, who, after the Prague Spring, broke the spells of orthodoxy and

---

[1] *The Mandarin*, 26 July 2017.

the privileged life of an insider, and then led an itinerant and dissident life in the main universities of the West. I used to possess his three-volume *Main Currents of Marxism* (I sold it in a fit of poverty in Canberra the year the Berlin Wall fell), and absorbed its deep aversion to the totalitarian spirit at the heart of that hydra-headed monster. I am forever grateful for the lifelong immunisation against that spirit, and look warily on spruikers of the revival of Marxist ideas in our troubled times.

Those ideas are resurgent in response to growing concerns with inequality, the disappointments of growth, and the predations of a merchant elite. Kolakowski's essay recognised the truth in socialism, without succumbing to that instinct for one-party rule, for intellectual domination of society by the vanguard of the proletariat. He wrote that a socialist believes: "That it is absurd and hypocritical to conclude that, simply because a perfect, conflictless society is impossible, every existing form of inequality is inevitable and all ways of profit-making justified."

But his essay also saw the truth in liberalism. The ambidextrous liberal believes that the State must play a role in security, and that security should be extended to health care, education, employment, and a basic income. But they also believe that "human communities are threatened not only by stagnation but also by degradation when they are so organized that there is no longer room for individual initiative and inventiveness'. Today, Kolakowski might also see a threat to strangle communities through the strictures placed on thought and speech by a radicalism that seeks to cleanse humanity of its traditions, affiliations and improvisations because they inevitably contain errors, guilty associations and unexamined habits.

That cultural repository is the domain of the conservative: the garden which serves as a refuge from a troubled world. Kolakowski gave the conservative three truthful propositions. Firstly:

That in human life there never have been and never will

be improvements that are not paid for with deteriorations and evils; thus, in considering each project of reform and amelioration, its price has to be assessed. Put another way, innumerable evils are compatible (i.e. we can suffer them comprehensively and simultaneously); but many goods limit or cancel each other, and therefore we will never enjoy them fully at the same time.

Secondly,

That we do not know the extent to which various traditional forms of social life—families, rituals, nations, religious communities—are indispensable if life in a society is to be tolerable or even possible. There are no grounds for believing that when we destroy these forms, or brand them as irrational, we increase the chance of happiness, peace, security, or freedom.

Thirdly,

That the *idée fixe* of the Enlightenment — that envy, vanity, greed, and aggression are all caused by the deficiencies of social institutions and that they will be swept away once these institutions are reformed — is not only utterly incredible and contrary to all experience, but is highly dangerous.

These nostrums speak to our times. In this year we have seen increasingly shrill debates between progressives, conservatives and radicals in a house they no longer wish to share. We have seen a backlash of populist nostalgia for ordinary ways of life. This is a revolt against the Enlightenment purity of economic reformers and their dangerous vision of a society ruled by contracts between individuals. This idea has dominated elites for thirty years. I have seen it up close. It has ravaged the institutions of government, and filled the halls of power with amoral *condottiere,* who ceaselessly mouth inanities about change and reform, but do not comprehend what they have undone. We have seen a radicalised sexual politics, with its utopianism of the bedroom foisted onto classrooms, that is every bit as scary as

Marcuse's polymorphous perversity. We have seen a return of sacred violence, which can only be understood by acknowledging the power of traditional forms of social life, and especially religion. We have seen domineering autocrats, with no respect for the subtleties of our cultural inheritance, rise to power on the back of resentment. This resentment has been fueled by the attacks of reformers, corporations and identity politics on the *lebenswelt* of their fellow citizens.

Kolakowski's invention of the ideal pluralist political thinker – the Conservative-Liberal-Socialist – is a gift of wisdom to our troubled times. It provides a way through the confusion of this moment of cultural disintegration that is infecting our political institutions. In this weekend's *Australian*, the doyen of Australian political columnists, Paul Kelly, has published a piece entitled, "2017: West challenged in a spinning world." It begins:

> Our age of disruption, decay and transformation reached a peak in 2017 and unleashed a shower of contradictions: democracy looks ineffective, politics has surrendered to an era of strong men, and the quest for enhanced individual autonomy now drives the culture.

Like all columns by political journalists, it improvises interpretations of events as they pass before us. Just as, I suppose, we bloggers do. While I do not share all of Kelly's unease about the defeat of the Christian tradition, I agree with his three principal ideas: our political system is collapsing into dysfunction; our culture is experiencing deep losses and decay, and these two trends are deeply intertwined. "The problem of our dysfunctional political system," Kelly writes, "does not relate just to politics, finance, parties or the parliament. It is also about the public culture and where that culture is ultimately heading." Nietzsche was more lapidary: "We are definitely ephemeral."

#

Silenced Voice of the Bureaucrat

On the traumatic origin of Machiavelli, *The Prince*

From *The Burning Archive* blog, 11 November 2018.

I have watched *Medici: Masters of Florence* and *The Borgias* over the last fortnight, and remembered some of my knowledge of Renaissance history, which I never formally studied. Both TV series take some liberties with history, but nonetheless present a fresh account of these grand families.

The most intriguing figure of Italian Renaissance history for me, however, is Niccolo Machiavelli. He has appeared on occasions on this blog, and makes an appearance in series one of *The Borgias*. The actor plays well, if to stereotype, the wily and worldly wise secretary to the rulers of Florence. This old historian's lament is that stereotypes about Machiavelli are sticky.

The image of Machiavelli and his reality are much different. His period as a notable bureaucrat and diplomat was brief – from the 1498 to 1512. In late 1512 the republic of Florence, guided by Piero Soderino and and his notary, Machiavelli, collapsed under the pressures of rival city states, nations and the besieging forces of the Medici family. The Medici did not only restore their dynastic rule in Florence. A few months after their reconquest of their city-state, Cardinal Giovanni de Medici became the Pope, as Leo X. As Machiavelli wrote, in his *History of Florence*, "This was in fact a ladder by means of which his house was enabled to mount to heaven itself."

The restored rulers of Florence took their revenge on those who had exiled them from their ancestral home. Many notable officials of the regime in which Machiavelli served were executed. Machiavelli was more fortunate. He was jailed, and tortured, subjected to the *strappado* for two months, and then dismissed from all office and sent to home detention in his country estate. He would never truly return to serve the state, despite his many entreaties to the new despots of Italy and the Church to reinstate him.

Disgraced and traumatised, his world turned upside down, Machiavelli turned to writing to process his trauma, and, with the inconsistency of great writing, to beg favours from his torturers. Out of this morass of pain and self-pity came that enigmatic celebration of autocracy and devious politics, *The Prince*.

If you know the traumatic origins of *The Prince*, then you will not easily fall victim to the illusion that Machiavelli was the master politician, the great wily fox of the Renaissance city-state. You will not, like so many of the professionalised political advisers of the last thirty years, imagine yourself writing *The New Prince* to celebrate the bowlderisation of governing by modern marketing techniques. You will not engage in fatuous conceits of cynical mastery by writing to mediocre aspiring leaders under the rubric of 'what would Machiavelli say'.

You will know that Machiavelli's work of that summer of 1513 was submitted to the scions of the Medici family, but was never published in his lifetime, as with most of his writing. He had to make do with mere reflections on politics, because his dismissal from the Florentine state was never reversed. You will know too that his more authentic, sometimes fatalistic, voice emerges in the *Discourses on the History of Livy*, where he wrote,

> a city which owing to its pervading corruption has once begun to decline, if it is to recover at all, must be saved not by the excellence of the people collectively, but of some one man then living among them, on whose death it at once relapses into its former plight; ... the reason being that hardly any ruler lives so long as to have time to accustom to right methods a city which has long been accustomed to wrong.

The voice of *The Prince* does not command like the successful political master; rather it whispers like a victim of trauma, failure and dissociation. As one historian commented,

> Under the sign of trauma, this individual [the Renaissance man] emerges neither as a coherent "classical" subject nor as a Burckhardtian configuration of the Nietzschean "superman". Rather we glimpse a restless and fragmented subject, compulsively seeking unity (but never finding it) in flights of abjection and aggression.[2]

It is this restless and fragmented voice, prowling the cells of his imagination in search of the ordinary virtues of governing well, that I admire in Machiavelli.

On the renunciation of the political world

(From *The Burning Archive* blog, 17 March 2019.)

Since I was very young I have been drawn, like a moth to light, to the world of politics. It has not done me much good. True, I have made a career of sorts in the margins of government; always on the periphery, even when I was truly close to the fabled centre of power; and never accepted by the executives who live by a modern warrior code. But politics has always disappointed me.

They say that disappointment is a great teacher, and points to the frustration of expectations. My expectations of politics were laid down sometime in my childhood for reasons of which reason knows nothing. I remember as an early primary school schoolboy I listened to the political news on the radio, absorbing into my very character the intricacy of calculation and the grandeur to shape events of the world

---

[2] Alison Frazier, "Machiavelli, Trauma, and the Scandal of 'The Prince'," *History in the Comic Mode*, eds. R. Fulton and B. Holsinge (2007)

through nothing but orders and words. I recall, when I was somewhere between 10 and 12, I played in the local park a game, adapted somehow from king of the hill, where I imagined myself the ruler of a principality or city state bounded by pine trees and BMX tracks.

I went on through adolescence to read the *Palliser* novels of Anthony Trollope, and to identify with the rising, young Anglo-Irish member of parliament, Phineas Finn, and then, even more so, with Plantagenet Palliser, the conscientious, intelligent, shy, awkward aristocrat-politician who eventually became, through the rivalry of other candidates and the compromise of events, the Prime Minister. Yet Palliser was too sensitive to perform the role, and ultimately was driven from office by the more worldly, less noble characters who knew how to conspire, cheat and grasp whatever they want. Palliser was like Arjuna hesitating before the great battle of the *Mahabharata*, but no Krishna whispered the truths of *dharma* into his ear. Palliser was both driven and destroyed by his belief - or was it a dream? - that the unworldly can make a life of virtue in the world of politics. And so certainly have I been driven, if not yet destroyed.

In late adolescence I got involved in student politics, briefly circling around, in painful introversion, some young stars of left-wing politics, one of whom would later go on to be a rather disappointing Prime Minister. Again, I felt drawn to this world, but did not belong and could not reconcile the perspectives I had gathered from books and life on the strangeness of the psyche from the uncomplicated ambitions of these apprentice politicians. They would listen to Bruce Springsteen and talk about unions and pragmatic economic policies, but I would go back and listen to Nick Cave or The Pop Group and think about Foucault, madness and redemption through literature. I was fortunate to be defeated in a student election. After my defeat, I turned away for the first time from the political world.

I let go of my political friends – or associates, to be more accurate – and committed myself to the life of scholarship, writing and experiment in thought. These were good years, even if racked by despair and disorientation in this world of academic careers, where I was unable to find the patrons needed for success and unwilling to ally my ideas with any gang of professors. So, the world of politics came looking for this wanderer again, in the form of a second – or was it a third? – career in the bureaucracy.

Now, nearly thirty years later, the disappointments have accumulated like a library of great books, and I am standing at my window wondering whether to renounce the outside world of politics, or to turn to the inner light and study my disappointments like holy writ, or to find some other place in which to lead a responsible life of ordinary virtue.

Yet there are other choices, other ways of finding engaging meaning in the greater world beyond politics, government and bureaucracy. I do renounce these worlds as places in which I strive to fulfil an obscure, beating desire. I may still make my way through these worlds, like a wandering mendicant teacher. But my mind will turn to the more meaningful worlds I encounter in the immediate reality of my limited life and in the infinite conversation of literature, narrative, history, and reflection on the deeper questions that make for a meaningful life. On this longer journey, which may take the rest of my life, the world of politics will change its colours, as from summer to autumn, and become not the *saṃsāra* of drifting, defeat, and disappointment, but rather the source for the greatest books of my life. As it is written in the *Bhagavad Gita*,

> Weapons can cleave it not,
>
> Fire can burn it not,
>
> Waters can drench it not,
>
> Winds can dry it not,
>
> Eternally stable, immobile, all-pervading,
>
> Unmanifest, unthinkable, immutable it is...

Bhagavad Gita (II, 22-25)

Or again, I may learn from Shen Zhou (沈周, 1427-1509), who indeed renounced the world of official service during the brilliant Ming Dynasty to care for his widowed mother.

> White clouds sash-like
>
> wrap mountain waists,
>
> The rock terrace flies in space
>
> distant, a narrow path.
>
> Leaning on a bramble staff
>
> far and free I gaze,
>
> To the warble of valley brook
>
> I will reply, whistling.

Free speech for public servants and Mandelstam

(From *The Burning Archive* blog, 11 August 2019.)

During the week the High Court of Australia passed judgement on a case in which a public servant was sacked for an anonymous tweet, critical of government but made in her private life, that was said to breach a code of conduct for government employees. The lower courts had found that this action was an unjustified constraint on freedom of speech. The Commonwealth Government appealed.

The High Court found that it was justified as a means to uphold the role of an apolitical public service in responsible government. The Court's summary judgement read:

On appeal, the High Court unanimously held that the impugned provisions had a purpose consistent with the constitutionally prescribed system of representative and responsible government, namely the maintenance of an apolitical public service. The Court also held that the provisions were reasonably appropriate and adapted or proportionate to their purpose and accordingly did not impose an unjustified burden on the implied freedom.[3]

The judgement has been interpreted widely as confirming the restriction of freedom of speech, not only of public servants but all employees who their employers seek to control through codes of conduct and organisational policies.[4] We truly have entered the realm of Havel's post-democratic society in which the fat controllers of petty organisations are able to enforce living in a lie.

I am no lawyer, but I doubt the quality of the Court's judgement on the substance of the claim that these kinds of rules maintain an apolitical public service. In truth, the public service is wrecked by political patronage, especially among the senior executive ranks who enforce these codes of conduct. It is ruled by an ethos of courting Ministers and their advisers, rather than determining the public interest apolitically. It is infected with too many communications executives, expedient consultants, venal office-holders and zealous advocates. Its intellectual traditions are ruined and its moral virtues compromised. These betrayals of an apolitical public service are the results of actions by the leadership of these organisations, much more so than by any sporadic, private tweets or blog posts by public servants who still, in some parts of their lives, wish to live in truth. These observations are true of governments run by left-wing and right-wing parties. They are all based on my observation of the decay of the Victorian public service over 30 years. The truth is there is no longer an apolitical public service to maintain in our distressed republics, and

---

[3] Comcare v Michael Banerji, High Court of Australia, 23 August 2019.
[4] Anthony Forsyth, 'Will the High Court ruling on public servant's tweets have a 'powerful chill' on free speech?' *The Conversation,* 7 August 2019.

codes of conduct are merely used to enforce living a lie.

Despite the chilling effect of this ruling, I will not be gagged. I will not be intimidated any longer. I would call, if anyone is listening, on mass civil disobedience of this code, but I know these rulings do intimidate. I know from my own experience. This Banerjee case led me to take down my anonymous *Happy Pessimist* blog five years ago, together with my craven wish to enjoy the privileges of political patronage. I see how how my own courage failed, how I yearned for political favour within this institution, and how I feared the meagre favours dispensed to me would be withdrawn because of my thought-crimes put down on paper.

So, as an act of defiance of the new *nomenklatura* of our post-democratic society, I am reposting a set of essays from that suppressed blog of thought-crimes. These essays (included in this book as 'The Crisis in Australian Politics 2010-13') began to sketch an interpretation of the crisis in Australian politics from 2010 – the Rudd/Gillard/Rudd, then Abbott/Turnbull years. These essays certainly criticised governments, parties and institutions, but they were not thoughtless spasms of bias. They were a free and open attempt to make sense of what was going wrong with government. They did not compromise my ability to perform my duties as a professional public servant.

So will our time's petty enforcers of post-democratic rule come for me in the way that bureaucratic enforcers came for Mikhaila Banerjee? Will they hunt me like Joseph Stalin came for Osip Mandelstam when the Russian poet wrote his poem, 'Stalin Epigram', that threatened the reputation of that government's executives?

> We are living, but can't feel the land where we stay,
>
> More than ten steps away you can't hear what we say.
>
> But if people would talk on occasion,
>
> They should mention the Kremlin Caucasian.
>
> We shall see what retribution comes .

Oh Henry, what have you done?

(From *The Happy Pessimist* blog, July 2010.)

The ABC's *The Drum* staged a discussion of lessons of the Rudd Government's neglect of the recommendations of its much trumpeted Henry tax review. What does this overlooking of the actual advice of the current Secretary to the Treasury, Ken Henry, mean about how the real business of governing is discussed and reported in this country?[5]

I confess myself that I have only flicked through parts of the vast document. It may well be a good starting point for discussion of new proposals for reform. I should promise to read and reflect on it, but I have reservations. Tony Abbott, the Leader of the Opposition, commented that the review report had large numbers of recommendations that were of 'only theoretical merit'. Abbott did give more weight, however, to proposals closest to Henry's core expertise.

The report ranges over such extensive policy domains that it cannot but at times read a little over-stretched, and a little like a textbook for Treasury officials. It will be interesting to watch whether this review report becomes for our many budding policy wonks the great text of the unrealised vision that could be, if only the real world conformed to the assumptions of our dear economists.

The other curious aspect of the review was the appointment of the Treasury Secretary to run it, in both name and fact. The traditional approach would see the Head of Treasury manipulate some prominent business leader or academic or consultant, from behind the scenes and through bureaucratic ventriloquism, to present an 'independent view' to government. By appointing Henry to lead the review, the Government forced an unusual openness about the ideas of our leading

---

[5] *The Drum* (current affairs television), abc.net.au 26 July 2010.

bureaucrats. I liked this aspect of the review's process. A more prominent role in the discussion of political or policy ideas by our leading bureaucrats may improve the quality of public discussion. It may push it beyond the limits of sound bites and talkback, and also demand an ethic of responsibility from the academic and consulting worlds.

Writing between the lines

(From *The Burning Archive* blog, 23 May 2021.)

> Persecution cannot prevent even public expression of the heterodox truth, for a man of independent thought can utter his views in public and remain unharmed, provided he moves with circumspection. He can even utter them in print without incurring any danger, provided he is capable of writing between the lines.
>
> Leo Strauss, *Persecution and the Art of Writing* (1941).

So wrote Leo Strauss, the American (if that is quite the right descriptor) political philosopher, amidst a world war and a holocaust of his people. His writing insists uncannily, despite all his erudition and esotericism, on being heard as much today as in that earlier crisis of authoritarianism, induced by Germany's descent into hell. At the outset of "Persecution and the Art of Writing", Strauss wrote,

> in a considerable number of countries which, for about a hundred years, have enjoyed practically complete freedom of public discussion, that freedom is now suppressed and replaced by a compulsion to coordinate speech with such

views as the government believes to be expedient, or holds in all seriousness.[6]

He observed that most people in these previously democratic societies accepted the orthodox views propounded by what we might today call mainstream news and the woke. So much so that even the limited form of freedom of thought for the majority was practically constrained. In Strauss' judgement this freedom was limited to 'the ability to choose between two or more different views presented by the small minority of people who are public speakers or writers'. Without this small choice, however, societies enter the realm of persecution, marked out by the belief that the culturally invested do not lie. The majority fall into line with this theatre, much like Havel's greengrocer in 'The Power of the Powerless', who put out his sign calling on Workers of the World to Unite. But there is a small minority who preserve genuinely independent thinking against the corrosion of this persecution by Red Guards, official orthodoxy, propaganda, distributed talking points, woksters and mainstream news. Strauss called this minority 'the intelligent minority, to distinguish them from such groups as the intelligentsia'. This persecuted minority sustain free expression, in practice, both by sharing thoughts with benevolent, trustworthy and reasonable friends, and, when they do dare to express their thought, by doing so artfully. The artful expression of their outlandish thoughts, evades the guards who roam in the public domain. It is this practice Strauss called 'writing between the lines'.

Strauss is known for this idea of writing between the lines, of esoteric writing. But his idea is widely misunderstood. It can be perceived, by both detractors and supporters, as celebrating the secret small seminars of an exclusive minority, who encode and decode their heterodoxies in conjured thought and who disdain the common reader. It can seem stupidly elitist, but not if you appreciate the centuries of intelligent resistance to persecution that it honoured. Strauss was an

---

[6] Leo Strauss, 'Persecution and the Art of Writing', *Social Research* 8:4 (1941), p. 488.

expert on Maimonides (1135-1204), who practised a double life of faith in Islamic Spain until he fled to Morocco, amidst the persecution of the Almohads, who practised a fundamentalist form of Islamist ideology.

Such persecution has driven writers for centuries to speak indirectly, and so to outwit censors and to find an audience of intelligent unknown readers, not merely their own acquaintances. Strauss observed how persecution can vary in form from the Spanish Inquisition (an index of banned books and public burnings of heretics) to mild social ostracism. He listed some of the political philosophers from Plato to Kant, who witnessed or suffered persecution, more tangible than social ostracism, and who knew in their bones that free inquiry was dangerous. Liberal democracies might have forgotten the rub of this halter on their necks, but those who attended to the writings of East European dissidents, the actions of the Red Guards in China, and the sophistry of television journalists, who claim to be trusted sources when delivering the latest hoax, never forgot how persecution sits well with our social instinct to conform, to mimic and to scapegoat.

In the eight decades since Strauss wrote his essay, the tides of persecution have risen and fallen. We are clearly experiencing a stormy high tide right now – cancel culture, deplatforming, media hoaxes, twitter bans, social media rages, justice system breakdowns, soft authoritarianism, excessive public health rules, mask mandates, media manipulation, frequent calls to control 'misinformation' and crackdowns on thinking aloud in ways that are not endorsed by the swarm. If the infinite conversation is to go on, it may well need to be conducted through the new *samizdats* and esoteric writing of our times. Never has Leo Strauss, for all his strange arcane art, been more relevant to the intelligent minority who sustain truly independent thought in our time of troubles.

Silenced Voice of the Bureaucrat

Chapter Three Thirteen Ways of Looking at a Bureaucrat

Thirteen ways of looking at a bureaucrat

(From *The Burning Archive* blog, January to March 2017.)

> *Psychoanalysts don't usually write essays; they tend to write lectures or papers or chapters, or what are called, perhaps optimistically, contributions.*
>
> (Adam Phillips, "Coda: up to a point"*)*

If Phillips' invitation, masked in the form of a provocation, is true of psychoanalysis, how much more true is it of my own profession - public servant, civil servant, bureaucrat. Bureaucrats do not write essays, or so some people might believe. They write briefs, presentations, summaries, or talking points, in descending order of intellectual significance. Indeed among many of the bureaucrats among whom I have made a kind of living, like some transplanted flower placed by a bumbling gardener in too much sun or too much shade, in the acid soil, where its roots soak all day in water, to write an essay is a phrase to denigrate a staff member who has put too much thought into a paper, and simply cannot reduce it down to memorisable talking points to be scanned for performance in front of your superiors. "Don't give me an essay," they will say, "just tell me what I need to know."

Is it because of the general contempt in this profession of contumely for the most inventive, flexible genre of prose that fiction writers have left us many caricatures, but few grand characters who are bureaucrats? A few years ago I recall a lifeless panel run by the local institute of public administration that asked the latest bunch of mini (very) celebrity bureaucrats what books they felt best represented life in the bureaucracy. The responses were so pallid, except for one, from a genuine reader, who nominated Hilary Mantel's rich portrait of that man of affairs, Thomas Cromwell, in *Wolf Hall* and its sequels. When you search google for best novels about the bureaucracy, you get a rather tired old list. Kafka's *Castle*. Heller's *Catch 22*. Gogol's *Dead Souls*. Then, a few references to satires of communist bureaucracy, as if it were only an East European institution. Before slipping in a reference to *Yes, Minister*, or similar light television comedies, including *Utopia*, in the Australian context. A few mention David Foster Wallace's *Pale King* or *Infinite Jest*, from which I recall surely one of the funniest literary names for a government department, the United States Office of Unspecified Services (USOUS), which you may well pronounce as "youse owe us."

But these representations of life in the bureaucracy have never really registered with me as genuine engagements with the life of the mind as it is practised in our government offices. Yet, it is that very culture, with its foibles, traps and few moments of genius, that I have dedicated the greater part of my working life to. It is that life of the mind in which I have experienced problems as deep, ethical dilemmas, and in which I have made thorny, practical judgements as meticulous as any second-rate university research seminar. But the world would not know this, because bureaucrats do not write essays.

So maybe they should, and maybe I should, and maybe I have already begun. Adam Phillips is an inspiration to me in this task, this attempt, this essay, in more ways than one. He has stepped outside the sterile code of his profession and lifted from its place, discarded on the floor, one of the traditions that exceed the profession's histories. After all, Freud was a great essayist, perhaps a greater essayist than a psychologist (the opposite may be said of his disciple, turned rival, Carl Jung). And within my profession - with some flexible interpretation of its boundaries across a long and diverse global history - there have been some great essayists, some great investigators of the human spirit as it is tested in the public life of the mind. There are the Chinese ancients for a start. Confucius was, after all, a public official dismayed

Thirteen Ways of Looking at a Bureaucrat

at the demoralisation of conduct in public office, who roamed the country for years with his teachings that sought to inspire a nobler spirit of duty. There were the great Byzantine scholar-bureaucrats. Indeed, there is the extraordinary Anna Comnena and her portrait of her father, *Alexiad*. There is Francis Bacon; although we might grant him the title of statesman and grandee, still government official he was. His essays speak still across the centuries to the peculiar obligations, duties and privileges of the bureaucrat who offers advice to a modern-day prince. "The greatest trust, between man and man," Bacon wrote around 1600 "is the trust of giving counsel."

So if Bacon's essays can endure these 400 years, and preserve a wisp of this peculiar, secreted and yet all too human life that I have led as a government official, surely I should honour this tradition by picking it up from its dusty corner and finding a new reinvention of the essay form to speak of the true experience of bureaucracy.

Long ago - maybe ten years ago - I took it into my head to write one such essay about the real life of the mind of bureaucrats - at least the kind of public official that I aspire to be - that would take its cue from Wallace Stevens, "Thirteen ways of looking at a blackbird." Over the years the yearning to express the true spirit has grown stronger as I have watched public institutions and public culture decay around me, and read other testimony of such decay, as in Francis Fukuyama, *Political Order and Political Decay*. The first impulse of this essay was to speak as a wistful, even comic, challenge to the many "stakeholders" I had met over the years who had treated me and other faithful public servants with sneering contempt. Take a look at the world through my eyes for a minute, if you will. Think of me as Stevens' manifold blackbird, and do not fixate on a cardboard cut-out image of who I am, what I do, and, especially, how I think.

As the years have rolled on, however, my thoughts on the essay have turned in different directions. I have wanted to write a "J'Accuse" to all the treasonous clerks who have profited from office, sought to break the greater traditions of the profession, and betrayed the higher purposes of public service. Some even proclaim nonsense like the "public purpose sector" to describe all the consultocrats and tax-farming firms who thrive on advantageous government contracts, tolls and partnerships. In yet another mood, "Thirteen ways of looking at a bureaucrat" is an elegy for a kind of life of the mind that has died around me. I sing my sad songs and hope the gods will resurrect this tradition. But the odds on that seem to grow slimmer by the day.

Still, what is writing for, if not to write sad songs that honour the traditions that represent the best of who you are? And who can say that my laments may not inspire at least one of my fellow officials to rise above the muck of daily talking points, the ill-considered decisions, the bluff and bluster of those consultocratic courtiers who know no better way?

So with those questions, let me end for tonight, and promise a mini-series of posts, 13 in all, each prompted by that great poem by Wallace Stevens on perspective, "Thirteen ways of looking at a blackbird."

I Vigilance among stillness

> Among twenty snowy mountains,
> The only moving thing
> Was the eye of the blackbird.
> (Stevens, *Thirteen Ways of Looking at a Blackbird*)

We citizens flatter ourselves sometimes by believing that government, Big Brother, and ultimately some bureaucrat somewhere in a police or intelligence agency, is really watching us. The ever vigilant state is more a paranoid dream of libertarians, artists and entrepreneurs - all rebels against bureaucratic rule - than a genuine historical phenomenon. Yes, there have been states where individuals and their errant minds have been tracked down, followed, and described in exacting, excruciating detail. Anna Funder's *Stasiland* recounted the underworld of eternal vigilance created by one such state. More powerfully, I recall that Anna Akhmatova's *Requiem* was painstakingly written on cigarette papers, committed to the memory of her friend, and then silently burned so that no all-seeing eye of the KGB would detect her lament of dissent.

It is also true that we live in times of both unprecedented scrutiny and uninhibited exposure of our digital communications. The collaborations between national intelligence agencies and large information technology firms, exposed by the leaks of Edward Snowden and to a lesser extent Julian Assange, have created not an ever-twitching, omniscient eye, but a vast and messy drain in which all the banal facts and words and digits of our lives swoosh down into a dense black big data mess. We are told that clever algorithms and super-smart graduates of the best universities can see patterns in this oozy, sticky mess. I wonder if this is just massive multiplayer online Rorschach blots.

In any case, the super-spies huddled over their super-computers are a rare, atypical form of bureaucrat. Their form of vigilance is not the only kind practised by other bureaucrats. For the most part bureaucrats observe their field with the same tools we all have - publicly available information, intuition pumps that read social behaviour, the ready-made ideas that circulate in the popular press and magazines, the cultural memes of our times. This great majority of bureaucrats content themselves with recycling and rehearsing the mantras of the day - whether those mantras are taken from some inept consultant's report, the editorial of the *Financial Review*, or the opinions and prejudices fostered by their social circle. They draw their interpretations of the world from a common stock of ideas that

13 Ways of Looking at a Bureaucrat

requires little searching for truth and little investigation of deeper questions. These ideas find their confirmation quickly, and reflect the governing consensus of their patrons and the powerful kingpins who guide the networks to which they belong. These bureaucrats are the conformists and lackeys of those zombie ideas that so dominate our governments, especially after the degradation of public intellectual culture over the last 30 years. They are the managers who cannot find a better argument in favour of the changes they propose than that change is always happening and you can't fight change. Ironically, they cannot see that the same change undermines their calls to reform the world in the static image of their own utopias and interests.

But there are some other bureaucrats, perhaps a small but significant minority, who are less like squawkish parrots with their imitative cries, and more like the eye of Stevens' blackbird, restlessly searching a vast immoveable world of snowy mountains for a clue to the unfolding of this world. This kind of bureaucrat seeks out contrary opinions and conflicting information. This kind of bureaucrat regularly scans the best academic journals of their field to find an idea that is better than their own. This kind of bureaucrat speaks after a meeting to the quiet voices in the room, and looks carefully and meticulously at the surprising data, that does not fit neatly the line graphs of progress or decline. When this kind of bureaucrat is challenged by their Minister to find some kind of model of cultural change - "someone must have one, surely?" - they will look outside management journals, and read deeply in anthropology, biological sciences, behavioural psychology and history before realising that we are posing again the enigmas of Heraclitus, but with no patience for oracles. Such a bureaucrat will pose to themselves everyday fundamental questions that try to make deeper sense of the social patterns they observe in their reading and in the social and cultural worlds around them.

I know such bureaucrats exist; because I have been one. It is true we are a small, and likely dwindling minority. Yet are not all of our most precious cultural heritages the same scarce, endangered species?

Thirteen Ways of Looking at a Bureaucrat

To preserve this tradition is essential if our societies are to be governed well, and our great intellectual traditions are to be conserved against degradation by the chic, stupid mantras of people on the make. It is given to a few perhaps to be the seers: to observe the things that others cannot see, and then to find the words to communicate them so that the great ship can keep sailing on. Those seers are rarely the grand mandarins who control large organisations. They do not receive the medals and the gongs. Their photo-shopped faces do not appear on the Mandarin news website. Nor are they the self-confident consultocrats who trade up their reputations with the latest fashionable nonsense. They suffer the exile of all prophets, and are often found wandering wounded, lame, even blinded, in the organisations that neither like nor support them. They do not even promise utopia and transformation. The long vigil has taught them of the limitations of the human animal. But if we see them, if we find a way of truly looking at this kind of bureaucrat, if we hear what they have learned through their long years of vigilance, then perhaps we can save our bureaucracies from the depredations of management that mistakes ambition for thought.

II The three-eyed raven

> I was of three minds,
>
> Like a tree
>
> In which there are three blackbirds.
>
> (Stevens, *Thirteen Ways of Looking at a Blackbird*)

In *Game of Thrones* the three-eyed raven is the seer who is withdrawn from the world, and yet travels, embodied as a raven, to witness the world's events, even though he already knows everything, from the beginning to the end. His third eye multiplies his perspectives exponentially. It gives him a greater vision of both the past and the future, but no more ability to influence events. Indeed, his knowledge humbles him. He does not seek to change the world, but only to be a compassionate witness, a servant to the fates, and to find his successor in the seer's tree, Brandon Stark.

Game of Thrones is a melodrama of power, about a world in which power is dictated by warrior codes of honour, family, and renown. It is not a world of power peopled by many bureaucrats. There are the maisters, like the loyal servant of the Starks at Winterfell, who is pledged to serve Theon Greyjoy despite his bloodlust and his folly. There are the spymasters and social climbers, like Little Finger and Varys. But is it possible to see the three-eyed raven as a symbol of a certain kind of bureaucrat?

Another fable of sorts may sharpen the image. Winston Churchill once said that if you put five economists in a room, you get five opinions. Unless, that is, one of the economists is Mr Keynes (John Maynard Keynes), in which case you get six.

I doubt these days if you put five bureaucrats in a room you would get five opinions. You would be lucky to get two. Some would say we can do whatever you wish Mr Churchill. Most would take their lead from the first to express a view, lock in behind it, and then reassure the Prime Minister that this was a big idea that would secure long-term reform. One or two might quibble about certain risks, but be careful to ensure they were not being seen as sticks in the mud, sceptical of the benefits of change. "I am sure our communications people can hammer out some lines - just a few dot points - that will manage this, Minister," they might say.

There is, however, at least so I hope and dream, within the scarred and decaying world-tree of government some trios of blackbirds, ready to sing some different songs. They are hard to find, these trios, since so many have been driven out over the last twenty years when the intellectual culture of the bureaucracy has succumbed to waves of bad ideas, grunted by thugs disguised as clerks. But in a few places, not least in my mind, they endure. What do you see when you look at such a bureaucrat?

You see a person of a genuinely open mind, who is capable of generating multiple perspectives on an issue. Such a bureaucrat might, for example, be tasked with devising ways to reduce alcohol problems in the community. They will look around and see quickly that the stakeholders are grouped into armed camps, each convinced in their convictions. On one side is public health, convinced that if you control availability - tax and ban - the problems will go away. On the other side, is industry who will say you need to do something about the problem drinkers, and with a sometimes mixed conscience assure you that regulations always fail. Such a bureaucrat will ask, is there not a third way, or a fourth, and even a fifth? They will investigate each of the many alternative paths, even if no-one accompanies them along that way. And they will come back and ask - what do the drinkers have to say about this? What about the principle of nothing about us, without us? Since such bureaucrats can speak many tongues, they will hear the subtleties in every case of special pleading. They will reach across the barricades of entrenched groups, and ask attentively about conditions there. They will present each piece of advice not as a "case for change," but as a scene from a never-ending drama. The characters will be vividly drawn. They will speak in their true voice. The conflicts will be fundamental - like Weber's warring gods of ultimate values - and the audience will receive no trite fable. They will be asked to search their own depths for their own most authentic answer, and will know they have responded to a deep question. "What shall we do, and how shall we arrange our lives?"

I cannot be sure how many share my sense of such a vocation of bureaucracy. I know we appear today to be scarce, and even under siege. But I live in the faith that this fragment of culture - and governing is culture, a form of human conduct - is worth preserving. It is a tradition that may be imperiled, but cannot be allowed to die.

These figures must persist: the three blackbirds in the tree who give choices to how we arrange our lives together, the three-eyed raven who sees the manifold possibilities of past, present and future, the bureaucrat whose inquiry makes possible choices, compromises and peaceful cohabitation in our society, which is so fragmented into pluralistic totalitarian bands that neither listen, nor speak, nor open their minds to strangers.

Inlaid on the marble floor of the Queen's Hall of Parliament House in Melbourne are these words from *Proverbs 11:14:* "Where no Counsel is the People Fall; but in the Multitude of Counsellors there is Safety."

III The craft of the cameo actor

> The blackbird whirled in the autumn winds.
> It was a small part of the pantomime.
> (Stevens, *Thirteen Ways of Looking at a Blackbird*)

Imagine yourself at a crowded and vexed public meeting. A few hundred ordinary people, that legendary *topos*, have gathered to discuss an issue that is causing concern in the community. It could be any one of the myriad of issues governments must decide in a fog of conflicting opinions, where complex layers of political, institutional, legal, professional, interest group and moral decision-making grind up against the life-worlds of these ordinary people. It might be about the siting of a new prison, or a proposal to redesign an important local medical service, or a provincial government's plans to extend a train network in a way that damages some residents' amenity. It might even be about more elevated topics - the directions of a country's foreign policy, ways to promote new industries or to anaesthetise dying businesses, how to protect people against violence, or ways to promote social cohesion in a world of disarray. The issue does not matter: let us focus on the roles of the actors on stage.

There will be a spokesperson for the government, under whose authority proceedings are convened. It may be the Minister. It may be a Minister's trusted adviser. It may be a proxy in the form of an eminent person, a representative of the community, the chair of a review panel. Whoever they may be, they are the focus of the attention, and they are the person for whom the performances of this pantomime are made (to echo Stevens' poem ironically, since this theatre is far from comic, far from pantomime). There will be the protesters, armed with placards, t-shirts and slogans. There will be a few quietly intrusive representatives of the private interests which are most disturbed by any decision on the issue. These sleek fellows will usually be dressed in suits (if not ties, since they appear to be going out with the dodo at such events) and seated towards the front. They will speak in calm and insinuating terms, suggestive of an unwanted intimacy with decision-makers, and present themselves as a reasoned contrast to the abusive, angry protesters. There may be one or two academic experts, some of whom will have sided with one or other of the disputants. They may even have been invited to speak as an expert to help inform the audience, in a rite of evidence-based policy.

In the shadows and the wings, there will be a few bureaucrats. They may not say much. Then again, they might say a lot. They may be put on the spot by the outraged community activist, who is exasperated with decisions made without us, and challenged to find the best methods to defuse and deflect anger. They may be asked questions by lawyers with attitude, which these advocates know they cannot answer without embarrassing their Minister. Then again, they may perform a part with calm assurance: quickly bringing a long and convoluted question to the nub of an issue; concisely summarising the key points of debate; displaying a virtuoso command of the statistical and scholarly information that can help guide a war of passions. Their assurance may be completely silent, like a playwright gently nodding approval of the acting troupe's fine realisation of his script.

However well or poorly performed, this is the whirl in the autumn winds. The flight of the bureaucrat in this flurry can only be made with craft. Craft is the enemy of management and tactless innovation; but craft is the ally of those who seek to govern well. We will know the ordinary virtues of governing well only through the craft skills of the bureaucrat. We will applaud the fine performance - even if we do not know we do so for this reason - not only because of the striking poses of the leading men and women, but in response to the subtle tissues sewn by the acting craft of the scarcely known cameo artists whose careers are made in shadows.

IV In unity is death

> A man and a woman
>
> Are one.
>
> A man and a woman and a blackbird
>
> Are one.
>
> (Stevens, *Thirteen Ways of Looking at a Blackbird*)

The supreme fiction of government is the unity of politics and administration. This fiction is told through many conceits and many variations. Sam Finer's glorious achievement, his multi-volume *History of Government from the Earliest Times*, written after his retirement from the university, distinguished between decision-makers and decision-implementers. Woodrow Wilson, long before entering politics, as a young doctoral student, looked to the Prussian bureaucratic tradition to imagine a science of administration that was not dirtied by "the poisonous atmosphere of city government, the crooked secrets of state administration, the confusion, the sinecurism and corruption ever and again discovered in the bureaux at Washington."[7] There, in an unworldly puritanism sickened by the patronage of politics, the field of public administration was born.

Weber composed his conceit differently, with a more tragic foreboding, as rational-legal authority. Duller economists compose mathematical formulae on the principal-agent problem to seek to explain away messy human problems. Both hide away in rules or in contracts the divisions between politics and administration. The Westminster system itself, that common resort of scoundrels among the top echelons of the bureaucracy, vests this fiction in myths of Ministerial responsibility and meritocratic appointments. And then there are the true believers in political will, reform, integrity or leadership, who dream that their vision of the world can be imposed through government as one. The leader, their Cabinet, the top officials, the minor officials, the public sector unions, the stakeholders will all get on board as one, and the great Reform, the last Utopia, will reveal itself to the world.

Two cannot be one. Nor can three, and even less any higher number. We live in unresolvable plurality. Our lives are long acts of distinguishing ourselves from others. It is by finding the differences in our being and living together with them that we find authentic identities and life-giving freedom, not by confusing our leaders with 'unifying intelligence', as the regrettable Secretary of the Victorian Department of Premier and Cabinet, Chris Eccles, imagined. And it is only by abandoning the supreme fiction of unity that we can see truly the presence of the bureaucrat in governing.

After all, it is not as if bureaucrats have been much loved by the politicians who are the true rulers of governments. Both the *Oxford English Dictionary* and Stein Ringen define a government as a body of

---

[7] "The Study of Administration" (1887), quoted Fukuyama, *Political Order and Political Decay: from the Industrial Revolution to the Globalisation of Democracy* (2014).

persons who govern a nation. That body of persons is formed of Ministers of the ruling party. To distinguish the government from governing, or the vast strange web of governance, is to see clearly the blackbird flying into view like the holy spirit. As Ringen wrote:

> we need to unwrap the system that generates governance and explore what goes on inside it. For me, the relationship between the political bosses and their civil servants, for example, is very much a part of the mystery of governance, and I don't want to hide that mystery away in a definition that says that both bosses and servants are parts of the same thing.[8]

To see the differences, we need to look past the nice compliments and befuddling stories of cohesion traded by serving and retired witnesses of high politics. Behind closed doors, or when pressed by recurrent failures, the venom and the hatred of difference comes out. What better example than that great advocate of reform and vision, Tony Blair, who Ringen magisterially assays as a master of "activism in all things, and accomplishment in none." A master of appearing across his brief, Blair's unifying intelligence could never grasp why the institutions at his command did not unify before his fluffy will. His whipping boy was the civil service. He would describe them as the "sinecure cynics who despise anything modern and are made uneasy by success."[9]

His recurrent sallies at reforming the National Health Service all failed, so that he resembled some latter-day Don Quixote, who had lost touch with reality through reading too many business magazines and crisply titled consultants' charts. He surrounded himself with advisers who comforted him in his delusions, but he could not ever really see the real people in the institution and how it might be made to work better. The civil service was always wrong, always a problem, always in need of reform and modernisation. Tom Bower's remarkable account

---

[8] Stein Ringen, *A Nation of Devils: Democratic Leadership and the Problem of Obedience* (2013).
[9] Tom Bower, *Broken Vows: Tony Blair - the tragedy of power* (2016).

of Blair's tragic years in power is informed by many interviews with senior and lowly officials who served in Blair's sofa court. Through their testimony they make clear that Blair ran a government at odds with itself, and with any decent culture of governing. Politics itself was fragmented, and his intellectual divorce from the "traditional culture of government during his decade in Downing Street" undermined all achievement. His undeclared civil war within government itself led to the tragic failures of Iran and Afghanistan; but more Bowers concluded,

> We now realise that the path to the two wars was not an aberration but all of a piece with the way his government behaved across its entire domestic agenda, especially in the areas of health, education, energy and immigration. In a tragic sense, Blair had been consistent.[10]

Unusually, Bowers in his biography of Blair left the last word to a bureaucrat. There were three top civil servants, Cabinet Secretaries, who served Blair, all competently and loyally in Bowers' judgement. All of them, after witnessing the strife of politics and administration and Blair's many questionable acts, later judged that "Blair had not been a laudable guardian of the public's interest." The book closes with the reflection of longest-serving of these Cabinet Secretaries, Richard Wilson,

> There are events during my period as Cabinet secretary that make me shudder at what I remember because we had high hopes and we were so disappointed. He promised so much, but in the end so little was achieved.[11]

More disappointment had been harvested from the supreme fiction of government. What might have been, if this illusion had been dispelled, and stronger leaders of public institutions had acted with a belief that in unity is death?

---

[10] Bowers, *Broken Vows*, p 594
[11] Bowers, *Broken Vows*, p. 594

13 Ways of Looking at a Bureaucrat

V The beauty of the bureaucrat

> I do not know which to prefer,
>
> The beauty of inflections
>
> Or the beauty of innuendoes,
>
> The blackbird whistling
>
> Or just after.
>
> (Stevens, *Thirteen Ways of Looking at a Blackbird*)

The idea that there is beauty in the acts of a bureaucrat may seem a shocking idea. Querulous. Contrary. Quixotic.

Are not bureaucrats grey, banal, the enemies of the great things, dull in their aesthetic sense, collectors of the petty and mean? Is this not the verdict of Hannah Arendt, the priestess of the public intellectual, on that archetype of the bureaucrat, the accounts clerk of the death camps, Adolf Eichmann. Did she not find radical evil clothed in the banality of an unthinking, compliant bureaucrat?

Bureaucrats are commonly presented in comedies of muddling through. Fair to middling, mediocre, not beautiful, not striking a pose of lasting value. They are the shackles on the visions of the great artists, the exquisite leaders, the entrepreneurs. They are the measurers, the schemers and the quibblers, not the creators, the inventors, the performers of beautiful theatre.

To claim beauty in the bureaucracy, somewhere on that vast incomplete canvas of grey oils, is a thought at odds with my own reflections that the modern bureaucracy is a confederacy of dunces, an affront to its intellectual traditions, a terrible disappointment to those of us who believed we were joining an institution of mandarins, schooled in essays on practical moral judgement.

Certainly, the prospects for acts of true beauty and lasting cultural value from our decayed institutions seem poor. They have been overrun by patronage of the consultocrats. They are plagued by leaders who mistake their ambition to impress their patrons with boldness of purpose, clarity of vision, and persuasive thought. A head of a department will decide that they can prove their mettle to their political leader by using a tragic, deadly and rare event to force the institution they lead to do things it will not do. They will bend it to a different purpose, twist its laws against its principles, and turn hard cases into bad law. A problem that does not exist will be decorated with powerpoint charts of flimsy concepts - cohort segmentation, process maps of unique events, service models for half-baked ideas - and whenever someone stops and questions the quality of the thought, what is the response? "Well the head of the department is very ambitious... They stand back and take a wider view.... They are pursuing 'opportunistic reform'."

Such thoughts, such projects, such pandering to the court are the antitheses of work of lasting value. Actions like these are destroying our public institutions, turning them into a vanity theatre for a meritless, parasitic court. They are acts of vandalism, turning institutions with a cultural life of their own into the playthings of rootless reformers.

But I would not feel so strongly if I did not have an attachment to something at once both profound and connected to enduring value. Surely that attachment is to some kind of beauty that survives in these ravaged institutions. The subordinated people who must try to make some good from these fanciful reform projects, fudge, dissemble and prevaricate in the hope that their more enduring ideas might survive these dark times. They raise their doubts. They question the speed with which all such follies rush to their bad conclusions. They sympathise with their fellow subordinates, perennially excluded from the club of the powerful, who sit around in rooms and speak ignorant contempt of their staff. They find a way to endure and survive. They repeat to themselves, when they cannot sleep at night, wracked as they are by these pantomimes of ambition, looking for some kind of comfort in profound thought, the words of Robert Conquest's third law of politics: the simplest way to explain the behaviour of any bureaucratic organisation is to assume that it is controlled by a cabal of its enemies.

They cannot confront the court or its ambitious grandees. Heroic gestures of defiance will only bring ruin on their heads, and in any case are contaminated by the empty heroic gestures of their leaders. Pity the country in need of heroes? To conserve what matters most of the discovered genius of their institutions, they must practise not heroic, but ordinary virtues. They must practice not an art of declamations on a well-lit public stage, but an art of innuendos and inflections. They must write *samizdat*.

They learn to suspect the forms of beauty that are beloved by the politicians, senior executives and consultants, who leech their work. These self professed masters of the universe admire design thinking, like Keating's clean pure lines and beautiful sets of numbers. This is a beauty of power and dominance, of the kind that clears the slums in cities and finds in boxed PowerPoint cartoons the driving causes of human behaviour.

The beauty of the bureaucrat is humbler, messier, more intricate, quieter. It is a beauty of dappled things:

> All things counter, original, spare, strange;
>
> Whatever is fickle, freckled (who knows how?)
>
> With swift, slow; sweet, sour; adazzle, dim;
>
> He fathers-forth whose beauty is past change:
>
> Praise him.
>
> (Gerald Manley Hopkins, 'Pied Beauty')

The god of the consultocrats is change. They worship it like a cargo cult. They use it to warn, intimidate, cower, and to excuse their thoughtlessness. Yet with all their change, they accomplish nil.

Thirteen Ways of Looking at a Bureaucrat

The authentic bureaucrat pursues a beauty that is past change. It is a beauty found in stooping to drink from the river of life, and other acts of humility. It is a beauty found in situations that are messes; that force all who act in them to stumble and to drop all preconceptions. It is a beauty of perplexity, of thoughts that are intricate and hard to express. This kind of beauty is imperilled by the reign of terror led by the reformers and grand designers, the well connected pontificators, and the consultocrats. It is an endangered beauty amidst political disorder and institutional decay.

Yet it is also a kind of beauty for which we must feel in the depths of our soul a lifelong, painful loss. For only in the fires of that grief can we reforge our will to conserve, cherish and fight for the pied beauty of the bureaucrat.

VI Through barbaric glass darkly

> Icicles filled the long window
>
> With barbaric glass.
>
> The shadow of the blackbird
>
> Crossed it, to and fro.
>
> The mood
>
> Traced in the shadow
>
> An indecipherable cause.
>
> (Stevens, *Thirteen Ways of Looking at a Blackbird*)

However much I may wish to make the figure of the bureaucrat familiar, for many people the way of seeing the bureaucrat will be, as in Stevens' poem, like a shadow moving inexplicably and ominously

13 Ways of Looking at a Bureaucrat

behind a frozen screen of barbaric glass.

In ordinary life we see only tightly framed glimpses of the bureaucrat in action. They are not one of the professions known to every schoolchild - a doctor, nurse, lawyer, scientist, teacher - whose role in making our shared life is immediately clear. Nor do they tend to the daily domestic needs like the trades we learn in rhymes - baker, builder, cobbler, candlestick maker. Bureaucrats serve hidden, more abstract purposes, shadows of an indecipherable cause.

Through this small window we see the bureaucrat flutter from side to side in a seemingly busy yet meaningless dance. There is always paperwork to complete, processes to follow, protocols to complete, budget bids to make, risks to manage, and reform projects to make believe in, even when they never quite find the articulate voice who can define their purpose. They fly from side to side, reinventing titles, and changing the structures of their organisations according to the latest pedantic cries of fashionable madmen, and so create a maze of ever greater impenetrability.

We see only their shadows through that glass, and do not hear their songs. The rules of the republic demand they act as dumb mimes. We do not know the chatter that occurs about the deeper things in many office cubicles, when forced to confront our shared lives' most difficult corners - containing the mad, bad and dangerous to know; consoling the broken, the addicted, the frail and the traumatised; corralling the corrupt, the ambitious, the conceited and the grandiose. Bureaucrats turn to each other to find comfort that someone else knows how it really is.

Those conversations, as between two prisoners condemned for their insight into the illusions of the outer world, can provide comfort, but can never proceed in full freedom. They can provide epiphanies: as when a lowly under-castellan will speak truths about human frailty; or the compassion required to endure a long life in institutions; or the limits of that ruthless modern deity, change. But these whispered truths are not known by the frenetic grand blackbirds above, who fly energetically from one banality to another trite lie, checking their phones, exchanging their ill-informed positions, and perfecting their gestures at court. These whispered truths endure for the survivors in the institutions, the practitioners of the ordinary virtues. They provide moments of dignity that can create little acts of freedom and small thoughts of kindness. These moments of dignity establish a survivors' code that is the hidden poetry of our troubled modern polities.

But these conversations in the dark can also turn sour. Sure in the world's misunderstanding, the insiders begin to resent always doing the dirty work that the great actors, the good and the great, the rich and the famous, do not acknowledge and will not do. This is the way of dark brotherhoods and dark sisterhoods who say: it is we who make your damned stupid laws work; it is we who cop the blame when others do wrong; it is we who need to mop up each and every social disaster, whether they be insolvent businesses or troubled families, violent youths or criminal minds, failing schools or mismanaged trains, escaped lunatics or rogue justices, drunken crowds or corrupted councillors. Behind their frozen trap, the dark brotherhoods and sisterhoods ruminate on their captive, poisoned state, and make of their resentment a virtue. They forget that the voyager through the underworld, who carries his lyre among shadows, searches to find his or her way back to infinite praise.

Surely though, as there is a season for all things, a time will come when the icicles on this frozen trap will melt away? Summer will come, and thaw away the barbaric ice, the shackles of our modern, decaying political institutions. These icicles have formed over the last 30 years, as the state has been colonised by party political marketing machines. A change in the way of governing has frosted the glass. Hard, obscure icicles have appeared: talking points, spoken by numberless witless advisers, a loss of capability in political leadership; the rise of the merchant elite and its fawning companions, the consultocrats; the cannibalisation of the university; the impoverishment of public debate in turns through panel shows and shock jocks; and the abandonment of intellectual culture by political leaders and senior bureaucrats themselves. The list of woe could go on, but that is work for another day.

Still if winter has come, can spring be far behind?

VII At the feet of thin men

> O thin men of Haddam,
> why do you imagine golden birds?
> Do you not see how the blackbird
> Walks around the feet
> Of the women around you?
> (Stevens, *Thirteen Ways of Looking at a Blackbird*)

Bureaucrats do not figure much in political utopias. Lawmakers do. Political leaders do, with their marvellous abilities of vision and will. But bureaucrats? They appear in utopias, if at all, only as exiles from the dreamt republic.

Utopias though are dangerous things. Golden illusions that lead us astray. The beautiful clean lines that insist on being etched in blood on human skin. Utopias, dreams of progress, pining for the restoration of a former time, ideals, grand visions of a better world and a purer democracy. Or merely, the reforms pursued by the thin men of Haddam. They are all temptations to straighten the crooked timber of humanity. They are all manias to make order out of chaos at least in our minds. They are all failures of looking at a bureaucrat.

To see the bureaucrat in the political world, we must be

comfortable with a messier, more mundane interpretation of the real. We must see the blackbirds feeding at the feet of the women of Haddam.

VIII Involved in what I know

> I know noble accents
> And lucid, inescapable rhythms;
> But I know, too,
> That the blackbird is involved
> In what I know.
>
> (Stevens, *Thirteen Ways of Looking at a Blackbird*)

It was Mario Cuomo, now dead former liberal democrat, governor of New York, who first said that "you campaign in poetry, and govern in prose." It is a phrase that has become a licence for political deceit. After all, poetry is grand, and prose is dull; are they not? So surely the public must understand that the political vaudeville is compressed. Surely they must accept that imaginative words that carry us away from the hard, prosaic accounting of compromised governing?

There is a misunderstanding in Cuomo's words, that is never questioned when this licence to deceive is repeated to excuse every broken promise, every disappointing decision. Poetry and prose overlap; they are not separate realms. Poetry can be beautiful, and it can have a terrible new beauty. Poetry can be like God-given speech, and it can be machine-written. Prose can be exquisite, of some other world, like Thomas Browne or his modern echo W.G. Sebald; and prose can be execrable, unintelligible, devoid of all sense, purpose and beauty.

I have known moments of lucid inescapable rhythms in my working life as a bureaucrat. Once indeed I was called upon to write some poems. The Cardinal once decided that the Australia Day oath was not to his liking. A talk back host had objected to its corny lines, and the Cardinal wanted to impress his master with a better result. So he asked me to write some alternative poems to replace the oath. I wrote three. The one I liked best, which lilted to a Presley song and conjured toes curling in the sand of a summer beach, was rejected, and another took the place of the doggerel oath.

Other times, action has had noble accents. I have stood vulnerable before drug users and wanted to make changes to how we treat addiction to consecrate their pain. I have stood in this life and been confronted with the deepest questions (what is culture? How do we change it?), and gone on to answer the call responsibly as best I could.

In all these moments, the bureaucrat has been involved too. Beans have had to be counted. Forms filled out. Commands obeyed. Details checked. Poetry and prose intermingle in the culture of governing.

IX Servants of Utopia

> When the blackbird flew out of sight,
>
> It marked the edge
>
> Of one of many circles
>
> (Stevens, *Thirteen Ways of Looking at a Blackbird*)

There is a strange book out there, which, if I ever develop these blogged posts into a more scholarly collection of essays, I suppose I will

Thirteen Ways of Looking at a Bureaucrat

have to read, and it is called *On the Utopia of Rules: on technology, stupidity and the secret joys of bureaucracy*. Written by an American activist academic, David Graeber, who describes himself as an "anarchist anthropologist", it declaims the "total bureaucratization" of the world. This is the utopia of rules, in which there is a strange marriage between the worst of Capitalism and the worst of Bureaucracy, both accented with pantomime capitals.

It is very much a view from outside bureaucracy; the libertarian anarchism that seems so prevalent in American culture, and the resentment of constraints by rules and resources that is so common among modern salaried professors. As a way of looking at bureaucrats, it is strangely unconvincing.

For a start, it misses the mark in describing the people who it caricatures. There are plenty of Graebers who I have encountered within the bureaucracy, who make it their mission to deregulate and strip away all constraints on the creative destruction of the merchants who they adore from afar. Far from utopians of rules, some bureaucrats are utopians of markets. I am not claiming there are not silly rules in all forms of modern bureaucracy, but these accounts of petty, rule-bound bureaucrats obsessed with process and paperwork are little more than thoughtless sneers. They bring us no closer to understanding the importance of law, as a repository of Edmund Burke's compact between the past, present and future; nor do they really help us understand the strange, more pervasive role of utopian fallacies in modern bureaucracies.

These ways of looking at the bureaucrat suffer a conceptual hostility to the state that is itself utopian, or at least suffers from the born free fallacy described in Roger Scruton's ever-useful, *The Uses of Pessimism: and the Danger of False Hope*. John Gray's review of Graeber's *The Utopia of Rules* isolated the book's account of bureaucracy as a utopian vision of the world ruled by rational principles. Graeber extended his anarchist vision to believe in the deformation of the true "insurrectionary moment" by the deviation of revolutionaries from their true lawless path through the maze of bureaucracy. So Graeber quoted Lenin's scornful wish to run the Revolution "like a postal service". And John Gray scornfully corrected Graeber; only an academic useful idiot could believe such martinet exclamations were the real cause of the Revolution's disappointments.

The state, law and strong bureaucratic institutions are gifts of the political world. They are the artefacts that make freedom possible, not the curses that suppress it. They are the associations in which negotiated solutions to our many conflicts may be discovered, beyond the limited vision, however utopian, of any one mind. As John Gray observed,

> But does it follow that state power is always and only repressive? Can't it sometimes also be liberating? Turning away from these awkward questions to a fantasy of unfettered freedom, Graeber joins hands with the neoliberals he scorns.[12]

John Gray has in mind some specific examples of bureaucratic institutions, such as the United Kingdom's post-war National Health Service, that are threatened by both the libertarianism of the merchants, the follies of the spin-doctors and a more pervasive utopia of Reform. And it is here that I begin to see more connections with my own experience.

> In Graeber's neo-anarchist view, the state is a demonic force thwarting human freedom. This seems to me a simple-minded philosophy, but perhaps it explains why he says so little about the public services that were created as part of the postwar settlement in Britain. Not entangled in government directives as almost every public body is at the present time, these were genuinely autonomous institutions. Regulated by those who worked in them, they weren't burdened by the bloated bureaucracy that

---

[12] Gray, "The utopia of rules on technology, stupidity and the secret joys of bureaucracy," *The Guardian*, 6 May 2015

strangles them today. But they were able to enjoy this freedom only because a public space had been created for it by the use of state power.

I work in one deformed successor to such an institution, although its origins are further back in the nineteenth century. The Health Department of Victoria has had many incarnations, and like public health departments around the world, it has long been at the heart of the modern state. It has used public resources, rules, professional expertise, imaginative action and the authority of the state to improve the lives of the community it serves. There is no clearer measure of this than the exceptional growth in life expectancy since the mid-nineteenth century.

Yet today this public institution and its best traditions are entangled in overheated grand plans, a bloated senior executive court, and a poisonous growth of bureaucratic utopianism. This poison is not Graeber's Utopia of Rules, but a Utopia of Reform. It is a poison of grandiosity, not of pettiness.

This Utopia of Reform is not an exclusively bureaucratic phenomenon. The Utopian plans, visions, "systems reforms" and targets to eliminate all blights on the human condition come from many sources – politicians, activists, lawyers, academics, the not-for-profit sector, even some business leaders. There is not a single Utopia pursued, but many Reforms – projected into a "future state" which these once prudent, proud institutions now kowtow before. All of these reform ideas commit the utopian fallacy, as Roger Scruton described it,

> Hence the utopian fallacy, which tells us that the ideal is immune to refutation. We need never turn back on our utopian aims, since utopia itself can never be realized and thus never disproved. It serves instead as an abstract condemnation of everything around us, and it justifies the believer in taking full control.[13]

---

[13] Scruton, *The Uses of Pessimism and the Danger of False Hope* (2012)

13 Ways of Looking at a Bureaucrat

It may seem surprising to describe the upper courts of bureaucracy as infected by Utopianism, but that is what I see around me. It is not necessarily a Utopianism without pragmatism, without cynicism, without opportunist careerism. To present yourself as a reformer, as an advocate of "change", is the badge that marks belonging to the executive class of the bureaucracy today. And like group markers everywhere, this apparent idealistic, enthusiastic embrace of change is a declaration that those outside the club are the enemy of all their striving.

> The ideal remains forever on the horizon of our experience, unsullied and untried, casting judgement on all that is actual, like a sun that cannot be looked at but which creates a dark side to everything on which it shines.

The blackbird files out of sight of the institutions which they have coerced into their dreams, and marks the edge of the future circles from which the actual people of those institutions are excluded.

Is it any wonder that there are political revolts around the world against these Utopias of Reform that have come to dominate our bureaucratic and political elites over the last thirty years? People realise, as Scruton wrote, that "Behind the utopia there advances another aim altogether, which is the desire for revenge against reality."

This virus of reform cannot be effectively opposed by dreams of liberation from the state, but by a restitution of the institutions of law, good government and bureaucracy. It requires a defence of the tradition of bureaucracy, governing and authority that I am groping my way towards understanding in these posts. This is necessary since, as Scruton argued, the reform solutions of the bureaucratic utopians destroy the institutions that enable us to resolve our conflicts one by one.

Rather than pursue the disappearing circles of our utopian blackbirds, we need to restore a bureaucratic tradition of sober judgment, cautious authority, prudent thought, and respectful talking to strangers.

> The solution to human conflicts is discovered case by case, and embodied thereafter in precedents, customs and laws. The solution does not exist as a plan, a scheme or a utopia. It is the residue of a myriad agreements and negotiations, preserved in custom and law. Solutions are rarely envisaged in advance, but steadily accumulate through dialogue and negotiation. They are a deposit laid down by the 'we' attitude, as it unfolds through norms of mutual dealing. And it is precisely this deposit, in customs and institutions, that the utopians set out to destroy.

The antidote to the Utopias of Rules and the Utopia of Reform is thus not liberation, freedom or markets, but law, institutions and a modest belief that we are all blackbirds.

X Flight in green light

> At the sight of blackbirds
> Flying in a green light,
> Even the bawds of euphony
> Would cry out sharply.
> (Stevens, *Thirteen Ways of Looking at a Blackbird*)

It is not often that the average educated reasonable person catches a glimpse of bureaucrats in flight, out in the open, for all to see, their black wings starkly beautiful in a soft green light. They are told it is not their job to take the limelight. They should keep away from public stages, television lights, and open-ended discussions with media identities. Most are harshly disciplined for talking out of school, even for making critical comments on Facebook about the upper hierarchy of their organisations. Free speech – even perhaps all elements of freedom of thought, conscience and religion as defined by the *International Covenant of Civil and Political Rights* – is something bureaucrats routinely, in my experience (yes, limited to a tolerant democracy of moderate quality), defend for others, while not enjoying themselves.

An effective invisibility cloak and a great cone of silence – that evergreen metaphor of broken, mundane conspiracies created by Mel Brooks in *Get Smart* – screen out bureaucrats from the great conversations on matters of public importance that shape the moral lives of our distressed republics. Those republics suffer for it. They suffer through a lowering of standards of public speech and political thought. They suffer through the gradual humiliation and disordering of the great public institutions of bureaucracy, which are at their strongest when they enjoy a strong, open and accountable relationship with the people they serve. That relationship should not be funnelled through the cell phone of a whizz-kid political adviser and the mindless demands of the 24-hour political media machine. They suffer from the diminished pool of knowledge shared to solve our many common problems of coordination. They suffer through the loss to the public stage of some of the best informed, articulate and compassionate minds. In their place we get panel shows of partisan left/right think-tankers, meretricious lobbyists and journalists endlessly talking to journalists about what journalists think of the issues in the papers of the day. Truly, the bawds of cacophony.

Could it be another way? I recall several years ago a serious current affairs television program announced that it would interview the head of the department responsible for child protection and family services, then called, with no conscious irony, the Department of Human Services. The department had been heavily criticised on many matters. The still quite new Government, then within the first weeks or months of its office, had even made something of a major election issue of the failings of this department and promised a major and fundamental inquiry, quite an unusual reordering political priorities. The head of the department was also not some mere courtier, but had worked on the front lines of child protection in her early career. She held a deep knowledge of the dilemmas, and had some real polish in speaking clearly to many audiences about how things ought to improve. Moreover, it was she who had been responsible directly and personally for many of the failures and many of the successes in child protection over maybe 20 years. It was right that she should face the tough questions, not some Minister newly briefed and with only a helicopter view of the problems. Surely, she is the best person to ask, on principle because of both her knowledge and accountability.

But when it came time for the interview, the capable, polished and assertive Minister appeared in the studio and live to air. The first question of her, was why would you not let your most senior bureaucrat speak directly to the program? The Minister's response was that I am the elected official and the Minister responsible, and it is appropriate that I represent the Government's views to the public. This is the Westminster system, but more it is a narrow code of operations enforced with rigid, thoughtless discipline entrenched by political and media advisory staff over the last thirty years.

It is not that the Minister was not capable and within her rights to speak on behalf of the Government. But was she really within her rights to silence her most senior official, and to prevent any form of direct relationship between the leaders of bureaucratic institutions and the public they serve? The Minister, after all, would have many more opportunities to speak to the media. The provincial government I serve releases five or more media releases every day. But they are the cheap and bowdlerised verse of the bawds of euphony. It is surely time to silence their cries; to sit back and to observe the blackbird in flight in these strange and rare lights.

13 Ways of Looking at a Bureaucrat

XI People who live in glass coaches

> He rode over Connecticut
> In a glass coach.
> Once, a fear pierced him,
> In that he mistook
> The shadow of his equipage
> For blackbirds.
> (Stevens, *Thirteen Ways of Looking at a Blackbird*)

At first, the image of travel in a glass coach, magically through the harbour towns and rural havens of Connecticut, might seem an image of bureaucratic isolation. Don't they live in a bubble, a fragile bubble, sealed off from the more robust world of rule-breakers, creators and destroyers? Do they not live in a privilege of immunity from the crush and hungry treading of the world and its markets?

But in a way, all who live in the affluent degraded democracies of the once liberal world order, do travel in a glass coach across the soothing countryside of New Haven. Our worlds are inundated with wealth, images and information, and anyone of us can summon to our palaces our very own glass coach from which we explore in transparent isolation our soothing, yet troubled, world.

Of course, this coach casts a shadow, even if faintly through its frames and joins. Even the simplest of our abundant pleasures have side-effects and preconditions. Every trip in isolation down the country road already assumes the *we*, who made the road, who set out the signs, who explained the rules of driving (even in magical vehicles, safety rules keep more people safe), who plotted the countryside, and who kept the titles by which its dwellers claim it as their own. So much organisation, so much responsibility, so much bureaucracy for every freedom ride.

But we suppose ourselves born free, unchained from tradition, loosed from all institutions and unaccountable, in our splendid glass coaches, to the *we* who created our ride. We travel in Romantic splendour in a glass coach of change, of innovation, of the latest; and we do not want to be reminded of the mundane work of stability, without which our glass cage of freedom would shatter.

So, we shriek in fear. So, we see the ominous blackbird of bureaucracy staining our lives. Dull, lifeless, not at all a friend to man. What does the fearful shadow tell us? That we are all bureaucrats?

XII The thaw, the flight

> The river is moving.
> The blackbird must be flying.
> (Stevens, *Thirteen Ways of Looking at a Blackbird*)

I dwell in a land where the rivers are always moving, except when they dry out, when they would be called dry creek beds, not rivers. To imagine a place where a river is not moving is to imagine a place without life.

I have travelled to lands where rivers do not move because they freeze, and so, I read, Stevens' mind of winter has stopped life, time, flight for this moment before the thaw.

But in my world the river never stops moving. Some call it change. Some call it events. Some call it power. Some call it culture. If the river stopped moving, the sun would parch us to death. The river is always moving. The sun always rises in the morning.

And so too the bureaucrat is always in flight. Never still. Always scanning the world. Always swooping by the water. Bound to the flowing river, until the exhausted blackbird falls from the sky. Then a new blackbird begins to singest of summer in full-throated ease.

XIII The long waits of winter

> It was evening all afternoon.
>
> It was snowing
>
> And it was going to snow.
>
> The blackbird sat
>
> In the cedar-limbs.
>
> (Stevens, *Thirteen Ways of Looking at a Blackbird*)

Our working lives are long, and yet our culture's celebration of youth is stronger: the energetic, the passionate, the believers and the ambitious displace those who know better, and who are resented for knowing better. After a certain time, all bureaucrats are passed over, treated like yesterday's failed lieutenants, and pushed into some dark corner where they wait out the evening all afternoon long.

There they sit in the cedar-limbs, bristling against the snow. Cold, alone, forgotten, the despised part of their accursed kind.

How many years might this long winter snow continue? I ask myself this question since surely this is now my fate. But am I not the same blackbird whose mobile eye chased down the still world? Am I not the same blackbird who performed his cameo parts perfectly in the theatre of power? Do I not still have visions? Can I not still sing of

Thirteen Ways of Looking at a Bureaucrat

innuendos and inflections? Can I not be one with any man or any woman? Fly in green light, or swoop behind a glass coach in Connecticut?

    I am. And the long years that I have to wait still in these cedar-limbs will be as truthfully, beautifully the way of a bureaucrat as the other twelve manifestations, or as many more as you might imagine. If the snow that I know will be coming does not kill me, it will make my winter's mind stronger.

13 Ways of Looking at a Bureaucrat

Chapter Four   Governing the Drunken Commons

Governing the drunken commons

In 2006 I took a job running an alcohol and drug policy unit in the minor provincial government in which I serve as a lowly under-castellan. It turned out to be a very rewarding experience, at least if you count the intrinsic rewards of work as the most important. I met some remarkable people – Robin Room, Stefan Grunert, David Best – and also struggled with some of the hardest questions, so it seemed at the time, of public policy. Alcohol, so my colleagues kept telling me, was one of those wicked problems. For me though, coming to terms with the difficulty of alcohol policy was something more of a personal journey of recovery.

Serving the wayward and the drunken, it turned out, did very little for my career. I plunged deeper and deeper into a kind of career crisis, in a smelly eddy far away from the flow of success. But I also accomplished many things, and not the least of those things was a kind of understanding of my conservative disposition in which grew my attachment to the ethos of my institution. It was that ethos that I saw forgotten and dishonoured all around me. It was the realisation that I had fused my identity with a culture that was disappearing from the world that would in time lead me into despair.

About a year or so after leaving the alcohol and drug policy job, in 2014, I wrote a conference paper that tried to make sense of it all. I gave this conference paper to the Kettil Bruun Society conference, a minor academic society dedicated to the impact of alcohol on society, policy and health. The Society is named after a Finnish social researcher who during the 1960s, 1970s and early 1980s influenced many alcohol control policies in Scandinavia and around the world. The conference I spoke to had a particular focus on how consensus views of alcohol researchers could be translated into real alcohol control policies. Most members of the audience were frustrated, even dumbfounded, that the policies of governments differed from the advice of researchers. I spoke to them as something of a kindly, compassionate heretic.

Some time later, a student interviewed me about the experience when another great city took fate in its hand and succumbed to the grand follies of controlling the availability of alcohol.[14] Now having left government in 2022 I can share my thoughts more openly. Here is the essay as it could have appeared if I had ever pursued the option of an academic journal.

---

[14] 'How to break a city's heart in three easy steps,' *Lot's Wife*, 10 May 2016.

Why is alcohol policy difficult? Reflections of a bureaucrat

Introduction

This paper asks two questions: why does alcohol policy so often fail, and what makes it difficult? Responses to these questions underlie how both researchers and policy-makers conduct and converse about alcohol policy research that aims to have an impact on policy. I reflect on some historical examples of failure and my own personal experience of failure. I draw out from my interpretation of debates on alcohol policy three explanations of policy failure - dominant interests, weak ideas, and wicked problems. While each explanation contributes insights, ultimately I prefer a fourth explanation. The difficulty of alcohol policy is rather, in the tradition of Bernard Crick's defence of politics, the noble difficulty of politics. Good alcohol policies, then, require less evidence based-policy, and more good government.

My paper is not a standard research paper, but rather the personal reflections of a former alcohol policy bureaucrat. In that role I read much research and thought deeply and daily on alcohol, or the 'drink question'. The forms in which my thought and research found expression, however, were very different to conference papers of the academic world. In the role, I also had the good fortune to work closely with Professor Robin Room. When I left the role, Robin encouraged me to write something about my experiences. I thank Robin and the organisers of the Kettil Bruun conference for accepting this paper, which is a stepping stone towards a more complete reflection on my experience.[15]

If not a conventional research paper, it is also not a conventional official's presentation. I have no dot points, and have rather enjoyed

---

[15] I imagined as I wrote this sentence in 2013 that I might find my own way to an academic position and complete a book-length study of the conflicts over alcohol policy. I have abandoned that project.

writing paragraphs of more than three sentences. I have tried to make sense through reflection of some frankly difficult experiences. The views expressed here, I need to state, are my own. They are not the views of the organisation I work for, nor are they the views of the Governments I have served. I have asked neither for any comments or endorsement of this paper. The paper is presented in my after-hours capacity as an independent scholar, rather than on behalf of my institutional affiliation. Moreover, I no longer play any role in alcohol policy, having moved on to another field in the department, so I offer this interpretation merely as a critical, but irrelevant, friend. Yet, I still speak with the restrictions of the public service code of conduct and rules on disclosure of confidences, and so sometimes speak a little indirectly. Moreover, these views are puzzled out while writing, and reflect my own deep uncertainty about the answers.

Temperamentally, I am with Vaclav Havel who urged those who seek to live in the truth to "keep the company of those who seek the truth, and run from those who have found it." When I ask why is alcohol policy difficult, I am seeking but have not found the truth. But framing these questions and essaying some answers, however partial, are essential tasks to bridging the unfortunate misunderstandings between the worlds of research and governing. Policy impact from alcohol research can only come by bridging those worlds through mutual respect for different manners of thought, not digging in with certain beliefs about what works and translating research into practice.

The Kettil Bruun tradition of alcohol policy

In 1972 Kettil Bruun gave a lecture here in Melbourne, the same city hosting this conference. He was sponsored by the Australian Alcoholism Foundation, then chaired by Weary Dunlop, the celebrated doctor who lived through and helped prisoners of war at Changi and subsequently helped many ex-soldiers who struggled with the drink.[16]

---

[16] Kettil Bruun, *Dilemmas in Drug Control Policy* (Melbourne: Alcoholism Foundation of Victoria, 1972).

Governing the Drunken Commons

Dunlop symbolised the post-war Australian society and elite that, in 1972, was in the midst of a major transition. Within a few years the Australian Alcoholism Foundation would soon change its name to the Australian Drug Foundation. Bruun was about to challenge this society with his speech on the theme of how to conceive and to prepare a good alcohol policy.

Bruun outlined three dilemmas that needed to be dealt with in order to prepare a 'systematically planned alcohol policy'. I will discuss just the first dilemma, that is, should the object of policy be alcohol or alcoholism? Bruun argued in favour of targeting the product, and not the disease, which may not have been good policy news for the foundation named after the disease. Bruun said that to choose this objective (policy more alcohol control, instead of less alcoholism) "represents an attempt to influence not only alcoholics and the coming rate of alcoholics, but the societal level of drinking, which may be manipulated by such factors as prices and availability." Bruun anticipated an objection, while still making light of it. It would be difficult to set such an objective to control the production and sale of alcohol, so difficult that the attempt may fail, and so deter government action. Such attempts, Bruun argued in the very different ideological climate of the early 1970s, stood in contrast to 'the Western world's ideology of free enterprise'. Regrettably, therefore, Bruun's experience was that many governments in many countries did not heed his advice and instead pursued policy that 'seems to fall into line with the philosophy of controlling alcoholics rather than that of the economic interest'. This interest, he elsewhere said "endeavours to raise the level of consumption," the exactly opposite aim of alcohol control policies. But Bruun kept hope alive, and in this lecture said that he sought to reawaken 'the historical development of an advanced philosophy in regard to the importance of excluding private profit from the liquor business'. This approach was exemplified in the Gothenburg system, the method of alcohol control through government-operated alcohol stores and local rationing that was established by some Swedish local governments in the nineteenth century. Intriguingly, Bruun primarily made his argument on the basis of principle, rather than effect. In other words, he did not attempt what we might call today 'evidence-based policy'. "Specific control measures have not provided much evidence of effect," he admitted; but Bruun took consolation in a methodological argument. It was too difficult to single out 'one particular detail of control' in order to demonstrate the impact of his wished-for policies in the real world. Ultimately, Bruun's argument rested on a political point: "in countries which are trying to develop an alcohol policy, an awareness should exist of the importance of controlling the economic interests connected with the production and sale, along with discussion of the practicability of abolishing the right to advertise, and to control prices and availability." In other words, it is not a question of what works, but of who does what to whom.

I imagine that Bruun's talk that night in 1972 gave birth to the ideas about alcohol policy that still shape modern public health policy arguments today. In the forty years since Bruun's Melbourne declaration, scholars such as Robin Room have elaborated these ideas, and pursued the philosophy of 'excluding private profit from the liquor business' despite a world of political ideas remade by Reagan, Thatcher, Clinton, Blair, Hawke and Keating. The political world after 1989 became increasingly hostile to the political principles that underlay Bruun's argument. His ideas of social control of the means of alcohol production have struggled in the political contest, but they have generated a rich tradition of scholarship, with thousands of research projects detailing dimensions of the control philosophy. They have also steeled a large public health lobbying industry that won an honourable victory over the tobacco industry, and is fighting the same war to solve the 'drink question'. The Finnish general laid out the battle plan to persuade governments to tax, restrict and ban.

For seven years, I worked by the long fertile river that flowed from Kettil Bruun's ideas, and in the fields so ably irrigated from this river by Robin Room. There I ran the alcohol policy unit in the Victorian Government in one of those recurring times when the 'drink question' spilled over from private drinking rooms to the political cabinets of the nation. Good and bad ideas were debated fiercely, and implemented both weakly and well. My seven years was a mere apprenticeship compared to the lifetime of research by Kettil Bruun or Robin Room. But my seven years were part of longer quarter-century career as a policy bureaucrat; in which I dealt with policy questions, large and small, advised governments, strong and weak, investigated issues, dull and contentious, and assessed ideas, favoured and opposed. My time in alcohol policy was not only a period of active inquiry about alcohol issues. It was a lesson in the nature of governing. It was seven years in which I learned from small, modest successes, and, more deeply still, from large, visible policy failures. It was a fruitful time for reflection on how to respond to the 'drink question', on how to govern well, and on why it is difficult to do both well together. When I finished my time there, I said to Robin Room, 'Perhaps I should write a book about what it all meant?' This little reflective essay is a first public step towards that work.

I wonder today how Kettil Bruun might judge the success or failure of the program he laid out for alcohol reformers that night in 1972. With the greatest respect to the distinguished scholars who work in his memory, a case could be made that his program has been a policy failure. If we look merely at Australia, few governments have adopted his ideas, notwithstanding the exuberant and never stilled chorus of the public health lobby. Indeed, they have generally adopted an opposing program, symbolically represented in Victoria at least by the liberalisation of liquor licensing laws through the Nieuwenhuysen review of 1986. Yet 42 years on from Bruun's program, despite decades unwinding the control model, with more advertising, more availability, some lower prices, and fewer regulatory controls, Australians drink less alcohol than they did in 1972. Australians have reduced average alcohol consumption by a quarter over those four decades.[17] There is

---

[17] Australian Bureau of Statistics, *Apparent Consumption of Alcohol, Australia* 2014. Indeed, Australia achieved much of the debated WHO target to reduce per capita consumption by 10% by 2025

growing evidence from regular surveys of drinking habits that fewer young people are drinking, that they are drinking less, and that future falls seem likely prospects. This paradoxical policy success has occurred in the face of deep opposition by public health advocates. In the world of health policy, does such a misdiagnosis count as a failure?

Alcohol policy's history of failures

If we judged Bruun's program to be a failure, then he would be in distinguished company. Alcohol policy has a long, distinguished multi-party history of policy failures. By 'policy failures' I mean attempts to change societies through public policy that lead to major unanticipated consequences or that are defeated by ferocious resistance. There is a rich literature on policy failure, if no final explanation. Failure need not be shunned. I found it to be part of the daily grind of life as a bureaucrat. There are many examples, such as British Prime Minister Thatcher's poll tax. But the archetypal case of policy failure (perhaps in all policy, not just alcohol policy) is alcohol prohibition in the United States of America.

Prohibition was no accident, no political whim. It resulted from decades of global campaigning, accumulation of evidence and passionate advocacy by the temperance cause. In this state of Victoria, the Maine Law (an early predecessor of prohibition implemented in the 1850s in the American state of Maine) was being debated in the Victorian Parliament in the 1850s.[18] Yet despite good intentions, evidence and strong coalitions of support, prohibition had disastrous consequences. The 1919 Volstead Act, which formally implemented prohibition in the United States of America, may have caused reductions in drinking, but more certainly led to resistance and subterfuge, moonshine and corruption, disaster and unplanned side-effects, and crime and unsafe products.

---

[18] *Victorian Parliamentary Papers* (1853); John Singleton, *A Narrative of Incidents in the Eventful Life of a Physician* (Melbourne, 1891).

Governing the Drunken Commons

The political history of alcohol contains other examples of failure. In my role, I would study these examples as an antidote to the historical ignorance of today's public policy discussions, in which a line graph of data for the last ten years is commonly the deepest reflection you get on the past. I would steel myself, when planning community education or social marketing campaigns, with the case of the 1950s French President, Pierre Mendès-France. Mendès-France assembled all the evidence on the harms of liver cirrhosis and the costs of alcohol-related hospital admissions, and presented the facts to the war-impoverished French taxpayer. He then launched a campaign to persuade the French to drink milk, not wine. He quickly failed, and was forced to retreat from a barrage of accusations that he pandered to dairy interests, and from a guerilla campaign of sneers and cat-calls in every café on the left-bank. But his intervention marked a symbolic turning point from which French alcohol consumption began a long-term decline after a post-war high. Perhaps the message got through, even if the policies did not. Another case I would console myself with when advising on arguments to change the drinking culture by adjusting licensing rules, was the tale of British Prime Minister William Gladstone's election defeat in 1874. It was a time when alcohol taxation was a much larger share of government revenue than today, and Gladstone sought both to open the trade of wine with continental Europe and to encourage a civilised, European culture of wine drinking in crude England. His changes to licensing rules pleased neither brewers nor temperance advocates, and he badly misread the mood of the newly widely enfranchised public, who declared their love for their own drinking habits. His miscalculation on alcohol policy led to his defeat at the following election. Gladstone commented afterwards that, "We have been swept away literally by a torrent of beer and gin."[19] Over the seven stormy years I worked as an alcohol policy bureaucrat, there were many times that I feared that I would similarly be washed away in a torrent of vodka cruisers and Red Bull.

---

[19] Richard Shannon, *Gladstone: God and Politics* (2008), p 258.

13 Ways of Looking at a Bureaucrat

The historical example of failure, however, that I paid closest attention to was the saga of early closing hours in Victoria and its unintended consequences of the six o'clock swill on drinking culture. Australia has had a long policy obsession with trading hours and outlet density (the number of alcohol retail shops in an area, whether they are pubs, wine shops or supermarkets), and similar alcohol control measures, as favoured by Kettil Bruun. Victoria never introduced Prohibition, although the idea was first investigated in its first democratic Parliament in the 1850s as the 'Maine Law'. In nineteenth-century Melbourne, temperance advocates knew well 'the drinking bill' and all its hidden harms, and used tallies of the social cost of alcohol to justify restrictions on hours and outlets. Incidentally, they also initiated public inquiries into the misuse of opium, but were less concerned about tobacco, which was mainly seen as a problem when it was used as a cheap adulterant for watered-down beer. By the 1880s a rapidly growing, prosperous Melbourne had given birth to strong social reform movements that advocated temperance. They petitioned Parliament for local laws to cap hotel numbers, and one-quarter of the adult female population signed the petition. In 1885, trading after 11.30 pm was stopped. Temperance conferences began to debate the Gothenburg system of local government controlled supply of alcohol. Their opponents, the brewers, anticipated a policy solution, which has been revived in the 21st century, and, in the early 20th-century, organised, together with the Victorian Government, a first minimum price for alcohol scheme. It might have helped drinkers drink less, but it certainly helped the newly consolidated Carlton and United Breweries to eliminate some unhealthy competition. Soon after, in 1906, the notorious deal-making politician, Thomas Bent, succumbed to both temperance advocates and the interests of hoteliers to introduce controls on outlet density. He established a liquor licensing buyback scheme to reduce the number of hotels. In the first years of Federation, the scheme was quite an expense for Victoria, as it struggled to recover from the Great 1890s Depression and Federation Drought. Looking back, you would have to ask what social benefit was gained by spending public money to reduce competition in the brewing and hotels industry, especially since Victoria would later endure 40 lean years of wars, depression, economic difficulty, and public retrenchments. But the difficulties of war and economy did not dissuade the temperance advocates. In the crisis of World War One, amidst the deep social and sectarian divisions of the conscription referendum, the mainly Protestant social reformers secured their alternative to Prohibition. In 1916, they persuaded the Victorian Government to declare six o'clock in the evening to be the mandatory closing time for all hotels.

These apparent alcohol policy victories on trading hours and outlet density were, however, still not enough for the temperance advocates. Prohibition was the end game, even if it was a step too far for Victorian politicians. The advocates' persistence and influence, however, secured a critical compromise. The Premier agreed to hold a referendum every five-to-ten years on whether to introduce prohibition or local laws in Victoria. There has been no other issue, to my knowledge, that has attracted such an enduring plebiscite in Victoria, or indeed Australia. It is proof perhaps that alcohol and drugs have long been a 'whole-of-government' and 'head-of-government' priority in Victoria. But while the referenda continued for decades, the temperance advocates never secured the vote they sought. The highest 'yes' vote in support of prohibition or local laws was in the 1930's when not quite one-third of people voted 'yes'.

Unwinding the World War One early closing hours deal took decades, and much political frustration. It was not until the 1950s that Premier John Cain Senior (Labor Party) removed the requirement for a referendum. Cain lost office after the Labor Split, and In 1956 the freshly elected Henry Bolte (Liberal Party), began Victoria's longest-serving Premiership of 17 years. According to legend, Bolte would plot his strategies while sharing a good cigar and a bottle of whisky with his closest advisers. In 1956, Bolte tried to convince voters at a referendum to remove six o'clock closing. Even so, he only dared propose a temporary end to early closing during the 1956 Melbourne Olympic Games. But Victorians refused to loosen up the tight alcohol controls that the temperance advocates continued to support from their powerful places in charities, social services, churches and other institutions. This period was a time in Victoria when a 'wowser' was feared, and not ridiculed. But Bolte was wily and patient. A decade later in 1965 he established the Phillips Royal Commission that investigated closing hours and recommended an end to the temperance advocates cherished regime. So Bolte and Phillips undid 50 years of law that had created the drinking culture of the crowded 'six o'clock swill', which surely was a great Australian ugliness.[20] They also confronted the monster that temperance or public health advocacy had created. Phillips commented that:

> the issue of hotel bar trading hours seems to me to be one arousing great public interest. I formed the impression that defence of the existing situation had become, in some cases, an act of faith. Defeat on this issue was important, not so much because it would open the way to an increase of specific social evils or accentuate existing ones, but because it would register defeat for the forces standing for morality and victory for selfishness and self-indulgence. To 'Stick to Six', was not solely a programme dictated by a weighing of sociological considerations, but a required resistance to the forces of darkness.[21]

The monster was confronted, but not slain. Phillips had defied the 'wowsers', and proposed a new partial dispensation of morals, freedom and responsibility that suited 1960s Australia, no longer chained to the world view of the Protestant churches. But the ideas of alcohol control lived on. They found a place in the hearts of new generations of less

---

[20] Tanja Luckins, "Pigs, Hogs and Aussie Blokes: The Emergence of the Term 'Six O'Clock Swill'," *History Australia* (2011); Anna Blainey, "The 'Fallen' Are Every Mother's Children: The Woman Christian Temperance Union's Campaigns for Temperance, Women's Suffrage and Sexual Reform in Australia 1885-1905," PhD, Latrobe University, 2000.

[21] *Report of Royal Commission into the Sale, Supply, Disposal or Consumption of Liquor in the State of Victoria* (1965), p. 24.

religious, more progressive social reformers. Six short years after Phillips' report, that visiting Finn, Kettil Bruun, issued his call to arms for advocates of government control of drinking supply. The monster of this alcohol policy failure prowled government offices again.

Today, you could see Bruun's intervention as exquisitely badly timed, although fertile ideas are rarely timely. Alcohol consumption would shortly reach its post-war peak in Australia. There was fair reason for Bruun and his audience to be concerned, but from the mid-1970s alcohol consumption began a long decline. The intertwined market and social revolutions of the 1970s began to change the worlds of politics, business, government and plain ordinary life in Australia and Anglo-American countries. Policy experiments of Nordic local governments from the nineteenth century were no longer welcome guests in these worlds redefined by Germaine Greer and Margaret Thatcher, Milton Friedman and Michel Foucault, Bob Hawke and Steve Jobs. In the late 1970s, a tiring Victorian Liberal State Government tried briefly to protect hotel business interests against price cutting by supermarkets by introducing a minimum price scheme for beer, but it did not work and it did not last. Finally in 1986, under Labor Premier John Cain Junior's leadership, and with a young Jeff Kennett supporting as Liberal Opposition Leader, John Nieuwenhuysen reviewed and fundamentally reformed liquor licensing, setting aside the alcohol control model. So Nieuwenhuysen finally laid to rest the noble policy failure of alcohol control Nieuwenhuysen began his final report with the symbolic comment that his report:

> is signed on 31 January 1986. That is exactly twenty years since the end of the half-century rule of 6 o'clock closing in Victoria. In the two decades since 1966, many changes in public taste have occurred. The 1968 Act has been pliable enough to accommodate some of them. But the Act is in many ways unsatisfactory. It should be repealed and replaced with a much simpler system reflecting the ethos of today, not that of a society just emerged from fifty years

of 6 o'clock closing.[22]

To this day, public health advocates have neither forgiven nor understood Nieuwenhuysen. The battlefield of ideas had changed. The public health advocates were stranded, and stuck with battle plans taken from old generals who had fought earlier wars.

I have narrated this history of the failures of alcohol policy in Victoria in some detail since I found few, if any, who know the whole story. During seven years in my role as an alcohol policy bureaucrat, only a rare few old hands knew much of this whole sad story. Instead, in my experience, the loudest voices were the most partisan. They built their often passionate arguments on fairy tales, not documented history. But I do it with respect and modesty to aid understanding, not from any sense of immunity from failure. It can be difficult for bureaucrats to speak openly of the government policy failures to which they contributed, but it is a routine part of governing life. I too failed in my seven years as a policy bureaucrat.

In 2008 the Victorian Government released a comprehensive policy to deal with alcohol covering the full gamut from prevention, regulation, law enforcement and health care actions. The policy was known as *Restoring the Balance: Victoria's Alcohol Action Plan 2008-2013*. I was responsible for its development and implementation. Like any policy document, it was a compromise, but it marked a shift in direction. Like many policy documents, when it approached its conclusion and final approval by Cabinet, some senior forces were keen to push an agenda, and to sharpen the political message of the document. A 'law and order' package was added to the balanced, if dull, compromises of 'evidence-based policy'. This package was designed to 'cut through' in the tabloid press and talk-back radio, where the 'punters' were worried about young people's binge drinking and alcohol-fuelled violence. It was pitched with three big, hairy actions: the freeze, the crackdown and the lockout. The sharper 'law

---

[22] *Review of the Liquor Control Act 1968* (Melbourne 1986), p. 1.

and order' package got up, and the plan, armed with dull detail and an attention-grabbing lockout, sailed through Cabinet to the delight of the Minister and Premier. The policy got the headline the Cabinet wanted. On the day of the launch, the *Herald-Sun*'s front-page screamed 'Booze Party Over' but that was the lockout's last success.

The 2 am lockout required all licensed venues in Melbourne to close their doors to new customers at 2 am. It was based on an example from the smaller city of Brisbane, and much smaller regional city of Bendigo. Many licensed venues challenged the legality of the action, and the Supreme Court ordered an injunction within weeks of its implementation. In addition it provoked the largest public protests in Melbourne for many years. The lockout was abandoned within the year.

The lockout had been the part of the package that provoked the most internal debate. Ministers and officials argued and sought to persuade each other on its likely effect on policy ('would it work?') and its likely effect on polls ('how would people respond, especially young people?'). On both issues, the strategic calculations proved dreadfully wrong. It did not work at all, not least because there were legal problems from the start, and it provoked a furious backlash. Until the COVID years, it was the only government action I was directly involved in that provoked large protest marches. Before too long people twigged that this was not a 'policy experiment', as the public health advocates liked to say, but an imposition on some people's way of life that had no achievable objective. It was an idea born of a policing mindset that was embraced by policy activists who sought to command and control drinking behaviour. Police, leading doctors, VicHealth and the Australian Drug Foundation all spoke out in favour of the experiment in public. I was more cautious, and never proposed nor advocated the lockout. I have always regretted however, being too timid in these internal debates. I did not, during the confused and scattered conversations that settled on this policy, say strongly enough and plainly enough, that it was a bad idea that would not work.

13 Ways of Looking at a Bureaucrat

The lockout very quickly unwound. All this late appendix achieved was diversion of effort from achieving the major goals of the policy. While the headlines produced by the announcement on the first day pleased some people in leadership circles, those good headlines disappeared quickly, and the resistance soon blossomed. Within weeks, thousands of protesters had joined a "No 2 AM Lockout" Facebook page. Large protest marches gathered around Parliament House. Many bureaucrats, who also enjoyed a good night out, looked on in sympathy from behind our steel and glass offices. Licensed venues challenged the decision and the local administrative tribunal suspended the government's bold, if rash, decision. Trouble on the streets went up, not down. The newly-defined problem that justified the action (young people 'venue-hopping', that is moving between bars late at night) rapidly disappeared from discussions soon after the lockout decision was made. As with too many policy arguments, the 'law and order' package, including the lockout, served a purpose of pitching a posture, not solving a problem. New bids for more police resources and powers soon followed, along with high visibility policing operations. But the discontent grew. Licensed venues had to employ additional security staff for late-night hotels to manage the discontented customers complaining about the 2 AM swill. One owner of an iconic institution of inner city drunkenness, the Tote, claimed that these additional costs were forcing him to close his hotel. Faced with the prospect of losing the pub, where many professionals had once danced at some late night gig, people lost their reason. Protesters marched down Bourke Street and carried signs saying, 'I want to get drunk at the Tote again'. Cold panic ran through government media staff when a rumour spread that Australian rock icon, Paul Kelly, and the global rock icons, AC-DC, who were then touring Melbourne, would reprise their famous 'It's a Long Way to the Top' performance on a truck down Swanston Street, together with protesting young voters. Before long, in the corridors of power, no-one would admit to previously suggesting or supporting the lockout. The troubles were used by some in the bureaucracy, perversely, to attack and to sideline those who wanted to deal primarily with the health problems of excessive drinking. The live music industry blamed a conspiracy of culturally insensitive 'wowser' bureaucrats. In fact, it was just a failure, a complex mistake. It was a classic example of the strange forms of misdiagnosis and group think that can infect politicians, bureaucrats, including those bureaucrats who wear police uniforms, and advocates alike when governing the drunken commons.

Three unsatisfying explanations of policy failure

All round, it was a dismal experience. I could wallow in the failures, or become distant and cynical; or, worse still, I could arrogantly delude myself that my actions made no contribution to this mistake, that it was caused only by others, by those who ignored 'the evidence', by those who over-sold this fiasco. But the fact is I made mistakes. We all made mistakes. We all, those of us in government, and those outside, made mistakes. Governing is a people business, and people make mistakes. To admit mistakes, moreover, is to begin to learn some deep lessons of the difficulties of alcohol policy. We are most likely to understand the nature of the policy problem and how to make an impact on it if we acknowledge failures and difficulties of all kinds, and then ask, why did we make these mistakes? Why is alcohol policy difficult?

The long track record of failure in alcohol policy, after all, impacts on the likelihood of future success. It weakens the ability of advocates and bureaucrats alike to convince political actors to take action on the issue. Why would politicians wish to bring a 'torrent of beer and gin' or a parade of lockout protesters down upon their heads? Failure seeps into the folklore of government and politics. It influences the sense of what is possible in the art of the possible. Political players take on lessons of past failures and retell the stories of farce or tragedy to advise their colleagues on the battles they are likely to face and the limits they should set on their goals. Every political leader who is urged to show 'political will' or 'leadership' or 'crash and crash through' will listen politely, but adamantly ignore those chest-beating, delusional advisers in future. Every institutional leader in business or bureaucracy or research or community organisations absorbs these lessons too. Be careful what you wish for. Be wily to defeat over-zealous opponents. Obfuscate your own mistakes by slurring the motives of another institution.

So how do we explain these failures? Over the course of my time in alcohol policy I heard many explanations proffered for why one or other policy case did not succeed. I synthesise these explanations into three main strands of argument, using plain terms. These three explanations are dominant interests, weak ideas and wicked problems. Each may explain part of what is going on, but each I find ultimately unsatisfying.

Do dominant interests explain policy failure?

The first explanation of failure is dominant interests. Alcohol policy is difficult because entrenched and powerful interests oppose good policy. In less polite language, this explanation blames failure on the self-interested motives of your bastard opponents.

This argument has its sources in the known facts of the role of private interests in politics, and more specifically for alcohol policy in the experience of many public health advocates during the long campaign to reduce tobacco smoking. There were many cases when advocates had to prepare responses to specious claims put out by the tobacco industry. Shutting out the dominant interests of 'Big Tobacco' is understandable in relation to that industry. In recent years, the same rhetoric has been used in Australian alcohol policy, with the label of 'Big Alcohol' used to attack differing points of view and to offer a comforting explanation for unsuccessful lobbying. Anti-tobacco tactics and leading advocates have migrated across to the drink question. Governments have been accused of making bad policy because they rely on 'alcohol industry revenue' - a rather ridiculous claim in the case of state governments - or political donations. Researchers have been accused of taking tainted money, and there has even been an attempt to portray a worldwide 'alcohol industry' conspiracy to buy favourable research results. Policies have been accused of fundamental failure because bureaucrats have actually spoken to the diverse range of businesses that produce and sell alcohol.

This is a kind of frenzied group-think that does Kettil Bruun's tradition no good. In both its crude and subtle forms, it is no more than an *ad hominem* argument, and a hypocritical one at that. We all have our interests and our biases. While such arguments may sometimes appeal in the hurly-burly of politics, they do not offer satisfactory explanations of failure, except to the already converted.

It should also be pointed out that there is a dark mirror image of the dominant interests argument. This argument is presented by the industry to besmirch good public health people. This can be described as the 'Sock Puppets' argument.[23] Here the interests are not large commercial revenues, but influence, prestige and public research funds in the world of ideas. This exact argument is made by some representatives of alcohol-related industries about the good people gathered here at the Kettil Bruun conference.

Across the desk of a bureaucrat these angry missives from both sides fly, and there is much mutual misunderstanding. In my experience, these kind of hostile, mutual misunderstandings and caricatures contribute more to policy failures than any undue attention to commercial interests. Of course, interests do lobby in off-stage arenas, but the interests that do so are not only commercial interests, and include public health and research organisations. In my experience, the culture of good governance and public duty is also very strong, although certainly decaying.[24] There are few public officials who cannot see a self-serving argument. In my experience, Ministers and

---

[23] See Christopher Snowdon, *Sock Puppets: How government lobbies itself and why* (2012).
[24] In 2023, I no longer believe the culture of good governance and public duty is as strong as I believed it was in 2014.

bureaucrats do not make the complex and difficult decisions that lead to policy failures because of the last person they met with from a lobbying firm acting for the alcohol industry or for that matter with the Alcohol Policy Coalition, the public health group. A deeper explanation is required.

Do weak ideas explain policy failure?

The second hypothesis is that alcohol policies fail because the underpinning ideas, policies or research are too weak or poorly founded. In other words, things go crook because leaders fall for dumb ideas. There is a particular version of this explanation that supports the fashion for 'evidence-based policy'. In this account, there are certain kinds of policy ideas that have the unusual characteristic of being based on evidence, and others that are not.

Unfortunately, we live in a world of too much information, too much evidence, and too few ideas. Ideas chase evidence; evidence does not generate ideas. A clear idea of how things work is always a good thing. But we should be wary of overstating the insights into complex operations of human societies offered by even the most sophisticated and best quantified concepts. Their ability to predict the outcomes of strategic interactions between players and conditions is simply not good enough.

Researchers who aspire to policy impact can go astray in the adamant pursuit of models based in the pure elaboration of strong ideas, validated in academic research. Sometimes the ideas just do not explain or predict that much. Sometimes defending the idea becomes more important than responding to the situation. Worse still it descends into an argument about the elevated prestige and authority of expert opinion. What begins as an argument about evidence, quickly becomes an assertion about who has the authority to interpret the evidence.

This becomes particularly challenging when policy assumptions are turned into statistical models. Models are a particularly common way today to market the strength and coherence of thinking. Presenting supposed connections between social phenomenon with equations and lots of data creates an impression of discipline and intellectual command. Few poor bureaucrats or Ministers have the time or the inclination to unpick the model. But in public policy terms, a model is rarely more than a more or less complex spreadsheet, with a long list of readily challenged assumptions. While models seem sometimes to work like magic charms, they bring a false precision. It takes a moment's thought, and a few days or weeks of harder work, to unpick most policy models. In my experience, I witnessed the failures of being carried away with mental models in the arguments for alcohol taxation and minimum pricing.

It is commonly argued today, including by the opinion writers of *The Economist* magazine, that many difficulties of the global financial crisis were created by the blindsiding of key economic policy-makers and regulators by their own mental models. Shifts in the structure of the economy, the strategies of institutions, and the expectations of economic actors were simply not factored into the models. A similar problem has occurred in Australian alcohol policy in recent years. After all, we have supposedly had the 'perfect storm' that our mental models tell us would mean drinking is going through the roof. Prices are falling. Availability is increasing. Marketing is ubiquitous. Some harms by some measures and in some groups appear to be increasing. Yet the annual Australian Bureau of Statistics figures on average alcohol consumption show the amount we drink on average is gradually and persistently falling. The facts contradict the fundamental hypothesis of the alcohol control model). This truth is inconvenient for the public health groups who want to claim political and media attention for their issue. These groups regrettably have obscured these facts with professions of faith in a model that over-states the problem. In the process, advocates with good intentions overlook the emerging patterns of social behaviour that should lead us to revise the assumptions built into our models. Rather than reconsider policies, we persist with the same old mental models. We stay locked into certain convictions, cornered into defending positions, trapped into not compromising with opponents who may, it seems, have a point. Our ideas themselves become our idols and our interests. Our ideas no longer work well as tools to reveal the actual world that is unfolding before our own eyes.

In the face of this evidence, all who advise governments and seek to influence governments should show more modesty about the quality of the ideas and models we use. Conviction itself is not a compelling argument for change. To claim with a smooth and compelling voice that the "evidence shows this" may fool some of the policy makers some of the time, but will never fool all of them, all of the time. It will become clear, sooner or later, that such facts and certainties are merely interpretations of interpretations.

But we should not despair or fear that all policy ideas are empty illusions. Many governments and many advocates have charged into policy failures led by the fallacies of clever ideas, but there have also been occasions when their judgement and intuition broke an evil charm, when they freed governments to respond to reality. I see the 1965 Phillips Royal Commission into liquor laws in Victoria as one such occasion. In this inquiry, the senior judge saw through the conviction and passionate intensity of experts and campaigners. He did not take at face value their faith that their ideas were superior. Justice Phillips stared down a group of advocates who were adamant that their ideas were superior and their claims beyond scrutiny. Phillips, however, tested each claim. He subjected himself to an evening of alcohol consumption to assess directly its effects on bodies and perceptions. He tested statistical evidence that was presented to him, and he examined the complex, moral, philosophical arguments that sat beneath most appeals either to control or to liberate the supply of alcohol. Yet still, he encountered exceptional ardour on the part of the 1960s successors to the temperance movement, who were certain that that opening hotels and liquor stores after six in the evening would devastate Victorian society. His report included a brief maxim that admonished advocates who get carried away with the certainty of their own convictions, and that should guide any prudent decision-maker in government. It was expressed in blunt language that I wish was still part of public discourse: "In general, men are as incapable of evaluating their own ideologies as they are of smelling their own breath."

Is alcohol policy a wicked problem?

So I come to my third unsatisfying explanation of alcohol policy failures. Some problems are hard to solve because they are not simple, not technical, not well-defined, but rather, as they say, because they are 'wicked'.

The term, 'wicked problems', has its origins in an early 1970s work by Aaron Wildavsky that was attempting to explain why so many policy intentions are not successfully implemented. Four decades later, wicked problems have grown like weeds. The wickedness of the problem is now a ubiquitous explanation of all sorts of policy difficulties, rather like a bad crafter blaming those damned tools. Wicked problems are said to be those kinds of problem where opposing parties cannot agree on the nature, terms and dimensions of the problem; where standard 'technical' solutions do not suffice; where situations are complex and dynamic so that the effects of interventions are highly uncertain or even 'non-linear'; where the problem can only be solved by how people think and act together about the problem. Sometimes wicked is simply used as a synonym for intractable or just plain hard. It is the eternal optimist's label for a problem that cannot be solved, but can only be managed, as indeed Aaron Wildavsky initially put it. It is a way to defy pessimism about such intractable problems, and express faith in the vision and the powers of that special kind of leadership that delivers magical 'reforms'.

Complaints about wicked problems are presented frequently at policy conferences. Techniques to solve them are taught at schools of government. Wicked problems have become fully integrated into ideas about how hard it is to govern today; to succeed, officials need 'adaptive leadership, and that peculiar form of policy thinking that is designated with the honorific of 'strategic'. It is a terribly seductive idea, especially for the more intellectually inclined within the bureaucracy. After all, exquisitely educated, expensive bureaucrats are needed to navigate us through the dangerous waters beset by so many wicked problems.

It can also be a very productive idea. There are many benefits from a set of ideas that encourage people to see the world in all of its bewildering complexity; to view opponents not as monsters but as companions in adversity; and to set humble limits on the power of government policy-making. In some respects, much of the work I did in alcohol and drug policy would not have been possible without this idea. When I worked in alcohol policy, I largely explained failures in this way too. I aspired to success with staring down the wickedness by redefining problems, facilitating multi-stakeholder dialogue, changing the terms of the debate, and nurturing cultural change. I believed, and probably still do, that if you are not part of the problem, you cannot be part of the solution.

But over time, I found that the appeal of the idea wore off. Mercifully, there are at least a few simple problems in government, but 'complex systems thinking' tends to label every minor problem in government as wicked. At the other end of the scale, in some respects, every issue that requires deliberation by Cabinets is complex, riddled with conflict, beclouded by incomprehension, and thoroughly imbued with interpretations of interpretations. All problems are wicked problems now, and not much is really gained by naming them so. The fondness for complexity can also lead both bureaucrats and politicians astray. There is currently a plague of waffle about complexity and 'systems" in government circles that I fear obfuscates, more than it illuminates. As the Norwegian sociologist Stein Ringen has observed,

"The problem with the analysis of systems is that people tend to disappear except as collectives and masses."[25]

If governments are to respond well to how wicked problems affect their citizens, they need more than befuddled abstractions. They need some kind of simple, compassionate, kind response. Governments cannot wait till the final research study comes in, or the latest complex statistical model is built and tested, or the day when everyone finally agrees on moral questions that have been disputed for centuries. By the end of my time in the role, therefore, I felt that all the sophisticated talk of wicked problems, complexity, adaptive leadership and systems thinking conveniently obscured crude policy instincts that only caused more policy failures. As Stein Ringen has observed of such talk: "They are really doing little more than using fancy language to tell us over and over again that complicated systems are complicated... We learn more by asking simple questions than by being sophisticatedly theoretical."[26]

Politics as an explanation of both failure and success

The talk about complexity and wicked problems also lets governments down. Complexity talk leaves political actors exposed and unable to do that which they must to respond to difficult problems for citizens. Waffle does not help political leaders to persuade, educate and inspire people, both their friends and their enemies, to do things they do not want to do. Complex systems do not guide people through the chaos of events, resistance and political battles. Complex battle plans break down quickly and do not last beyond their first day on the political battlefield. Complex theories yield to stronger, simple sentiments. Sophisticated research ideas about natural experiments, random controlled trials or agent-based simulations can be popular among social scientists, but citizens are not lab rats and do not

---

[25] Stein Ringen, *A Nation of Devils: democratic leadership and the problem of obedience* (2013), p. 11.
[26] Stein Ringen, *A Nation of Devils*, p. 41.

cooperate, mostly, with plans that conceive them so. People protect their interests, their agreements, their ways of life, their own sense of justice, their familiar attachments; and so, before long, 'political will' confronts more enemies than it can handle.

So I think the best explanation of the many alcohol policy failures is not bad interests, weak ideas or wicked problems, but that they fail the test of politics. They fail to see that in all major policy debates governments must support a claim for political authority and democratic legitimacy. Policies must not only be decided, but decided and acted on rightfully, and seen to be sufficiently so by those who oppose them. Good policy must not only be done, but be seen to be done.

The best route to achieving policy impact then is to understand the demands of politics, and to adapt alcohol policies to the fundamentally political nature of ideas about freedom and responsibility. Some popular concerns go to democratic legitimacy, often expressed in terms such as 'nanny state', which speak to a felt order of freedom and responsibility. If these concerns are lightly dismissed as ideological smokescreens or industry propaganda, then alcohol policy advocates only set up themselves for failure. And governments see the trap. A better response is to acknowledge that successful alcohol policy must engage with politics in its best sense. By politics in its best sense I mean the inherently creative, if difficult and frustrating, process of compromising between divergent interests, interpretations and values through a just process of public reason. For alcohol policy advocates to do this successfully they must shed a little certainty about the solutions and the evidence they propose, and adopt a little more modesty about the capacity of political leaders to govern deeply entrenched social and cultural patterns of behaviour, such as drinking. Policy impact will not be achieved by a chorus of expert judgement or the translation of "evidence based policy". It is more likely to be achieved by befriending politics.

Governing the Drunken Commons

Today, of course, there is a common refrain that our political institutions are weak and the culture of politics tepid. In various ways, many observers describe the system as broken. One response to this problem is to seek to insulate decisions from the world of politics through expert panels and independent bodies. You see this across many fields – economics, business, climate change, health, and, I regret, alcohol policy. There is a strong temptation in the alcohol policy world to over-value the opinion of the expert or the expert authority over the judgements of ordinary citizens and their democratically expressed social demands. People will argue that 'the experts say' this or 'the evidence shows' that, and so governments should 'just do it'. The experts urge governments to ignore the doubts, the emotions, the complaints or the plain facts that the proposal simply is not what the democratic public want. It is as if the experts never studied the lesson of Gladstone's torrent of beer and gin.

To befriend politics we might remind ourselves of Bernard Crick's *In Defence of Politics* (1961). Crick was a British political theorist and democratic socialist who believed politics was "ethics done in public". He advised British Labour Party leaders and governments, and admired, indeed wrote a biography of, George Orwell, who also saw politics in ethical terms and crystal-clear language. In his long essay, *In Defence of Politics,* Crick wrote:

> There are two great enemies of politics: indifference to human suffering and the passionate quest for certainty in matters which are essentially political. The quest for certainty scorns the political virtues – of prudence, of conciliation, of compromise, of variety, of adaptability, of liveliness – in favour of some pseudo-science of government, some absolute-sounding ethic, or some ideology, some world picture in terms of either race or economics.

Crick wrote, in particular, on the role of the expert in politics. He sought to emphasise the importance of democratic public reason and political judgement in sorting through the values and choices pursued

13 Ways of Looking at a Bureaucrat

by government.

> Politics defines what the inhabitants of a state think should be the problems to be solved. They may not all be capable of solution. But it is a pity that so many of the experts or technologists who are called in to attempt the solution of some of these problems feel that they know best what order of priority should be attached to these attempts, and feel that politics impedes, rather than clears the way for, their use of their techniques. So many problems are only resolvable politically that the politician has a special right to be defended against the pride of the engineer or the arrogance of the technologist. Let the cobbler stick to his last. We have a desperate need of good shoes – and too many bad dreams.

But though such a message may seem discouraging to the many experts who work on policy problems, Crick's argument is good news. He shows that politics, in its best sense, explains and helps us to accept the difficulty of alcohol policy. Alcohol policy advocates and researchers are not alone, nor uniquely special, in experiencing the troubles prompted by the 'drink question'. All fields of governing encounter failure. But recurrent failure wears away at trust, authority and legitimacy. Ringen observed this consequence in his discussion of the importance to democracy of governments actually getting things done: "Governments falter and dysfunction feeds back into the population as a confirmation that politicians are useless and government a mess of interferences, inefficiency and unfairness."[27]

The lesson that I drew from my time leading alcohol policies as a lowly bureaucrat, was that policies will have the most impact, not if they are based on evidence, but if they follow a respectful way of governing. Alcohol policy is not alone in this, and Stein Ringen makes a plea to adopt a different approach across government in general. That different approach is:

---

[27] Ringen, *A Nation of Devils*, p 154.

to work normatively: to influence people's mindsets, beliefs and preferences so as to neutralise antagonism and lure people into wanting to do as they should so that they do it by their own volition and do not have to be forced. Ministers must inform and educate their people and touch their souls and stimulate their will.[28]

This job is difficult, and, in truth, our institutions of government face some major challenges in implementing such an approach in a sustained and continuous way.

There is, however, especially in the wake of the financial collapse and regulatory oversight failures in 2008, a growing chorus joining a debate about how to govern, and how to improve democracy. These debates may over time generate significant improvements to our institutions. Researchers need to appreciate these challenges if their work is to have 'policy impact'. If they do, then ideas, practices and institutions may develop that show more humility about the academic enterprise, and a little more insight into the problems of governing.

Towards a new alcohol policy tradition

So let me return, in conclusion, to Kettil Bruun and his advice in 1972 that Australian governments establish policies that 'influence not only alcoholics and the coming rate of alcoholics, but the societal level of drinking'. His third dilemma concerned controls directed at the individual alcoholic, especially issues of encouraging or compelling treatment. He argued that "the number of alcoholics in the industrialised western societies is so great that these societies have to live with their alcoholics, and avoid measures that are in conflict with individual rights to freedom. Manipulation of the situation of alcoholics should be a matter of general social policy."[29] By general social policy, Bruun meant matters like employment and housing policy.

---

[28] Ringen, *A Nation of Devils,* p. 73.
[29] Bruun. K, *Dilemmas in Drug Control Policy*, p. 9.

13 Ways of Looking at a Bureaucrat

I do not share Bruun's early 1970s confidence in the ability of such general social policies to 'manipulate' the situation of alcoholics. It is, of course, an enduring aspiration of policy and 'social science', but it is a dream that disappeared for me at some forgotten time during my 30 year career within the belly of the Leviathan. It is also a reinvention` of the manipulative and controlling objectives of temperance advocates, and wowsers, and most certainly does not involve in decisions about their lives those who are most affected by those decisions. Bruun's choice of manipulative, temperate democracy, moreover, spurned the very people who might form the basis of a better form of social coordination of drinking problems: the people who drink too much. Bruun and his public health audience chose to 'manipulate' the situation of these drinkers (who may compose between 10 and 80 per cent of the population, depending on your standards) through social conditions. These stern controls would be enforced with the very best of intentions, and the most rosy assumptions about how much governments could effectively engineer general social conditions to improve the life circumstances of a person chained to the booze. This confidence in the capability of governments would evaporate over the 1970s and following decades. Social movements moved away from expert-driven agendas towards an approach of 'nothing about us without us'. But the public health alcohol groups chose a different approach. They had some good reasons. Locking people away as drunks or alcohol dependent persons while providing no effective treatment to them did little good and attacked the human rights of these people. But the choice of the public health or alcohol control advocates had one major, regrettable consequence: the long term neglect of the drinker and the drunk in the policy proposals of the alcohol control tradition. This choice abandoned the drinkers to their cups. It also deprived the alcohol control movement of a strong basis of legitimacy or justice for its arguments. In the end, they advocated an abstract argument to manipulate price and availability, and not practical justice to help struggling drinkers recover.

If alcohol research is to make an impact on policy, governments and voters, it should return, against Kettil Bruun's advice, to concern with the drinker, the drunk, and the individual alcoholic. It should pay less attention to price, advertising and availability of the drink. My advice, as a critical friend, is that governments can do a lot more to provide more help for the drinkers, but can do very little more to control the drink itself. This simple change of focus in advocacy and health groups is most likely to support a surprisingly large proportion of the community who experience drinking problems. Two examples of policy success, which sprang from such a change of focus, are the active recovery movements in the United States of America and improved responses to mental illness in Australia over recent decades. Both cases suggest to me that such an approach may also have a decent chance of both political and policy success.

In summary, alcohol policy is difficult because governing is difficult. This is not an excuse, but rather a call to accomplish higher standards of governing. This is not a counsel of despair, but rather a request that alcohol policy researchers study more deeply the institutional and political challenges of governing when they advocate various policy research ideas. Our governments and our societies can achieve much more to reduce drinking problems. But such policy success requires two small changes in perspective: a little less certainty about what works, and a little more respect for the rightful reasons for not implementing policies that people do not want.

13 Ways of Looking at a Bureaucrat

Chapter Five   From Flashbacks to Testimony

From Flashbacks to Testimony

Reflections on the Child Abuse Royal Commission

In September 2016 I delivered a paper to a conference sponsored by a major research centre on the history of emotions. It was a bold out of hiding for the bureaucrat who never spoke in public and did not share the depth and range of his thoughts. I hoped it might launch me on the path not taken, and so lead me back to my early career aspiration to be an historian.

But that was not to be. However, I did receive a pleasing response to the paper from the conference attendees. The paper concerned the Australian Royal Commission into Institutional Responses to Childhood Sexual Abuse, which between 2013 and 2017 inquired into the many cases of child sexual abuse in the churches and other institutions, schools, government welfare services, dance schools, yoga centres, sports organisations and so on.

The Royal Commission had an enduring, unusual and beneficial impact on Australian public life. In contrast to the general discourse of public institutions, which has descended over the last decade into a degraded, spiteful, tit-for-tat conversation about all that is petty, this Royal Commission found a way to speak in the most dignified, profound way about issues that are distressing and difficult. I portrayed this enigma in the paper, and I sought to connect it to the recent field of history, known as the 'history of emotions'.

The American philosopher, Martha Nussbaum, has written important books on the use of emotions in public and political life. She stressed how 'tragic spectatorship' can gather in one shared theatre the herded cats of democratic societies. Just as classical Greek drama provided catharsis to the demos of Athens, so well-staged democratic 'tragic spectatorship' can release and relieve the difficult social emotions that bring our public life down. This way of staging emotions in public offers a 'better way to be angry', Nussbaum argued, in the wake of Donald Trump and the 'populist revolts' of 2016. Finding a better way to be angry is surely a task for our times. Precisely this artful staging of difficult emotions was the foundation of the Royal Commission's achievement.

For a few years I considered writing a short book or a long essay on the Royal Commission, that reflected on what I observed and learned when I worked within the Victorian Government to respond to the Royal Commission between 2013 and 2015. Eventually, I abandoned the plan. To stare into the abyss of childhood sexual abuse became too much of a burden on my mental health. It was not a task I could realize alone and with little support. But I did share my paper as a submission to the Royal Commission, and I am now sharing with the world the full text of my talk at the conference on Children's Voices in Contemporary Australia.

The remembered child who speaks of trauma

(Paper delivered to Children's Voices in Contemporary Australia Conference, held by ARC Centre for the History of Emotions, University of Melbourne, Session - Voices that Testify, September 9, 2016.)

The Children's Voices in Contemporary Australia Symposium explored the status of children's voices and their ability to tell their own stories. The symposium heard from neuroscientists, historians, legal scholars, literary scholars, mental health and child welfare practitioners, and most importantly children and young people themselves. My contribution is a little different since it looks not at the voices of today's children, but the remembered voices of children, as spoken by the adults who have testified at the Royal Commission into Institutional Responses to Child Sexual Abuse.

Children's Voices and Royal Commission Testimony

Sometimes during the many survivor testimonies at the Royal Commission, you can hear summoned from the memory of a 40 year old, a 60 year old, even an 80 year old, the voice of the traumatised child. Though spoken by adults, they are children's voices nonetheless, even if filtered through all the prisms of memory, later experience and narrative reconstruction. To attend so carefully, at last, to these voices is one of the great achievements of the Royal Commission.

Although they are not strictly contemporary children's voices, the way the Commission puts them on the public stage is demonstrating new possibilities for how we all respond to children today. Indeed, the example set by the Royal Commission through its inquiries, public hearings and most significantly its private sessions is reshaping community attitudes and institutional responses to children. Fragile, sometimes dissociated, remembered voices of traumatised children are no longer brushed aside as sob stories from too long ago. And so the Commission has borne witness not just to the facts, but also to the emotions carried in these voices.

More than that, the Commission is reshaping our emotional responses to trauma, even inventing a new emotional regime, to use the term of William Reddy, the historian of emotions. Here I think the ARC Centre for History of Emotions could play a role

There is in historical writing a booming field of the history of emotions. This field has diverse origins in the study of the mass psychology of crowds and irrational irruptions of violence in civilised societies. The field has explored contrasts between modern rationalised societies and their medieval or anthropologically remote counterparts, the birth of manners and civility, the emotional experience of family, art and many quotidian experiences. Since the 1980s, the field has received great impetus from discoveries and borrowings from the life sciences, as many disciplines learn from new understandings of how the nature of the brain, cognition, emotion and culture are intertwined in human evolution and history. Socially, too, it has been spurred by the diffusion of self-help groups across many social movements and health concerns, and this practice has prompted historians to ponder the existence of "emotional communities" - affinity groups of akin styles of expressing and acting on emotion. This opening out of historical writing to felt experience, and its examination of how emotions are shaped and adapted over time, how cultures and institutions give rise to particular patterns of emotional life, and how they enable particular ways of understanding, expressing and acting on the shifting impulses of feeling. It has led to a boom of studies of fear, anger, shame and violence that can deepen our understanding of the community response to the Royal Commission, and go beyond general arguments about social attitudes or indeed lazy clichés like "moral panic" which, in the past, have been tagged to people concerned about child sexual abuse.

William Reddy is among the most distinguished practitioners of the history of emotions. In a strange irony, Reddy's *The Navigation of Feeling* was, in fact, published the day before the terror attack on the twin towers buildings in New York on September 11 2001, and the history of emotions has ever since perhaps spoken to the anxieties of our time. Reddy has coined two terms 'emotives' and 'emotional regime,' which can be used to examine the articulation of emotion through the Royal Commission. 'Emotives' refers to a certain characteristic of utterance of emotion - mid-way between an unacknowledged instinct and a fully intentional expression of a known self. It is an exploratory and incomplete articulation of feeling, whose point is its own experiment with expression, not revelation of truth or purpose. In an interview, Reddy explained:

> Emotional expressions, in this sense, are neither constative nor performative, in Austin's sense. They are a

third kind of utterance: this is why I coined the term "emotives" for them.... An emotional expression is an attempt to call up the emotion that is expressed; it is an attempt to feel what one says one feels. These attempts usually work, but they can and do fail. When they fail the emotive expression is 'exploratory' in the sense that one discovers something unexpected about one's own feelings.[30]

Reddy defined emotional regime as "the set of normative emotions and official rituals, practices and 'emotives' that express and inculcate them." In the *Navigation of Feeling* he explored contrasts between the emotional styles or regimes of Revolutionary France and later nineteenth century France, and argued that each regime led to different qualities of emotional suffering, with the regime in nineteenth century France offering more choices and hope to the individual.[31]

This way of thinking about how societies shape and use emotions, or indeed how emotions shape and use societies, is of profound importance to understanding the Royal Commission. It is a truth commission that is not solely investigating documentary and analytical truth, but the truth of felt emotion. It is cultivating ways of speaking of the intimate shame of victims, bringing to light new truths about the failures of our social institutions, and new truths about how we can go beyond them. Shame is not an emotion that has been extensively investigated in the history of emotions, but it is central to the more philosophical work of Martha Nussbaum. In *Hiding from History: Disgust, Shame and the Law* she explored how responses to shame and disgust reveal profound social and political distinctions, and through 'projective disgust' can readily lead to derogation of the rights of others. By accepting our embodied, vulnerable and animal states, we become more accepting of others, more compassionate. But if shame

---

[30] "The history of emotions: an interview with William Reddy, Barbara Rosenwein and Peter Stearns," *History and Theory* 49 (May 2010), pp 237-265.
[31] Reddy, William, *The Navigation of Feelings: framework for a history of emotions* (2001).

leads to the separation from the strange, disgusting other, then some of the worst cruelties of humanity follow.

Nussbaum also explored systematically the role of emotions in public political institutional and cultural life. Her argument was that there are two main tasks of political emotion in liberal societies. The first task is to cultivate love, sympathy, and strong commitments to worthy projects that require effort and sacrifice. So, a prime example is to cultivate the compassion for others that underpins paying taxes to support others in a full range of activities, and to redistribute some resources to the poor and frail. The second task is to hold at bay 'tendencies to protect the fragile self by denigrating and subordinating others,' especially in the ways that societies handle fear, disgust, envy, and shaming others.[32] Emotions do not simply exist as passing feelings within an individual's psyche. They find cultural and symbolic form. They form myths that motivate movements and found institutions that respond to common human dilemmas. Hence, governments need to craft the use and institutional form of emotions carefully along two tracks. Nussbaum wrote:

> In other words, government may attempt to influence citizens' psychology directly (for example, through political rhetoric, songs, symbols, and the content and pedagogy of public education), or it may devise institutions that represent the insights of a valuable type of emotion— as a decent tax system, for example, could represent the insights of a duly balanced and appropriately impartial compassion. ... the motivational ... is always in dialogue with the institutional.[33]

The Royal Commission support Nussbaum's argument with a deeper, more emotional case study than the tax system. The Royal Commission is establishing institutional arrangements to support

---

[32] Martha Nussbaum, *Political Emotions: why love matters for justice* (2013), p. 2. See also "A Better Way to Be Angry: Advice from Philosopher Martha Nussbaum." CBC Radio, February 24, 2017.
[33] Nussbaum, *Political Emotions*, p. 20.

victims, perpetrators, and bystanders to speak of their difficult emotions. By its example, and in response to the widespread public discussion of the many stories from the Royal Commission, it is triggering a change in our history of emotions, prompting the formation, from thousands of individual and institutional responses, of a new 'emotional regime', in William Reddy's term. This term refers to the modes of emotional expression and thought that are dominant in a particular time period and cultural context. An example of changes in an emotional regime is the turn to a more effusive emotional style in the decades before and during the French Revolution, associated with sentimentalism and Rousseau's writings, including his *Confessions*. We are unlikely to experience a political revolution today, but the willingness to speak openly about trauma and childhood sexual abuse does overthrow an emotional regime.

Unless we do create a new emotional regime to respond to trauma, we will not establish the flexible, robust and supportive responses to children's voices that we aim for. It is part of the practical genius of the Royal Commission that it has focused not solely on a new regime of laws, policies and systems, but has nurtured practices, stories and changes in heart that can support such a new emotional regime.

About the Royal Commission

For three and a half years since April 2013, the Australian public have grown accustomed to regular, headline news stories from this Royal Commission. Over that time we have heard many moving , distressing accounts of child sexual abuse in every major social institution with responsibility for children. 45 of 70 case studies have been heard. The most widely known cases involve Cardinal Pell and the Catholic Church - which for a week earlier this year put the Commission in the global news spotlight. But the Commissioners have investigated poor responses by many other institutions - various faiths, churches and their affiliated welfare services, schools for the elite and the disadvantaged, orphanages, disability services, hospitals, health regulators, sports organisations, State child welfare departments, youth justice centres, the YMCA, child care centres, and the police; still more institutions are to come.[34]

It has been an extraordinary reckoning with a troubling past, ongoing failures, and some difficult questions of why? Why did this occur, and can it be prevented in the future? Why do people do these terrible things? Why do children not speak up or are not listened to? Why can it take decades before a person can disclose abuse? Why do good people fail to act when they know about them?

How I became connected to the Royal Commission

I was introduced to the work of the Royal Commission from an unusual perspective. For about two years I was coordinating the responses of the Victorian Health Department to the Royal Commission, including examining our archival, historical records for evidence of any past failures in Victoria's health institutions.

While there was some abuse in health institutions, it appears to have been much less common than in orphanages or out-of-home care, religious institutions and schools. As a result, my work and my advice refocused on the broader interpretation of the Royal Commission. What was the significance of this public event? What impact was it having on the community, especially the health of the tens of thousands of survivors of abuse? Now, I am no longer in that role, but I left the role remaining curious about what the Royal Commission told us all about our shared emotional life, and those difficult questions of 'why?'.

The Royal Commission seemed to be like a great rolling scandal that revealed the spirit of the times, like the Dreyfus case in nineteenth century France. So I conceived the idea of writing a book about the

---

[34] Royal Commission into Institutional Responses to Child Sexual Abuse, *Redress and Civil Litigation Report* (August, 2015), and *Interim Report* (June 2014). The full final report has since been published.

Royal Commission. It would share the remarkable stories from all the people who appear at the commission - the victims, the perpetrators, the bystanders, the leaders of institutions, and try to explore some of the perhaps unanswerable questions that the Commission, with its obligation to develop careful legal argument and actionable recommendations, could not address. And this paper is a first public venture of some of the ideas for that project.

Silencing children and the context of abuse

The Commission has exposed so many failures by so many institutions. As Justice McLellan said in a 2015 speech,

> There has been a time in Australian history when the conjunction of prevailing social attitudes to children and an unquestioning respect for authority of institutions by adults coalesced to create the high risk environment in which thousands of children were abused.[35]

The actuarial assessment is that 60,000 survivors will come forward to seek redress. We do not know how many have already died from suicide, crippling shame, alcohol and drugs. This great tragedy was a 'system failure', to use the term the Royal Commission prefers, although I find it desiccated. People in responsible positions failed because they did not "provide appropriate policies to guide the institution and practices to inhibit the actions of offenders."

Perhaps the hardest thing for the Royal Commission to come to terms with is how perfectly ordinary and common this failure was. It was not just evil-doers or a dark Vatican conspiracy; but good people who did good things, and yet failed to respond effectively to this great epidemic of human suffering. The hearings show over and over again, that "well-intentioned people did not understand and did not respond to failures which should have been obvious in the institutions of which they were part."

---

[35] Royal Commission into Institutional Responses to Child Sexual Abuse, Speeches, accessed from www.childabuseroyalcommission.gov.au.

13 Ways of Looking at a Bureaucrat

This failure cannot be explained without thinking about the history of emotions, and how emotional regimes drove responses to the children who spoke of their abuse. So, if, as Julia Gillard said, the Royal Commission will 'change Australia', that change will occur not only in what we do (the policies, laws and systems we administer), but also in how we feel (the expressions, repressions and actions we make of those emotions). Most of all it will change how we feel about shame and the difficult emotions provoked by childhood trauma and abuse.

We need an emotional regime in which difficult emotions in tragic situations that involve vulnerable children do not drive people, whether they be victims, perpetrators, bystanders, or witnesses, into frozen, silent shame that can ignore any rule book of good policies and procedures. I do not see much evidence yet that the history of emotions as such is on the radar of the Royal Commission, although as it completes its final report perhaps it should be. In some ways, however, the Royal Commission's practice is ahead of its theory on this issue. In its most important role of bearing witness to victims, the Commission has shown sensitivity to emotional truth, and developed practices that have created a safe stage on which the remembered voices of childhood trauma can be spoken.

The Commission has devised a certain way of speaking trauma to power through its private sessions, its case studies, its preparation of witnesses, its support services for witnesses, its publication of a hundred stories of abused individuals, through the kind, firm conduct of the Commissioners, and the respectful processes followed by the lawyers from all parties. The Commission has instructed victims in simple forms of retelling their stories that have brought these private histories of trauma safely into the public discourse. Yet in doing so, it has not tampered with the fragmented, dissociated and vulnerable voices of trauma. It respects the conflicted emotions. It honours the lapses and faults in memory. It stands as a guardian for the voice of trauma that can now speak despite its fears, and the threats and the intimidating authority of the courtroom, and indeed of the Royal

Commissioners as the supreme representatives of investigative powers of the state, of the symbolic blessing of the Crown. The courtroom is transformed from a site of retraumatisation to a place of healing where victims can speak of their difficult histories. In so doing these voices are heard beyond the private and become a public cathartic drama for us all.

Parramatta case

I want to give just one example of the appearance of this remembered voice of trauma. It is from Case Study 7 which examined the Parramatta Training School for Girls and the Hay Institution for Girls. Both institutions have a quite shocking record of abuse. They disciplined the girls harshly, and the Hay Institution in particular went to extremes. As the Royal Commission reported:

> Witnesses said that girls were subjected to military-style discipline and forced to march everywhere with their eyes to the ground. They were only allowed to talk to each other for 10 minutes a day. At both institutions, girls often faced severe punishments for disobedience. They might be deprived of food or told to scrub floors. But the worst punishment at Parramatta Girls was being sent to an isolation cell.[36]

Here girls were sent for periods of weeks in an underground isolation cell, known as the 'dungeon', where girls were regularly physically and sexually abused by staff, including the superintendents of the facility. Again, I do not want to focus on the details of the abuse, but as we have learned to expect, this abuse has long term and devastating impacts on life opportunities and mental health. The former residents of these institutions experienced ongoing psychological trauma, including depression, stress disorders,

---

[36] Royal Commission into Institutional Responses to Child Sexual Abuse, *Report of Case Study No. 7: Child Sexual Abuse at the Parramatta Training School for Girls and Hay Institution for Girls (October 2014)*, pp. 5-6.

flashbacks, trust issues, relationship conflicts, alienation from the community, and suicide attempts.

One 65 year-old survivor, Coral Campbell, gave evidence on the final day of the four-day hearing on Parramatta. She told the Commission: "I walked through the big green door of Parramatta Girls as a little girl and I came out of its big green gates a slut and a prostitute."[37]

She still suffers flashbacks and horrible memories. These flashbacks are often triggered by the number 11, as she told the Commission, because number 11 was her nominated number at the institution. The staff spoke to her using that non-name. Like many victims, she did not tell anyone in authority or the police about the abuse because she did not think she would be believed. Indeed, like many, she did not say anything about the abuse until much later in life when she was 55 years old, 43 years after the events. Whenever she heard the word Parramatta or 11 she would freeze in a flashback:

> It opened up that Pandora's box that I tried not to think about. Little things would click and I'd go back. I'd go back.... From the dungeon at ground level sat a little girl at night-time, looking through those bars. You could see the hospital. Very frightening to be on your own, not knowing what to expect next time or what's coming up.[38]

The abuse led to great confusion in her mind. Was she a 'good' girl, or was she a 'bad' girl? She went on:

> And I'm still confused today. When I first reported my statement, wrote my statement, for the Royal Commission, I was scared. I was scared. Will they believe me? Would anybody believe me? I never even told my mother and father what happened to me in that home.

---

[37] Royal Commission into Institutional Responses to Child Sexual Abuse, *Transcripts of Public Hearings for Case No. 7*, Campbell, *Transcript Day 50*, p. 5141, lines 43-46.
[38] *Transcript Day 50*, pp. 5143-44.

From Flashbacks to Testimony

What happened next in the courtroom was both moving and revealing of the changes in practice that the Commission has introduced. The Commission had indeed gained Ms Campbell's trust through a private session where she received the welcoming attention of two Commissioners, including Commissioner Atkinson (a former Police Commissioner). Building on that trust the Commission offered therapeutic and legal assistance to prepare her statement. Nonetheless, when Ms Campbell stood in the witness box, the Counsel for the Commission wanted to draw attention to the topic of redress, or financial compensation as one of the systemic issues being investigated by the Commission. Had she ever applied for compensation?

> Oh, Mr Atkinson asked me that in the private session. I said to him, "I don't want compensation. All I want is a funeral by the State, a wake for my friends and family and a headstone saying that Coral was a good girl. That's all. What can money buy? What can any financial situation - if you did get it, what can it buy? It can't bring back that little girl that I was looking for but could not find.

This testimony highlighted the exceptional thing about this Royal Commission. The Commission allowed this very strong, yet very fragile voice of the remembered child to speak without challenge on the public stage. Indeed, this voice received greater respect than all the lawyers, government officials and senior church figures who traipsed through the court, and yet still could not speak with such gentle vulnerability and raw power. There in front of the assembled silks of New South Wales, in front of a long table, where sat overpaid, over-briefed barristers, this one brave woman sought not a legal claim, but only restitution of the shame she suffered as a child.

Ms Campbell's testimony showed how the Royal Commission is staging public emotions that Martha Nussbaum discussed.[39] In *Political Emotions,* she described this work as 'tragic spectatorship'

---

[39] See also Martha Nussbaum, *Hiding from Humanity: disgust, shame and the law* (Princeton, 2004).

and argued that this work creates bonds of compassion, love and justice within a community. Its staging of these public emotions brings the voices of power and recalled trauma into dialogue within a joint sitting. By hearing the voice of the remembered child, the Royal Commission is bringing lasting change to the emotional regime of our society. Its 'tragic spectatorship' dissolves authority's frozen shame about its dark history of child welfare. Its newly created institutionalised practices cradle the voices of traumatised children, at whatever age they choose to speak. They cradle the difficult emotion of shame. They give voice and form on the public stage to these tragic stories of remembered children. Thus, the Commission achieves an important task. For thousands of survivors, it has sensitively and justly turned their insistent traumas of childhood into safer histories of abuse. The Commission and the survivors together have turned flashbacks into testimony.

From Flashbacks to Testimony

Notes on history of child sexual abuse in Victoria

In 2013 and 2014 I was assigned a role coordinating the Victorian Department of Health's response to the Royal Commission into Institutional Responses to Childhood Sexual Abuse. This major inquiry investigated the scandal of sexual abuse of children by Catholic priests and religious, by many other churches, by teachers, by sporting coaches, by government welfare organisations, by hospital staff, and and by other institutions. It was a great rolling tragedy, although the primary motivation of the senior officials who assigned me to the role was to minimise risk and to protect the reputation of the government, and numerous officials, especially in child protection. I had one great advantage for the role. I was a historian, and knew my way through an archive.

I responded to the challenge of the Royal Commission with different motivations to my senior leaders. I wanted to get to the truth of this great trauma. I wanted to understand the perspective of victims, perpetrators, and bystanders to the abuse, after the model of Inga Clendinnen in *Reading the Holocaust*. I searched the archive as a 'due diligence' search to discover if there were any major scandals in this history of the Victorian health department. There were few, but not of the weight and number of my department's estranged partner, the child welfare department, the abstractly named Department of Human Services. With little 'risk' to manage, and very little engagement from senior leaders with the work I undertook, I began to focus on writing an interpretative history of this great traumatic event of childhood sexual abuse. My roles as writer and bureaucrat fused in unexpected and uncontrolled ways.

The history was written in adverse circumstances. If I strayed into their terrain, other protective departments would react hostilely. My masters were not interested in my essays, nor long, boring 'history lessons'. Even the Royal Commission itself seemed satisfied with the most superficial historical interpretations, derived from social work specialists. Consultants were employed to write a historical background paper for the Victorian Government, but their work was shamefully poor. In these circumstances, I struggled to complete my work, find a voice, and share my testimony.

I did, however, prepare a paper, which was attached as a background paper to one of those tedious positioning papers that bureaucrats write to their inattentive executive committees. Noone commented. After the remarriage of health and human services, my work, which had focussed on trauma and victims, was largely disparaged. My masters moved me off the project so that the protection of reputations could resume. I handed over the files. But my little history survived as my personal notes. I would in my private time extend these notes to something like a research proposal. From time to time, I adapted these notes, and for some time imagined I might write a book on the meaning of trauma, the historical experience of childhood sexual abuse, and how we might govern the emotions provoked by both trauma and abuse. The book overwhelmed me. In truth, I suffered from vicarious trauma, and the scale of the research required was too great for my part-time, besieged and bestormed writing life.

Still I have saved from the burning archive of my government career, this fragment of writing about government, and to government, that is yet not writing of government. I present it here in incomplete, lightly edited form.

Introduction

Childhood sexual abuse takes many forms. It is a sin, a crime, a moral lapse, a cry for help, an act of cruelty, trauma, memory that shapes identity and distorts feeling. It occurs within institutions and without, within families and without, between known persons and strangers. It is perpetrated by priests, professionals, peers and family members, and by persons who themselves sometimes are children, and themselves sometimes are victims. The acts themselves are varied. The consequences too are unpredictable and sensitive to circumstances, culture and how the institutions that surround victim and perpetrator respond.

Many of these facets of child sexual abuse have been known for centuries, and cases of abuse have prompted moral, legal and social condemnation for varied reasons and with varied ardour for centuries. But there is not measurable data on how common abuse is and how it might vary over time. Even today, we have no definitive way of measuring the rate of abuse in the community. Speculation on changing rates of abuse over time then can not be resolved with clear facts. However, given both individual and environmental factors both play a role, one would expect patterns of abuse to change over time as different cultures and institutional settings create environments that favour or restrict acts of abuse, that support or make more vulnerable the victims of abuse.

The extent of public discussion waxes and wanes, and the concepts and language used to describe abuse changes, so equipping people acting in diverse institutions with ways of responding to abuse that vary in their principal concerns, their empathy for victims or offenders, child or adult, and their disposition to prevent, punish, cure or cover-up.

As a result over centuries our society has developed complex institutional responses to abuse. All of these responses are embedded within broader social institutions that educate, guard, provide custody, employ, offer services to, care for, provide spiritual guidance, discipline and treat children, their families and the people who sometimes abuse them.

None of these institutions take as their primary and sole focus the immediate and longer term therapeutic recovery of the child who is abused or the adult who remembers that trauma. Other goals are served, as they ought to since they are the essential functions of those institutions. Doctors treat other patients. Teachers educate children on other issues. Judges weigh justice in other cases. Child protection workers prevent other types of abuse, especially physical abuse, and support families with other complex problems. The service of those broader aims – the reputation, security, the rights of adults, and the efficiency of those institutions – have too often been prioritised over the rights of too readily silenced child, and the crucial importance of responding to an abused child immediately with truth, justice and healing.

All of these institutions can respond better to child sexual abuse by bearing witness to the suffering of the child, and making therapeutic justice its first priority in responding to childhood sexual abuse.

These institutions have already begun to do so. To do so more effectively, more comprehensively, more justly is the task this Commission presents to all institutions of Australian society that serve children.

To do so they must make joint restitution for the injuries and wrongs they have made. Restitution of these wrongs does not require a full understanding of the past. But reshaping institutional responses systematically does require an understanding of the complex and diverse heritage of ideas and institutions that led individuals to make choices that wronged children. Understanding the history of our institutional responses can free us to decide which parts of that heritage to keep and which parts to abandon. Some of that heritage is very old indeed. The Roman Catholic Church established the rule of celibacy for the clergy in 1139 with the Second Lateran Council. Many parts of the Victorian institutions response emerged after 1985. Some ideas – such as trauma-informed care - are much more recent, and not yet embedded in institutional responses, despite their promise.

This brief account of the historical development of responses to child sexual abuse in Victoria – with a focus on the role of Victorian Government, its institutions and the services provided on its behalf – tells the story of how there is an historic opportunity for the Commission to make the most of developments already under way and still to institute enduring changes to benefit children and the adult survivors of abuse.

Strands of the history

Child sexual abuse is a complex problem and so there are many intertwining strands in the history of its development. These strands have produced diverse institutional responses over time, themselves marked by major political, social and cultural events.

The Commission has indicated it will focus on systemic issues. A focus on systemic issues is welcome. There is, however, no single system to prevent and respond to child sexual abuse; nor can there be. There are rather many other institutions, each with their own characteristics, influences, value, and patterns of response to child sexual abuse. 'Systemic reform' is best targeted at redirecting the responses of these diverse institutions to be more focussed on the experience and recovery of the child, not inventing a new system.

Child sexual abuse cases themselves are the first strand. Documented cases of abuse extend back to the nineteenth century. The terms used to describe and evoke child sexual abuse have changed over time. Research on child sexual abuse in Victorian England shows this. While there is little reliable historical data on prevalence, this problem has been known for a long time. Over time particular cases, including especially in the last thirty years international cases involving religious organisations, have informed Victorian responses.

Institutional responses are shaped by community, culture and faith. This includes changing, diverse ideas about moral conduct, family life, childhood, healthy adolescent development and sexuality. Facets of the culture shaped the institutions in which abuse could occur, the nature of the arguments people have had about sex between adults and children, and how the attitudes of the persons in those institutions have responded. There have long between diverse views on these issues in the community, and there will long continue to be such debates.

There are multiple strands of Victorian Government institutional responses to child sexual abuse. Four strands stand out health, education, welfare and justice. These four strands all have their own history of development, and ongoing issues of their relationship between each other. For example, the school medical service and disability services were from 1890 to the 1980s administered as part of the Department of Health and its predecessors.

This brief narrative history focuses on health institutional responses, and draws in key aspects of these other strands. It presents the co-evolution of institutions and diverse social norms that guide them.

Periods and Narrative History

Seven broad periods are described to make some sense of the pattern of development. The Commission itself indicates it will trace history back to 1890. There are, however, some relevant developments in the nineteenth century. The history since 1985 is broken into two periods. 1985 is a crucial year for several reasons.

1854-1890 Early patterns of state, church and charity protection of children

Victoria formed a separate colony in 1851, and was granted responsible government in 1855. The first Victorian Parliament elected on a male, but otherwise democratic suffrage, met in 1856. Yet even before this first meeting of the Legislative Assembly, the institutions of the State were acting against child sexual abuse.

In May 1854 William Thoroughgood was hanged for the rape of a seven year old child. The Melbourne newspapers reported that the child "through its innocence was unable to give the evidence usually required in such cases. The medical man, however, clearly proved the commission of the offence. He was found guilty, and His Honor passed sentence of death upon him, without hope of mercy. The prisoner, at the conclusion of the sentence, said, "Amen," and appeared to feel the situation in which he was placed."[40] A further six executions for rape, carnal knowledge or sodomy of a child occurred in Victoria before 1900.

Child sexual abuse was not discovered in the last decade, or the 1990s or the 1970s, but was known, if with different language and ideas, from the beginning of Victorian institutions. It was in 1857 that the leading forensic doctor of his day Auguste Tardieu published in France his documentation of child sexual abuse.[41] Tardieu's early account of child abuse would trouble many contemporaries, but would lead to physical abuse or 'battered baby syndrome', later being known also as Tardieu syndrome. Much of the discussion of abuse in the nineteenth century was less direct, and appeared through discussion of issues of child prostitution, social purity, moral danger, contagious diseases (including sexually transmitted infections), temperance, infanticide, or cases of larrikins (originally a nineteenth century word for youth gangs) engaging in gang rapes.[42]

The conditions for the development of healthy children were also quite different. Children were a much larger share of the population in the 19th century. Many worked from an early age. Childhood diseases and deaths in childbirth were far more common, and the early death and disabling of parents were also common. The majority of Victorian families were migrants, and they shaped a distinctive culture in the

---

[40] *Argus*, 17 May 1854. Peter J. Lynn. *From Pentonville to Pentridge: a History of Prisons in Victoria*. (1996) lists the executions.

[41] The State Library of Victoria holds A. Tardieu. *Etude Medico-legale Sur Les Attentats Aux Moeurs*. 7e ed., 1878, suggesting knowledge of it was available to Victorian doctors from the 1870s.

[42] Louise A. Jackson. *Child Sexual Abuse in Victorian England*. (2000).

colony that saw the emergence of social services and government policies for children through a form of partnership between state, churches and charity. This partnership would lead to social experiments to promote a free, secular and democratic state that sought to introduce institutions and ideas that would create opportunities for more, if not all, Victorian children.

Health administration began in Victoria in 1854, when the Central Board of Health was established, although arguably the Chief Surgeon or Medical Officer had played this role since 1835. It was primarily focused on controlling infectious diseases and quarantine. It also performed some other functions. In the 1880s, for example, the Board of Health distributed pamphlets to parents on how best to prevent common infectious diseases of children. It kept this form until 1890, when, after a major Royal Commission into the Sanitary Conditions of Melbourne, a new Department of Public Health was formed.

Hospitals and health services were established in this time with the institutions that would become the Royal Women's Hospital (1856) and the Royal Children's Hospital (1870) being established. A number of Royal Commissions into the operation of charitable institutions investigated the nature of State support for these charitable institutions Royal Commissions on Charitable Institutions were conducted in 1863, 1871 and 1890-85. Both hospitals and charities were loosely overseen by the Chief Secretary's Department.[43]

Mental health services were provided in asylums that provided some care, but mainly detention, for the mentally ill. There was considerable scrutiny of these asylums during the period with a number of boards of inquiry investigating conditions, complaints of mistreatment, and unexplained deaths. These concerns culminated in a major Royal Commission led by Ephraim Zox (a leading Jewish politician and financier), during the mid 1880s that would lay the

---

[43] Until the 1970s, the Chief Secretary was a Minister. The Department administered police, jails, mental health, child welfare and other functions.

groundwork for the development of mental health institutions until the 1950s. It separated care for mental illness and intellectual disability. It proposed a separate institution for the criminally insane, and it established obligations concerning the conduct of institutional staff and inspection of institutions. Much of this plan was not implemented until the early twentieth century due to the impact on public spending of the 1890s depression.

In the 1870s, Victoria established its system of public education complemented by faith-based education systems supported in particular by the Churches. In particular, priests and religious orders continued a long established role in education, and this was especially important for the development of separate Catholic education institutions staffed by religious orders, and not supported by state aid. It was not until the 1960s that the state aid and lay teachers in Catholic schools began to displace the preeminent role of religious orders in the education, supervision, discipline, and, as we now know, in some cases, abuse of children in these schools.

From the 1870s the arrangements for neglected children were formed. Initially state run orphanages were established, but public inquiries exposed major problems including harsh discipline and mistreatment of children. This led to the establishment of the 'boarding-out' system which was the precursor of foster care or out-of-home care. It directed children through short term congregate care in Catholic and Protestant orphanages to foster care, and aimed to provide education and training in the industries of the colony, especially agriculture. Importantly, Victoria developed an approach that was consciously and proudly different to Ireland and the United Kingdom, as stated in a 1891 report by the head of the Neglected Children's Department. This report also noted that the arrangements were criticised by the Catholic Church, which had a preference for institutional care. This was a significant contrast to Ireland where there was an overwhelming focus on Catholic residential institutions, with foster care or boarding out not being implemented in Ireland until the

1980s.

These early developments may seem far away, but they were foundational. As late as 1976, the Norgard Child Care Inquiry (which primarily focused on state wards, residential and foster care) stated that most of the ideas and principles of Victoria's child welfare system were based on these nineteenth century arrangements. They were also distinctive and aimed to improve life for children. In their own terms, they believed they had developed a significant social advance – the boarding out system – that kept children away from prisons, and institutions, which even then were perceived as prone to abuse or 'schools of crime', while protecting children from abuse and neglect.

The relationship between health services and the Neglected Children's Department similarly was established early and was at times strained. Many of the neglected children were referred to the Royal Children's Hospital, and in the 1880s negotiations between this hospital and the Neglected Children's Department led to a specific agreement concerning arrangements access, priority and payment. The hospital frequently complained that the child protection department's predecessor frequently abused the arrangement to insist on priority treatment for its clients.

Key welfare and religious institutions were established in Victoria in the colonial period between 1854 and 1890, and would endure with their names and forms late into the twentieth century. Church acts enabling canon law in the Anglican church were passed in the 1850s, but there was no single established church in Victoria, and political leaders came from several faiths. Key welfare institutions established in this period include all the major Protestant and Catholic welfare missions that would later be merged in the 1990s into larger organisations, such as Anglicare and MacKillop Family Services. Berry Street, the Charity Organisation Society, and The Salvation Army were formed in this time and worked with the government.

The state established a loosely supervised mode of working with churches and community organisations to conduct social policy in this period. From very early on in Victoria a close working relationship developed between government, churches and charitable organisations to deliver a wide range of health, education and welfare services. Indeed, in many ways developments in Victoria pioneered approaches to social reform and partnerships with the charity sector worldwide. This can be seen in the example of the Salvation Army .Grants provided to the Salvation Army in Victoria for 'fallen women' and 'child rescue' were among the first provided in the world, and were used to convince General Booth to extend the Army's mission from a religious evangelical mission to a social welfare mission.

There were close links between these various institutions and health practitioners, and Dr John Singleton is emblematic of this. Singleton founded the Royal Children's Hospital. He established the Collingwood Dispensary that would ultimately become Collingwood's community health service. He made large donations to the Salvation Army. He was a leader of the temperance movement, and was a regular prison visitor, including being Ned Kelly's doctor. What today we would understand as social policy was largely described in terms of Christian mission. These values and institutions would shape how Victorians responded to child sexual abuse. As society changed in the 20th century these institutions would both adapt and resist changes. New language, ideas, methods and problems would develop through the twentieth century, but this should not obscure the complex 19th century foundation of the institutions investigated by the Royal Commission.

The deep Depression of the 1890s deeply affected Victoria. The number of children in Victoria and through the 1890s the Federation debates led to the formation of the Commonwealth Government. Some of the developments that were emerging in the late 1880s would be taken up again after Federation.

These years were also very important to the Aboriginal protection system and related institutions, as described in Richard Broome's work.

1890-1919 Social reform and child welfare

The Social reform movement that developed in the 1880s and was at its strongest in the 1890-1919 period had three broad related priorities - women's suffrage, temperance and sexual reform.

Other issues to discuss in this period: Temperance; Age of consent raised and increased interventions; Catholic Law Trusts; Emergence of infant welfare and kindergarten movement; Growing flavour of eugenics to social reform movement; Growth or Emergence of paediatrics as a speciality; Growing concern about declining birth rate; Initiatives to control venereal diseases and to improve supervision of asylums; Public health, local government and sanitation; Hostility of medical profession to abortion; Sectarianism related to Irish rebellion (1916), conscription (1917), and pandemic (1919).

This period culminates in various social reform measures that would sit uneasily with the society that tried to re-establish itself after the war.

1919-1945 Darkened renewal of closed institutions

Issues to discuss in this period: Conscription debate and sectarianism; Returned soldiers; Modern public health principles and legislation; Infant welfare and other movements; Royal Commission into cruelty at Kew Cottages; Police Strike and corruption issues; Gun Alley case; Depression; Establishment of disability institutions (in response to over-crowding in part); Eugenicist in charge of mental health; Spread of sexology ideas and practices; Sectarianism flowing through to early development of child welfare and education institutions.

Eugenics Leading light of eugenics established a clinic to conduct intelligence tests and cranial and other measures of defectives. No treatment was offered. In 1920 new psychiatrist specialist who began to establish a more social and emotional perspective, including at Royal Children's Hospital.

1945-1969 Professions, new institutions and the emergence of modern society

After World War Two expanded health and social services developed confidently within an inherited framework of institutions and reliance on charitable institutions and professional services. Emergence of a technically driven approach to social problems. Other issues to discuss in this period: Migration, population and economic growth; Impacts of family, society and social services; End of period Vatican 2; Scientology case 1965; Emergence of Bowlby 'good enough', attachment and child guidance models after post-World War Two refugee crisis; Emergence of community mental health model; Child Maltreatment and neglect inquiry (early discussion of mandatory reporting); Menhennit ruling on abortion; 1962 Canon law interpretation; Significant development of Commonwealth services in housing, health, social welfare and education from 1950s; Resolution of state aid debate in 1960s and impact on Catholic institutions; Growth of social work profession and tertiary education; Mental health reviews and rebuilding of mental health and intellectual disability services by Cunningham Dax and Alan Stoller; Prisons reviews; Example of visiting rules for Royal children's hospital; Combining of social welfare functions with youth justice.

1970-1985 Institutions challenged and the blooming of diversity

Period of major questioning and challenging of many institutional responses, and establishment of significant innovations in health and social policy. Conscious adaptation of law, institutions and services to a new self-understanding of contemporary society and contemporary welfare.

Institutional arrangements however remained in flux for much of this period. 1970 saw creation of a Social Welfare Department as a separate administrative entity. Other issues to discuss include: Wainer, abortion and police corruption; Whitlam social policy changes; Medibank and changes in health system; Development of CASAs in health services; Administrative changes to health, welfare and education; Beach inquiry report; Family Law; Rape law reform; Feminism; High tide of progressive law reform; Cain Government administrative changes including Auditor-General performance audits; Initiation of major reviews and inquiries that would culminate in realignment of institutions.

1985-2005 Open and competing institutions

Issues to discuss in this period: Community Services Victoria and Health Department change; Hewitt paper on child sexual abuse; Gauthe case; Mt Cashel case; 1996 Melbourne Response; Law reform in social policy; Institutional reform in disability, mental health and health services; Changes to professional regulation, legal protections and open scrutiny of these services; Transfer of statutory child protection service from Children's Protection Society to Community Services Victoria (later Department of Human Services); Amalgamation and competitive tendering of welfare and health services, which in turn leads to significant restructuring of main charities; Renewed challenges to institutions and a new opportunity of crisis?; 2005 Children, Youth and Families Act; 2006 Sex Offences Act; Working with Children Check; Justice reform, sexual assault reform; Mental health reform; Growing gap with response to victims.

This period sees a return to a period of questioning of the adequacy of responses without certainty about the institutional arrangements that can best suit the diverse community.

***

I no longer can carry forward the thread of this story and these traumas. These incomplete notes may assist some historian of the future. These notes may even assist some poor bureaucrats who want to understand, rather than protect the reputation of, the failing institution that they serve. They may even assist some historian who has the courage to contemplate the great trans-generational trauma of childhood sexual abuse, and how governments, institutions and society responded. If any historian does take up that task, I can only apologise for the incomplete and confused research proposal that I have prepared. But, with courage, even these fragmentary notes may be turned into a deeper story of memory, history and forgetting, that honours this great tragedy of Australian history.

Chapter Six   Ordinary Virtues of Governing Well

Ordinary Virtues of Governing Well

Good government starts today

(From *New Samizdat* and *Burning Archive* blogs, February 2015 and July 2019.)

Earlier this week I got a message from WordPress that I had passed my 11th anniversary as a blogger on the platform. I began with an anonymous blog, *The Happy Pessimist*, which I began during a spell of doubt about my public service career. In response, I embraced the political essay in the new form of the post as my best way to exercise leadership.

That blog continued for four years, and it traced the political crises of Australia from 2009 to 2013, which saw a series of leadership changes of the national government, the downfall of Rudd, the installation of Gillard, and Rudd's final revenge. I eventually abandoned it, in fear. I was afraid that the opponents of free speech and enforcers of employee codes of conduct would punish me for speaking my mind. I still imagined that I might network myself into a position of high status, and so I feared my blog would ruin my chances. So I abandoned *The Happy Pessimist*, closed it down, removed its digital traces, but saved the texts, which together formed a small manuscript of political history and philosophy. For a year or more, I put aside history and philosophy, entranced by the illusion that I might finally find my place at court.

I soon discovered the grandees whom I sought to court were liars, cowards and executioners, to use the line from Herbert's 'Envoy of Mr Cogito'. There were no honours awaiting me at court. I was rapidly down-ranked from herald of change, who might expect graces and favours from court, to despised outcast. So, began my *annus horribilis*, 2015. But in that year, I reclaimed my writing, and, after a night journey, was reborn in fire. First, I began the *New Samizdat* blog, which I conceived as political writings for a real democracy. I wrote this blog for three months in early 2015, but then collapsed in a depression, provoked by my ostracism in the Department of Hell and Human Suffering.

Then in July 2015 I began the *Burning* Archive blog, initially while in the depths of acedia, but more actively and strongly from October. So today, I calculate, this blog celebrates its fourth birthday. In this blog, I gave up my earlier practice of writing under the cloak of a pseudonym or avatar, such as my old favourite, Antonio Possevino. I also wrote across the full spectrum of my interests, not just politics or policy. I wrote in all my chosen forms, and did not conceal who I was. I let myself be carried forward by the great rivers of culture and tradition that flowed through me. It was here that I became comfortable with my voice, and believed, at last, I was contributing to the infinite conversation.

Who knows if this blog will grow in its reach or impact? The fact is I do not seek outward recognition, since I accept exclusion from all halls of power, whether in government or culture. I wander like Parsifal. I serve the real aims of life, the pursuit of meaning, the expression of ideas, the love of the best, the protection of the endangered specie of our culture.

To celebrate this anniversary, and the courage of living in truth that writing this new form of samizdat has brought me, I am reposting three posts from my earlier masked, pseudonymous blogs, *New Samizdat* and *The Happy Pessimist*.

Today I am posting an early meditation from 2015 on the virtues of governing well, prompted by yet another leadership challenge in Australian politics, the beginning of the end of Tony Abbott's period as Prime Minister.

Ordinary Virtues of Governing Well

Good Government starts today

(originally posted February 22, 2015 on the *New Samizdat* blog)

In February 2015 the Australian Prime Minister stared down a threat to his leadership. A vote in his party room for a leadership spill, when there was no declared rival candidate, was defeated 60 to 40, but this majority was padded by the obligation of the Prime Minister's Cabinet to remain loyal in their vote, if not in their thoughts. In truth, up to 60 per cent of the backbench voted against the leader, and most opinion on the next morning proclaimed the stigmata that the Prime Minister wore: Tony Abbott was now a dead man walking. His leadership was lost to his undeclared rival, not if, but when. One wit declared that a political leader had lost a ballot to an empty chair.

This collapse in authority dismayed political observers, and new courtiers in the media, public service and lobby groups who gathered around the state. It was only a few years since journalists, political leaders and top bureaucrats preened themselves on Australia's 'economic miracle' and governing genius that fashioned an 'age of reform,' which, they claimed, pulled the country out of near bankruptcy to become the envy of the world. This 'age of reform' saw the rise of a new elite, who were drawn from the world of business, media and political marketers; who were practical and market-driven; who the reforms set free from the disciplines and moorings of traditional institutions; who ruthlessly concentrated on productivity and market economics; and who proudly displayed their contempt for citizens' ordinary, messy worlds of caring, culture and just copin'. They shared with architects of fascism and French monarchs a preference for the elegant, clean lines of economic reform. For a time, they had appeared to have 'made history' when the 'Australian moment' saved the country from the global financial crisis, and at once set to redeeming the planet from its 'greatest moral challenge' of climate change.

Then, as things do, it all fell apart. China and America spurned poor, pathetic Kevin Rudd's zeal at Copenhagen, and left him a broken man, unable to face his own shadows and stripped of the moral courage to lead. The fiasco of climate change policy undid him. His public displayed towards his economic policies the ordinary ingratitude of politics, and the Great Helmsmen of the GFC grew to resent this callow, ignorant public. They, in turn, suspected Rudd was spooked by shadows, or grandiosely solving the financial problems of other countries by throwing imprudent wads of cash at them. Their suspicions were confirmed when they saw the implementation problems in their suburban lives: the shonky businesses who installed deadly pink batts, the schools halls built needlessly; and the ceaseless pestering telemarketing calls about solar panels. The mameluks of the Labor party lost their way, and unleashed four years of madness and court assassinations on the country's government.

Paradoxically, the tragedy of Tony Abbott's collapse in authority stemmed from the wrong in the Rudd/Gillard/Rudd years that Abbott had discerned correctly and expressed with such rhetorical skill: a great country had been let down by a bad government. But Abbott's collapse was doubly tragic because it had occurred with such speed and with full knowledge of the failures of the Rudd/Gillard/Rudd years. The cruel fates tormented the new leader with the same suffering of the opponents whom he had crushed. The collapse of Abbott's authority was sudden and sharp. In the 2013 election the Coalition parties led by Abbott had won 90 of 150 seats in the main lower house of the Australian Parliament. His Labor Party opponents had been utterly discredited and institutionally weakened. He had inherited a state with some weaknesses, but essentially strong conditions, and his first steps were to repeat mantras of good government: be calm and methodical; do not talk too much; be serious-minded; look for the deeper and darker forces of history that shape the fates of nations and states. Here was an Australian Prime Minister with the gifts of a writer, deep connections to ordinary experience, and knowledge of high culture. With these capabilities, he seemed poised to interpret the nation to itself.

Ordinary Virtues of Governing Well

But it all fell apart so quickly, so ineptly, so ridiculously. He assembled a Cabinet that spurned the half of the country who are women. He mocked basic sentiments that the governors of the country should include the diverse character of the people. He vested power and authority in his chief of staff, and so offended basic moral principles of rightful authority He confused the prerogatives of political marketers with the principles of democratic government. He let loose the vandalism of a Commission of Audit, led by a mediocre business clerk who had no ideas to contribute to government or public life, except his C-suite scorn for those who suffer illness, frailty and hardship. He breached, time and again, fundamental cultural values of fairness in the budget: co-payments undermined universal health care; tax and transfer changes skewed to the rich; unconscionable restrictions on paying social security benefits oppressed the young unemployed; higher education fees saddled students with debt to indulge the enterprise ambitions of vice-chancellors. He made that inequity worse by pursuing the sullen resentments of the right-wing think tanks with a Quixotic folly, despite the plain facts that they would never be implemented through the Senate. He forgot the wisdom that when governments pursue foolish ideas that cannot be done, they only destroy their authority. Lastly and most ridiculously, he succumbed to the occasional madness of isolation in the court, perhaps stirred by reading too much Churchill and by worries about the mortality of all monarchs, when he conferred a knighthood on a foreign prince to mark a national day.

So, Prime Minister Abbott suffered this sudden collapse in authority. This people's champion crumbled when he let himself be infected by the resentment of the great and the grifter towards the poor and the weak. He was humiliated before an empty chair. His fall shocked and dismayed those who believed they knew how to govern. Greg Sheridan best expressed the shock. Sheridan is Tony Abbott's friend, who rightly praised this thoroughly decent, genial, cultured and compassionate man. For decades, Abbott had been Sheridan's companion in journalism, conservative politics, and analysis of a dark, troubling world. On the night of Abbott's defeat by the empty chair, Sheridan said that he had thought that the loss of the 'art of rule' was a feature of the Rudd/Gillard/Rudd years. But now, Sheridan candidly observed, the loss of this art was the cause of this political crisis, more than Abbott's personal failures. Business had lost all authority. Unions were corrupted. Sources to recruit political leaders to the major parties now only produced people talented in the wrong things. Social media had turned political talk into an over-excited digital repetition of the murderous French revolutionary crowd. Parties had lost all deep connection with people other than the narrowly ruthless and shallowly skilled political professionals who act as the minders of political offices. Ideas are not debated. Arguments are not constructed. The universities have descended into the same pit of marketing pulp. Economists confuse analysing data on everything with valuing anything. Journalists have abandoned reporting of facts to chase self-promotion through endless, pointless opinion panel shows. The public service had long ago betrayed its purpose to become reactive slaves to addictive ideas, pushed by gangs of advisers. It has been sapped by viral political patronage. So, Sheridan lamented, 'we have lost the culture of governing well.'

Perhaps, Sheridan shared this thought privately with the Prime Minister since Mr Abbott declared at the press conference, which followed the party-room revolt, that "good government starts today." This rhetorical reboot, however, was soon mocked by his opponents, in politics and journalism. 'What, after all,' they asked, 'had he been doing for all the other days in government?' But sarcasm does not discern the more tragic truth in this new year's leadership resolution. None of the clown's parade of politicians and opinion journalists could explain, if tested, what good government is. Nor could they defend it against many enemies, who have taken up positions outside and within the state. Sheridan may have exaggerated. Cultures change, and rarely die. An optimistic observer can still say the culture of governing well is not lost yet, even if it is crumbling and at risk of collapse. Its custodians are mistreated, forgotten and maligned. Its true texts are neglected. Its defenders are isolated, hungry, and yet passionate. It is time for those defenders to come down from the mountains and rebuild the traditions and ideas of good government. Good government may not start today. But the first shot of a long battle of ideas has been fired.

From political decay to ordinary virtues of governing well

(From *The Burning Archive*, 18 July 2016.)

Francis Fukuyama has recently argued that Western democratic states, especially America, are suffering political decay. The causes of this decay lie in institutions and culture. State capability, law and accountability begin to work against or to undermine each other. They do not combine as complementary components of the political order of Western or liberal democracy.

Fukuyama's case is strongest with the 'vetocracy' of the United States of America, but similar problems are apparent in Australia. The Senate blocks executive mandates. The parties have hollowed out and become parasitical on executive government, raiding bureaucracies for announcements to market the brand of the party and to promote the careers of a new *nomenklatura*. The quality of political talent is in decline, and large parts of the senior level bureaucracy have abandoned the ethos of an independent public institution to become a modern court, obsessed with favour, relationships with advisers, and the signalling of virtue and rank. The public dialogue about the issues of governing is degraded. Nowhere is this more apparent than the fall of the ABC's *QANDA*. It began as an adventure in democracy, and has become a frenzy of social media outrage.

So how can this change for the better? The answer does not lie in systems or institutions or leadership. It lies, I think, in simple ordinary virtues that the meek, humble and people outside of "leadership positions" can act on. The answer can be found in ordinary virtues that underpin governing well.

Ordinary virtues were described by Tzetvan Todorov, a French-Romanian literary critic who studied the horrors of the twentieth-century.[44] Todorov defined ordinary virtues in contrast to heroic virtues. He praised them as part of his exploration of moral conduct in the extreme circumstances of the Nazi death camps. The traditional heroic virtues of defiance, bravery, combat and self-sacrifice, were only one rare response to such an overwhelming experience. Todorov celebrated the small actions of daily life that allowed for endurance of the extremes. In them he found three cardinal ordinary virtues: dignity, caring, and the life of the mind.

Caring, especially today, is a virtue more widely practised, if rarely celebrated. But it is a virtue that 'leaders' in their bubbles rarely know well. It may bring anonymity, but that is not the test of this virtue. In an interview, Todorov commented:

> If money does not make one person more deserving of living than another, neither does a commitment to the life of the mind, even though history may remember the names of poets and scholars and not those of the people who brought them tea in their bedrooms or sewed on their buttons.

The life of the mind, dignity, and caring are virtues that can be cultivated again so that we can govern well again. Todorov suggested his three ordinary virtues are the foundation of living with others.

> Wisdom is neither hereditary nor contagious: one attains it more or less, but always and only alone, not by virtue of one's membership in a group or a State. The best regime in the world is never anything but the least bad, and even if it is the one under which we live, everything still

---

[44] Zbinden, Karine, and Tzvetan Todorov. "In Praise of Nuance: An Interview with Tzvetan Todorov," *Salmagundi*, no. 141/142 (2004): pp. 3–26.

remains to be done. Learning to live with others is part of this wisdom.

There are other virtues that need to be discovered if we are to reverse political decay: talking to strangers, scrupulous pessimism, humility in both tradition and prediction. But what other virtues do we need to rekindle not just among the leaders, but among all those who play a part in governing democratic states?

On humility

(From *The Burning Archive*, 11 June 2017.)

For many years I have believed, as Carl Jung once said or wrote, that, 'You must stoop to drink from the river of life.'

But Google has taught me humility. Or perhaps, after a long week at work, which has also taught me humility, I more simply do not have the energy to hunt down my quarry quote with professional literary scholarship. In any case, I get nothing whenever I type these words into Google's search bar.

I do not need either Jung or Google to know, however, that humility is one of the Christian virtues, which might make a reader sceptical if he/she were steeped in the writing of Nietzsche or Machiavelli or any kind of post-modernist. Can such a Christian virtue be known after such knowledge provided by the critiques of the philosophy of slaves or the ideology of those without power and fortune, or the grand narratives of naive realists?

The case of Machiavelli suggests it can. Though he denounced the sanctimony of the powerless, he practised a kind of intellectual humility, when he was not flattering the Prince. He knew the trauma of being humbled. We might think of him today as perhaps the most famous bureaucrat of all time. But this fame was posthumous. He served the Florentine republic, but the oligarchy removed him from power. Machiavelli was humiliated, tortured and dismissed from his public office, and sent into a kind of internal exile. He would never return to power and status. He turned instead to the humble craft of writing, and produced the insightful, yet puzzling tract on politics and power, *The Prince*. In the dedication to that text, he introduced this enduring enigma: from the viewpoint that the humble may not inherit the earth, but they can observe the battlefield of power and the rivalry of princes:

> Nor do I hold with those who regard it as a presumption if a man of low and humble condition dare to discuss and settle the concerns of princes; because, just as those who draw landscapes place themselves below in the plain to contemplate the nature of the mountains and of lofty places, and in order to contemplate the plains place themselves upon high mountains, even so to understand the nature of the people it needs to be a prince, and to understand that if princes it needs to be of the people.

The Prince is not the work of a successful celebrity official on a speaking tour to promote his new book on leadership to aspiring executives. It is an imaginative response to the trauma of Machiavelli's torture and downfall. That poet-philosopher-philologist, Friedrich Nietzsche, also knew a thing or two about failure, self-destruction and ostracism. He gave up his chair to write his books, and those books were published to a yawning world. *Thus Spoke Zarathustra* sold fewer than a hundred copies when published in the 1880s. His ideas, his temperament and his syphilis ultimately sent him mad in Turin.

What would these thinkers, who had a lived experience of humiliation, make of the vast cult of 'Leadership' in organisations today? New aspirants to be *Übermensch*? Everyone in today's organisations wants to be a 'Leader'. Even in the bureaucratic halls that

I wander through like a reviled exile, leadership is summoned like a magical spell. It appears in almost every job description, and is urged in every banal dilemma. Its ubiquity cheapens the currency. Most often the most admired attribute of the leader is to 'manage up', to master 'impression management' so that the leader appears always in control, but never too far from the pack, always in conformity with the wishes of the true masters. In the vast literature on leadership, humility has become fashionable, contemporaneous with the humble brag. Yet humility struggles to be expressed authentically. It becomes lukewarm, understated modesty that is happy to share the limelight with other members of the club. For example, this randomly selected article on the '11 characteristics of great leadership', advises the leading practitioner of humility to avoid false modesty.

> Humility: There's nothing wrong with accepting praise for accomplishments so long as there's as much willingness to accept criticism, to declare weaknesses, to seek opportunities for personal development, and to value others as much as oneself. That, in essence, is balanced humility.[45]

But the true virtue of humility is not spoiled by this modern pseudo-secular celebration of leadership. If management advice substitutes for religion, a culture is displaying symptoms of ruin. But we can find our way out of the ruins and back to the true virtue of humility, as consecrated by many older, longer and deeper traditions, if we can practise humility as one of the ordinary virtues.

Ordinary virtues were described by Tzetvan Todorov in his accounts of responses to the degradation and inhumanity of the German concentration camps. He contrasted ordinary virtues that, in these circumstances, allowed some to endure the unconscionable. In those destitute times, the celebrated heroic virtues of defiance, bravery, combat and self-sacrifice, which many honour today as 'leadership',

---

[45] Adonis, James. "The 11 Characteristics of Great Leadership." *The Sydney Morning Herald*, February 16, 2017.

would have led the suffering inmates to compromise or death. By contrast, the ordinary virtues reasserted in the camps the simple, small actions of daily life. Todorov identified three cardinal ordinary virtues: dignity, caring and the life of the mind. Yet Todorov also assumed the humility of those practising these virtues. These virtues were practised by those who suffered the regime, not those who administered the suffering, let alone those who led the regime. But the ordinary virtues can be practised in less extreme settings. They can even be practised by lowly and despised bureaucrats. Over the course of my failed career as a very minor government official, I have witnessed and tried to practise this simple virtue of humility in the outer halls of power.

In my early years as a public servant, I witnessed this ordinary virtue practised by the then head of the Department of Premier and Cabinet in Victoria, Mr Peter Kirby.[46] It was an era of more formal communications, prior to ubiquitously digitised email, texting and chat messages. Mr Kirby would give instructions to his direct reports through neatly handwritten sentences, which he squeezed elegantly into the margins of letters and briefs. Each instruction would begin with a formal salutation, and a polite request. 'Mr Moran, please advise.' But this formality was outweighed by the humility that I recall in another memory I have.

The Government offices in Melbourne are nearly all squeezed into the Treasury block at the Paris end of Collins Street, where there are many places for lunch to meet every budget from banker to lowly young bureaucrat. When I would get my takeaway sandwiches I would spot several days each week, Mr Kirby, the most powerful and respected official of the land, lunching with a relatively low status person within the Department, Fred Warmbrand. They ate and chatted like old friends in a modest cafe restaurant where all could see them. The exact purpose of these lunches? I never really knew. They might have been the familiar habits of friendship or a way to 'feel the pulse'

---

[46] "Public Servant Stood Tall among Greats." Peter Harmsworth and Zana Smith, *The Age/Sydney Morning Herald* 23 April 2012.

without surveys or fuss. But the lunches of Mr Kirby, like his other 'leadership' habits, sat down with the ordinary and the humble, even when he occupied one of the most powerful positions in the state. I rarely, if ever, saw his successors in the position do the same.

The qualities I admire in my heroes are the endurance of difficult experiences, and humility. My greatest political hero is Vaclav Havel, former dissident who became President of Czechoslovakia and then the Czechia after the fall of Communism. In the decades before the Velvet Revolution, Vaclav Havel was stripped of status, denied access to privileges, and imprisoned for his words. Yet he sustained a secular faith in simple virtues that would become the foundation of a new state. He was, at least until 1989, the embodiment of the ordinary virtues. If we could topple our modern courtiers, and restore public institutions to the ways of governing well, those ways that Mr. Peter Kirby practised when Vaclav Havel became President, we would not reach nirvana, just as Havel did not. But by installing an ethos of compassion, dignity, the life of the mind, and humility, we would have restored some rare and precious things.

Republics in distress

(From *The Burning Archive*, 6 August 2017.)

As I look around the world at the state of politics, I conclude that our democratic republics are in distress.

This judgement is not a reflex to oppose Donald Trump or Brexit. It is not dressed-up disappointment that my preferred leader or team has lost the electoral lottery. It is a long-held view about the decay of our political, governing and public institutions. It is a view I have

13 Ways of Looking at a Bureaucrat

gestured towards occasionally on *The Burning Archive*, but never fully articulated. The full argument is the work of a long essay or a short book, but let me at least stammer out some brief fragments here this morning.

1. Politics has turned into a spiteful shouting match, little more than highly conventional panel shows.

2. Our political leaders chant mantras of grandiose reform, overwhelmingly about the economy, not humanly measured care for our fellow humans. They have abandoned the true grounds of democratic politics, that is, practical morality, concerned for our neighbours and strangers alike. Instead, they preen themselves before the merchant masters of the universe.

3. Governments have lost authority. People mistake loss of authority for a loss of trust by citizens in political leaders. But trust is the basis of personal transactions. Authority is the basis of politics. Authority is earned by rightful action. While the governing may claim authority, it can only be bestowed by the governed. Today the governed no longer grant their elites such mandates. Our republics have lost the Mandate of Heaven.

4. Political elites have become parasites on government. They no longer direct the institutions of the republic towards commonly agreed goals, but use those institutions to market themselves to their followers. Large camps of followers now make their careers through the exploitation of the resources of government in this way. These are the despised 'elites', although this term may be too kind a description.

5. Political parties have become husks of their twentieth-century functions to mobilise ideas and networks towards a purpose. They have become hollow marketing machines that are sustained only by commandeering the resources of government and dispensing patronage to the hollow men of the parties.

6. Governments in these conditions fail to deliver the basic, if ever

evolving, services and infrastructure people want. This is Fukuyama's judgement too. It is for this reason that public trust is so low. The elites may blame toxic social media or fickle misinformed voters, but the inconvenient truth is that low trust is a function of poor performance by leaders.

7. Political patronage, marketing and managerial ideas have cannibalised public institutions, which were once among the independent platoons of democratic society. These institutions, including the public service bureaucracy, professional services and universities, have become spiritless shells of their former selves.

8. Public debate has plummeted with the dominance of professionalised party machines, marketing and spectator media. The public institutions that could be sources of better public debate have been sidelined in favour of celebrities, spin doctors and automaton politicians with talking points.

These are gloomy points on a gloomy winter's morning, and I may refashion over time my responses to these conceptual and ethical dilemmas. But how else should one respond to our republics in distress? To respond with populist sentiments and to shout, 'Power to the people!,' would be naively heroic. To respond with partisan sentiment and to declare blindly that 'Party X is the best, most responsible, most progressive, most credible alternative,' would be heroically naive. To respond with serene optimism and to assert that 'The evidence shows we have faced crises before and will find our way through this one," would be Panglossian and stupid.

My responses tend towards endurance, withdrawal and dreams of renewal. Our civic problems of governing have escaped our control. We cannot stop the disintegration of our political institutions, and all the adverse consequences of our broken tools of governance. Each night on the news we glance at cascades of spite and failure. The reports give no realistic hope that we can stop climate change, economic inequality, cultural decay, social fragmentation and the unravelling of empires.

13 Ways of Looking at a Bureaucrat

When such gloom descends, I imagine we are entering a new Dark Ages. But there is surprising hope in that thought. The history of those times may provide a lamp to guide a long walk to a better life. In the monasteries and margins of the Dark Ages, new ways of 'living in truth' took hold. We do not want to recreate such times, but can look for similar actions within our control that may be wellsprings for new ways of living. This blog is one such practice that protects the culture I hold dear from the destructive flames. Care of my family is another daily practice of renewal, and at work I practice the ordinary virtues (dignity, compassion, humility, respect for human frailty). In acceptance and commitment therapy, I also see a path. There, you deal with life's adversities by taking committed action that approaches your values. So, in our distressed republics, a committed life will only destroy itself if it tries to break the wheel of our decadent politics. Rather, in each of our lives, we should turn to the simple actions that preserve, protect and sustain a more virtuous politics for renewal in a better time.

The antidote to our republics in distress is the commitment by each of us to live in the truth. How each of us lives in the truth will be unique. But this ethical stance of dissidence, in which our spaces of freedom, such as these blogs and the new digital *samizdats*, creates a sanctuary from the flames for at least one seedling of a virtuous life.

As Vaclav Havel wrote, and as I have drawn on his inspiration before,

> I favour... Politics as one of the ways of seeking and achieving meaningful lives, of protecting them and serving them. I favour politics as practical morality, as service to the truth, as essentially human and humanly measured care for our fellow humans. It is, I presume, an approach which, in this world, is extremely impractical and difficult to apply in daily life. Still, I know no better alternative.[47]

---

[47] Havel, 'Politics and Conscience,' *Living in Truth (1986)*.

Ordinary Virtues of Governing Well

To repair republics with big ideas or ordinary virtues?

(From *The Burning Archive*, 31 March 2019.)

My old boss, and sometime mentor, Terry Moran, has given an oration in which he sets out a diagnosis and remedy for today's troubles of government and democracy. Terry is the former head of the Department of Prime Minister and Cabinet in Australia, and, less impressively, the Victorian Premier's Department where I worked with him nearly twenty years ago. Indeed, I wrote his speeches back then. His speech is titled 'The Next Long Wave of Reform – where will the ideas come from?' It was published in slightly edited form on the blog, *Pearls and Irritations*, hosted by another former head of the Prime Minister's Department, John Menadue.[48]

It is said that great leaders are people of common opinions and uncommon abilities. This description fits Terry well. There are few more capable practitioners of the art of governing. He has decisively shaped Australian governments over his career beginning in the 1970s. He has brought a quality of strategic judgement that has lifted the focus of Cabinets beyond trashy politics to the greater purposes of good government. He has led people with finesse, skill and compassion, both in organisations and in a vast network of influential relationships. In essence, government is a people business, and Terry has been the best in the business. Yet the big ideas that he has yearned to focus on are rarely more than commonplace aspirations of the business or managerial executive elite. They are the sentimental attachments of centrist-progressive politics. Divorced from his situation as a leader, his ideas themselves will not remedy the troubled state of disordered republics.

---

[48] Moran, Terry, "The next Long Wave of Reform — Where Will the Ideas Come from? Part 1." *Pearls and Irritations* (johnmenadue.com*)*, March 26, 2019. Part 2 is from same source.

13 Ways of Looking at a Bureaucrat

Terry has shown great courage in speaking of his dismay at the state of those republics. He says plainly we have pursued a wrong course in undermining the integrity of the public service over thirty years:

> We must return to a public service able to provide frank advice to Ministers while securing continuity in our system of Government. This must involve respect for the culture and values of the public service, a significant investment in its capability and, acknowledgement that the untested and supposed superiority of the private sector is actually an illusion cultivated by rent seekers monetising service delivery opportunities, constraining advice in the public interest or pretending that efficiency and nothing else matters. Security for the most senior public servants such that they may safely offer tough, independent professional advice in the face of stakeholder blandishments, whims and aggravation at the Ministerial level, must be reintroduced.

He states plainly that we are on a descending path of distrust in our political institutions.

> In my view, a big problem is the absence of agreement on the big ideas to drive the next long wave of policy reform designed around an Australia which citizens aspire to live in. Certainly, institutions and delivery need reform but this is best done in the light of agreement on where we are to go — what the light on the hill is, and where that light is....To be clear: we've reached the end of a nearly 50-year policy cycle, dominated by ideas derived from macro- and micro-economics.

This diagnosis is structured around the idea of a 'triple helix of democracy', with the three strands being institutions, big ideas and delivery. This political philosophy is that of a plain speaking, practical manager. The meaning of institutions is clear enough. By 'big ideas', he means responses to 'the long term challenges [that] give birth to major policies and the effective program initiatives which define what governments do in the community and the economy.' This definition of 'big ideas' reflects Terry's cast of mind and practical experience. He has always concentrated on the strategy of governments, which he would always tell me, is best understood by Michael Porter's definition of 'strategy', the relationship of a business with its external environment. 'Delivery' is an unusual choice of word for a discussion of concepts of democracy, at least for most, more philosophical traditions. But by this term, Terry means 'the efficacy, honesty and accountability of public administration and the institutions of which it is comprised and the quality of their services.' In essence, 'delivery' means execution of tasks or performance. My gloss on Terry's triple helix then is that he has articulated a managerial philosophy of democracy – organisation/structure (institutions), performance (delivery) and strategy (big ideas). As he would always say to me, strategy is preeminent because it drives the results achieved by the helix.

In Terry's political theory, the chief executives of democracies need to define a vision, informed by what customers want, that can launch the business on its next wave of growth. He proposed to fix our deep cultural and political malaise with that blighted memory of managerial gobbledegook, the strategic mission statement:

> My view is Australians want government to seek tailored, smart, creative solutions that draw on the experience of civil society, business and the public. They want missions.

My cast of mind is very different. More poetic and historical, than managerial or strategic. This idea of missions to solve our broken republics leaves me cold. The list of potential missions are deeply uninspiring and unpersuasive to the eccentric mind that I have. Decarbonising the economy. Training the workforce 'to succeed in the new digital era' (whatever that means). Rebalancing our diplomatic relationships with China and the USA. Integration of diverse communities. Adoption of the *Uluru Statement from the Heart*. National competitiveness goals (to help our big exporters). And that old furphy of 20th century Catholic social thought, subsidiarity, so that we can 'find comfort and support in local connection.' The missions do not hit the mark of what matters most to me.

To be fair, Moran did not propose these missions as the final word, and invited a community dialogue about them. The silence around here is deafening. I suspect my older, more capable, more bureaucratically accomplished boss made a mistake of ideas and strategy. He sought to harness the carriage of democracy to these missions and these 'big ideas'. But, from my perspective, these commonplace ideas and grandiose missions have caused the dilemma we are in. They cannot be the tool to repair our distressed republics. Michael Oakeshott would say that Terry has fallen into the trap of enterprise thinking. He has treated the state, or the polity, as an enterprise, as a business with a single-minded mission that all can work to. By contrast Oakeshott considers the state or the polity to be an association. It does not fix on one purpose. It hosts eternal conflicts on missions, and is kept civil by consensual rules and institutional procedures that hold the sparring parties within civil bounds. Practical judgement every day arbitrates the disputes between between big ideas and small attachments in this Oakeshott's vision. My old boss's mistake is understandable. To view the state as an enterprise is a mirage induced by too many years at the top. It is the habit of generals to see armies marching as one. It is a habit shed if you spend most of your time with the Good Soldier Schweik in the blood-running trenches of our broken republics.

There may well be a triple helix of the virtuous republic, but it is not the three legged manager's stool put forward by Terry Moran. Institutions would be there, and proper care would be given to them, more care than Terry is inclined to do. Moran dismisses concerns with institutional repair as 'embroidery at the edge of the real debate we need to have.' Perhaps, he has confused fashionable ideas of citizen's juries and participatory techniques with real attention to the culture and *habitus* of institutions. Such attention would bring to the fore the view of the state as an association formed by culture, not an enterprise led by missions.

Ordinary Virtues of Governing Well

But Terry's other two strands of 'delivery' and 'big ideas' would not be there. Delivery refers to the execution of a task, rather than the political effect of the action of a ruler. So I would replace this strand of the triple helix with the concept of 'authority'. Authority, not trust or competence, is always the central question of a virtuous republic. Do our rulers, great and small, exercise their power in a rightful way that leads us to bestow authority on them? More on that another day.

In place of 'big ideas' I would propose 'ordinary virtues'. We do not need out-sized ideas among a dominant few, but rather virtuous action by the humble many. Those simple, humble acts create the culture of a virtuous republic. They are carried in the pockets of citizens and soldiers in the trenches, not in the spare knapsacks of visionary executives, whether such would-be missionaries are found in government departments, corporations, think-tanks, NGOs or philanthropic foundations.

I will return to these ordinary virtues in a longer essay, but I imagine twelve: compassion, loyalty, restraint, duty, dignity, humility, courtesy (talking to strangers), courage, the life of the mind, scrupulous pessimism, judgement, and truth-telling.

Cultivating these virtues is the most important thing each of us can do, and that each of us can demand of our leaders. If we put aside big, rare ideas, and take up small daily virtues, we will revive traditions of civic virtue from many civilizations, including Confucian ideas of virtue and the exemplary person – *de, junzi* and *ren*. Confucius, indeed, began his preaching of true political virtue in response to a breakdown in authority and political order, that has family resemblances to that which the republics of the West experience today.

13 Ways of Looking at a Bureaucrat

On human frailty in governing

(From *The Burning Archive*, 7 July 2019.)

Ten years ago, I gave answers to one of those personal profile questionnaires that aimed to help people know more about their colleagues at work. It asked questions like 'How would you describe your childhood?', 'What film changed your life?,' 'What are your favourite books?' and so on. I put some effort into it since I knew I was not liked by most of my colleagues, and they had only the most superficial understanding of who I was.

One question I replied most succinctly to was, 'How would you describe your ideal workplace?' My answer was 'One that respects human frailty.' This is a modest ideal. It went against the grain of the common progressive utopias, and proposed instead the simple restraints of compassionate virtue and tragic pessimism.

My workplace today, the minor halls of the minor provincial government of Victoria, does not respect human frailty. It trumpets its firsts in the march of progressive illusions. It preaches leadership , reform and engineered outcomes, which are certain to be achieved, if we just overcome our human weakness. It proclaims the possibility of the impossible, the necessity of the vainglorious policy goal, the virtue of the grandiose announcement that can never be realised. This pod of leviathans, this catacomb of organisations, misshapen by client-patron relationships and ill-conceived transformations, even pronounces itself, like a parody of an impotent authoritarian, 'One VPS [Victorian Public Service]'. Yet despite, or because of, all those Utopian ambitions, it treat its frail people without respect. It venerates the change-makers, and destroys the objects of their change. It amplifies the cruel sneer that progressives snicker whenever faced with the frail

Ordinary Virtues of Governing Well

affections of ordinary people for the weak actual, rather than the all-powerful possible.

Since I am confronted with such sentiments and actions every day, I take some comfort in what Michael Oakeshott described as the 'conservative disposition'. He wrote in 'On Being Conservative' (1956),

> To be conservative, then is to prefer the familiar to the unknown, to prefer the tried to the untried, fact to mystery, the actual to the possible, the limited to the unbounded, the near to the distant, the sufficient to the superabundant, the convenient to the perfect, present laughter to Utopian bliss.

Surely such a disposition is not such an alien way of being? Perhaps I share this disposition, and it signals to me that I should leave behind this workplace of ambitious change agents? In my time in the bureaucracy, these managers of change, endless change, have taken control of the institution, and deformed it. They have instigated cultural and political decay. Ronald Reagan once said, 'I did not leave the Democrats, but the Democrats left me.' He described his own experience of starting his political or public service career in the Democratic party of the 1950s and 1960s when it was still led the 'Greatest Generation' of post-war Americans. But he moved over the course of the 1960s, in a climate of progressive Utopianism, to the Republican party that espoused, for all its faults, a coherent outlook on governing. So, he defined a new group of voters in the 1970s and 1980s, the 'Reagan Democrats'. Over recent weeks, I have said to friends and mentors, that I am not leaving the Victorian public service and government, but that it has left me. It has abandoned the ordinary virtues that I observed, and learned to respect in the 1980s and 1990s. My friends and mentors generally assent to the idea.

This insight shows the way to live in truth, and may have profound consequences for the choices I make about my working life over coming months. The Department of Hell and Human Suffering wants to spit me out; and this Jonah wants to survive the ordeal within the belly of the Leviathan. But whatever my fate, the disposition to act within the constraints of human frailty matters for the culture of governing.

Take the recent 2019 Australian election, for example. One party (the Australian Labor Party) told itself and the world that it was energised by policy vision, busy with a full agenda of change, and determined to wrought grand transformation across all fields of life – energy, climate, education, health, retirement, child care, identity, gender, electric cars, symbols of shared national life, the constitution, the republic, and so it went on. It told the electorate not to care about the cost of these visions. It said to count the cost of climate change policies was for petty 'little men', who did not understand big ideas and grand missions. This party's leaders clothed themselves in the uncertain grandeur of the past, the mantles of their grand fallen leaders. Mr Shorten even soared like Icarus to emulate Gough Whitlam's 'It's Time' policy launch, like a great leader riding the dragon of reform. The hollow men of the party rolled out the true believer, former Prime Minister, Paul Keating, who tried to convince himself that this gaggle of party hacks was a team of champions. Gareth Evans, former Foreign Minister, toured clubs, cafes and consulting offices to tell ageing Partisans of Reform that this team was 'the most talented shadow cabinet since Hawke's first Cabinet'. The party chanted in chorus Keating's old nostrum that 'When you change the government, you change the country.' They did not see the madness of the former leader who mistook the views from the Cabinet room for the real world. No one around the party elite could see the real, frail world. The parasitic media, the arts community, the progressive intellectuals, and the consultant hangers-on all whirled in their mystic dreams of how they could change the country, with nothing more than an idea. And how badly they wanted to change Australia. Petty, old, racist, self-interested, sexist, nationalistic, dispossessing, tradition-bound, stupid, anti-intellectual, anti-reform, climate-denying, unambitious, frightened Australia had it coming. Labor and the unions were going to 'Change the Rules'. The progressive *nomenklatura* were going to change the rulers in power.

But, the country said, 'No.' Voters said to the Labor Party: it is not the country that must change, it is your bad ideas to change the country that must change. Preacher, heal thyself. If you despise us that much, why do you want to lead us? If you hate the lives we lead, why should you be responsible for them? If our modest successes are not grand enough for you, what makes you think that you are able to do better when everything you do depends solely on us. If we must change, how will you show that you can change for the better, especially when we have not forgotten the progressive farce of the Rudd-Gillard years. The re-elected Prime Minister, Scott Morrison, had sensed the mood, and represented the emotion of the decisive moment perfectly in his speech acknowledging his victory. 'How good is Australia?' he said, not how badly does Australia need to change. This outcome is a 'victory for the quiet Australians', he said, not for the loud, privileged reformers of other people's lives. This result was 'all about you', the voters, he said, and not the realisation of the ambitions of big ideas, professional politicians and true believers.

This too was a kind of fairy tale. Like any election, in truth, it was a close result, a game of inches. Yet Morrison's echo of the voice that was heard that night seems inescapable. Ordinary people do not want sketchy daydreams of grandiose progress. They do not want to live in denial of realistic acceptance of human imperfection and frailty. They do not want manifestly flawed, unsavoury political elites running their lives to a managerial reform project plan. If governing elites are to repair the breach of authority with ordinary people, they must accept, and indeed love, human frailty. Change must evolve, not be engineered by newly marketed masters of the universe.

This great lesson from the 2019 Australian election, which may indeed also be one lesson of the victories of Trump and Brexit in 2016, has not yet been learned by the rejected progressives of Australia. They remain sour-faced, spurned and resentful champions of their failures.

Everyone is to blame except themselves. Self-interested voters. The least watched news outlets. The 'little men' of Australia who failed to embrace their brave, bold and botched policy vision. They still believe they lead from the 'radical centre'. But this centre is out of this world. This radicalism has mesmerised intellectuals because it cloaks in grandeur their low contempt for the dilemmas, virtues and affections of ordinary people in their imperfect and frail lives.

Able Archer, virtue and human decision-making

(From *The Burning Archive*, July 2018.)

Over the weekend I read Taylor Downing, *1983: the world at the brink*. It gave me new perspectives on the dimly sensed fear of apocalypse that I remember from my youth.

In the early 1980s, the Cold War rose to a late crescendo as Ronald Reagan poked the Russian bear into vengeful fury. The story of how this crescendo almost overwhelmed the world is told in *1983: the world at the brink*. Downing narrates this story clearly with all its many points of view and the complexity of motivation of Reagan, and indeed Chernenko, Gorbachev and the double agent spies on all sides.

At the heart of the book are the fatal miscalculations provoked by the NATO war game exercise, Able Archer 83, which took the world to the edge of apocalypse. Buried deep in their compound near Brussels, the NATO generals had no idea that their simulation to practice nuclear launch protocols heightened the fears of the leaders of the USSR, who were already threatened by Reagan's rhetoric, strategic posture, nuclear missiles in Europe and Star Wars strategic defence initiative, which seemed to make a USA first strike nuclear launch feasible. The ailing, defensive, even at times paranoid Politburo perceived NATO as staging a cover for a real nuclear launch against

Ordinary Virtues of Governing Well

Russia. In response to Able Archer, and signs that launch protocols were being initiated, the USSR put its entire nuclear missile armoury on combat alert.

The world has never been closer to a nuclear winter. Downing makes clear that it was ultimately moments of human intuitive decision-making that held the world back from racing over the cliff. One American military officer stationed in Germany observed the heightened military activities of the USSR forces, as they prepared to counter a nuclear strike. If he had escalated in response, the Russians would have had their suspicions confirmed, and a nuclear miscalculation would likely follow. But his intuition called for calm, and his peaceful response helped to prevent a crisis.

A few weeks prior to the crisis, a Russian military official was in charge of the nuclear missile warning systems he had helped to design. They monitored the USA launch sites, and would provide warning of any flash indicative of a launch. To his horror on a shift when he was responsible, the system warned the USSR: 'LAUNCH! LAUNCH LAUNCH!'

With the prospect of nuclear annihilation in minutes, the Soviet official sensed something was wrong. He rebooted the system to check for errors. Still, it screamed, 'LAUNCH!' And then once more. Faced with mechanical alarms, the officer decided to rely on human intelligence, not artificial intelligence.

He was right. The warning had been triggered by a flash of light in the atmosphere. But being right did not save this humble officer, this practitioner of the ordinary virtues. He was drummed out of his job, and relocated into a pokey flat. He was humiliated and excluded because he did not follow procedure.

But he had been right. He had humbly served the truth. Despite all his losses, he maintained his dignity. Later in his life, when retired and in his modest home, he pointed his rare visitors to a globe in a sculpted hand. On the globe was written an inscription from the Secretary General of the United Nations, Kofi Annan that honoured the unknown, uncelebrated, minor government official: "To X, who saved the world."

Ordinary virtue, indeed.

On the virtue of not knowing

(From *The Happy Pessimist* (18 October 2010) and *The Burning Archive*, 27 July 2019.)

Today I repost from my earlier, retired blog an essay from 2010 that reflected on the thought of Vaclav Havel, who was then still alive, and who had survived jail under Communism and power under Liberalism in order to witness the apparent defeat of the masters of the universe in the global financial crisis.

I also read Havel's famous long essay, 'The Power of the Powerless', during the week, and I watched a memorable photomontage that connected Havel's great essay to images of our own times, when we too live in lies. Havel's essay was a diagnosis of the post-totalitarian societies of Communist Eastern Europe, and a search for the conditions and forms that could revive ethics and politics rooted in the real aims of life. Havel called out as lies some mantras we hear today, like 'systemic change' and 'reform'. He found the true power of the powerless in the humble ways that citizens could live in truth, not the indulgent mastery of systems.

It is often lost in the West, that Havel's essay did not only dissent from oppressive communist regimes. Havel believed communist Soviet and Western advanced capitalist societies shared a fate, the modern oppression of Being. Havel wrote:

> The post-totalitarian system, after all, is not the manifestation of a particular political line followed by a particular government. It is something radically different: it is a complex, profound and long-term violation of society, or rather the self-violation of society.[49]

Havel's essay on the malaise of powerlessness was made possible by his decision to focus on the 'problem of life itself', rather than politics. This problem is the bridge that links the fates of late communist societies, and what we we might call 'late democratic' societies. Indeed, Havel himself called the West a post-democratic society.

> There are times when we must sink to the bottom of our misery to understand truth, just as we must descend to the bottom of a well to see the stars in broad daylight.... In democratic societies, where the violence done to human beings is not nearly so obvious and cruel, this fundamental revolution in politics has yet to happen, and some things will have to get worse there before the urgent need for that revolution is reflected in politics.[50]

Surely, we must wonder if we have reached this low point today in our post-democratic societies. This is not because of Trump or Brexit, but rather the scrap heap of more than 40 years of rule by merchant elites, tech giants, mercenary political activists, celebrities, identitarian intellectuals, intelligence agencies, the military industrial congressional media complex, and the institutional corruption of post-democratic societies.

Havel saw deeper roots in the crisis of both post-totalitarian and post-democratic societies. He referred to Heidegger's diagnosis of technology's rule over Being, and Solzhenitsyn's critique of the illusory freedoms of the West.

---

[49] *Living in Truth*, p. 88.
[50] *Living in Truth*, p. 89.

> But to cling to the notion of traditional parliamentary democracy as one's political ideal and to succumb to the illusion that only this 'tried and true' form is capable of guaranteeing human beings enduring dignity and an independent role in society would, in my opinion, be at the very least shortsighted.[51]

So, Havel turned his hope to an "existential revolution," not a political program. He celebrated the uncontrollable, organic, plural diversity of the real aims of life that would be pursued through such an approach. And so in this essay/blog post from 2010 I turned to one aspect of such an insurrection of virtue in a society oppressed by the dreadful certainty of management and the terrorism of change: the virtue of not knowing.

On the virtue of not knowing

During the week I read some remarks by Vaclav Havel at the opening of his Forum 2000 conference and an earlier speech to the European Parliament. Havel has long been one of my heroes ever since I read of *Charter 77* as a teenager, and continuing on through the extraordinary Velvet Revolution in 1989. I have never read his plays but only his political writings and speeches. He mixes oddly his pragmatic application of thought to the world as he encounters it, with a striving to dwell with the mysteries of being, and so finds ways of being that can help us all. Whether his thought has all the rigour of the more rationally oriented thinkers of the world has never mattered to me because it is his animation of the parts of life that are beyond reason, and yet generate its form, that is most creative and provocative in his reflections.

How unusual is it to have a former long-serving President of a nation writing about Being? How provocative is it to see reflections on

---

[51] Havel, *Living in Truth*, p. 117.

the global financial crisis which do not show politicians preening themselves about their foresight, their penetration of the mysteries of these complex transactions that unpicked the world's economic system, or that immediately propose certain solutions within days of revealed ignorance of the problems?

Havel's approach is different. He points to the malaise in modern thought and modern ways that the global financial crisis revealed. Too many forget that nothing is self-evident. "We have totally forgotten," Havel writes, "what all previous civilisations knew: that nothing is self-evident." We assume too easily that we know and can know. We take for granted that our behaviour and the behaviour of our worlds is explicable, and waiting to be manipulated. This theme is the hallmark of Havel's thought, and reminds me of Heidegger's writing on technology and being. But Havel is not seeking in these aspects of life an exit door to a quiet life in the black forest. He seeks there rather a clearing ground, a meeting place for dissent and assertion of eccentric truths by all those who, like him, will not allow life to be destroyed by reason.

There is a beautiful parallel between his essay, 'The Power of the Powerless,' and the unforgettable theatre of the Velvet Revolution, when Czechoslovak citizens, opposed to the fully elaborated reason of an authoritarian state, shook their key-rings together in Wencelas Square, and so brought down the communist state. In his essays of the 1970s, Havel did not advocate the triumph of free market liberalism over the communist regime, even if that was what the 1990s brought. He saw as many weaknesses in the market democracies as in the communist authoritarian regimes. When he was President, he wrestled with the self-certainties of economists who presented to his office in Prague castle (Pražský Hrad). In *To the Castle and Back*, he wrote of his regret that, when dealing with the economists, especially the most ardent, self-certain bully of them all, Vaclav Klaus, he did not dissent with his common sense doubts about these self-certain plans, built on abstract economic theories. During the Global Financial Crisis, he sees the same problem at play, but has no qualms to call it as it is:

> Most economists relied directly or indirectly on the idea that the world, including human conduct, is more or less understandable, scientifically describable and hence predictable. Market economics and its entire legal framework counted on our knowing who man is and what aims he pursues, what was the logic behind the actions of banks or firms, what the shareholding public does and what one may expect from some particular individual or community. And all of a sudden none of that applied. Irrationality leered at us from all the stock-exchange screens. And even the most fundamentalist economists, who – having intimate access to the truth – were convinced with unshakeable assurance that the invisible hand of the market knew what it was doing, had suddenly to admit that they had been taken by surprise.[52]

The masters of the universe were taken by surprise, but did not allow doubt to weaken them for long. We see the same behaviour, even in Australia's response to the crisis. Arguably, the Australian officials had more inkling of at least some troubles ahead. But the journalistic account of Australia's GFC, *Shitstorm suggests* that the RBA and Treasury officials were truly blind-sided. The extraordinary crisis response was a testament to excellence in government to some degree; but it was also an over-reaction, based again on the fallacious assumption that the instruments could be relied on and the tools were within their control.[53]

Havel's successor as President was Vaclav Klaus, his long-term rival, even enemy. He represented for Havel the hyper-rational way of being that he opposed in the Czech Republic after and before 1989. We find the same way of being all about us in Australia in 2010. Many young men and women I speak to in government have this dreadful faith in their opinions, this over-bearing confidence in their analysis,

---

[52] Havel, Forum 2000 Conference Speech 2010.
[53] Lenore Taylor, David Uren, *Shitstorm: Inside Labor's Darkest Days* (2010).

and deceptive certainty that reason will yield the answers to the conundrums of life and of government.

Paul Keating's contempt for 'Balmain basket-weavers' infused a whole generation of apparatchiks and bureaucrats with a militant ethic of rationalism. Those who opposed this 'economic rationalism,' however, chose the wrong grounds for dissent. They jousted one self-certain idea with another. When I look back today, the issue in contest was not economic thought, but self-certainty itself. Neither side of the dispute accepted the limits of knowing and the need to release a way of life from the shackles of preconception, so it could explore the mystery of Being.

This argument does not lead to choosing one or other side of politics. The strains of conservative thought that are influenced by Oakeshott, which I have sympathy for, evoke the habits of life that are resistant to rationalism in politics. Rationalism in politics mistakes ways of being for social engineering. 'The economy is a tool, not the objective' is the title of one of the workshops at Havel's *Forum 2000* conference. This idea should inform how we think about our goals, and we should temper our goals with a greater knowing of the limits of knowing.

Personally, I have felt profoundly these limits for at least ten years. I have felt deeply that I do not, and cannot, understand how the world works, and yet I must act truthfully and respectfully within it. Ten years ago I worked on Nouriel Roubini's theories of the financial system (before he became famous), and tried to make sense of what they meant to government, and its economic policies. It was research prompted by the Head of the Department who had a suspicious hunch about the modern function of money. It was a strange kind of prescience, a fumbling and unknowing prescience, which now in retrospect I did not make the most of. But when I finished with that material, I did not leave with a conviction of being a prophet ignored, but rather a wanderer who was profoundly uncertain about the world and all that we shape within it.

So I praise Havel's call to reawaken the irrational basis for dissent against the degradation of the physical world, of human life, and expressive culture against the great, commercial, inhuman machine, made by a billion rational spiders that enclose us in their sticky web. This dissent begins with an act as simple as shaking key-rings in a crowd, or posting these words for all the world to see.

To govern does not equal to change

(From *The Burning Archive*, 6 October 2019)

In 2016, following the vote on Brexit, an American political journalist wrote:

> But what if progressivism isn't inevitable at all? What if people will always be inclined by nature to love their own — themselves, their families, their neighbours, members of their churches, their fellow citizens, their country — more than they love the placeless abstraction of "humanity"? In that case, the act of ignoring or even denigrating this love will have the effect of provoking its defensive wrath and ultimately making it stronger.[54]

His piece posed the problem of a kind of progressive fallacy: the illusion that things always get better, and that the arc of history bends upwards, and in accordance with the values of the righteous proportion of the population. Many writers are available to dispel this illusion. For example, John Gray, the English political philosopher, presents a more

---

[54] Damon Linker, "How Brexit Shattered Progressives' Dearest Illusions," *The Week*, June 27, 2016.

comprehensive, incisive account of the 'lie of human progress'. Gray's essays show the terrible consequences in recent times of progressive Utopianism, whether it takes the form of free marketeers on both left and right, the disastrous unipolar policies towards Russia, or the moral plague of censorious hyper-liberal identity politics. The antidote, in Gray's view, is a dose of political realism. Realists accept that some, if not all, political or social problems have no real solution; that disagreement on some values is the universal feature of human communities; and that conflicting purposes define the conditions of all polities.

Since May 2019 progressive Australia has gone through its own Brexit or Trump crisis. The progressive cause lost the 'unloseable election'. The crusade for fairness was stranded in Constantinople. The 'best shadow Cabinet since Hawke' failed to take command. They suffered the hubris of an encounter with the facts of history, and were not lifted upward by a rainbow of idealistic dreams. This Cabinet, drawn from one faction of the polity, has now learned they are but one faction that has fewer supporters than they imagined. They remain in shock that the people, who in other slogans they claim to put first, are not members of the elect who will enter the progressive heaven. In their rude shock, they lash out rudely. 'Australians are dumb,' mutter progressive celebrities. Australia has revealed itself to be in a 'backward-looking country'.

There is little sign that this group will learn from the surprising gap between idea and reality. Scapegoats will be found, such as the unpopular Bill Shorten. Facts will be reinterpreted in obvious but foolish ways, such as that only x votes had to change and the result could be different. The para-political mercenary class of advisers, consultants and marketeers will talk about branding, strategy and campaign techniques. Factions within the faction will defend their favoured policies, and sabotage those they never really admired. But very few, if any, will admit the fundamental weakness of the progressive cause when it aspires to govern the country.

13 Ways of Looking at a Bureaucrat

That weakness is the compulsion to mount the 'case for change'. Bill Shorten repeated this tired cliche of corporate life and progressive pitches at the Labor Party's campaign launch in May 2019:

> 'Our great country needs real change – because more of the same isn't good enough for Australia. Our case for change rests on all the great things we are determined to achieve for our country's future. Everything from equality for women, to getting the NDIS back on track. Our agenda is ambitious – it aims high. We are choosing hope over fear. We're choosing the future over the past.'

Alas, the people knew we don't really choose between the past and the future. Paul Keating cemented this progressive illusion into political dogma when he said, 'When the government changes, the country changes.' This claim was absurd as Shorten's choice between past and future. But its fallacy did not appear to the gazers within the hall of political mirrors. So too, the idea of choosing – truly, choosing?! – the future over the past only confirmed that Labor speechwriters misunderstand life around them, and are poorly read. They do not understand Edmund Burke's maxim that government is a contract between the past, present and future.

To govern a country does not require the government to change the country, and certainly not in the name of an unknowable future. To govern a country does not bestow privilege to one faction, who may represent the views of a mere 30 per cent of the country, to change the other 70 per cent who oppose or differ from them. The larger part of the country has its own multifarious affections, loyalties, traditions, cultures, memories, wounds and hopes. Progressives may stand on their soap box and shout, 'Be like me, or else!' But they ought to realise that the crowd whom they denigrate may then choose a leader who likes them. They may make this choice even if that leader is not quite like them. They may prefer this leader to the champion of change who seeks to reshape their ideas and character. They may seek a fair magistrate, who can govern the country, arbitrate its ceaseless conflicts, and negotiate settlements on its intractable problems. They may spurn the leader who seeks to change the country, but is bound in chains of illusion and self-interest.

The ordinary virtues of governing well

*(In episode 7 of *The Burning Archive* podcast (15 June 2021), I discussed a possible antidote to political decay; building a strong culture rooted in the ordinary virtues of governing well. Based on traditions of virtue ethics scattered from Confucius (Kong Fūzi) and Aristotle, to Alasdair McIntyre and Michael Ignatieff these virtues can help us all curb political decay. Can culture - simple virtues like humility, talking to strangers and the life of the mind – offer the best defence against republics in distress?)*

Welcome to the *Burning Archive*, the podcast where the past is never dead, the past is not even past, and where by thinking about the past we try to live better in the present. In this episode of the *Burning Archive,* I am talking about the culture or the ethos of governing. What is it like among our elites today, amidst political decay, democracy in decline, and republics in distress? And more hopefully, what can we find in our culture that might offer us a way out? That is the question for today's *Burning Archive*.

So today, I am asking what is our best response to political decay? Is it innovation or is it a renewal of an old tradition of virtue ethics? A tradition that I might call, the ordinary virtues of governing well. That is the question for today's *Burning Archive*.

My name is Jeff Rich. I am a writer, historian, podcaster, and a very minor government official, and, of course, this podcast is my own creative work, and not related in any way to my rather obscure and unimportant official role.

And also a shout out this week, and I guess a call back to an earlier episode on America as an empire in decline. During the last week or so, we have had some comments from Vladimir Putin on the state of America as, indeed, an empire in decline. And I will just play President Putin's remarks in the background there. Obviously, they are in Russian, so I will just keep the voice low, but the rough translation of what he says is this. When asked about what is going wrong with America, he says,

> You know what the problem is? I will tell you as a former citizen of the former Soviet Union, what is the problem of empires? They think that they are so powerful that they can afford small errors and mistakes, but the number of problems is growing and there comes a time when they can no longer be dealt with. And the United States with a confident gait and a firm step is going straight along the path of the Soviet Union.[55]

Vladimir Putin remarked on how empires, as political institutions, can get overwhelmed by problems, and lose the capacity to deal with those problems effectively. Those comments remind us that the theme of political decay is part of a nested set of themes that I am developing in this podcast. It is my interpretation of today's society and events from a historical perspective. And we are seeing all four themes play out in current events. We see the theme of imperial rivalry, in the summit between President Putin, one of the *Burning Archive* listeners, and Joe Biden from the United States. I am recording this podcast on the 14th or 15th of June, a day or so before the summit. There we can see Uncle Sam turning into bad Grandpa Joe, as a rather classic example of the links between political decay and imperial rivalry.

This podcast is my third episode on political decay. In the first of those episodes (*Episode 5. Doom, Disaster and Decay*), I talked about

---

[55] St. Petersburg International Economic Forum, June 2021.

Ordinary Virtues of Governing Well

Francis Fukuyama's *Political Order and Political Decay*. I discussed how the idea of political decay is not a normative judgment, but more a constant force of entropy in political institutions. The structure of those institutions and the culture that they work with need to contain and restrict that force. I discussed Neil Ferguson, *Doom*, which is a history of catastrophe with a focus on the pandemic, and how it illustrated how political decay can have catastrophic effects on societies. And indeed, perhaps the response to COVID is, at least in some states, or in some countries, an example of political decay hollowing out the capacity of political institutions to respond effectively to social and imperial challenges. Then, in the previous episode (*Episode 6. The True History of the Bureaucracy Gang*), I looked at how one institution, that is essential to good government, that is the bureaucracy, has developed over time, and how bureaucracy is important, in Fukuyama's judgement, to a well-functioning political order. I examined how the history of bureaucracy, the development of merit-based, relatively autonomous and capable bureaucratic institutions, played an important role in the Fukuyama's triangle of political order. That triangle is formed by accountability, the rule of law, and the capable state. All three elements are needed in the foundation of a well-functioning set of political institutions, in Fukuyama's view. Moreover, a well-functioning bureaucracy, that performs well against standards of political responsiveness and relative autonomy, is essential to curb political decay. And lastly, I expressed my judgement, that we have seen worsening conditions in those bureaucratic institutions, as capable, relatively autonomous institutions, over the last 30 years.

So this week, we are looking to the other facet of political order that can act as a curb against the entropy of political decay, as well as institutions, such as a good bureaucracy or strong parliament or whatever. That facet is culture. I view culture as what people have in their hearts and minds, the ideas and symbols in people's heads, and the traditions, heritage, and thoughts that they bring to bear to deal with situations. Culture helps people 'do the right thing' or perhaps

13 Ways of Looking at a Bureaucrat

contributes to them 'doing the wrong thing' when they govern states. And so we are looking at ethos or morality, the ideas that people bring to bear to how they govern or conduct politics. I think, a little bit like last week, without getting too much into details of the present day, I think there is a little bit of rot there today. Today's podcast, however, is, on the whole, an optimistic one, or at least I will talk about an optimistic path out of this situation. Because I think that culture can be repaired through what I call the ordinary virtues of governing well.

So we are talking about culture. That is a big topic, and a term that might need to be defined. Fair enough. I might need to address the meaning of that more when I talk about my theme of cultural decay in a later episode. But it does make me think of a time, several years ago, when I was working on some government policy statements on alcohol and drug policy. There was a lot of discussion about how, if you want to reduce alcohol and drug problems, you can not just make rules for people, and you can not just provide services to people, for example, to help them overcome their drinking problems. More than that, people said, you need to address the culture. You need to deal with the drinking culture, or the culture of drug use. I remember, when I was working on this policy statement, the then Minister was very interested in questions of culture, and how to change the culture. One day I was going down the lift, travelling between meetings, and the Minister and I happened to be in the lift together. She turned to me in the lift and said, "Oh look, you know, what we need is just a good definition of what culture is. Go out and get it, and put it into policy." I may not have recalled the words exactly, but they were spoken in that brisk, matter of fact way. And, of course as any historian or anthropologist could tell you, it turns out that culture is one of the most studied, most written about concepts in the social sciences and humanities. It is a vast, vast topic, which I am not going to bore everyone with here. However, in the end, I did boil the literature down to a useable definition that came from Clifford Geertz.

Geertz was an American anthropologist, one of the great American

Ordinary Virtues of Governing Well

anthropologists. I wrote a piece on my blog a year or so ago about his great essay on a Balinese cockfight. Incidentally, I actually wrote that blog post in Bali. Geertz talked about culture as a series of performative and symbolic practices, and, in one phrasing, as a *set of rules to govern human behaviour*. I can not quite seem to find the exact quote from Geertz today, but ever since the Minister said, "Oh, find the definition of culture," then I, being the sort of person I am, searched through the more fundamental texts to try to understand culture in all its rich meanings. I ended up rereading Clifford Geertz.

Ever since then I have always felt that the fact that culture is a set of rules to govern human behaviour should define a principle for how to look at governing itself. Governing is a culture, a pattern of behaviours, ideas and institutions, that guides the actors, as in the politicians, bureaucrats, citizens, and other actors, who interact together within any particular political order. There is an underlying code of government, a cultural code that emerges from historical events, traditions, and the various stories, symbols, rituals, and webs of meaning that are spun by political and social actors when they aim to rule over each other. It does not mean there is just one single set of ideas, but there are mental models, if you like, that can be shared, externalised, performed, handed down, and used to socialise people.

So for me, the idea of the culture of governing is quite important, and really important to understand what our current situation. I want to evoke this idea of culture when I talk about the 'ordinary virtues of governing well', because looking to the best of the culture, to the best myths of a political order, its best traditions of rule, might help give us the path out. For me, those best traditions do not relate to party politics. They do not relate to left or right, nor progressive or conservative or centrist, and not even technocratic or populist. It is less about the ideas or ideologies that people espouse. It is more about the behaviours, qualities, or virtues that one brings to bear on problems of government.

13 Ways of Looking at a Bureaucrat

It is not a question about values, but rather virtues and practices. And so again, to say that there is decay in the culture is not necessarily saying, "Well, I don't share the beliefs that other people have today." It is not saying that. It is more saying that people do not bring to bear the same set of virtues, skills and practices to resolve differences in the way that perhaps they once did and could do again. So there is a bit of a contrast, at least in my thinking, between virtue ethics and values ethics. This is important because often when people talk about culture, they talk about values. But to my mind, it is better to talk about virtues. This discussion brings up a huge topic in philosophy, the tradition of virtue ethics. It is indeed a whole topic of philosophy, which I am not going to get down to. But my main point is we have a choice of method to find our way out of our current experiences or problems. Should we focus on the values that are most important to us: freedom, democracy, progress, humanity, tradition or whatever they might be? Or, is it better to focus on the virtues that we might practice? Are there virtues that would enable more civil dialogue amongst ourselves, recognizing that we are never all going to agree on our values? Despite our quarrels, we still all need to live together, and make common cause on some issues, in some ways, within a state or a republic.

The other thing to note, of course, is the idea of virtuous rule, or wise government, is common to many traditions of political thought. Many political thinkers discuss how to restore virtue to governments, and we may learn from them to fix our republics in distress. This idea is found in Confucius, Aristotle, Machiavelli, and James Madison. In its own way, it has been evoked, in a famous book of philosophy by Alasdair MacIntyre, called *After Virtue*. MacIntyre explicitly argued that we need to move away from values debates towards virtue ethics. He argued that doing so was our only way out of the rather degraded form of modern political discourse was by doing so. That book was published in 1981. So I am picking up a long established idea to renew its application to our current situation. So, for example, in 1788, as part of the discussions of the foundation of the American republic, the founding father, James Madison, wrote, "Is there no virtue among us?

Ordinary Virtues of Governing Well

If not, we're in a wretched situation." He thought that virtue in the citizenry was a curb on wicked government.

That is one example, but an example that I have more fondness for is Confucius, to use the traditional Latinised name, or or more accurately Kong Fūzi. He advocated rulers adopt a virtuous way of doing things. I sometimes think I can identify with Confucius. Yes, he lived two and a half thousand years ago. But he served in a number of courts of his time, during a period of fragmented Chinese dynasties. He did not really like what he saw. He was deeply disappointed with all his rulers, and a lot of them were not all that fussed about him. And he had this perception of a diseased ruling culture, a failure to practice the best practices, let's say, the best virtues, the correct rites, the true ethics of a wise ruler that would keep people protected and well governed. But none of the rulers really followed his ideas or paid them much attention. He went wandering, taught his philosophy to whoever would listen, rather like some, you know, stray podcaster. Ultimately, it was not until after his death, when his teachings were formalized, and given structure by Mencius and others, that his guiding philosophy of a virtuous way, of fealty to the traditionally understood Confucian values, were mobilised into a single system. I am not saying that everything Confucius said was great. Let's face it, you know, he may have been a little bit inclined to be authoritarian. The Chinese dissident, Liu Xiaobo, who died in a Chinese prison something less than 10 years ago, had said that Confucius wandering China in search of the virtuous ruler was a stray dog who would have become a guardian dog, if he had found the right patron.

That is not what I am advocating. I am not looking for a patron amongst the powerful. I want to find the ordinary virtues that can be practised by a broad group, the many people, grand and little, who actually govern. To seek a single, just, wise ruler, is to discover disappointment. Nor do I seek to find virtues solely among the hardy, virtuous citizenry outside of government, among the citizens who shelter from government, like James Madison's farmers and yeoman soldiers. Rather, I seek the ordinary virtues of governing well that can be practised by citizens in self-government, and by the bureaucrats, even lowly under-castellans like me, who need to find the way to do the right things inside governments, despite all the pressures bearing down on them. And over time, if those virtues are taught and shared, there will assemble small platoons, so to speak, of bureaucrats and other people involved in politics, who choose to practice those virtues. As those small platoons grow, it will change who ends up climbing to the top and becoming the wise ruler.

So this concept of ordinary virtues is something I've read from at least two writers, one of whom is the Canadian author and former political leader, Michael Ignatieff. In a public lecture he described his work on the ordinary virtues.

> By ordinary virtues, I simply mean the virtues of ordinary life, and by ordinary people, I mean you. I don't mean some other group of people who are not in this room. I mean the ordinary reasoning, the ordinary display of moral behavior that all of us display. And the virtues that I'm looking at were, in a sense, the positive ones, pity, compassion, tolerance, friendliness, forgiveness. I'm interested in those virtues that make for moral order, that keep the show on the road. The microscopic interchanges between human beings that make for a moral world as opposed to a jungle. And everywhere, in every social setting, people are knitting together what I would call the moral operating system of their particular world. And by operating system, I mean it's a metaphor to computers and stuff. All I mean by that is when you turn the thing on, you forget about it. It's a sense of the tacit, the unstated, the implicit. That's what I'm trying to capture by the idea of a moral operating system. But these virtues, and here we set up the question that I was interested in, these virtues are very local. They're the virtues of a community. They're the virtues of small settings. And the question that we went around the world looking at was the relationship between the universal values, let me pick one, human

rights, and these local virtues. It is commonly assumed that the ordinary virtues are the source of human rights universalism. That it's some basic intuition we have about human beings that allows and structures and undergirds the idea of the universal values, like human rights. I was struck, on the other hand, by something very different, which is that the ordinary virtues and universal values are in much more tension than we like to admit. And a lot of the inquiry that we went over three years was looking at that tension in action, and I'll give you some examples of what I mean. So the kind of questions that organized this study were, what keeps a liberal democracy together? We have an institutional bias when we think about open societies or liberal democracies. We put an emphasis on rule of law. We put an emphasis on the Madisonian machinery that keeps this thing together. And we don't focus on the micro sociology of virtuous behavior and the operating systems reproduced in society that make these societies cohere. And I was interested in what happens when these operating systems are put under pressure. What happens in fragmented and divided societies? What happens when the moral operating systems and the local virtues are put under pressure? I was also interested, since these are private virtues and local virtues, what happens when political discourse starts to work on them? What happens when a Trump, a Viktor Orban, goes to work on people's emotional feelings? How does that impact the operation of the ordinary virtues? And then this question that I've already suggested, how do we handle the conflict between local virtues and universal values? The universal values of human rights, duties to refugees and strangers versus the local virtues, which are pride in your nation, pride in your community, preference for us versus preference for them."

I would summarise Ignatieff as updating the Madisonian (James Madison) concept of virtue for our current times. He is concerned that the public has turned against the elites, and so against the globalist, human rights-based, liberal political order Ignatieff associates with.

13 Ways of Looking at a Bureaucrat

The public has turned instead to a nationalist, populist sentiment. So, Ignatieff tried to find in that populist sentiment the good ordinary virtues that can be built upon, not just the negatives, such as resentment or xenophobia. His real argument is that we can find in some popular reactions to how countries have developed in recent times the right sentiments for a civil order. He encourages elites to find the good in how people are responding, and engage with the populist backlash' respectfully, rather than reject it as racist, xenophobic, or extreme.

Ignatieff then proposes a different idea of ordinary virtues to mine, because the ordinary virtues that I am thinking of are not qualities of 'the people', but practices of the people who do the practical work of governing. Ordinary virtue, in my concept, requires not just having your heart in the right place. It demands the actual practice of certain virtues that enable you to deal with the challenges of government. This idea of ordinary virtues I originally got from a French Bulgarian thinker, Tsetvan Todorov. He is a historian, philosopher, structuralist, literary critic, sociologist, essayist, and primarily a kind of literary critic. In 1991, he wrote a book called *Facing the Extreme Moral Life in the Concentration Camps,* in which he talked about the ordinary virtues. He contrasted ordinary virtues to heroic virtues. He did not praise being brave or being unrestrained or free. He honoured a humble, constrained sense of virtue. He detected these virtues in reports of life in the concentration camps, where people were able to keep their souls together, so to speak. Todorov wrote

> The manifestation of ordinary virtue reflects a regard for others that is marked by caring, a willingness to look after and even sacrifice for their welfare. It is an act not for humanity, but for an individual human being. It reflects bonds of civility that benefit other individuals rather than a cause.

And that's the contrast to heroic virtues. This is not people fighting for a cause. This is people responding to the immediate particulars of another person. These virtues forge bonds of civility that benefit other individuals, rather than a cause, and lie at the heart of a civilised society.

Todorov identified four ordinary virtues: dignity, retaining a sense of dignity, rather than pride; caring, looking after people in particular individual ways; sympathy or compassion; and the life of the mind. They were his four ordinary virtues, really thinking of people facing extreme circumstances, people living in authoritarianism or in the horrors of the concentration camps. Several years ago I took the idea and adapted it to life as a bureaucrat in the early 21st century, subject to political decay. Clearly, we are not in any way talking about a situation as dire as a concentration camp. Let's just be clear about that. But there is a sense in which I tried to think, with this term, about what is the power of the powerless, to use the phrase of the famous Vaclav Havel essay. I was thinking about different circumstances, such as today when there is more 'soft authoritarianism' than previously, or where people do not necessarily have a lot of control over their situations, but are directed by others, often not for the best of reasons. In these circumstances, what are the ordinary virtues? What virtues can they can practise that, as Todorov proposed, focus on the particulars of the individual, rather than the general cause of humanity or the state or the community or progress? How can they serve a particular situation rather than abstract principles? What practices will create a bond of civil good government, rather than tear it away?

So I took that idea and I came up with this list of ordinary virtues. The virtues on the list that I will not talk about today were compassion, which I took from Todorov, loyalty, strength, duty, humility, courage, scrupulous pessimism, judgement and frankness (or providing testimony). I also listed two virtues that I might quickly expand upon, and that are very important in dealing with our current sense of decay and any prospect of renewal. The first is courtesy or dialogue, which may also be described as talking to strangers. Ordinary virtue in government requires the ability to talk to strangers, and to talk to the enemy, so to speak. You need to talk at the extreme to the enemy, but also daily to many people who do not think like you. This virtue of courtesy or dialogue seems especially poorly practised in today's political culture. The second virtue is the life of the mind, which again I took from Todorov. This virtue may be described as wisdom or even high literacy, such as that old Confucian bureaucrats were educated in. When these mandarin scholars learned how to write essays infused with the Chinese classics, they did more than practise writing skills. They engaged with the deep moral issues that the Chinese classics presented. Their essays in examinations and performance of rites were not just writing exercises, they were actually an exercise in the life of the mind. They built the capacity to think beyond yourself, to think about bigger things and to practice that.

We can see the loss of these two virtues in many political events, certainly in my experience. When political, government or policy issues are discussed these days in the media or on Twitter, for goodness sake, or in Parliament or in public consultations, there is this tendency to caricature and to stigmatise people who have a different point of view. The ultimate version of that is cancel culture. This tendency does not proceed on the basis that, well, none of us are going to agree on everything, and so let's talk to each other, because we all have an interest in finding some settlement. We need to settle on some common ground where we can all learn to 'live and let live'. The intellectual standards in government and the public service are also seriously less than they were 30 years ago. If I really wanted to go into that, I could probably produce objective evidence for that; but I am not going to discuss details in the podcast because of speech code restrictions.

One other little reflection here is that ordinary virtues do not just live abstractly, nor are they just carried in a single mind. You cannot read something in Tsetvan Todorov, and, magic, there you go, you now possess the ordinary virtues. These virtues have to be practised in groups and in social practices. Since the topic of our conversation today is culture and how it can remedy political decay, we should note culture is intrinsically social. So much of our culture is formed by the groups that we are part of, including our professional groups. These rules apply to political culture too. Consequently, the sociology of the political system, as structured by the roles and interaction of many social groups, makes a big difference to the political culture and how it is passed on from one elite group to another. There is a book by a man called David Priestland, who started life as a historian of the Soviet Union, and his book is *Merchant, Soldier, Sage: a New History of Power*. Priestland makes the argument that those kind of groups - merchant, soldier and sage - are three archetypal castes. There is a hierarchical system of relative status based around social group. Broadly professional or occupational social groups are among the most important for political and social roles, and over time, in history, one or other of those groups (soldier, sage or merchant) are dominant within the political and social systems. So, for example, in feudal Europe or Samurai Japan, the soldier or warrior caste was dominant. In the Soviet Union, in a way, the sage was dominant, through a particular sort of alliance between intellectuals or sages and workers. In our political orders, since the 1970s, Priestland argues the merchant class or caste has been dominant. This group includes literally merchants or business people, but also merchant-like bureaucrats and politicians, who valued the entrepreneur or the skilled business manager. They applied that mindset and thinking to politics.

This book presents an interesting argument about how those castes use, let us call it, a 'house style' in their political order. Priestland used a technical term, drawn from French sociologist Pierre Bourdieu, called *habitus*, which means the learned ways of doing things embedded with and giving meaning to a social practice. Priestland wrote,

> caste is the term that I shall use in this essay or book for it allows us to see social groups not only as self-interested entities seeking economic advantage but also as embodiments of ideas and lifestyles which they often seek

to impose on others.[56]

What are the principal castes? Thinkers in many pre-modern, agrarian societies identified four castes: sages or priests, rulers or warriors, merchants, and peasants. Priestland uses these same fundamental groups, although he adds workers. His scheme is a categorisation that you can you can play along with, and make more or less complicated. But I think it is a really interesting idea. For me the key thing is, as I said last time about the political orders of western liberal democracies since since the 1970s, there has been this growing professionalisation of politics and the growing dominance of not just free market ideology or neoliberalism, but a growing dominance of the merchant caste within the political order. This dominance profoundly affected the bureaucracy. It has brought a different sense of what is valued as virtue, of what is good practice, and what are the ordinary virtues of governing well. Are such virtues the ability to run government like a business, or to know how to talk to strangers and to engage in the life of the mind?

For me that is one of the big social changes that underlies this sense of political decay. This merchant-caste dominated system has been in place now for quite a long time. It has lost some of its energy and creativity. It has become decayed. It is now full of spin doctors, consultants, and those kinds of people who, I think, have really degraded some older traditions of virtuous rule, and degraded intellectual and moral traditions of wise government, virtuous government or the ordinary virtues of governing well. It might be that I am just some weird kind of 21st century Australian neo-Confucian thinker. I do stand in the tradition of the sage or priest type class, but I am a very humble sage, a very very humble sage. If I were to articulate for this podcast a desire to have some kind of impact on the world, it would be maybe to build some group of people who would follow those ordinary virtues of governing well, and who would focus less on the business and merchant class, and more on the traditions of the sage.

---

[56] Priestland, *Merchant, Solider, Sage (2012)*.

Ordinary Virtues of Governing Well

Yet I also wonder, in a way, if that is just a reflection of the age-old tension, amongst the sages of the world, in the choice whether to pursue the *vita activa* or the active life in the republic, or whether to pursue the *vita contemplativa* or the contemplative life in the study. I recall Lu Xiaobao's comment on Confucius, and I do not think I will ever find the model ruler who will turn me from "stray dog into guard dog". I am more inclined to the *vita contemplativa*. Since I am close to the end of my career in government, perhaps it is best just to cultivate one's garden when the world falls apart. But for me, that garden cannot always be politics. It has to be the life of the mind and the infinite conversation of culture.

That really brings us to our third theme of cultural decay which we will get to next week. So to summarise today's episode, we have talked about the ordinary virtues of governing well to explore the theme of how culture can be a bulwark against political decay. If culture is used as a bulwark against political decay, it may be best to turn to traditions of virtue ethics rather than particular substantive ideas or values. Regardless of individual beliefs or values, what are the virtues that people might have that can help them act responsibly in politics and in government. I espouse a humble sense of virtue, taken from the works that I have talked about, in contrast to heroic virtues. To provide power to the powerless may simply reflect my status in the world, but those virtues need to find a vehicle through social groups, social practices and a life in institutions. They cannot be just dead letters in books.

That is the last of my podcasts on political decay. So, I introduced the concept, talked about one big institution, the bureaucracy, and then talked about virtues as a way of possible path away from political decay towards renewal. From next week, I will talk about the third big theme of my four themes, cultural decay. That is a bit of a welcome turn away from politics. It will be a little easier for me to evade retribution from the guard dogs of our rulers today, who might say that I am talking on matters that I am really not allowed to. But let me just invoke Vaclav Havel, the great Czech playwright, dissident and later president of the

Czech Republic, who during the 1970s was, in fact, imprisoned for 'living in truth'. He said of Lech Walesa, the Polish leader of Solidarity and later President of post-communist Poland, that a simple electrician with his heart in the right place can change the course of his country. Perhaps, if a few people practice the ordinary virtues, there might be some tiny, tiny, microscopic change in the course of this country. We will see.

I hope I gave you some insight into the traditions that inspire me, and, to some degree, I see in tatters around me. They are traditions that I would certainly like to save from an untimely death, so the past is not dead, it is not even past.

Ordinary Virtues of Governing Well

Chapter Seven The Crisis in Australian Politics

The Crisis in Australian Politics

Three dilemmas of government

(From *The Happy Pessimist* blog 22 December 2013 and *The Burning Archive* blog 22 July 2019.)

I am continuing my blog retrospective today with a repost of a small think-piece from *The Happy Pessimist* blog. If I have done my digital erasure correctly, you will not find any record of this blog online. I wrote it using the avatar pseudonym of Antonio Possevino, a Jesuit priest, diplomat and missionary of the 16th century. Possevino himself wrote using pseudonyms.

This piece on three dilemmas of government appeared just before Christmas in 2013. It enjoyed a brief flame of publicity when a longstanding cranky opponent of government, Vern Hughes, who claimed to run Australia's 'peak body for civil society' took it up as a 'brilliant analysis'. Vern did not and could not know the author was paradoxically the same snivelling, cowardly bureaucrat he had once insulted and abused after a minor dispute. Perhaps, Vern will read this book, and realise his embarrassment, but most likely he will not. In any case, Vern's outburst of praise saw this piece cross-posted, and led to a little flash of views, maybe even 50, and the peak of popularity for *The Happy Pessimist* blog. Soon after, I took the blog down in fear of retribution. I hope it is still of interest.

Three Dilemmas of Government

We have stumbled into dilemmas about government. Six years of incompetence from the Rudd-Gillard Governments disguised deeper problems about the institutions of government. Abbott's honeymoon and poll support has sunk inexplicably quickly, suggesting that the sense of malaise and disappointment relates to a deeper issue than who, or which party, governs. The malaise springs from how we are governed. So, we discover three large dilemmas about government.

Dilemma One. Governments do not satisfy us, but we long for them to do so.

Abbott's most effective line against the Rudd-Gillard era was that Australia was a great country, let down by a bad government. Labor's great failure in response to the global financial crisis was to confuse throwing away cash handouts and building projects with ruling in the public interest. Faced with the greatest political challenge to over-zealous market interests and unethical private behaviour, the Government chose to act like a banker in a sharp suit, pretending to knowledge of financial wizardry, splashing other people's cash, and doing deals to 'keep people in work'. When the illusion passed and no political credit came their way, they turned nasty and launched a class war. They blamed conspiracies in the media and among men, and descended into ill-disciplined tribalism. Abbott, in response, urged all the disaffected, who wanted better, to 'join us', but mistook a longing for the honest pursuit of the public good with the choice of him 'to put the adults in charge'. The dilemma now is whether Abbott and his Cabinet will see beyond the superficial political game; whether they can perceive the deeper public concern underlying complaints about how things are done. Only if they do can they strike out on a new path that pursues honestly that public good.

Dilemma Two. Private interests dismay us, but we cripple the public power that might challenge them.

Behind a succession of public debates since the election of the Abbott Government has lain a concern with how private interests distort how Governments work: the travel expenses saga, the restriction of information on refugees and 'on-water operations', the preference for old careerist men over women in the Cabinet, the out-of-control operations of security agencies, the ludicrous appointment of Tim Wilson to the Human Rights Commission (equalled, of course, by the as ludicrous appointment by Gillard of the less versatile, 'former Labor speechwriter' Tim Soutphammasane), and, most dramatically of all, the debate over corporate welfare through takeovers, Qantas, and Holden. The Government appears at times to be undecided whether to listen to, or to hold at bay, some ill-chosen friends, such as Maurice Newman or David Murray. Their public statements croon greed and private interests. Yet the Government has also said a firmer 'No' to the rent-seekers of Holden and Qantas. It might even finally send a dose of salts through the excessive corporate welfare of Australia. On the other side, Labor cannot end this habit of gambling with other people's money. If Australian Governments are to resist these siren calls of private interests, a renewal of public institutions is needed. At times, Abbott shows passing interest in that. Yet, at other times, he falls for the same old merchant illusion that 'business knows best'. His ambivalence reflects the wider political culture's shyness and ignorance of governing well.

Dilemma Three. Public debate's descent into sound bites, name-calling and think-tank posturing insults us, but we do not attend to the voices that can change the terms and tone of the discussion.

I know I watch too many news panel shows, but surely I am not alone in despairing at the endless recycling of the same witless dumb journalists and party-affiliated think tankers or business/union identities who appear over and over again. The only plus of Tim Wilson's appointment is that maybe he won't be on these shows as much. Barry Cassidy's now pathetically named *Insiders* perhaps should be renamed, *Clapped out 80's lefties journalistic insiders*? Surely, it is not so hard to choose other people. Surely, the producers can be less lazy, and search for guests outside the same old touts and pimps from talent agencies, think tanks and the diminished circle of their mates. Of course, this tedious conversation brings down the public discussion of the listeners. It is an echo chamber of stupidity. *QandA* began as an 'adventure in democracy' but has become tired, weak and predictable. Surely, in our educated community, which is saturated with communications and degrees, we can do better. Do we need to reinvent the role of journalist and media commentator for a different conception of the public interest? After all, the model they all pursue today is less than 25 years old.

We need to understand these dilemmas in the long view, as part of a story about co-evolution of the institutions and culture of power. Increasingly, I think a shock to the political, economic and social system is needed. The shock may come through future financial trouble. It may come from open dissent, or perhaps more private dissent. We could resurrect the spirit of *Charter 77*, Vaclav Havel and the *samizdat*, to inspire hope in our immediate political and social situation. But citizens alone cannot deliver on that hope. We need a government prepared to change both the institutions and culture of governing. Such a government would need a group of leaders ready to choose to rule differently, to forge new institutions of government, and, by talking about politics and government differently, to reshape our political culture.

Here are three steps that can be done.

Challenge the game play of the elites. Nothing will be gained by playing the same old rules, the same old games, and using the same old players. Most of all that means challenging the dominance of econocrats, spin-doctors and business interests.

Keep power under restraints. Power will fail if it over-reaches. Most community activist talk demands too much from ordinary people, and too much involvement in politics. We just don't have the time and the patience. But we do want to be mobilised in our working lives to do better for the public interest. So, we need a culture that restrains power, frames achievable goals, and focuses people's effort on the pursuit of meaningful improvements in social conditions.

Shift focus to wellbeing. Stop nagging the community about productivity, belt-tightening and wealth creation. Stop obsessing with living standards, and help people to live well.

In any local circumstance, there will of course be more particular steps. Governing well is about discerning the public interest in circumstances. But please, please, let us find a way through these three dilemmas.

The crisis in Australian politics 2010-2013

(From *The Happy Pessimist* blog 7 April 2013)

In the nineteenth century Alfred Deakin, who would later become Prime Minister of Australia, wrote a fascinating book, *The Crisis in Victorian Politics 1879-81*. It was a first-hand account of a parliamentary crisis in Victoria that had similarities to the national constitutional crisis in 1975, when the Crown dismissed Prime Minister Whitlam. Let's pull back a little from the strains of the three years since 2010, when a minority government was formed, and describe these events as one protracted crisis in Australian politics.

It has been a crisis of politics, rather than government. The institutions of government have, on the whole, withstood the collapse of legitimacy of the political elites. It is true that government spending is not being effectively restrained, and Cabinet government procedures have decayed. A merry-go-round of Ministers, especially in the last eighteen months, has exacerbated the decay of political authority. The Government has become a shambles, and has brought down some cheerleaders in the bureaucracy and government institutions with it. But the crisis has been overwhelmingly a political failure, the loss of advantage in the conflict between them and us, as marked by rhetoric, values and interests.

13 Ways of Looking at a Bureaucrat

The loss of political authority, and the failure of leaders to negotiate reasonable resolutions of conflicts with that authority, lie at the heart of this crisis. The rancorous dispute between Rudd and Gillard is very real, and very influential. Its roots lie, however, in the failure of both leaders to establish governing traditions, conventions, ideas and coalitions despite the extraordinary political mandate conferred on them in November 2007.

It is worth looking back at the euphoric praise of Rudd and Gillard when they entered office, and the mood that a new age had dawned. It spotlights the humiliating stumbles of this 'super-duo'. In November 2007, Paul Sheehan wrote:

> The utopian Left inside Labor and the Greens will have to come to terms with the reality that Australia will soon have a Labor Prime Minister who has a temper, an iron will, a fierce intellect and an enormous mandate, who has given the Australian electorate what it wanted... an end to the excesses and the hollowness of the Howard Government, not a deviation from policy pragmatism.

With prophetic and ironic words. Geoffrey Blainey wrote:

> The emphatic lesson of Saturday's election is that a successful political regime is bound to be in grave trouble once it approaches its 12th birthday. Having carried out its main tasks, it loses its sense of purpose and mission.

How strange that not yet three years later, Julia Gillard's infamous verdict on her infant government was that 'a good government had lost its way.' Gillard and Rudd together abandoned the secret of Howard's success, according to Geoffrey Blainey: to be the great persuader. In truth, the Rudd/Gillard Government from the outset confused celebrity with persuasion, and media announcements with ideas. The Government never really had a 'way' to follow or to lose. It soon revealed itself to be a gang full of sound and fury, lost in a drifting boat, with captain and merchant crew mesmerised by the siren songs of the sentimental intellectual elite. For a while, the show appealed to the crowd. Before long, the bright sets and vivid music could no longer hide the weakness of the performers. Then, it all dreadfully, magnificently collapsed.

The Seeds of the Crisis

The seeds of the crisis lay in this flop on stage. The Rudd/Gillard Government overreached, miscalculated and lost sense of how politics is moored in the sentiments and traditions of a common 'we'. Events cascaded, and carried the thrashing leaders towards the chasm. Each event entangled itself in the next. They sapped coalitions, and breached the sources of political authority, that is tradition, reason, law and charisma.

The Australia 2020 Summit

The first flop on stage was the Australia 2020 Summit. I recall the enthusiasm of the elites of a certain age in the months after Rudd's election. Every statement implied the boast, 'This is our time. We're the ones in charge now.' The Australia 2020 Summit was the début ball of the new great and good. It repeated Bob Hawke's famous summit in 1983 of government, unions and business. Twenty-five years later, in April 2008, Rudd gathered his great, good and grandstanding to hold the *2020 Australia Summit* in order to develop 'a strategy for the future of the nation'. The meeting was facilitated by a hive of management consultants who pretended to be public servants. In one stroke, Rudd and Gillard announced their separation from the common 'folk', and exposed their hollow political vision. The great, good and grandstanding tried their mettle, and failed.

They became hostages to the cartoon thinking of McKinsey and Boston Consulting Group, and their doting, insecure bureaucratic patrons. The rare idea that survived the butcher paper treatment quickly turned to mush. The participants, flattered at their elevation in the ranks of the new bunyip aristocracy, believed at last they could lecture the nation in 'clear air'. David Marr wrote:

it was worth a trip to Canberra to hear how the rhetoric has shifted and the faces changed. These are the early days of the post-Howard era, but it's already possible to grow a little nostalgic for elite bashing. All gone.[57]

But outsiders saw this summitry as the elite failure that it was. Rumours emerged that the consensus was fabricated. Bad Chairs bumped into the silly ideas they espoused. The energy in the room sank with an overwhelming feeling that government had been pushed into the format of 'games that trainers play'. But, enchanted by their elevated public importance, the elites overlooked their failure. Marr kept the faith, and quoted Rudd approvingly, this 'was just the beginning'. In fact, it was the beginning of the crisis.

In 1983, Hawke used his summit to confer depth on 'consensus', and to build coalitions to execute his mandate. In 2008, Rudd was poised to do the same. He enjoyed a 70 to 9 advantage over his opponent in the preferred PM rating. But he craved a mandate, not from the public, but above above all from above, from the 'smart and the famous', who could answer his prayer to create a strategy for the future. But the Summit revealed the government had no forceful political idea. It shattered its real mandate into a thousand pet projects of the great, the good and the grandstanding. The Summit gave birth to the meme of Rudd 'hitting the ground reviewing'. His approval ratings began running down that hill.

The Global Financial Crisis

The second event in the cascade was the ideological crisis of the Global Financial Crisis (GFC). At the Australia 2020 Summit there was little or no commentary on this event, or of the financial meltdown that would soon consume the Prime Minister. But the early signs of the GFC first appeared in 2007. The dramatisation of bad business news events into a political, ideological crisis did not peak until September and

---

[57] 'Glimmers of hope survive in the mush,' *Sydney Morning Herald*, April 21, 2008.

The Crisis in Australian Politics

October 2008, half a year after the summit of Australian illusions of futurism. Most accounts of the first round of action by the Australian Government, led by Rudd and his key Treasury bureaucrats, praise the timely, brilliant and exemplary response. It appeared to be a truly great accomplishment of a wise and insightful government, unlikely ever to lose its way.

Yet for months on end, Rudd and his Government turned this policy triumph into an ideological crisis. In February 2009, Rudd published his essay, 'The Global Financial Crisis,' in *The Monthly* magazine. Rudd had written this piece, so the news stories went, while on his 'holidays' at the Prime Minister's residence on Sydney Harbour. When I read it, I was expecting strategic insight, but instead found bad, confused writing. It read like the musings of a holidaying executive at his beach house after an exhausting year. I sensed a disordered mind in the writings of this pilot of the financial crisis. I feared he would be driven by obsessive ideas to make poor judgements and to live in the illusions of his dreams. He professed to have written it himself, although stories had been emerging for some time of his vexed and troubled relationships with advisers and writers. It was, Rudd claimed to his soft left audience in *The Monthly*, one of those rare moments in history when intellectual prophets emerge to change the course of history. In his grandiloquent opening paragraph, he wrote:

> From time to time in human history there occur events of a truly seismic significance, events that mark a turning point between one epoch and the next, when one orthodoxy is overthrown and another takes its place. The significance of these events is rarely apparent as they unfold: it becomes clear only in retrospect, when observed from the commanding heights of history. By such time it is often too late to act to shape the course of such events and their effects on the day-to-day working lives of men and women and the families they support.[58]

The global financial crisis, Rudd wrote, secure in his roost on the

---

[58] Kevin Rudd, "The global financial crisis," *The Monthly*, February 2009.

13 Ways of Looking at a Bureaucrat

commanding heights of history,

> called into question the prevailing neo-liberal economic orthodoxy of the past 30 years – the orthodoxy that has underpinned the national and global regulatory frameworks that have so spectacularly failed to prevent the economic mayhem which has now been visited upon us. Not for the first time in history, the international challenge for social democrats is to save capitalism from itself: to recognise the great strengths of open, competitive markets while rejecting the extreme capitalism and unrestrained greed that have perverted so much of the global financial system in recent times.

He compared himself by association with Roosevelt and Keynes. This spectacular over-statement was Rudd's most grandiose over-reach. He had become so absorbed in briefings and interpretations of events overseas, that he failed to observe the very different impacts of these financial events in Australia. Domestically, the GFC was not economic mayhem, but a mild disturbance. Australia's trade and fiscal position enjoyed protection, in large measure our trade with China, from the storms blowing from the Atlantic. But Rudd and his economic advisers were so obsessed with the over-heated world of 'saving capitalism from itself', that they did not look out the window to their ordinary suburban gardens. They were preoccupied with interpreting events that did not quite fit their usual understandings as epoch-shaking changes. But in the outside world, ordinary people had a different everyday experience of the economy. On the street, life went on, much as normal. On the screens of the masters of the universe, elites confirmed their bias that had had experienced a revelation of a world historical crisis. A vast credibility gap emerged. For the public, the GFC added marginal pressures on household budgets, but they adapted simply to mild changes. For the Rudd Government and its bureaucracy, the GFC was a hero's call and they were stationed at the 'commanding heights of history'.

The elites experienced the crisis as an ideological or semi-religious conversion. They fell victim to the gambler's fallacy. They came to believe government could predict markets better than business. This belief in their uncanny foresight led them to open the deepest pockets of government spending, and they convinced themselves this pre-emptive spending was the morally right thing to do because they would avoid mistakes of Keating's recession of '92. Rudd, Gillard, Swann and Tanner became victims of their own illusions. The ideological crisis created a political crisis because the interpretation by the Government of the actual circumstances of people's lives was just plain wrong.

This credibility gap caused the Government's problems with 'selling its record in responding to the Global Financial Crisis'. This was a mystery to the government: why did it receive so little credit for its success managing the GFC? It was not because it had not trumpeted myths about its track record from day one. They could have presented a more modest reading of events that did not inflate the Government's roles into the harbinger of a new epoch and redeemer of capitalism. If they had taken this modest approach, they would have spent less, and persuaded more. They could have argued that they had carefully navigated the ship of state away from the storm. But instead the Government claimed to be the omnipotent rider of the storm. The myth was brittle and just waiting to be smashed.

The smash up came as a result of the fiscal overreach provoked by the ideological crisis, and its combination with failures of budgets and implementation. To look ahead to the remaining sections of this essay, these failures devastated the Rudd/Gillard Government's credibility. Then came the political failure on the environment and the emissions trading scheme that, more than any other event, destroyed Rudd's reputation of moral integrity as a leader. Then I will examine three remaining roots of the crisis – health reform failure, the Henry taxation review fiasco, and immigration and cultural security. Finally I will examine the characteristics of this prolonged crisis of parliamentary and party government, before summarising what may endure and what will disappear from these events

13 Ways of Looking at a Bureaucrat

Fiscal crisis

So, quick recap. I am trying to make sense of this three-year period as a prolonged crisis in Australian politics, which had its roots in a series of political elite failures, which precipitated a collapse in authority of these elites and their institutions.

The first event considered was the Australia 2020 summit, which dramatised the modern labor party, despite its remarkable electoral mandate, as empty-headed, detached from social institutions, and bedazzled by media-driven celebrity. No-one better personifies this failure than Rhys Muldoon. This children's author, performer and very minor television star became, reportedly, a close confidant and strategic adviser to Prime Minister Rudd.

The second event was the ideological crisis provoked by Rudd's over-reach in his response to the global financial crisis. In presenting himself as the prophet of a new anti-capitalist epoch, he over-valued the agency of government, detached himself from the market reform traditions of the Hawke-Keating era, and decisively opened the credibility gap between the Government's economic rhetoric and everyday experience of life. The state was roaring at a mouse.

The third event was the fiscal crisis provoked by the GFC. In their panic, Rudd and Gillard opened the door to many huckster schemes. Their rhetoric of new epochs was too cheap to match the huge costs of these schemes. In particular, the blue-collar interests of the Labor Party, especially the building and construction union, pressed hard to 'save' jobs by funding what Labor advisers called 'nation-building' projects. While the first cash injection for households was a sensible response to the GFC, the second wave of grandiose 'nation-building' projects were slow to deliver, failed cost-benefit tests, and largely pandered to opening gambits of the principal unions, the AWU and CFMEU. All their special pleading blinded the government to the evidence all around that a repeat of Keating's '92 recession was just not going to happen. So were born the school halls, pink batts and NBN construction cargo cults.

As a consequence, the Commonwealth lost control of spending for policy purposes. Sites, such as the Catallaxy Files, have documented the growth in payments. And payments were the problem. A shallow dip in receipts in 2008/09 and 2009/10 did not continue beyond that point. By 2010, there was no policy control of the budget. Deficits increased dramatically. More importantly still, the loss of budget flexibility immobilised the government on the three major social policy priorities that could have saved the government's bacon: health, education and disability.

The Environmental Policy Betrayal

The fourth event was the environmental policy betrayal. I do not use 'betrayal' as a personal judgement, but rather as a characterisation of the emotional and political response of the public. Rudd/Gillard backed down and later failed on the emissions trading scheme, citizen's assembly and, ultimately, the carbon tax. It was this event beyond all else that exposed Rudd as an idol with feet of clay. At the time, Malcolm Mackerras said:

> This is about the fact that the electorate has woken up to the fact that Kevin Rudd is not the sort of leader that they once hoped he might be. I think three years ago the Australian people were so determined to get rid of (then conservative leader) John Howard that they looked for virtues in Kevin Rudd that were never there.[59]

Robert Manne made a similar point in his essay *Left, Right, Left,* even though he was preoccupied with redeeming Rudd's reputation and sheeting blame on Gillard and her backroom crew.

> The third strategic error of the Rudd government was to trust the Coalition and to cold-shoulder the Greens regarding negotiations leading towards its most important

---

[59] *The Telegraph*, 10 May 2020.

piece of legislation – the emissions trading scheme. Rudd placed faith in the capacity of Malcolm Turnbull to deliver bipartisan support. When Turnbull lost the Liberal Party leadership in November 2009, and when Tony Abbott made it clear that the Coalition would oppose the climate change legislation, the Rudd government began to lose its way. Rudd could have now opted for a double dissolution and negotiations with the Greens. Instead he allowed members of his cabinet – including his deputy, Julia Gillard – to talk him into postponing the emissions trading scheme for the next three years. Not only did it now seem as if Rudd believed in nothing. In considerable numbers left-leaning inner city voters now defected, probably permanently, to the Greens.[60]

The collapse in support, the diminished authority, and the creation of a war on two fronts created the political conditions of the crisis. Beneath these political conditions lay a deeper difficulty with the environmental policy agenda. It had been captured by economists, like Ross Garnaut and Martin Parkinson. These austere experts stripped environmental policy of its greatest asset. It had real moral, political and public appeal. But in Garnaut and Parkinson's hands climate change became a byzantine economist's puzzle, not a question of political values. Bureaucratic, business and political elites failed to imagine a moral response to the 'greatest moral challenge of our time'. As a result, Rudd took the fall. He was not without blame. The climate change debate was another case of Rudd hoisting himself on his own grandiose, apocalyptic, rhetorical petard. He failed to connect with the life-world of the public. He floated the bubble of ever more complex expert schemes to change the basics of people's lives. So, the trap was laid for a defining event of the crisis: Gillard's missteps on the citizen's assembly and the carbon tax.

The fifth and sixth events followed on from this shared failure of Rudd and Gillard. They thrashed government's policy arms wildly in a desperate search for a way to restore their lost authority. Fatally they

---

[60] *The Monthly* (March 2012).

saw their saviours in the avoidance of death and taxes; that is, in national health reform and the response to the Henry taxation review. Rudd engaged in a furious misadventure of PowerPoint driven policy, against a backdrop of his televised confession of failures, and lame attempt to connect with the felt language of the public. Remember "fair shake of the sauce bottle"?

National Health Reform

The fifth torrent of failure was national health reform. The early part of 2010 was dominated by photo ops of Rudd in hospitals. These stunts that sought to demonstrate that he really understood the dilemmas of the health and hospital system. He promised to present a plan 'to fix' hospitals. Bureaucratic discussions, to which I was a witness, became a vast guessing game. Did the PM really want to take responsibility for hospitals? Did he actually understand the significance of that? What was the plan? When would he share it with anyone outside his inner circle? Was there more to the plan than those few PowerPoint slides presented by a top-tier consulting firm to 'pitch the project'? Had anyone prepared a list of the legal and resource questions that would need to be resolved to reassign health institutions and budgets from the states to the national Government?

The well-informed observer might have noticed the same character appear in many of the PM's photo-ops and bureaucratic briefings. By Rudd's left or right shoulder on the many missions to the Premiers was a bureaucrat, Ben Rimmer, who was in charge of 'strategy and implementation' in the Prime Minister's Department. Mr Rimmer's great skill was to cook up hare-brained strategies, and then present himself as best in breed of the new 'best and brightest,' who would do whatever it takes to implement them. Sadly, his strategy was as confused as the PM's mind, and he knew nothing of implementation. So despite all the policy papers, COAG meetings, hospital tours, all the storming of the health administrators' buildings, all the bad-tempered stage management of consultations with doctors and nurses, Rudd's national health reform flopped disastrously. It delivered lots of bureaucratic arrangements, even more confusion, and next to no tangible benefits to the public. It was yet another case of political overreach and elite failure.

The Henry Tax Review

The sixth circle of hell in the political crisis was the Henry tax review. For many members of the economic policy elite, the Henry Tax Review is a bit like the economic rationalist's political manifesto of the early 1990s, *Fightback!* - the unacknowledged policy bible that governments are just too gutless to implement. It was born in the mist and murk of the *Australia 2020 Summit*. The Prime Minister made the brave decision to ask the Head of Treasury, a public servant who reported to him, to produce an independent report to Government. Near academic quality analysis was produced. Speedy but thorough consultation was undertaken. The small committee bound its recommendations in impeccable logic, and then handed its worthy, but dull, report to its boss. There it sat for months on end, while Mr Rudd sought to save his status as saviour of the health of the nation.

Now I am no tax or economic policy expert. I could not discuss the technicalities of tax regimes. But even I could see the problem the Prime Minister's neglect of this policy bible would become. The Government had invested so much in this exercise, but then let it sit neglected in a Treasurer's in-tray for months. When finally the Government relented and released the report, the Prime Minister and Treasurer had cooked up their own answer to the tax and transfer system. Just tax the rich, or at least the mining industry. The Government's published response to the review rejected pretty much the whole report, except for its adapted implementation of a mining tax. It looked weird. It confused everyone. It spoke of confusion.

Both the Government and the review authors, Mr Ken Henry and his fellow grandees, had let each other down. They all forgot that tax is the tap root of political authority. They were negligent in their political judgement. They ignored the debates about values that are embedded in debates about 'Who pays, and how?' They confused these basic judgements with technical policy tasks. Rudd, Gillard and Wayne Swann, the Treasurer, were a reckless crew. They sailed into the storm with no political strategy at all. They even failed to consult properly the mining interests they sought to tax, and the state governments who taxed them now. Such reckless conduct ignored a basic maxim in government, to collaborate with those who implement your orders. They failed a basic skill test of both policy and politics.

By targeting the mining industry, Rudd, Gillard and Swann also struck at the heart of the entrenched interests of the Labor Party, including its most powerful and iconic union, the Australian Workers Union (AWU). They did not notice the collateral damage they were doing to themselves because they had mesmerised themselves to believe the Big Miners were a soft target, a modern reinvention of Labor's long tradition of populist attacks on the 'money power'. The Minister for Mining was Martin Ferguson, and he had not been deeply consulted on the mining tax. This old-fashioned, but shrewd, former head of the union movement, and later paid lobbyist for the mining industry, identified the self-delusion in the Rudd Government's 'gang of four' political strategy. He remarked that Rudd and his inner core of Ministers believe they had developed a smart, popular strategy of 'class warfare'. The Government played at being David fighting Goliath, but in fact they were simply being naive fools.

Immigration and Cultural Security

The final event that created the political crisis was the debate on immigration and cultural security. The debate on immigration and border security in Australia dismays me often. However, it is an enduring feature of our politics. We should not be surprised. We live on an island country, where cities cluster on the coast of an inhospitable and dry continent. Those cities host an affluent country that suffers the deep cultural malaise of the shallow modern West without being nourished by the traditions of Old Europe and insane ambition of New America.[61] We are an insecure exile, encircled by an undefendable coastline, and dependent on migration and trade for economic growth. Immigration politics profoundly shapes the factions and internal politics of the Labor Party and the Liberal Party. Different experiences of migration and settlement in each region make different parties, politics and clients in, for example, Victoria, Western Sydney, or Queensland. Migration runs through the politics of economic policy too. Different visions of business growth, whether to choose growth through population increase or old-style protection, compete in both major parties. But it is especially strong in the Labor Party that attracts those most exposed to competition from labour migration, workers in the trades, semi-skilled and unskilled occupations.

It is difficult for the Labor Party to hold these political, factional, policy, and cultural tensions in harmony within its own institution. The difficulty of balancing these tensions when governing the nation exceeds their grasp. They add to their burden with a potent political myth, that conservative Prime Minister John Hoard exploited ethnocentric sentiments on the refugee issue. The myth assures the Labor Party that it lost the 2001 election because Prime Minister John Howard exploited the Tampa incident, involving a Norwegian boat that stopped to rescue a boatload of refugees and transport them to Australian shores. The myth is Howard used the incident as a wedge issue to expose the Labor Party's inability to choose between being soft-headed or hard-hearted towards refugees. But when in Government, Labor performed poorly on the refugee issue. Moreover, the Rudd/Gillard Government's poor handling of the underlying debates on cultural values from 2008 to 2010 was exposed over and over again by the border protection debates, the 'Big Australia' population debate, and the cultural name-calling (e.g. 'bogans') by the

---

[61]   John Carroll, *Ego and Soul: the modern west in search of meaning* (2010).

elites. Ultimately, all three issues would be personified in the personal struggle between Rudd and Gillard.

These debates exposed deep cultural fissures in our society. They magnified the consequences of issues and deranged people's assessments of disagreements. People would say, 'There are only a small number of refugees so why do we make so much of it?' The reason was every issue was refracted through the distorting mirror of cultural insecurity. But policy elites showed little appreciation of the emotional lifeworld of the bogan public. They mocked them, but could not imagine solutions that connected with them. Instead, they prescribed drab, technical policy interventions, even when they were sold as 'breaking the people smuggler's business model'.

In summary, these seven events broke open Australia's political institutions to a sustained crisis of authority and legitimacy. They created the background music of the political scene in the first half of 2010, the insistent, rapid beat of 'Rudd, the failure'. In May 2010 the online magazine, *Crikey*, reported laments of disappointed Labor voters that Rudd was damaged goods and was damaging Labor in turn.

> It's easy to say that Kevin Rudd has no one but himself to blame for his plummeting popularity. But he shares the blame with the cult of populist, principle-free propaganda that has come to dominate the ALP, pushed by the Right faction, not only but most noxiously in NSW.' Euphemised as "Spin", this cult bewitched the Carr government into photo-op/media-release atrophy, was exported to Britain, undermining good intentions and poisoning the Labour brand for the long term, and has managed to capture the Lodge under Kevin Rudd. It is a philosophy that admits only one hope, one goal: the exercise of power.[62]

How far had the hero of the 2007 election fallen? The hopes, the mandate, the authority had shattered in the shaking hands of Kevin '07. In 2007 political commentators as different as Geoffrey Blainey

---

[62] *Crikey*, 11 May 2010.

and David Marr saw Rudd as triumphant. Now he was a figure of fun, whose future was full of difficulties. The victorious Labor Party never liked a loser. Now the fragmented, patrimonial, factional, culturally adrift Labor party would turn this man into a martyr, and instigate the political crisis that today threatens the future of the party they lead.

The crisis in Australian politics 2010-2013 part two

So, we arrive at the crisis. But how might we define this term, crisis? I have not undertaken exhaustive research on how this term may be defined. I know enough of the warp and weave of its rich history. It has strands of theological concepts of the Last Judgement imported into secular, political history. Utopian thinkers conceived the unrealistic on the threshold of politics and governing with their use of the term. It has commonly been a weapon to subvert institutions that authors felt disconnected from.

My working definition of crisis is the situation of a complex system that is functioning poorly. The reasons for dysfunction may not be known by the agents within the system. But the poor functioning creates high levels of uncertainty among those agents, and threatens their accomplishment of high priority goals. In reaction, the agents press the system for immediate decisions to prevent further disintegration or downfall. Crises are often total, involving all social systems. But the crisis I am describing is more limited. It is quite specifically a crisis of the political party system, which infected, but did not subvert, the whole political system.

Cue June 2010. The political miscalculations of the Rudd Government have exposed the poor functioning of the Labor Party's modern factional and policy forms. The 'Sunrise candidate', as Rudd was derisively named because of his appearances on a morning TV show, is increasingly perceived as a parasite on the Labor Party. His armchair warlord detractors in the party said, 'The only faction that supported Rudd was Newspoll.' He was mocked because he had no defining ideas and no institutional backers in the Party. His solo attack on the Party had left him exposed, after the cascade of seven failures that I have described. The pressure grew to find a creature of the Party who could act as saviour for 'a good government that had lost its way'.

The creatures of the Party factions took action. But the dark quiet savagery of their execution of Rudd demonstrated to the public that this was a gang of political mercenaries who had long ago lost any moral compass. The 'faceless' power brokers acted against the parasite on their party, Rudd; but their raid on the leader exposed themselves as parasites on the political system. They worsened the crisis of legitimacy. They could not admit their mistake. They spent the next three years denying they ever conspired against the elected government, and spread misinformation that all these rumours of leadership tensions were conspiracies of the mainstream media. The coup failed to end the poor functioning of the party and political systems, but it continued institutional failure by other means. The plotters lunged at the King, and pierced the throne.

Policy misstep followed policy misstep. Some errors, infelicities or misjudgements were caused by the personal qualities of Gillard or Rudd - her political "tin ear", his psychopathology. But the crazed, haphazard deviation from the way of the government was caused by the character of the modern party political machine. It was parasitical, but loosely attached to society. It lacked both the constraints and freedoms forged in deeper connections with social institutions and traditions of thought. Within weeks of the coup, the Government was in a tail spin of spin. Political staffers confected 'big ideas' that died before the nightly news. The self-proclaimed political masters of the universe conjured illusions that only tripped themselves. Gillard's authority collapsed, and would cause more policy failure. The Prime Minister's proposal to warehouse refugees in East Timor lasted barely one week. Caving in on the mining tax negotiations crippled revenue

13 Ways of Looking at a Bureaucrat

for years.

Prowling in the shadowy halls of power, watching all these mistakes like a bitter critic, the undead Banquo whispered his dark poison. When Gillard called an early election within months of the coup, the problem of illegitimate authority was clear to all. The election was meant to be another quick fix. It became a slow burn because the unresolved crisis of legitimacy continued, and was exacerbated by the very poor performance of the disconnected political party elites. The most disconnected of those elites made up Gillard's inner circle, political advisers imported from Britain and party loyalists who had no life. This cabal created a confused, bizarre electoral proposition. Votes fell away with ridiculous proposals that seemed drawn from an episode of *Hollowmen*, the television parody of the modern culture of political spin. The Government announced it would solve the greatest moral challenge of our time, the climate crisis, with a 'citizen's assembly' and 'cash for clunkers'.

During this entire saga within the government, its opposition, the conservative side of politics, was burdened by the troubled awareness of its bad faith on the greatest moral challenge of our time. So votes from the Labor Party leaked to the Greens and the Independents, since people felt the major parties did not offer a choice between viable options. The 'plague on both their houses' syndrome, in fact, was its own form of self-delusion. It avoided in exasperation the fundamental character of governing. Decision-making is made in constrained and unfavourable circumstances.

Then, remarkably, electoral maths joined with political uncertainty to deliver the hung Parliament of 2010. Three years of dismal governing followed. It took, however, until the last last few months of 2013 for the combatants to speak clearly about how bad things got. Simon Crean, former Leader and veteran of a Labor dynasty, criticised Gillard's 'tin ear'. But he deflected the criticism to her staffers who, despite Gillard listening and responding with a sage 'mmmmm',

The Crisis in Australian Politics

managed to misdirect her from any true political judgement in favour of gimmicks, stunts and miscalculations, all designed merely to get a headline. Privately, Crean would say the Prime Minister, not the staffers, makes the decisions. Such is the decayed form of government the professional party political adviser system made.

But beneath the coded slights, some consistent accounts are emerging of the nature of modern Labor's rule. The accounts are similar to former Treasurer Keating's sarcasm about his Prime Minister Hawke's 'Manchu Court'. They portray dysfunctional decision-making in a broken system. The inner circle of rulers appear as a gang who are out of touch and disconnected from this country's political and social traditions. Such ill-formed rulers arise not only from bad personnel choices by leaders and staffers, but from the torpid institution that had bred, installed and fostered them. The rot of party government is at the core of the crisis. The problems will only end when party government ends, and we establish some other form of governing, more deeply connected to social institutions, cultural traditions and political associations.

For the time being, there is no doubt that the conservative side of politics will be the first to seize the opportunity to fashion such a model of government. There is something about Tony Abbott's conservative background, his way with language, and his roots in the plain forms of Australia's lifeworld that make me think he has the capacities to lead such a successful form of governing. But does his Cabinet? Does his Party? Do the networks of advisers, operatives and lobbyists who run our governments? Conservative governments in the states and territories have failed to do so, and that may be the more realistic prospect. It may be that an electoral defeat for the Labor Party may bring on system change or even collapse within that institution, and yet still leave unresolved the weaknesses of political legitimacy in the other parties. Or it may be that demotic forms of democratic politics – somewhat like those described by John Carroll – will refashion how Abbott and the Liberal party governs. We shall see soon enough, and a future post will examine if and how such a remoulding might occur.

Postscript in August 2019

I have not changed these predictions though they proved wrong. The Abbott and Turnbull Governments exposed an ongoing political crisis and a broader institutional crisis of governing in Australia, and other post-democratic societies. Maybe Scott Morrison is the harbinger of the demotic forms of democratic politics – "the quiet Australians" and "how good is Australia" – but I am more gloomy and uncertain about the future and my judgement of the present today than I was in 2013.

Untimely thoughts on the parliamentary crisis

(From *The Happy Pessimist* 30 August 2010.)

I am going to allow myself to express some radical, tentative and even unthinkable thoughts about the current political crisis. It is an interregnum in which we may direct questions to our beliefs concerning our polity, which is an old word that has oddly been spoken so gracefully in recent days.

Is there a crisis of legitimacy if neither major party, not even the 'independents', can claim a mandate or the right to govern? If we admit such a crisis, do all claims of majority rule lose value? If so, what are the grounds for authority of an executive government in a contemporary polity?

In liberal Westminster theory, Parliament is not the executive, but rather the assembly of members who choose between two stage roles, to govern or to oppose. But this election raises the question: what are the roles, limits and legitimacy of the member of Parliament? What truly is the function of the elected representative? How far is it diminished when elected representatives who govern propose that 'citizen assemblies' perform that stage role of deliberation instead of MPs? When, and how, may restrictions be placed on the role of the local member, and how might the rights and obligations of those members differ between those who choose to govern or to oppose or to profess 'independence'? Why should I obey the Independents? Who made them independent of my vote?

Government is formed by negotiation between fragments of elites. The independents are rebel elites who dare not say their names. They are elites who failed to sustain comity within the association of a party, but now expect to determine the composition of the Cabinet. Near Prime Minister Gillard remarked on the election result that 'the people had spoken but it may take some time to interpret what they have said'. Witty, but wrong, in this way. Popular opinion has not spoken with any intelligible meaning. There is simply no just outcome from this election, no claim for mandate from popular vote. We are left with a compromised Parliament and an illegitimate Parliamentary executive. From a confusion of messages, we may see a leader emerge, or we may encounter more confusion.

Good government is not equal to good parliamentary oversight of government. People have expressed both surprise and satisfaction that despite the absence of an elected government, we seem to be doing OK. The wheels of administration keep turning. One market analyst even reported the view, in business circles, that a hung Parliament would be good for markets. The markets are pleased that the Parliament is stripped of the authority to spring surprises, or to make strong decisions that defy even the slightest opposition or private lobbying. I read this contentment as code that the markets have concluded that the government's mining tax will be defeated, and they expect no more questioning of the great betting scam of international finance. But this is comfortable blindness; there will be a slow deterioration in the efficacy of government if this crisis of legitimacy continues.

This election featured few debates and a preference for 'people's forums' organised by rival television networks. Such forums organised by the media have replaced the more formal institutional debate of public issues and scrutiny of political actors. Panel shows, not parliaments, now govern the relationship between people, media and parties. But can they provide legitimacy to our choices?

The question will become what are the sufficient and necessary conditions for strong executive government? Can minority government and a hung parliament provide these conditions? If authority for a government cannot proceed from its mandate, popular vote or parliamentary support, what is the basis and extent of the authority for an executive government in these circumstances? Have our government institutions outgrown their parliamentary overseers?

Kevin Rudd's election disguised the decay of political elites on both sides. That decay became evident in this election, and especially in the factional administration of the ALP. The Australian-American political sociologist, John Higley, has thought more deeply on the problems of political elites than any other thinker alive today. Higley accepts the fundamental importance of elites to politics, and thus the necessity for some kind of moral code to influence, at least, a powerful fraction of the elites in order for societies to be governed well. Higley argues the performance of a consensual elite is essential to the health of democracy. If so, what does the observed decay of political elites in Australia mean for the values and efficacy of democracy. What does the degraded ethos of the sub-elite of the union movement and Labor Party careerists mean for the capacity to govern among this elite? During Julia Gillard's campaign launch, the Labor Party brought back its once virtuous leader, most successful Prime Minister, and representative of a tradition of a consensual elite, Bob Hawke. But his resurrection only highlighted the contrast between this elite leader's virtue and the crop of despised, factional union hacks, who aspire to replace him.

The Crisis in Australian Politics

We have a generous, and perhaps too generous, view of the scope of government activity in this country. Will we shrink that role as we cramp the legitimacy of the new Parliament and Government? Or will we find more open and direct forms of supervision of government that rely less on parliamentary contest?

Time for a real debate on debates

(From *The Happy Pessimist* August 2010.)

The rules of discourse we set ourselves shape the quality of thought we both expect and receive. So, it surely must be time to achieve a breakthrough on the debate on debates. Tony Abbott has supported the old Kevin Rudd proposal for a debates commission. For the record here is the agreed format of the USA's Presidential Debates Commission for 2008, taken from their website.

> *First presidential debate*: foreign policy and national security, moderated by Jim Lehrer Friday, September 26, University of Mississippi. Two-minute answers, followed by five-minute discussion for each question.
>
> *Vice presidential debate*: all topics, moderated by Gwen Ifill Thursday, October 2, Washington University. Ninety-second answers, followed by two-minute discussion for each question. Two-minute closing statements.
>
> *Second presidential debate*: all topics in town meeting format, moderated by Tom Brokaw Tuesday, October 7, Belmont University. Two-minute answers, followed by one-minute discussion for each question.
>
> *Third presidential debate*: the economy and domestic policy, moderated by Bob Schieffer Wednesday, October

15, Hofstra University. Two-minute answers, followed by five-minute discussion. Two-minute closing statements.

Surely, the implementation of such a simple procedure cannot be beyond us in this country, especially given our traditions of public service, and our more fitful record of quality journalism, broadcasting and public policy. Some adaptations would be made. On the face of it, there may be less time devoted to foreign policy and security. Then again, what is the 'refugees/stop the boats' discussion if not the emblematic foreign policy/security issue of this campaign? It would be good to extend the reach of the issues and arguments. Equally, there is more national debate of social policy in this country, or so it seems to me. The 'town hall' format on either the Sky News or QANDA format has value I think, although keeping it independent of particular networks would be an improvement. I have enjoyed seeing both leaders having to think on their feet to respond to real individuals who are actually involved and passionate about an issue. Nearly every time, the responses were thoughtful and respectful, and revealed how issues these leaders might decide an issue in the future.

It is disappointing to read that the Debates Commission proposal was nobbled by the Labor Government in this year. It made a proposal to the Press Council that three debates during the campaign be replaced by three debates 'over the election season', a much longer period when voters are much less observant. It also proposed to reduce the numbers of commissioners from five to three. Why? Well, who knows? But both these nobbles reek of political wriggles aimed to make the proponent withdraw their support, or provide maximum flexibility to campaign 'strategists'. I don't think the Debates Commission should just be the press or a not-for-profit organisation as in the USA. I think we might consider including senior and independent public servants. We might also introduce a debate between Treasurers, or a group of senior Ministerial portfolios, to fulfil the role of the Vice-President's debate in the USA. These conventions might have better effects on the quality of government than the ridiculous 'Charter of Budget Honesty'.

It might be difficult to choose the appropriate person, but candidates could be the Electoral Commissioner, a senior officer of the Parliament, such as the Clerk of the Senate, or even the head of a School of Government. I think we should ensure all those who have a real stake in quality political discourse be part of making it happen.

I also think the Commission might have a dialogue with the Press Council about certain journalistic practices in the campaign. Too often the media were a flock of sheep who followed the 'campaign bus' to write stories, but in reality the political parties kept the journalists in the dark till the last minute. These practices are questionable ethically and certainly not conducive to good reporting of political affairs, good journalism, or good political discourse. This is a simple but fine thing that surely we can make happen in this country. Whatever happens on Saturday, please Tony and Julia, make this one happen.

13 Ways of Looking at a Bureaucrat

Chapter Eight Journal of Some Plague Years

Journal of Some Plague Years

The Plague Year

(From *The Burning Archive* 19 March 2020 and 18 March 2021.)

One year ago, in the first quarter of the first COVID year, I wrote the post below on the likely effects of the coronavirus on our lives, our health and our governments. Like most people I over-estimated the health impact of the virus, and under-estimated its social and political impact. I certainly did not predict the sapping of democratic culture by expert elites. The year became as much a year of viral meltdown, a pandemic of fear, as a year of plague. Boccaccio had a much worse catastrophe to deal with.

The Plague Year

I have been following the emergence of the coronavirus pandemic since January, especially through the podcast *Warroom: Pandemic,* hosted by Steven K. Bannon. The world is now living in its modern plague year, and living through an exploding crisis that cannot be managed.

The great cities of the world – Wuhan, Beijing, Milan, Venice, San Francisco, New York – are going into quarantine. Tens of millions, hundreds of millions of people have been locked down. The bountiful markets crumble before mass hoarding and the shocked fears of consumers who, for the first time in their lives, know shortages. People call for kindness, and encounter fights in supermarket aisles over the last pack of toilet paper. Travel between countries is closing down. Travel within countries is winding down. I can even get a seat on my commuter train for the first time in years. The stock markets speed into a whirligig powered by automatic algorithms, and lose more value than the human-induced crash of 1929. The masters of the universe in the

13 Ways of Looking at a Bureaucrat

Reserve Banks, Treasuries and merchant banks pretend to mastery by nodding approval for billions or trillions of dollars in stimulus packages, but they soon discover their impotence. The pandemic is the final humiliation of the dismal science before the social facts of illness, biology, fear, survival, life and death.

Some projections suggest somewhere between 20 and 70 per cent of the world's population will be infected with this virus. The mortality rate? No-one really knows. There has simply not been enough testing or reliable studies; but it could be as low as 0.2 per cent or as high as 2 per cent. Whichever rate, the result is a lot of deaths. This is a once-in-a-century event, akin to the great Spanish flu of 1918. These two foreign viruses also shared the complications of entanglement with the American empire. Wartime censorship murkily obscured both the early reports of death rates and even the names of these pandemic viruses.

There is no treatment. There is no vaccine. There is no definitive refuge. We have all learnt the meaning of 'social distancing' and 'self-isolation', and we hope they will keep us safe. We trust. We hope. We urge our alchemists to find the cure, and their purpose may well merit our trust, even if their track record has not always done so. We put our faith in the pandemic planners and public health physicians, even if the speed of this spread – cases appear to be doubling every four to five days in my city – has taken them by surprise, and a few mad scientists thought they could treat the population as a herd to be immunised to try out their theories. Still, better, calmer and more reliable advice is coming from those leading public health physicians than from some of the less capable politicians and media panellists grandstanding before the cameras.

We all have our stories of our lives being turned upside down: schools closed down, home-quarantines, businesses suddenly abandoned by customers, travel plans cancelled, customary leisure lost, work conducted even more remotely from the space commanders of our organisations. My adult children have had their last year of university and plans for travel thrown up into the air. They cope with but do not enjoy online learning, the separation from community, the suspension of overseas campus exchanges, and the loss of part-time job opportunities. We wonder what we will do and think about when in self-isolation? Lists have gone up online of plague reading: Camus, Defoe, and, of course, Boccaccio, *Decameron*.

This crisis will have large effects on the economy, society and the culture. It will break some leaders in all those fields, and will make others. It is in large part a crisis of governing, and over the months of its unfolding I may return to that. But will this crisis also lead to events and adaptations of the decaying culture. Will we turn from constant consumerism, flippant influencers and corrupt, complacent elites? Will our culture regenerate? Will the onset of a biological event – the outbreak of a pathogenic RNA virus: lead to a transvaluation of all values?

The Great Seclusion

From The Burning Archive 22 March 2020.

Michel Foucault's history of madness described the decrees of 1656 that confined the insane, the unemployed, and the socially aberrant to the *Hôpital Général de Paris*, the former home of the lepers and the plague-ridden. It was part of what he described as the *Great Confinement*.

> It is common knowledge that the seventeenth century created enormous houses of confinement; it is less commonly known that more than one out of every hundred inhabitants of the city of Paris found themselves

confined there, within several months.... From the middle of the seventeenth century, madness was linked with this country of confinement, and with the act which designated confinement as its natural abode.[63]

He may have exaggerated and misinterpreted the historical events; but he did create an enduring historical metaphor, the *Great Confinement*, that described how a political order, economic drivers, an array of ideas, and a new pattern of disease could rapidly change the daily life of people.

Could we be living through another such moment? Millions of people around the world are self-isolating and staying at home to slow the spread of the coronavirus. Next week I will be among them, as I take into my own hands a more proactive response than is recommended by the public health authorities. Kevin Bacon has seized the social science concept of networks and social distance, which is forever associated with his name, six degrees of separation from Kevin Bacon. He galvanised a movement on Instagram to #stayathome, not to save yourself, but to protect others. Guests on panel shows do not appear together in the same room. Bondi Beach is closed by the police. The infinite number of eateries and cafes in our consumer-driven service economy are shutting down, in response to both government fiat and the citizenry voting for health with their feet.

Unlike Foucault's *Great Confinement*, this *Great Seclusion* is driven more by the ordinary person, who wants to protect their family and friends from unwitting infection, which they and the authorities can do nothing else about. This seclusion from below differs in large measure from Foucault's confinement from above, driven by the commanding heights of Reason. But there is a measure of panic below in response to the confusing directives from above issued by the governments and chief medical officers of the world. These experts have been jumped by a social problem to which they cannot readily

---

[63] Michel Foucault, *Madness And Civilization: A History Of Insanity In The Age Of Reason* (1965), pp. 38-39.

adapt their systems and institutions.

We do not know how long this *Great Seclusion* will last for, even though the communications initiatives speak of 15 days to slow the spread. It might last for six months or more, since we need to adapt to later waves of more transmissible or more deadly strains of this and other viruses. There will be many inconveniences and difficulties. There will be many deaths and losses. We may see serious strains in the economy and social order. We may see the spread of bad ideas, from both elites and the 'deplorables'. We may see more modern bread riots, when consumers fight over access to rationed goods in our modern capitalist supermarkets.

But might this voluntary *Great Seclusion* also give birth to something better in our cultural lives, even in the face of many deaths and great tragedies? Something that we will not want to give up when business and the authorities call us to return to normal, later in the year. In many traditions, seclusion has long been a practice of spiritual renewal. The American journalist, Andrew Sullivan, has compared in recent days his experience living through the AIDS epidemic and this more widely dispersed pandemic:

> Living in a plague is just an intensified way of living. It merely unveils the radical uncertainty of life that is already here, and puts it into far sharper focus. We will all die one day, and we will almost all get sick at some point in our lives; none of this makes sense on its own (especially the dying part). The trick, as the great religions teach us, is counterintuitive: not to seize control, but to gain some balance and even serenity in absorbing what you can't. There may be moments in this great public silence when we learn and relearn this lesson. Because we will need to relearn it, as I'm rediscovering in this surreal flashback to a way of living I once knew. Plague living is almost seasonal for humans. Like the spring which insists on arriving.[64]

---

[64] "How To Survive A Plague," *New York Magazine,* 20 March 2020.

Rod Dreher at the *American Conservative* has taken that thought further:

> We really are in an apocalypse, a word that means "unveiling." This plague shows us who we really are. It first reveals to us that we have far less control than we thought, and the things we believed were permanent are not permanent at all. It can all be taken away from us in a matter of days and weeks.[65]

What will *The Great Seclusion* reveal to us all? We can hope it will reveal some better ways to live, work and play than those we have institutionalised, over the last 50 years, in the Great Borderless Consumer Market. As Nietzsche wrote in *The Gay Science*:

> And while I shall keep silent about some points, I do not want to remain silent about my morality which says to me: Live in seclusion so that you can live for yourself. Live in ignorance about what seems most important to your age. Between yourself and today lay the skin of at least three centuries. And the clamour of today, the noise of wars and revolutions should be a mere murmur for you.

Plague notes

(From *The Burning Archive* 29 March 2020.)

The stay-at-home urging continues, and we are all doing the responsible thing. Order appears to be returning to the supermarkets. Yesterday, I was able to buy nearly everything that I wanted to, except a whole chicken. We are confined at home. Even young lovers are practising social distancing to protect their doctor parents: intimacy now means walking the park at night, 1.5 metres apart.

---

[65] "The Hard Road Ahead" *The American Conservative*, 20 March 2020.

Journal of Some Plague Years

New York is bracing for disaster, and Spain has suffered tremendously. Yet other countries – Germany and perhaps my own Australia – may be dodging a bullet. Variability in the local response and impact of this virus appears to be the order of the day.

Will social distancing work to an acceptable level? Most likely. The race for effective treatments is on, and looks like it will displace the evangelical public health epidemiologists, who are enjoying a few weeks or months in charge of society, from the front line of the response. That might be a little unkind. But over the weeks ahead we may see a shifting balance from public health controls to treatment, as the unavoidable wave of ill patients crashes on our overly efficient health care system.

We are all asking, how long will we remain in this new way of life, and what parts of it may be enduring? The crisis may last two months; or it could extend to 18 months or more in some of the extreme 'suppression' scenarios put forward by the Imperial College of London. If there are later waves of the virus, or even more deadly viruses, this new way of life may become institutionalised. If the crisis passes quickly, we may rush back to our old ways, and expel the puritans from our new Babylon. We do not know the length or enduring character of these changes. But here are some speculations on how this health crisis may seed a cultural renaissance.

The slap to the face of consumerism. For the first time ever in the West, and for the first time since the 1990s in many ex-communist countries, people have encountered queues, shortages and the denial of services. Going out to shop for shoes leads to public shaming. The shops are closed or operating on restricted hours; and we must resist our urge to rush out and buy ice cream after 8 pm at night. Retail therapy is being replaced by counselling via Zoom. For some of us that may lead to a constant change; but, if free-flowing wealth returns to our society, I suspect consumerism will surge back with only minor embarrassment.

13 Ways of Looking at a Bureaucrat

The trimming of the service economy. Life in the gig economy never looked so insecure or unrewarding. Nations who decided to live off the back of services, and not make their own face-masks and medicines, never looked so foolish. The Americans want to repatriate their manufacturing and send China a bill for the disease. Australian universities might need to stop being a major export industry, that fleeces international students more than it supports cultural missions at home. The ability to do practical things, including around the homes to which we are all confined, never seemed so important. I expect some recalibration; but not a return to manufacturing autarky.

Home working. If you can work from home, you must work from home, say our political leaders. And for those of us who are by nature solitary, we take the chance with both hands. Who among us would not like to avoid mass transit systems, unpleasant commutes, overcrowded cities, and unreliable colleagues who have low standards of hygiene? I suspect there will be an irresistible demand for many to work from home well into the future. When we are not confined to quarters after all, working from home will be even more enjoyable. But this will test the narrow competency limits of management in our large organisations.

A new humility to re-imagine purpose. The virus, a microscopic string of proteins, has humiliated the masters of the universe, those 'leaders' who aspire to command the heights of the economy and globalist institutions. We all live within more controlled spaces, more limited horizons, more confined perspectives. We have all learned we are vulnerable to new, uncontrollable biological events, and that death, illness and frailty await us all. But many of us, who have not succumbed to the maelstrom yet, have also discovered time to reflect, and to contemplate the deeper meaning, connections and purposes that make life worth living. The slow viral transformation of our characters induced by this global retreat may be the most fertile seed planted by this crisis.

Journal of Some Plague Years

Thucydides' tower

(From *The Burning Archive* 9 April 2020.)

Thucydides, one of the rival brothers who founded the Western tradition of history, who lived in the period 460 to 400 BC, was a general in a series of wars over 27 years that he would later name the Peloponnesian War.

He was a failed general ultimately, because, after a fashion, all human endeavour fails when it is of the complexity of military leadership. Thucydides' individual failure was to arrive late for battle, after he received the summons to save the town of Amphipolis. The town fell to the Spartans before Thucydides reached the city, and, for this failure, he was sent into exile, most likely in his family estate near Thrace.

There, Thucydides spent the next twenty years of his exile writing his *History of the Peloponnesian War*. The liminal status of the internal exile stimulated Thucydides to see the wars from multiple perspectives, and allowed him to gather intelligence far and wide on the social and emotional drivers of human history, which he contrasted to the supernatural, scandalous and divine fabulations of his great rival brother, Herodotus.

No-one quite knows the location of the estate on which Thucydides was exiled, nor can can anyone describe, from documents or ruins, the look of the building in which the exiled *strategos* wrote his masterful reflections on war, politics, and human conduct. However, I imagine, for small reason, that he wrote in a stone-walled tower above a garden that offered refuge from the disintegrating world.

So too, I imagine myself in a modern reconstruction of that tower; where I sit, read and wonder in internal exile; where I am separated from the interests and factions of the world in which I once played a minor part; and where I record in this history the meanings of the war's events and my defeats.

From the *History of the Peloponnesian War*, I recovered this strange echo of our own times, although the scourge of the plague then was more fearsome than this coronavirus now. Here is part of Thucydides' description of the plague of Athens:

> But the greatest misery of all was the dejection of mind in such as found themselves beginning to be sick (for they grew presently desperate and gave themselves over without making any resistance), as also their dying thus like sheep, infected by mutual visitation, for the greatest mortality proceeded that way. For if men forebore to visit them for fear, then they died forlorn; whereby many families became empty for want of such as should take care of them. If they forbore not, then they died themselves, and principally the honestest men. For out of shame they would not spare themselves but went in unto their friends, especially after it was come to this pass that even their domestics, wearied with the lamentations of them that died and overcome with the greatness of the calamity, were no longer moved therewith.[66]

Public health rules, OK?

(From *The Burning Archive* May 2020.)

The psychology of power is enigmatic and poisonous, and infects more than the ruthless and the mercenary. Principled men and women of medicine succumb, even at moments of apparent triumph, when the

---

[66] Thucydides, *History of the Peloponnesian War*, 2.51.

whole society kneels in submission before their authority, in the hope of a cure, or still miraculously, a vaccine for a new disease. Submission, however, transmits the infection of power. It inspires in the most compassionate medicine men and women the excessive belief in their remedy.

The virtue of clinical medicine, or the good practice of a treating physician, is empirical testing and observation; not models, not statistics, and not sweeping recipes for living divorced from all the particular affections to which we are prone. The religion of the true doctor, this *Religio Medici*, we might say, is not mathematical, not regulatory, but strange, peculiar and idiosyncratic. For each patient, there is but one truth, which may only be manifested in the dialogue of 'I and Thou'.

The same principle does not govern the behaviour of that unusual branch of medicine, Public Health. This discipline, under whose iron-fisted rule we all today shelter, shackled in our homes, describes itself in terms distinct from the good Sir Thomas Browne, who knew the fragile uncertainty of all knowledge, and the brittle experiments of all ideas:

> I could never divide my self from any man upon the difference of an opinion, or be angry with his judgment for not agreeing with me in that from which perhaps within a few days I should dissent my self.[67]

The *Oxford Textbook of Public Health* defined its field so:

> "Public health is the art and science of preventing disease, prolonging life, and promoting health through the organized efforts of society. The goal of public health is the biologic, physical, and mental well-being of all members of society. Thus, *unlike medicine, which focuses on the health of the individual patient, public health focuses on the health of the public in the aggregate.*

---

[67] Sir Thomas Browne, *Religio Medici (1643)*, Section 6.

> [emphasis added] To achieve this broad, challenging goal, public health professionals engage in a wide range of functions involving technology, social sciences, and politics. Public health professionals utilize these functions to anticipate and prevent future problems, identify current problems, identify appropriate strategies to resolve these problems, implement these strategies, and finally, evaluate their effectiveness.[68]

Public health doctors are not content to be mere physicians. Their ambition extends to be problem solvers, evaluators of their own solutions, engineers of society, or indeed engineers of the very soul. They do not treat individuals in their enigmatic and alone manifestations, but prescribe for populations in the aggregate, as those sums are revealed through the dull haze of statistics. They do not practise weak medicine, but perform a powerful brace of functions (technology, social sciences and politics) that seek not to cure disease, but to rearrange the organised efforts of entire societies. So, the dark dream of the non-medicine man is spoken.

In the telling of the sacred keepers of their tradition, public health emerged as the saviour of degenerate and unhealthy mankind, which before the revelations had been prone to infectious disease, until 2020 just a memory of distant times. The revelations came not in the form of prophecies or sacred texts, but in the patient, incontrovertible evidence of modest statisticians, such as John Snow. Snow was, in some eyes, the founder of that peculiar curse of our times, epidemiology and its weird sister, data science. In these accounts, John Snow, by looking at the data, traced the true source of the cholera epidemic in his district, the Broad Street Pump. So, Snow established the tradition in which Public Health doctors, by dictating solutions beyond the small circle of their individual practice of medicine, which in Snow's case was symptomatically anaesthesia, used political levers to save humankind from at least one horseman of the apocalypse.

---

[68] *The Oxford Textbook Of Public Health*, 5th Edition, eds. Roger Detels, Robert Beaglehole, Mary Ann Lansang, and Martin Gulliford (2009).

Journal of Some Plague Years

This hagiographical tradition of the history of public health tells of a golden age from 1880 to 1970, when public health rationales were relatively unquestioned. But it also complains of the rebellion of patients against the dictates of public health since the revolutions of the 1960s. Since then, people began to question doctor's orders, and to doubt their wisdom beyond their specialised field. A brief resurgence of the faith emerged in the 1980s when public health combined with social zealotry to outlaw tobacco smoking. But ever since, public health has complained to the few who had to listen of their frustrating inability to achieve much with chronic or non-communicable disease; unless they were brought back from the margins of government.

The outbreak of the coronavirus returned public health to the central powers of government. Suddenly, specialists in that dying category of medicine, infectious disease, surged back into public view. They sensed an unprecedented crisis, a population yearning for answers, and a moment not to waste a crisis. Within weeks, the technical terms of epidemiology littered popular media: exponential (but rarely sigmoid) growth, contact tracing, and social distancing. The tools of medicine changed again, in favour of the epidemiological non-medicine man. Distancing, not drugs; tracing, not therapy; models, not medicine, became all important. The specialists in these tools surrounded the powerful, and formed a new court of unprecedented power, in which they declared, on the basis of their own convictions, emergency powers that they would wield to defeat an enemy on a battlefield shrouded in the fog of ignorance.

One thin prophet from London came to symbolise this new power in the world, Professor Neil Ferguson. He was the epidemiologist, infectious disease modeller, professor of mathematical biology, 'Professor Lockdown', false prophet of the plague times. Emblematically for the field of public health, Professor Ferguson is the ultimate non-medicine man. His training was in physics, and his doctorate in theoretical physics. His topic was the 'interpolations from crystalline to dynamically triangulated random surfaces,' whatever that means (I confess my ignorance of science). Yet this untrained physician, who was more knowledgeable in derivative calculus than in disease cures, prescribed a mass quarantine for the entire world.

For a few short weeks, Professor Ferguson was giddy with fame, celebrity and power. His Imperial College model changed the course of politics and this pandemic. He was the prime expert on the curiously named SAGE group that advised the UK Government. But then, as things do, his model began to fall apart. His predictions lasted barely a fortnight before being walked back before a Parliamentary Committee. He cut his prediction of deaths from the virus by over 90 per cent, with no sign of embarrassment. People pointed out the false predictions he had made, based on the same mathematical fallacies, in past pandemics. Questions were asked about the reliability of his brittle, byzantine, occult code.[69] Then his own hypocrisy was exposed, when he was publicly shamed, like a wicked priest of old, for breaking the vows of isolation he had imposed on the world. He had made illicit visits to his married lover, when he had been infected with coronavirus. Bizarrely, he explained his breach of his own standards with this confession of being drunk with Faustian knowledge:

> *I acted in the belief that I was immune,* [emphasis added] having tested positive for coronavirus, and completely isolated myself for almost two weeks after developing symptoms. I deeply regret any undermining of the clear messages around the continued need for social distancing to control this devastating epidemic.[70]

The non-medicine man appeared to forget his ignorance of medicine. His models misled him to assume a knowledge of this infectious pathogen that was entirely impossible still.

So, we may hope that the quieter practitioners of true medicine might come to the fore before too long, and this brief Puritanical Commonwealth of Lockdown may come to the end. As Sir Thomas

---

[69] *The Daily Sceptic*, 6 May 2020.
[70] *The Guardian*, 5 May 2020, quoting Neil Ferguson.

Browne said, 'We all labour against our own cure, for death is the cure of all disease.'

Reflections on the current unrest.

(From *The Burning Archive* 19 July 2020.)

In today's world the falcon cannot hear the falconer. In the widening gyre of overlapping world crises, our minds have lost contact with our culture. We are hunters alone and adrift in terrain we have not mapped, and where we can not find our way back home. I will not repeat the well-repeated line, too often fenced, from Yeats, "The Second Coming" (1919), but will take it from there:

> Mere anarchy is loosed upon the world
> The blood-dimmed tide is loosed, and everywhere
> The ceremony of innocence is drowned;
> The best lack all conviction, while the worst
> Are full of passionate intensity.

Will there be revelation for us in this moment of crisis? Have events stirred some pitiless stone monster in the sands to take rough form, and then stagger from our neglected *Spiritus Mundi* in the desert to terrorise the feral cities of our decaying culture?

I do not know. I lack all conviction that some 'new normal' or some vision splendid of progressive control awaits us on the other side of the events of 2020. But I see many shysters putting forward a shallow view, and a few who might reconnect the falcon and the falconer.

Today, I thought I might use the virtues of the blog's

improvisational, fragmentary and iterative form to begin to formulate some hypotheses on what on earth is going on in the world. There are intersecting crises of health, security, geopolitics, authority, making a living and passing on culture. This post might begin a series. I have little time, and I must give testimony.

Today I may only formulate an initial list of partial theses. I may amend, correct and adapt these theses over coming days.

Ten theses on the crises of the world.

1. The resurgence of infectious disease has threatened our belief in invulnerability and the authority of medicine.

2. The American Empire is collapsing through cultural, political and social decay, and will suffer a century of humiliation instigated by China.

3. The multi-polar world is emerging but is breaking cultural and technological interoperability: we need to relearn how to talk to strangers.

4. A millennium-long trend of cultural convergence is reversing.

5. Our institutions in politics, media, education, government, commerce, arts, health and social service are corrupted and have lost the mandate of heaven.

6. The evolution of family systems and associated values in the Anglo-American world has generated a crisis of cultural fragmentation.

7. Education has prostituted itself to social stratification, and betrayed its authentic purpose of the getting of wisdom.

8. A mercenary caste system of political government in the West is collapsing.

9. The loss of meaning, or the poverty of collective belief among human groups, has produced a catastrophe of selfishness that confuses

political protest with stealing a pair of high status sneakers.

10. The habits and institutions of civil society have been replaced by the illusions and mistakes of social media.

Captain Ahab and lockdown in Melbourne

(From *The Burning Archive* 20 September 2020.)

Historians (and I am one) will search for cultural archetypes that explain the strange delusions of power that imposed captivity on the citizens of Melbourne and Victoria in 2020. In a state of 6.5 million people, there have been, on this day, 20 September 2020, a mere 14 positive tests for the presence of fragments, dead or alive, of an RNA virus, SARS-COV-2. Extrapolating from rates of serious illness and deaths, the likelihood is there will be no deaths and maybe one case of serious illness (SARS-COV-2) from these positive tests. And yet Melbourne, my city, remains in the longest and most severe lockdown in the world. It is subject to the first nighttime curfew in its history. Masks are mandated, even when walking alone in the sunshine. Grandmothers are harassed by police for sitting for a breath on a park bench. Pregnant women are arrested for posting reasonable concerns on Facebook. People are questioned, watched and abused by police for complaining about the loss of fundamental freedoms. Parliament is effectively closed. A legal regime of near martial law is declared. Human rights are breached consistently, flagrantly and thoughtlessly. The public health medicine is wildly worse than the disease. Why?

I am not at liberty to speak openly about my interpretation of events within the institutions of government, but I may ask about the cultural figures at play in this enigmatic scream at a mouse in the corner of the barn. What cultural virus has infected the minds of our ruling physicians and the Great Helmsman of Victoria?

It is curious that some commentators have turned to the resources of literature to make sense of the horrific tragedy unfolding in this state. In *The Australian*, John Carroll, the eminent cultural sociologist, explored the political psychology of the leader of the Victorian Government, and compared the Premier of the State to Captain Ahab from Hermann Melville's *Moby Dick*.

> Andrews looks more and more like a solitary figure on a spotlit stage, surrounded in the shadows by subservience, somehow believing he can take on the pandemic monster single-handedly but registering failure after failure, to which he responds with inflexible indifference as his state becomes the laughing-stock of the nation, condemned to a woeful short to midterm economic future. Is there some subconscious mythical identification with Captain Ahab, who devoted his entire adult life to a self-obsessed pursuit of the white monster of the deep, Moby-Dick?[71]

This article struck me for two reasons. First, the author is eminent, and was first recommended for reading to me by the great Frank Knopfelmacher. Second, the same figure from literature occurred to me just days before. Captain Ahab seemed to me the perfect match for the troubled, obsessed, vengeful leader of the St Petersburg of the South. Daniel Andrews has pursued the elimination of the SARS-COV-2 just as Ahab did the White Whale, after it cleaved his leg away. Carroll extends the same analogy:

> The ferocious giant whale had, on one encounter, reaped away Ahab's leg like a mown blade of grass. Moby Dick is of uncommon size and malignity; to chase him has become an act of superhuman impiety, and it destroys Ahab. The Andrews impiety seems similarly monomaniac, with the perverse twist that the more exhausted and

---

[71] John Carroll, "Brought Low In Pursuit Of A Covid Whale," *The Australian*, September 17, 2020.

rattled his own personal state, the more he seems driven to inflict ever more severe punishment on his victim, the Victorian public.

Who in Victoria will speak out, like Starbuck in the final chase? Who will confront Andrews to say: "'Oh! Ahab,' cried Starbuck, 'not too late is it, even now, the third day to desist. See! Moby Dick sees thee not. It is thou, thou, that madly seekest him!"[72]

From here to immunity: from pandemic to endemic

From The Burning Archive 18 October 2020.

2020 has proved a testing year for the culture and capacity of governments around the world. Many governments have failed. Governments, far away and close to home, have failed. The State of Victoria in Australia, which I call home, has failed more in proportion to the real spread of the virus among its resident population than most, and certainly more than the usual targets of criticism without facts, such as Donald Trump or Sweden.

Disease outbreaks arising from pathogens have disrupted regimes or even induced collapse of empires in the past. Examples are the Justinian plague weakening the Eastern Roman Empire, and the bubonic plague shocking the Mameluk sultanate, that elite of military governors of Egypt in the 14th and 15th centuries. Those disease outbreaks have been deadly serious. The Black Death of the 14th century killed one-third of the population. By contrast, SARS-COV-2 appears to have added seven days to excess mortality, and less in some countries. In Australia, there appear to be less death than normal in

---

[72] Herman Melville, *Moby Dick*, p. 465.

13 Ways of Looking at a Bureaucrat

this year of lockdowns and mass panic.

In January and February there was a genuine, reasonable concern that this blooming pandemic would have a dramatic impact on health, but also on the operations of the inter-connected global economy. Markets and governments acted in anticipation. Was this a black swan event that the masters of the universe would need to get on top of with rapid speed? Would we see a repetition of the 1918 pandemic that had a death toll estimated between 25 and 100 million people, when the world's population was 1.8 billion, one quarter of today? Or was it, as historian Niall Ferguson wrote, more likely, a Dragon King or Gray Rhino event?[73]

As February and March faded into April, May and June, the evidence accumulated that this virus would never have the direct impact on mortality of the direst predictions. It was likely a Gray Rhino, a predictable and manageable event. Nobel Laureates, epidemiologists and true public health experts such as Michael Levitt, Jon Ioannides, Sunetra Gupta, Carl Henegan, Jaya Bhattachara questioned the science. Historian, Niall Ferguson, out of curiosity, began to develop a 1000-slide powerpoint deck that would evolve into a powerful critique of the catastrophic errors of strategic judgement of many government leaders. These errors of judgement could have been prevented with a little dose of scrupulous pessimism and some perspective grounded in reading and interpreting history.

Instead, the bureaucratic and medical Utopians exploited some confused, opportunistic political leaders, who sensed a chance to lift their standing by seeming to save lives in an emergency. The Utopians misled the Cynics with that old saw of sorcery, attributed to Barack Obama's adviser, 'never let a crisis go to waste'. The only way to recycle the crisis, day after day, was to exaggerate the threat. As a result, the reaction to the virus has been more devastating than the virus and

---

[73] Niall Ferguson, 'Dragon Kings and Grey Rhinos: The World War of 1914-1918 and the Pandemic of 2020?' (Hoover Institution, 2020).

related disease themselves.

On the sniff of a snotty rag, large swathes of the governing elite decided in February and March that this virus was a Dragon King. Or perhaps more realistically, they decided to portray the virus as a catastrophic event in which they could pose as the Dragon Queen who would break the wheel. Political, bureaucratic and public health leaders jumped on the train that named this virus 'unprecedented' or '100-year event'. These leaders suddenly stood in the spotlight, and were cast as world leaders. It created a firestorm of political rhetoric and over-excited decision-making. Hugely consequential decisions were made with barely any facts or settled understanding of disease patterns. The public health leaders, however, from my direct knowledge, were too often mere statisticians, pretenders, or burnt-out doctors who did not want to see patients any more. They explained every disease by the 'social model of health', and urged these frightened leaders to devastate society on a hunch and a gamble. For the first time in human history, we could eliminate a new disease pathogen within a year. Like Daenerys Targaryen, they rode the dragon, drove themselves mad with power, and in righteous anger burned King's Landing to the ground.

Underlying this madness were false assumptions about the pandemic, some very bad history, and clumsy misunderstandings of mathematics. The saturation level of the virus in the population was assumed to be 80 per cent. This assumption was wrong; the more accurate estimate was near 20 per cent. The assumed deadliness of the virus was high and uniform. This too was wrong. The infection fatality rate appears to be in the range of 1 to 5 in a thousand, and heavily skewed towards the old and others with diseases that otherwise weaken their ability to fight off viruses. Everyone was susceptible; they assumed, wrongly. Many had protection from cross-immunity and other coronaviruses. The only immunity could come from antibodies and a sterilising vaccine. Wrong. T-cell immunity and other protections gained by resistance to the common cold also worked. The assumption that we could reliably test how many cases were infected was wrong.

13 Ways of Looking at a Bureaucrat

Reported cases from PCR-tests are vastly below even infections identified through blood tests. The pandemic was 'unprecedented' or a 'once-in-a-hundred year event'. Wrong, wrong and wrong again. The disease impact of the virus is closer to a bad influenza year. It had much in common with the influenza of 1957 and 1969. It was in a lesser league than the Spanish Flu of 1918, which occurred in the wake of a world war. Even the ubiquitous mathematical truism that the virus was spreading with 'exponential growth' was wrong. The spread of any virus follows a Gompertz curve with decaying and limited growth, as Professor Michael Levitt has demonstrated comprehensively.

Our Governments and governing elites will need to chart a course away from these disastrous policies on the pandemic. The new course must be guided by one simple idea: we are not stopping a pandemic wave, but we are living with an endemic virus. As Sunetra Gupta has stated bravely for months, the virus will reach a point of endemic equilibrium, and then life can return to the old normal.

Of course, we will have learned some healthy lessons: the value of good personal hygiene; the need for care for post-viral syndromes; ways that the elderly and vulnerable can be better protected against respiratory viruses; the importance of real work, rather than absolutely fabulous knowledge workers; the stupidity of forecast models constructed without understanding the phenomena they model. Most of all, we will have been warned about the folly and authoritarian temptations of our governing elites and the Public Health Rulez crowd.

The course our leaders should chart is that set out in the Great Barrington Declaration (named after the place where it was written, Great Barrington in Massachusetts). Let me quote its final paragraphs:

> As immunity builds in the population, the risk of infection to all – including the vulnerable – falls. We know that all populations will eventually reach herd immunity – i.e. the point at which the rate of new infections is stable – and that this can be assisted by (but is not dependent upon) a vaccine. Our goal should therefore be to minimize

mortality and social harm until we reach herd immunity.

The most compassionate approach that balances the risks and benefits of reaching herd immunity, is to allow those who are at minimal risk of death to live their lives normally to build up immunity to the virus through natural infection, while better protecting those who are at highest risk. We call this Focused Protection.

Those who are not vulnerable should immediately be allowed to resume life as normal. ... People who are more at risk may participate if they wish, while society as a whole enjoys the protection conferred upon the vulnerable by those who have built up herd immunity.[74]

I have signed the Great Barrington Declaration, and I encourage any readers to do so too. Our response to SARS-COV-2 and other pathogens should be modelled on its wisdom not some modeller's folly. Our health, culture and freedom depend on its ideas, and not the diseased rhizomes of lockdowns, fear and masks.

Report from a besieged city

(From *The Burning Archive* 12 February and 28 May 2021.)

Today, 12 February 2021, Melbourne and all the citizens of Victoria have been thrown again, with eleven hours notice, into a futile, fickle lockdown, that is not founded in evidence of effectiveness.

The reason? Five people who have tested positive and are assumed to have acquired the traces of the virus locally when over 24,000 test results have been received in the last 24 hours. That is a positive test

---

[74] *Great Barrington Declaration*, (2020).

13 Ways of Looking at a Bureaucrat

rate of 0.02 per cent. Not two per cent, but one-hundredth of that.

We are locked down again. The run on the supermarkets is on again. People's weddings, funerals, parties, everything, even friendly visits, have been stopped. People have been plunged again into despair. Again, the challenge is to remain sane.

To that purpose, I take down from my shelf Zbigniew Herbert, *Collected Poems 1956-1998*, and turn directly to the great poem from 1982, 'Report from a Besieged City'. Written and published in Poland under the martial law of General Jaruzelski, two years after the formation of *Solidarność* and seven years prior to the collapse of the regime, this great poem is a statement of resistance through writing in truth.

It begins with the observation that everyone has lost all sense of time, as we in Melbourne have too. The narrator of the poem has been assigned the task to report on events in his besieged city. He begins hesitantly, "Too old to carry arms and fight like the others—/ they graciously gave me the inferior role of chronicler/ I record—I don't know for whom—the history of the siege."[75]

Simple humble service of the muses is a path of hope. Czelaw Milosz observed that Herbert's poem exemplifies the life of the internal exile from communism, and the way in which the poetry of witness can provide the home of incorrigible hope. Faced with a total monster or a monster of totalitarianism, fear, depression and a sense of futility take over our collective and individual psyches. Writing a poem can be a mandarin gesture of defiance. It is a way to participate, to resist, to assert independence, to keep going on, even if only by calling that weak reed going, and that fizzle on. But to write a poem begins motion and ends the hopelessness of torpor.

Herbert's poem concludes: "we look in the face of hunger the face of fire face of death/ worst of all—the face of betrayal/ and only our

---

[75] *Zbigniew Herbert: The Collected Poems 1956-1998* (2007).

dreams have not been humiliated." I will write on. Melbourne and Victoria will outlast this siege. Poetry will defeat the besiegers. Our dreams will not be humiliated. General Jaruzelski was overthrown.

12 February 2021

Alas three months later, another report from the besieged city of Melbourne – locked down, its people 'fleeing the Qin'.

28 May 2021

Dr Cogito endures Melbourne's fifth lockdown

(From *The Burning Archive* 18 July 2021.)

Dr Cogito, a persona I know who inhabits the ghost of Zbigniew Herbert's *Pan Cogito*, writes to me:

> The city in which I dwell, Melbourne, and indeed the state in which I am a citizen, if of a subordinate ghostly status, that is, Victoria, in the south-east corner of Australia, has entered its fifth lockdown. In the middle of last week, news spread that there had been a handful of positive PCR tests in Melbourne, and the usual panic, scapegoating and virtue-signalling began. Among ordinary people, fear and demoralisation set in. But the leaders and journalists fell over themselves cheering for testing records, just like how the old *nomenklatura* would celebrate the achievement of industrial targets, while the people stood in long queues for bread. Everyone knew that the Government here would lock us down, regardless of the actual health consequences of this small number of infections. The maskers and neo-authoritarians and relentless government advertising, paid for and undisclosed, urged

13 Ways of Looking at a Bureaucrat

> it on. The radio hosts on state media engaged in transparent personality cult worship of their man, never disclosing, of course, their behind-the-scenes collaboration with the media staff and commissars of the government. We are a besieged city again, terrorised by the Saint-Justs and Robespierres of the Committee of Public Health. All conscripted to fight a war against a virus that can only end in hunger, humiliation and defeat. (Dr Cogito, *Private Correspondence*)

How long this fifth lockdown lasts no-one really knows. Dr Cogito writes it has been staged with all sorts of political theatrics, to keep us all waiting every day on our leaders' grace, virtue and heroism. Will you release us from prison this week, master? He suspects we may endure more weeks, if not months, of this imprisonment, serving the ambition of a handful of public health bureaucrats to eliminate the virus. We are in this real prison to sustain their fantasy-land, where they are celebrated as 'best in the world' in COVID zeal.

I have no way to know if what Dr Cogito says is true, but, as it happened, I turned coincidentally this morning in my daily reading of a random poem to the inventor of the persona of Mr Cogito, the great ancestor of Dr Cogito, Zbigniew Herbert. There I read from Herbert's poem, "Mr Cogito on Upright Attitudes."[76]

Herbert placed Mr Cogito in the city of Utica in the state of Carthage, besieged by the Roman Republic and the general Scipio Africanus, in the year 204 BC. The siege would end in heavy casualties and mass slaughter for the citizens of Utica. But Herbert went to the state of mind of these citizens besieged by fear and self-abasement.

> In Utica
>
> the citizens
>
> don't want to put up a defence
>
> in the city an epidemic broke out

---

[76] *Zbigniew Herbert: The Collected Poems 1956-1998* (2007).

of an instinct of self-preservation

In this poem from 1970s Poland, Herbert captured the psychology of the besieged citizens of Melbourne today (at least as reported by Dr Cogito observations to me). Citizens sew white and blue flags of submission on their faces and teach their children to lie. They do not put up a defence of their own freedom and dignity.

It is not as if it is easy, not to succumb to this new terror of our age. In the second part of the poem, Herbert went on to describe Mr Cogito's own struggles to act with courage. He relied on an inherited concept of courage, from epic poems and Stoic philosophy. He glared at fate in the face of this humiliation by power and the siege of the Roman Republic. Mr Cogito wanted to rise to the occasion, but had not the means or the will to take the Stoics' path of suicide, and perhaps he rightly suspected self-harm to be a theatrical pose of courage; fear dressed up as self-destruction. So instead of plunging a sword into his heart, Mr Cogito walked to the window, looked out on the sun setting on the Republic, and contemplated his choices to act. He noticed a way that was less courageous, but filled with a more ordinary virtue.

> not much is left to him
>
> really only
>
> the choice of the attitude
>
> in which he wishes to die
>
> the choice of a gesture
>
> the choice of a last word

And so it seems, the people of Melbourne again must endure this impoverished choice in their lives, as they endure another siege by public health. But such infinite possibility is there in those choices: of attitude, of gesture, of a last word.

13 Ways of Looking at a Bureaucrat

Cease the endless war against the virus

From The Burning Archive 8 August 2021.

Generals are always prepared to fight the last war. So, Winston Churchill said. Their early experiences of combat, their intellectual training, and all received wisdom shape how they read the battlefield. Their expert consensus lays out how they ought to interpret the most recent conflicts. These decisions constrain the strategy. Constraints also come from the interests of the institutions that accumulated and encrusted the generals during the last war: the war machine, its dependent controllers and industries, the military-industrial complex, the security state, the academic expounders of orthodoxy. These constraints limit the tactics chosen by the generals in the fog of war.

Usually, the last war was different to the one before our eyes. It had different opponents, different allies, different battlefields, different weapons, different balances of forces, different popular sentiments, and, most importantly, different war aims. But the differences only emerge when reality tests the generals' assumptions, thought, decisions, prejudices, motivations and abilities. The realities of lost battles, tactical failures, soured relations with other countries, and loss of morale eventually kick in, but at great cost, with deep suffering. It is usually the foot soldiers and the citizens who pay the highest price, not the generals.

The generals do what people do. They defend their initial judgements. They deploy the weapons they know. They look for whatever evidence they can find in the confusion of human events to confirm their beliefs. They define themselves as 'in charge', and exclude those who dissent or who challenge. Unity, after all, is essential. 'We are all in this together,' they say to critics and rivals. They excuse their errors and deceptions with their noble intentions.

They fail. We all fail, but the generals use victory parades and propaganda to hide their failures.

Usually, reality grinds out a slow siege against the generals' grand illusions. History is full of long wars that went on too long and did not go to plan. In some cases, the war becomes the plan, and then we have the endless wars of the United States of America, Iraq, Afghanistan, and NATO's undeclared war against Russia since 1945. In endless wars the generals dare not stand down from their posture because it would reveal there was never a clear war aim. They never had a coherent strategy. They never made an open-minded assessment of the costs and benefits of the plan, which they inherited from the last war. They cannot change the posture because it would require the admission, they had failed. In the panic and fog of the onset of war, they do not heed the most essential advice dispensed by Clausewitz to military strategists: "No one starts a war–or rather, no one in his senses ought to do so–without first being clear in his mind what he intends to achieve by that war and how he intends to conduct it."[77]

Sometimes, however, a civilian leader emerges who does not wait for reality to challenge the generals, but tests their strategies in the command room. After all, that is why military leadership is subjected to civilian command. The great civilian leader does not merely follow the military advice. They test, challenge and overthrow it. They sack their generals, who, after all, like all fallible humans are tempted by the power, patronage and favour of the court. Lincoln sacked many generals before he came upon the unlikely, morose, alcoholic Ulysses S. Grant, who would actually win the civil war, not use their office to promote their status and exploit the war for some other political, ideological or economic interest. Churchill too sacked generals and challenged advice, and it was this exercise of judgement, command and inquiry that was the essential attribute of his supreme command. At least some historians believe that Churchill exercised the important function of a war leader by testing military plans and claims against the

---

[77] Clausewitz, *On War*.

13 Ways of Looking at a Bureaucrat

standards of rare common sense. It was a common sense that grew from decades of study, wide reading and experience of war. It tested his relationships with his commanders, and was made possible by his willingness to pick commanders who disagreed with him and who could do so vehemently.

At the onset of the coronavirus pandemic, our civilian governments and public health leaders decided they were generals in a war against the virus. The airwaves were bombarded with talk about the war against the invisible enemy. Even the United Nations Secretary-General, the world's supposed number one peacekeeper, got fired up by the opportunity to fight a career-defining war. In a statement on 26 March 2020, António Guterres said:

> We are at war with a virus – and not winning it. The next 100,000 happened in just 12 days. The third took four days. The fourth, just one and a half. This is exponential growth and only the tip of the iceberg. This war needs a war-time plan to fight it. Solidarity is essential. Among the G-20 – and with the developing world, including countries in conflict. That is why I appealed for a global ceasefire.[78]

All human wars would cease, the world's statesmen and stateswomen declared, and a new war against a barely understood RNA virus begin. This war was declared without knowing much at all about the enemy. Our generals did not know its nature, its origins, its armaments, its tactics, or its chosen battlefield. The war was declared against a non-human entity, a pathogen, not even an agent that has objectives, despite all the absurd rhetoric of this wicked, smart and unerring virus.

Mr Guterres spoke for global leadership when he defined the three aims of this war. First, with costly ambiguity, he declared the war aim 'to suppress the transmission of COVID-19 as quickly as possible'.

---

[78] UN Secretary-General's Remarks At G-20 Virtual Summit On The Covid-19 Pandemic.

Second, with studied vagueness, he declared, 'We must work together to minimize the social and economic impact.' Third, with compound cliches, he set the world's sights to 'work together now to set the stage for a recovery that builds a more sustainable, inclusive and equitable economy, guided by our shared promise — the 2030 Agenda for Sustainable Development.'

The first war aim was especially fatal. This aim would inspire the newly empowered generals of public health to believe, despite all they did not know about the enemy, that they had invincible weapons and they could eliminate the virus. Here was born that fantasy of omnipotence, the zero-COVID strategy, pursued as an undeclared war aim by the unelected public health committees of so many countries, including the Australian Health Protection Principal Committee. Here was revealed how the generals would fight the last war, or at least misread the enemy and the battlefield with old biases, entrenched interests, ideological fragments and prematurely closed science.

In retrospect, we should all have been alarmed when the figurehead of the United Nations declared preemptively that 'suppressing' the virus, as much and as quickly as possible, 'must be our common strategy.' No debate here. None of Churchill's searching for an alternative view, or even two, like those offered by Mr Keynes ("If you put two economists in a room, you get two opinions, unless one of them is Lord Keynes, in which case you get three opinions." Winston Churchill'). Guterres locked down the essential elements of the generals' strategy, hastily assembled in those first weeks of the war:

> It requires a coordinated G-20 response mechanism guided by WHO. All countries must be able to combine systematic testing, tracing, quarantining and treatment with restrictions on movement and contact – aiming to suppress transmission of the virus. And they have to coordinate the exit strategy to keep it suppressed until a vaccine becomes available.[79]

---

[79] UN Secretary-General's Remarks At G-20 Virtual Summit.

13 Ways of Looking at a Bureaucrat

But did any of our civilian leaders really challenge, like Lincoln, like Churchill, the judgements, the thinking, the battlefield assessment of these newly appointed generals? Did any leader notice how the generals were drunk on their new fame, power and celebrity? No, they did not. And so the endless war against coronavirus began without an achievable objective. It has been waged now for 18 months, and the enemy has natural mutation on its side. Every few months new allies, some damnable wild variant, join the axis of sniffle. We forget this endless war began, in part, because wartime leader failed to perform their most important responsibility. As Clausewitz said,

> The first, the supreme, the most far-reaching act of judgement that the statesman and commander have to make is to establish... the kind of war on which they are embarking.

Now the generals' armies have limped into the second half of 2021. The invisible enemy has taken many casualties. Their chosen methods to fight this war have inflicted so much collateral damage, and taken so many victims of 'friendly fire'. There have been so many compromises with the truth, and so many noble lies. Surely, it is time for our public health generals to face reality. The vaccines are a miracle, achieved despite the skepticism of the generals. They work, but imperfectly. Treatments are neglected. The mass mobilisation of testing, tracing and isolating is not sustainable, except in the early stages of small outbreaks. Lockdowns do not work. The treatment is worse than the disease. Universal strategies exhaust us all, consume too many resources, and do not work except in the simulated world of epidemiology. They cannot be sustained. This endless siege will destroy the city, its people and the besieging army.

The public health generals and their civilian supreme commanders need to heed Clausewitz's advice: 'The best strategy is always to be very strong; first in general, and then at the decisive point... There is no higher and simpler law of strategy than that of keeping one's forces concentrated.' The generals in charge of the endless war against coronavirus have over-rated their strength, misread the battlefield, deployed their forces in the wrong places, and pursued grandiose and unachievable aims. They have pursued a universal strategy, as is the bias of public health, not a targeted strategy of focused protection as proposed by the Great Barrington Declaration. They have deluded themselves they can protect everyone, and neglected to treat anyone. They have wrought tremendous damage that will in time be recognised as one of the great catastrophes of the twenty-first century.

It is time for the true statesmen and stateswomen of the world to stop hiding behind this public health advice, and to start to challenge it. It is time to cease the endless war against the virus.

13 Ways of Looking at a Bureaucrat

Chapter Nine   Political Disorder

Political disorder and decay in Australia

(From *The Burning Archive*, 29 November 2015.)

> If there has been a single problem facing contemporary democracies, either aspiring or well established, it has been centred in their failure to provide the substance of what people want from government: personal security, shared economic growth, and quality basic public services like education, health and infrastructure that are needed to achieve individual opportunity." (Francis Fukuyama, *Political Order and Political Decay*, p. 524)

Governments are failing in Australia, and yet there is next to no insightful commentary on the underlying reasons why. There is much noise and puff about failings of the political class, and tiresome predictable conferences on reigniting 'reform'. There is an endless circle of meaningless commentary by self-regarding journalists and panellists, who perform no useful function other than their own self-promotion.

Occasionally, there is discussion of trust, of disengagement from 'mainstream' politics and the media, and of a need to establish new processes and institutions to renew democracy. Much of this material comes from former political advisers, such as Nicholas Reece and Mark Triffit, at the Melbourne School of Government. Their proposals include ideas such as participatory budgeting or new forms of media engagement. Some of this discussion receives sponsorship from wealthy patrons, like the Belgiorno-Nettis family foundation that sponsors forms of citizen deliberation.

These ideas are worthwhile innovations, but in the end are minor changes in process. They will always be of marginal concern. They can provide for entertaining workshops, now and again, for people with boundless enthusiasm and restricted responsibility. But they do not offer a way to reshape the ordinary, enduring duties of governing. They do not consider the deeper institutional and cultural foundations of the problems they discern. Small changes in process will not address profound failures in political order. To rectify the course of democracy it is important to understand the roots of the decay that has taken hold in the contemporary political order.

This is the task performed by Francis Fukuyama's *Political Order and Political Decay*. As Fukuyama indicates in the quotation above, the loss of trust and discontent with democracy is at its foundation a failure of performance: modern democratic governments are failing as political orders because they do not provide the substance of what people want. They pursue 'reforms' to pander to media and elite audiences, but do not deliver the substance of what people want from their governments, that is, real improvements in their connected lives. As Stein Ringen commented in *A Nation of Devils*, the best explanation for a loss of trust in governments is that governments have not acted in trustworthy ways. It is not a newly fickle public, but a long, slow decay in governing that is at the heart of our democratic disorders. It is not a failure of 'reform' vision that is the problem of Australian political culture, as argued most insistently by Paul Kelly, but a betrayal of democratic substance by political elites whose careers are grounded in a new patrimonial political order.

For Fukuyama, a successful political order stands evenly on three legs: accountability, rule of law and state capability. But in contemporary democracy, this balanced order is not achieved. Most of the discussion of democratic renewal focuses on process changes in accountability. Indeed, these attempts at renewal can sabotage state capability by investing new authority and resources in non-state actors, such as citizens groups, charities, social businesses, social entrepreneurs, or democratic 'monitors' in the form of public or private oversight organisations. The appeal to philanthropists and 'independent' persons is evident, but these changes have minimal impact on the prime institution bonding political elites to the ordinary citizen, parliament and other forms of democratic representative assembly. Similarly, the rule of law becomes a process driven diversion because 'the worship of procedure over substance is a critical source of political decay in contemporary liberal democracies.' It becomes a stalemated game of lawyers who prosecute political elites, too little and too late. The grossest example of a deformed institution of the rule of law in Australia is the New South Wales Independent Commission Against Corruption. Despite high profile indictments for minor misdemeanours, it has systematically failed to prevent gross, pervasive and destructive corruption in that state.

Rule of law and accountability are common themes in most public discussion of the ingredients of successful democracy. But Fukuyama's third essential ingredient, state capability, is rarely mentioned. This makes *Political Order and Political Decay* an important contribution. States must be effective if they are to be authoritative. If they are not authoritative, they cannot impose democratic order on reluctant others. Democracies must project authority and command obedience. They are not a vaudeville show for gadflies, journalists, think-tankers, and media critics.

Moreover, there is an embarrassing, inconvenient truth about state capability. Capable states have emerged as from both authoritarian origins, cultures of dissidence and citizen participation. For example, Britain's hallowed Westminster system was the product of a tightly organised aristocratic elite that opened itself to new talent from a commercial, technological elite. It developed prior to significant widening of the democratic franchise. Germany is another example of a capable state that had an effective bureaucracy which persisted through various forms and deformations of the rule of law and accountability. Fukuyama shows how well-functioning bureaucracy is essential to political order and democratic success. His analysis ought to underpin wide-scale institutional change in today's bureaucracies in

Australia.

It is the disease in state capability in contemporary democracy that I know best. Twenty-five years in the Victorian state government bureaucracy has given me direct experience of the decay of an institution, the public service, and the deformation of a culture, an ethos of governing well. Slowly, without anyone really noticing, over the last thirty to fifty years a model of governing, rooted in economic and social developments, has emerged triumphant within its enclosed walls. But its triumph has undone state capability, entrenched an elite consultocracy (squads of advisers, job-hopping executives and consultants) through new forms of patronage and clientilism. This consultocracy is befuddled by its own rhetoric and rites. The more it talks about reform, the less it contributes to the performance of a capable state. It is the unacknowledged legislator of Australia's political crisis of recent years. Fukuyama's analysis of the deformation of contemporary democracy by new forms of patronage, clientilism, kinship affiliation and reciprocal altruism shows how these bureaucratic gangs have taken over and sabotaged Australian public institutions. This is the treason of the clerks.

Citizenship is a spiritual experience

(From *The Burning Archive*, 23 July 2016.)

The most insightful, curious article I have read in the weekend papers is by Paul Kelly of *The Australian*. Kelly has written a piece that appears to be part of a journey of discovery. He has recently castigated the political class and the Australian people because they spurned 'sensible economic reform'. At times Kelly has written like a spoiled and petulant child. But his more recent commentary has opened a way to reflection on the deeper roots of political identity and the more chthonic origins of political drama.

The occasion of the piece is criticism of Prime Minister Turnbull for not attending war commemoration events in Fromelles and Pozières. But Kelly's deeper insight is that mantras about economic plans fail to define any 'emotional, moral, or spiritual quest on behalf of the nation'. Economics, law and planning is not enough. Man does not live by bread and business alone. Who knew?

In support of his argument, Kelly quotes Michael Oakeshott. The British conservative political philosopher wrote, 'Citizenship is a spiritual experience, not a legal relationship.'

Kelly's late turn to the conservative Oakeshott comes now, when, in our troubled times, democratic publics are in revolt against elites. All the technocratic plans and econocratic reforms leave the public cold. They are moved instead by fears of terror, fervours of new religions, and hissing fissures breaking apart traditional identities. This emotional crowd feels abandoned by cultural order. The liberation of this chaos, and abandonment of the public to this disorder, are the great betrayals by those who govern us today.

Oakeshott was the great critic of rationalism in politics. He understood that the conduct of governing, that distinct experience, could not be reduced to rational ideas, nor the plans of intellectuals. The experience of this form of human conduct had to be respected, and sympathetically understood. The conduct of governing is not promulgation of an idea, nor declaration of an edict, nor planning of an enterprise. Rather, Oakeshott wrote that, when governing, people:

> sail a boundless and bottomless sea; there is neither harbour for shelter nor floor for anchorage, neither starting-place nor appointed destination. The enterprise is to keep afloat on an even keel.

The aphorism, quoted by Kelly, that citizenship is a spiritual experience, comes from Oakeshott's recently published *Notebooks*. Oakeshott published little in his lifetime. He stood against the spirit of the times. He strove always to sound the deepest caves of human thought, and aspired to be part of an aphoristic tradition. He is one of the enduring sources of traditions of thought that can lead us on our frail bark away from these dark and troubled waters.

Myths of power: merchant, soldier, sage...?

(From *The Burning Archive*, 6 October 2015.)

David Priestland has written a provocative book, *Merchant, soldier, sage: a new history of power*. His main idea is that power is controlled by 'castes', which he defined as social orders formed by occupation, a prevailing social ethos and characteristic ways of wielding power. These castes or elite groups cycle through positions of dominance or alliance with each other. The waxing and waning, combination and permutation, rise and fall of these castes makes political history. Regimes, societies and periods of political history take their characteristic patterns of rules, social values and blind spots from the ruling order of castes.

Priestland defines four castes, with the methodological assumption, inherited from Weber, that these castes are ideal types, and there are many historical variations on these themes. The four castes are merchant, soldier, sage and the workers. The last caste has rarely ruled, and so slips from the title of his book. But Priestland is an historian of communism and the Soviet state. He knows that even workers have had brief times of rule. Our current age is the regime of the merchant. Both 1950s America and theocratic Muslim states were, in different ways, regimes of the sage. The sage, as with the other castes, can appear in different costumes at different times. In 1950's America, he was the sage technocrat, who might have been resurrected as the econocrat, if the economists had not sold their rather cheapened soul to the merchants. The sage has appeared commonly as the priest, the wise one, the law speaker. The soldier leader we have known many times, and, I fear, will know again.

There is, in Priestland's account, something of an eternal turning of the kaleidoscope, as these patterns of caste are refracted through the changing light of social conditions and the ceaseless struggle of their incompatible values. There is a deep, long bass note of hope in his account of today's regime of the merchant, where free markets have free reign, where unshackled merchants dominate, where all who seek life without prices are banished. The turn of the cycle means their rule must end sometime. Priestland did write his book, after all, in the wake of the financial collapses of 2008.

Of course, such a simplified story of power, which brushes aside all its multifarious intricacy, is a form of myth-making. But such myths are powerful and necessary, as Georges Sorel argued with the idea of the social myth. Sorel defined the social myth as a pragmatically necessary fiction formed prior to and enabling action. I agree with Priestland's fundamental idea that power crystallises around certain dominant social orders, and his insight that these orders are activated not mainly by interests, but by an ethos which can shape common purposes and activities.

It is a commonplace observation today that we are grouped in 'tribes', largely defined by what we do, and that there is often a chasm of misunderstanding between 'people like us' and those lesser people we shame on Twitter. I think though that there are more patterns in the glass. Each dominant social order is shaped in contention with a shadow, and not only by itself, whether its interests, ethos, symbols or power. I would propose then some variations on Priestland's theme.

13 Ways of Looking at a Bureaucrat

The soldier is shadowed by the criminal, the thug or the terrorist. Regrettably there are those who use violence for anti-social ends; and sometimes the soldier leader comes from the criminal. Is this not the story of Mao and Stalin?

The merchant is shadowed by the libertine, the spendthrift, the extravagant consumer. The acquisition of money is negated by burning through the stuff, and all courts have at least one libertine.

The sage is shadowed by the artist, the clown, the fool. The high priests of knowledge are shadowed by the high priests of feeling.

The worker is shadowed by the carer. Yes, there are no gendered social roles in Priestland's history of power, or more precisely there is no-one at home cooking dinner. The celebration of the dignity of labour is so often a flight from the necessity of caring and waiting on the sick, the young, the old, the frail and the vulnerable.

So I could imagine a variation on Priestland's hypothesis that defines not four castes, but eight phenotypes, which develop in tension with both their rivals and opposing types. Then, we might create a truly mythic cosmogony of power. It would provide a richer story of power than the stereotypes I find so often in even the best literature.

Perestroika

(From *The Burning Archive*, 19 November 2016.)

Towards the end of Mikhail Gorbachev's *The New Russia* (2016), Gorbachev recounted an anecdote told in a speech by Richard Pipes, the American historian of Russia and a former Cold War warrior, although this appellation is rather a simplification. Pipes was tasked with a speech in honour of Gorbachev, many years after Gorbachev's remarkable years of presidency of the USSR. We still carry from those remarkable years the words *glasnost* (openness) and *perestroika* (rebuilding). Pipes explained that, in 1987, before the walls had come down across Eastern Europe, he had reviewed Gorbachev's account of what he was striving to do, his book *Perestroika: New Thinking for our Country and the World*. Pipes criticised the book as too tepid. He did not think it went far enough.

Twenty years later, the two older men faced each other, and Pipes offered a *mea culpa*. He did so by recalling an anecdote from the reign of Catherine the Great, who kept at her court a salon of French *philosophes,* who were living ornaments for her Hermitage and stimuli to her project to rebuild a greater Russia. Denis Diderot acted then like public intellectuals in all times do. He snarled with no fangs at his great patron because she did not pursue political reforms as bold and pure as reason dictated. Catherine the Great responded in a letter, 'You, M. Diderot, propose sweeping changes, but you write on paper, which is very durable, whereas I must write on human skin, and that is very sensitive.'

Two centuries later, across the Atlantic, Catherine's words returned to Pipes. He spoke that night in the complacent comfort of a conservative American think tank *soireé*, in the confident days when a few ageing elite Americans began to doubt the USA really was the indispensable nation. Pipes said to Gorbachev, 'Now, I understand you better.'

Gorbachev wrote New Russia in his 80s, and died in 2022. *New Russia* provided an insightful account of the troubled course his country took after the fall of *perestroika*. Gorbachev held a corrective mirror to the complacent West, who during a twenty year spree of spending stock market wealth, believed that the market had solved all fundamental problems of human social coordination.

In one chapter, Gorbachev provided an extended response to

Richard Pipes's earlier doubts. He reasserted the relevance of the 'New Thinking' of his *perestroika* to the world, which we still struggle to understand and to act together in. Gorbachev repeated of this New Thinking, which he fashioned in the 1980s, that the world 'still very much needs it today'.

This New Thinking is not 'a set of dogmas or a code of practice', and it evolved in response to new ideas and adapted to world events. But its basis was a stable core of three values: "recognition of the interconnection and interdependence of the world, of the indivisibility of global security, of the importance of human values and interests."[80] He quoted his 1992 speech that expressed the hope that from the challenges of globalisation a new 'symbiosis' of the world's people's and cultures, including those cultures that resolve civil disputes that we know as 'politics', can emerge in a world at peace. It would be a multipolar world that places greater value on healthcare, culture, and human personality, rather than the ceaseless machine of production and consumption at the service of financial markets.

It is to this optimistic belief that Gorbachev returned, despite all the difficult turns of his own own country's history, towards the end of his book. He repeated his argument that

> The twenty-first century will either be a century of disastrous intensification of a deadly crisis, or the century in which mankind becomes more pure and spiritually healthier. I am convinced that we are all called upon to do our part to ensure the triumph of humanity and justice, to make the twenty-first century an age of renaissance, the century of mankind.

In a way, the courage and resilience of Gorbachev, who has nourished these convictions through many difficult years, is an inspiration. Surely, it is an inspiration that deserves a Nobel Peace Prize, more than many of the empty gestures of recent years.

---

[80] Gorbachev, *New Russia*, pp. 293-294.

Political Disorder

In another way, I wondered if America has not chosen in Trump its own Yeltsin, who with populist charisma and manifest deficiencies in rule, may deliver America to its own time of troubles. But what is bad for America may be good for the rest of the world.

So from difficulties made in the USA, from the death throes of American illusions that it is the one indispensable nation in the world, may emerge Gorbachev's promise of a new symbiosis of multi-polar world, committed to humane and democratic model of development and of governing the world.

The Meaning of a coup

(From *The Burning Archive*, 2 September 2018.)

Barely a week ago, Australia was gripped in political drama when a clumsily organised coup unseated a Prime Minister. News stations had 24/7 coverage, in which rolling panels of journalists talked non-stop to unfolding events. Breathlessly, they read out texts from conspirators on-air, and yet still claimed they had no part in the fiasco that had become Australian politics. There was much usage of 'unprecedented' and 'poisonous', but very few reflections on the events of the past, even the very recent past that had seen three other Prime Ministers succumb to similar insurgencies. Exasperated words amplified disbelief, amplified because this coup did not enthrone the journalists' preferred leader. Its only success was the destruction of Malcolm Turnbull, who had become an icon of moderate, centrist government, and so a hated figure for the frenzied, confused conservatives who engineered this messy coup.

'What was all that about?' media people asked, and were echoed by the people on the streets. I sat with colleagues who watched the climax of the reportage on the internet screens at work. The outgoing Prime Minister accurately captured the mood of the nation, not his strongest skill ordinarily, when he said Australians would be 'dumbstruck and appalled' by these events. Above all, the public asked what was the meaning of this coup? I take that question one step deeper, and ask: why have the political institutions of this wealthy democracy become stained by the compulsive repetition of such symbolic violence?

Coincidentally, I have been reading over the same time Simon Sebag Montefiore's astonishing, page-turner history of the dynasty of the Romanovs. It is a work of fine scholarship that is advertised with both commendations from fellow scholars, and this squeal of excitement from Oprah Winfrey, no less. 'Turn off thy Kardashians. Pick up thy Montefiore.' This book is remarkable for its craft, but mostly for its content: the truly astonishing sequence of stories of the Romanov Tsars, Tsarinas, and Tsarevichi, and their courts and conspiracies.

The dynasty began in the near extinction of the Russian polity during Russia's First Civil War, the early 1600s Time of Troubles. It ceased in the clumsy extermination of the Romanov family in a cellar near Ekaterinburg, after the Bolshevik revolution of 1917. Along the way, we read how fathers and sons, wives and husbands, brothers and sisters, courtesans and barbers, courtiers and generals all betrayed each other, killed each other, conspired against each other, and together succumbed to the monstrosity of power.

Against such a backdrop. the ham-fisted organisation of a party ballot is much less melodramatic. Prime Minister Turnbull, after all, left the building smiling, kissing his family, clutching his grandchild, ever optimistic, with a wealthy man's confidence about the future. He was not killed. He was not brutally bashed, nor strangled in his bedroom like Emperor Paul. He was not imprisoned and isolated in a remote dungeon like the deposed infant Emperor Peter. He was not

Political Disorder

tortured by his own leader and father in the way that Peter the Great tortured and killed his unfavoured son, Alexei. Things could get a lot worse.

And yet, there is surely something rotten in the state of Australia. The explanations proffered by the participants – personal animosity, vengeance, an ideology of conservatism, a betrayal of party identity, the dismay of the base, the stopping of the bleeding of votes to minor parties – all circle around the decay of the political party system. Turnbull, like Rudd, former Labor Prime Minister and fellow coup victim, was an outsider to this system. They both sought to govern beyond the parties. They were both ultimately unsuccessful. Gillard and Abbott, by contrast, were the leaders of the partisans. They were both representatives and instruments of the modern, professionalised, but hollow political party.

While the party system has decayed over recent decades, it has created the conditions for unstable contests for control at the top. Australia has witnessed this unstable leadership of its governing parties since 2008, and among its opposition parties for longer still. The Rudd/Gillard years of instability, after all, came after a longer sequence of temporary Opposition leaders of the Labor Party. This bitter Byzantine bickering was memorably described by one deposed Labor Leader, Mark Latham, in an appendix to his *Latham Diaries*. The world has known for more than a dozen years how party politics is a death trap of entrenched minor factional warlords, who pursue fragmented, incoherent, sectional goals.

Even so, the public and elites have not drawn the right conclusions from the phenomenon of the decline of political parties as institutions. In all the drama and the personalities of the coups, the sombre background music of broken institutions is not noticed. But it is the broken institutions that have made these coups over the last ten years more likely. The crumbling ethos of these institutions contributes to the lack of purpose and the absence of moral constraints on the competitive gangs, who politely call themselves factions, that run the parties. The declines in standing, performance and membership of these institutions lead to a smaller pool of viable elites, and weaker systems to select leaders from those elites. Parliamentarians are recruited from a small, stagnant pool of social roles. They are rarely subjected to the real tests of leadership ability, that is, tragic life experience, defeat and adversity. Faced with the immense difficulty of coordinating large social problems and directing major institutions of government, these second-class elites shrink into lazy media stunts and easy factional games. The decline of the parties spins the vicious cycle of waning confidence in democratic institutions. The powerless lose what little power virtue gives them. After all, what can ordinary citizens do, except to shake their heads and mutter the words, 'dumbstruck and appalled'? There are, of course, some performances on TV of *mea culpas* from the defrocked leader and faceless party hacks. They apologise that they 'spent too much time talking about themselves, and not enough about the wishes of the electorate'. But no-one is fooled.

Sadly, problems of institutions and culture are not fixed easily. Coups may bring a brief thrill of accomplishment to the flailing elites in parliaments, but they are seen elsewhere as a sign of despair. The educated citizens of the wealthy liberal democracies have many more years ahead of this sad story of distressed republics. At most, we can remind ourselves that not everything is politics, and seek to salvage something from the wreckage of our cultures, and turn to our deeper selves to create a garden of beauty. As Catherine the Great's enlightenment plaything, Voltaire, said through his characters in *Candide:* "We must take care of our garden... Work then without disputing. It is the only way to render life supportable."

Political Disorder

The political ghosts of literature

(From *The Burning Archive* 28 October 2018.)

I have been reading some fragments of Maurice Blanchot, the enigmatic 20th century French writer who haunted Derrida and Foucault. I read *The Madness of the Day, The Writing of Disaster*, and some essays assembled in *The Gaze of Orpheus*. I was trying to make sense of the discrepancies in his story, and how it has encountered my own.

Certain phrases from Blanchot, such as the *infinite conversation*, have become talismans for my own interpretation of the world. But it is only fragments of Blanchot that mean much to me; perhaps appropriately since as one critic has said,

> If Blanchot came to belong anywhere it is to the tradition (although "tradition" is hardly the word) of fragmentary writing that began with the Jena Romantics and which includes such figures as Gertrude Stein, Wittgenstein, and Paul Celan.[81]

Yet even many of these fragments are tedious. His novels, such as *Thomas the Obscure*, are even duller. Stripped bare *récits*, they read like Beckett, without the wit; or Kafka, without the eerie imagination.

It is really his writing on writing that has the greatest fascination, even if it is clogged with endless paradoxes of abstraction. Literature is a form of moral paralysis when reclusive Blanchot evokes the space of literature. The writer's task is a form of Sisyphean labour, or, even more tragically, the impossibility (one of Blanchot's tedious talismanic words) of the Gaze of Orpheus.

---

[81] Leslie Hill, Brian Nelson, and Dimitris Vardoulakis (eds.), *After Blanchot: Literature, Criticism, Philosophy*, University of Delaware Press, 2006.

The act of writing begins with Orpheus' gaze, and that gaze is the impulse of desire which shatters the song's destiny and concern, and in that inspired and unconcerned decision reaches the origin, consecrates the song. But Orpheus already needed the power of art in order to descend to that instant. This means: one can only write if one arrives at the instant towards which one can only move through space opened up by the movement of writing. In order to write one must already be writing. The essence of writing, the difficulty of experience and the leap of inspiration also lie within this contradiction.[82]

Experience and inspiration, however, are thinly scattered in Blanchot. His work was most powerful when he connected the themes of other writers, such as Kafka, Rilke, and Proust, to his own strange madness of writing without purpose or hope to communicate. When he turned to fiction, the poverty of his imagination and of his experience showed. But in his criticism, his encounters in the infinite conversation, over and over, Blanchot evoked the perfect uselessness of writing. It is that impossibility that makes literature possible.

There is also a ghost that haunts Blanchot's writings on literature, on thought, and his paltry writings on politics. In the 1930's Blanchot espoused fascist, anti-semitic and anti-democratic political ideas. He wrote trashy political journalism for ultra-right wing journals in France, such as *Combat*. The fragmentary evidence suggests – despite some of his best friends being Jewish, such as Emmanuel Levinas – that Blanchot collaborated with the German occupation of France. During the war he wrote articles such as 'Terrorism as a Method of Public Safety'. Like his friend Bataille, he enthused about very Nietzschean transvaluations of all values, to be led by *übermensch* among the aristocrats of literature, such as himself. These great souls would suppress all organised political discussion, and the petty bickering of the *petit bourgeoisie* in such mundane institutions as parliamentary debate or civil dialogue.

---

[82] Blanchot, *The Gaze of Orpheus*, p. 104.

Political Disorder

After the war, when literary collaborators, such as Robert Brasillach, were executed, Blanchot pursued a reclusive life. He avoided public appearances, and made a living by writing literary criticism that worked private obsessions and philosophical questions into an enigmatic writing of disaster. He turned dramatically to the left in the 1950s, yet still pursued a form of millenarian hatred of democracy. To be a communist in the democratic West during the Cold War, after all, was a better moral choice than to be a collaborator with Nazi Germany in occupied France. But it still demanded writers live in lies.

Still, many radical literary critics perceived Blanchot's turn to the communist or anarchic left as a form of redemption.

> From 1958 onwards Blanchot's engagement is in a movement of the radical left. It is here that he reflects on the essential part that literature plays in the realm of the political, driving at a formulation of 'literary communism'.[83]

Blanchot was not the only extremist who had oscillated between left and right hatred for the ordinary virtues of democracy. I must suppose his long meditations on the errors of his youth had some sincerity. Yet I am also struck by a false note of profundity in Blanchot's writing on the relationship between literature, or thought, and politics.

Haase and Large, who celebrated Blanchot's literary communism, praised his fragments of the 1970s and 1980s, *Unavowable Community,* as a problematisation of liberal democracy and the information society. Blanchot circled through the space of literature, looked for a form of political experience that he could celebrate, searched for a pure community to house the same paradoxical impossibility of his literature, and found it in the pure community of his literary communism, the 'communist exigency'. He looked at the

---

[83] Ullrich Haase, William Large, *Maurice Blanchot* (2001).

ideas of communism and community, which were words he placed side-by-side, with regret for the "grandiose miscalculations of history... disaster that goes much further than mere ruin."[84] He sought to redeem his millenarian longing, which surged deeply below his temporary attachment to right-wing or left-wing radical politics.

> As I write this, I am reading the following lines by Edgar Morin which many of us could make our own: "Communism is the major question and the principal experience of my life. I have never stopped recognizing myself in the aspirations it expresses and I still believe in the possibility of another society and another humanity.[85]

But it is a shadow play of communism or community that we encounter in Blanchot's essay. There are fragmentary reflections on Bataille, Marguerite Duras, Tristan and Isolde, de Sade, and Levinas. But, there is no declaration on De Gaulle, Vichy, or Hitler. There are cryptic reflections on Bataille's experimentation with a literary induced blood sacrifice. But, we know from other sources Bataille and Blanchot once believed such a rite would commence a revolution against all common sense, led by the *Acéphale* group. There is never a word on gulags, or the Cheka, or the Party, or contempt for the idiocy of rural life. These silences make this collection a strange meditation on the unavowable beliefs of Blanchot's past. Only briefly do real world events impinge on this space of literature, when Blanchot celebrated the carnival of May '68:

> May '68 has shown that without project, without conjuration, in the suddenness of a happy meeting, like a feast that breached the admitted and expected social norms, *explosive communication* could affirm itself... as the opening that gave permission to everyone, without distinction of class, age, sex or culture, to mix with the first comer as if with an already loved being, precisely

---
[84] Blanchot, *Unavowable Community*. p. 1.
[85] *Unavowable Community*, p 2.

because he was the unknown-familiar.[86]

Intellectuals are attracted to the idea of politics as a permanent carnival of ecstatically induced illusions. But the idea does not bear the slightest examination by anyone who governs. This illusion can only survive in a fevered world of paradox, which forever turns away from the lived world of the true other: those damned, petty, ordinary people. They, out of necessity, lead humble lives and practise ordinary virtues. They must dwell together with strangers in compromise and conflict. Such ordinary politics has no place in Blanchot's unavowable community. Rather, his idea of politics survives by evading the past. It is the elaborate illusion of the literary man. Obscurely, Blanchot looks into the abyss of his own lies to himself. But does he see there some guilt for his ineffectual, embarrassing beliefs about politics:

> The *unavowable community*: does that mean that it does not acknowledge itself or that it is *such that no avowal may reveal it*, given that each time we have talked about its way of being, one has had the feeling that one grasped only what makes it exist by default? So, *would it have been better to have remained silent?*[87]

Or perhaps, would it have been better had Blanchot practised a different kind of thought?

I have long lived a strange life in the shadows of both literature and politics. The dream of a new politics, cleansed and redeemed by literary or philosophical miracles, never appealed to me. I have known the strange worklessness of writing that Blanchot evoked, but would never confuse it with the tasks of politics. Those tasks require ceaseless talking to strangers, ordinary virtues of practical judgement, patient resolution of conflict, and endurance through muddy compromises. And community, what is that? Is it anything but nostalgia in today's worlds, when identities are fissured, cultures are fragmented, and societies feel uncontrollable?

---

[86] *Unavowable Community*, p 29-30.
[87] Blanchot, *The Unavowable Community*, p. 56 [my emphasis].

There is something profoundly ridiculous about literature professors who pronounce on the politics of the day. For example, Stephen Greenblatt, also an historian of sorts who should know better, finds in Shakespeare's plays resources for the resistance to Trump.[88] An example closer to Blanchot, is Julia Kristeva, renowned radical literary critic of the Tel Quel circle and May '68. There are recent revelations that she was a Bulgarian spy, who supported her life of privileged radicalism, during the carnival of May '68 and cultural deconstruction, by serving the authoritarian police state of her real home's communist state. No domestic spies appear in Blanchot's unavowable community, and Kristeva, it seemed, was not even a very good spy. Such hypocrisies and secrets of literary radicals continue to this day.[89]

The portrayal of politics in literature is so often dull and uninformed, and full of tired tropes and fictional caricatures. I don't know if these two worlds can be easily brought together. Perhaps the true impossibility of literature is the art of the possible itself?

Identity crisis: some theses on identity politics

(From *The Burning Archive* 18 November 2018.)

What are we to make of the phenomenon of identity politics? Here are some exploratory theses.

There is a vast debate on the merits and meaning of identity politics. This debate springs from the common use of claims of an

---

[88] Stephen Greenblatt, *Tyrant: Shakespeare on Politics* (2018).
[89] Richard Wolin, 'Was a Renowned Literary Theorist Also a Spy? The strange case of Julia Kristeva', *Chronicle of Higher Education,* June 20 2018.

exclusive political authority that is grounded in the lived experience of one or other shared attribute of a group of persons, whether race, gender, sexual character, disability and so on. The debate has taken a sharp turn in recent years. We have moved from second wave feminism to debates on transgender bathrooms, and from rainbow coalitions to deplatforming Germaine Greer.

Thesis 1. The politics of social movements has not always been based on concepts of identity, but in the last two decades has transformed into an aggressive politics of exclusive, narrower identities.

This form of political argument has become pervasive across many advocacy groups, and has moved to the front of the political stage. It has brought prominence to issues previously considered unworthy of the attention of parliaments and governments. In many countries, including my own, there have been central debates on gay marriage, a quintessential topic of identity politics. But this form of argument changes the tone of politics.

Thesis 2. Identity politics transforms the political into the personal, and converts politics from a tradition of compromises into a theatre of confession.

Identity politics has also become increasingly aggressive or exclusive, even within its own coalitions. Its aggression is rarely displayed through violence, but through intimidation and attempts to control the language and thoughts of others.

Thesis 3. The characteristic tactic of identity politics is to invent a new political language to describe identity, and then to claim the inherited language of others as inherently discriminatory or subjectively oppressive.

Gay and lesbian are replaced each year with variants on LGBTIQ+. Even the common words of man and woman become questionable. They assume a meaning that denies or "erases" the existence of those who claim fixedly a fluid gender.

Thesis 4. Identity politics is the political form of cultural fragmentation, and is corrosive of some features of an effective democracy: social cohesion, talking with strangers, and working across the aisle.

While identity politics is not new, it has become more salient over the last ten years, and with a growing awareness of its negative consequences and risks. This debate on the problems with identity politics has escalated with debates on race in America, the defeat of Hilary Clinton's rainbow coalition, and the emergence of Trump's blue-collar nationalism. Now identity politics has become not only a theology of the left, but a virus threatening democracy.

Thesis 5. The three talismanic claims of identity politics are: nothing about us without us, the personal is political, and I am oppressed because of who I am.

'Nothing about us without us' is a claim for involvement, voice and authority. Yet it also denies the ability to cross cultures, to move between identities, and to make social compromises through empathy and communication.

"The personal is political" reorders the priorities of governments, and expands the domain of political conflict into matters of private life. Freedom, after all, requires a refuge from politics, and a willingness to live and let live. "I am oppressed because of who I am" brooks no argument. It condemns us to an echo chamber of self-professed political authority.

Thesis 6. These claims of identity politics invest lived experience as a fourth source of political authority – to replace charisma, tradition and law. This new authority can be liberating, and it can be authoritarian.

Identity politics is a politics of minorities. It makes claims not on the basis of traditional utilitarian or majoritarian calculus – the greatest good for the greatest number but on an inverted calculus of the greater injustice that belongs to the most invisible.

Thesis 7. Identity politics does not claim we are the 99 per cent, oppressed by the 1 per cent, but we are the 1 per cent made martyrs by the blindness of the 99 per cent.

It is also a politics of identification. This politics demands a ceremony of coming out. The political actor comes out to the clearing of awareness, where light shines on the attribute of identity, and on the lived experience that defines both their experience and the truth of their politics. But this emotional regime of confessions and separate identification creates an engine of division and fragmentation. In this way, identity politics is a fissiparous transformation of an older politics of *ressentiment*.

Thesis 8. Identity politics does not enable a plural, shared identity of the past, present and the future. It is a "we" who are the same, and not a "we" who are strangers dwelling together despite our differences and our histories.

It becomes a denial of all forms of authority beyond the lived experience of the oppressed. Activism corrodes institutions, and there is no good government without strong institutions. Thus identity politics is a politics of opposition, and not a politics of governing.

Thesis 9. A politics of identities is antithetical to institutions, and so struggles with the ethic of responsibility that is required to govern.

Fukuyama argued that identity politics is a demand for dignity and a struggle for recognition, rooted in the human drive for *thymos*. This theme may be restated more accurately. Identity politics is a distortion of the demand for dignity.

Thesis 10. In identity politics, dignity is sought in victimhood, and the demand to others is made through the self-regarding authority of lived experience.

Can we find an a way of acting with dignity that goes beyond narrow personal identities, and that extinguishes the self in the common good of an inherited culture?

Frankenstein's children

(From *The Burning Archive* 22 September 2019.)

In 1815, Mount Tambora, on the northern coast of the Indonesian island of Sumbawa, erupted in the largest volcanic explosion in recorded history. The vast amount of ash and gas thrown into the atmosphere led to strange weather being recorded across the world, in China, in India, in America, in Europe, and even presumably in Australia. In central Europe, this faraway volcano caused, together with any other random climatic fluctuations, a 'Year without Summer' in 1816.

In the shadow of that dark summer, some English literary friends huddled in the gloom of their holiday house on the shores of Lake Geneva. To entertain themselves without boats, sun and frivolity, they told each other horror stories. Mary Godwin, later known as Mary Shelley, when married to Percy Bysshe Shelley, told and later wrote the story of *Frankenstein*.

Frankenstein is a story of human powers that escape our control. It is a tragedy of how our own cultural, social or scientific creations find drives and needs that we cannot easily satisfy. Victor Frankenstein, the archetypal mad scientist, created a Creature through the reanimation of corpses. The Creature pleaded with Victor to make him a female companion of his own kind, a reanimated corpse, whom the Creature might love. Victor agreed reluctantly, and made a negligent deal that the Creature pledge to disappear with his newly forged companion into the South American forests. But Victor reneged on his agreement, when he became aware this Creature of his own making was evil, and would not do as he promised.

Victor's broken promise enraged Frankenstein's evil child. The Creature pursued his Creator in anger. The Creature threatened Victor's bride to be. He murdered an innocent, which crime led Victor to be tried for the murder. In pursuit of justice or absolution, Victor pursued the Creature, with a determined plan to destroy him. The Creature strangled Victor's promised bride, and provoked his father's death. In grief and rage, Victor pursued the monster of his own creation to the North Pole. There the powerful scientist was caught in pack ice, that caused the deaths of his crew, who were led by Captain Walton. Victor lectured his wavering men that great undertakings demand hardship, but when the boat was freed from its ice trap, Victor was too weakened by cold and hypothermia to go on. Captain Walton decided to return South, and Victor died, with a last minute recantation of his ambition. He told Captain Walton to 'seek happiness in tranquility and avoid ambition'. Then Walton found the Creature, deprived of love in his existence, stranded on his ship, grieving for his destroyed creator. His revenge, spite and crimes had not brought the Creature relief or happiness or peace. He was now completely alone, and Walton watched him drift off on an ice raft 'lost in darkness and distance'.

Such a powerful story. It has fuelled the modern horror movie, if in bastardised form. It has worked as a prescient omen for climate change. It has served as a metaphor for science and technology escaping our control. It has served as a metaphor for artificial intelligence. It has served as a metaphor for the revolt of the emotions against a life too governed by reason and ambition, and for the impact of childhood without a loving mother or parent.

And I am going to turn the story to a different use again, and make it a metaphor for the modern professional political operatives whose revenge, spite and crimes drive the rolling crisis of Australian politics, or even global politics. But I know the Australian case well. Since 2007, until perhaps an uncertain conclusion in 2019, these political operatives have played out a horror story of Australian politics. The story of Prime Ministers Rudd, Gillard, Rudd, Abbott (Credlin), Turnbull and maybe Morrison too is a story of a peculiar kind of loveless monster, the party political mercenary.[90] This mercenary was created by the modern political party machine, in the full blush of its over-confident ambition. The machine believed that it could control human events because there were some early successful experiments in the 1980s and 1990s, after the mercenaries seized control of the institutions of power.

These are Frankenstein's children. As the story goes, they will, in the shadow created by climate change, turn against their creator, destroy the government institutions they inherited, and then destroy themselves.

The impeachment of the republic

(From *The Burning Archive* 24 November 2019.)

Over the last week I have had some illness, which led me to convalesce in bed for four days, to listen to podcasts, and to watch YouTube. The bed rest, in turn, led to some insomnia, when I woke anywhere between two and six AM, and, with my eyes wide shut, tuned into many hours of the Donald Trump impeachment hearings in Washington.

---

[90] In 2023, we might say, maybe, Albanese too.

Political Disorder

My sleepless attention led to these summary judgements. There appears to be no substantial case to impeach Donald Trump, however flawed or abrasive a character he may be. By contrast, there appear to be many claims of corruption that involve the Biden family and Burisma. And who guards the guardians? There has been some outrageous conduct by the FBI, CIA and officials. It is reported that this conduct includes tampering with the evidence that initiated the whole Russia-Gate fiasco.[91]

The impeachment hearings themselves are a travesty of a legal process. Distinguished constitutional scholars, like Jonathon Turley and Alan Dershowitz, have stated clearly that the impeachment case is narrow, has a poor evidentiary basis, has been rushed, and simply does not establish a crime. Turley says 'contemptible' should be distinguished from 'impeachable'. Dershowitz pleads for an end to the criminalisation of political differences. Dershowitz says:

> I'm a liberal Democrat. "And I'm on the side of Donald Trump on this issue... There's no crime there. You can argue that maybe there is an abuse of the foreign policy, but there is no crime there.[92]

Moreover, Dershowitz goes on to lament the descent of political discussion into a partisan chorus. Speaking of the various political commentators who mistook the outcomes of this poor legal process for clear legal verdicts, he says:

> They're just partisan political operatives or spokespeople who just make the law come out the way they want it to. I've become very unpopular among my liberal friends because I'm telling it the way I've always told it.

It seems, indeed, the impeachment process is backfiring badly against its proponents and zealots. There has been a stunning loss of support in opinion polls for impeachment coinciding with the hearings,

---

[91] The Durham Report on this fiasco was published when I was finalising this publication, but I have included no details. The reader can look it up.
[92] *Washington Examiner*, 22 November 2019.

13 Ways of Looking at a Bureaucrat

notwithstanding the extraordinarily biased reporting from outlets like CNN. Indeed, support for Trump has increased, and Trump has come out fighting, urging a trial in the Senate. That removal trial, presided over by the Chief Justice of the Supreme Court, will not be conducted as a show trial. It will not give credibility, as Adam Schiff ludicrously did, to the idea that hearsay evidence is superior to direct evidence. It will not be a platform for grandstanding pseudo-bureaucrats. It will almost certainly test the motives for the so-called whistleblower claim, the validity of concerns about misconduct associated with Hunter Biden, questionable decisions of officials loyal to the resistance to Trump's redirection of American foreign policy, and apparent collusion of numerous witnesses to the impeachment hearing in the cover-up of those apparent misdeeds. It could turn out very badly indeed: people in glass houses should not throw stones.

My impressions on the assessment of guilt, or predictions about the ultimate political and legal outcomes, are not the only observations I have made on this impeachment hearing. In many ways, the Congress has set out to impeach the President, and accidentally found itself impeaching the republic.

It struck me that at the heart of the impeachment hearings is a breakdown in the institutional role and professional conduct of the public service, or the bureaucracy, in its relationship to elected government and the professional political class.

The Democrats sought to present witnesses who were true public servants, and dress them up, with moving back stories, as heroic patriots. As the *Washington Post* put it, in a headline following Dr Fiona Hill's testimony: "Public servants use impeachment hearings to offer lessons of history and military service in rejoinder to Trump." On the other hand, many conservative commentators cried that these witnesses are just resentful bureaucrats, who mistakenly believe they determine foreign policy, and bristle at direction by the sole, constitutionally legitimate authority on foreign policy, the President.

Political Disorder

The weak evocation by witnesses of the 'interagency policy consensus' only confirmed this judgement of the bureaucrats. It supported the argument that this impeachment hearing really is a response to a dispute over foreign policy within the foreign policy establishment. It may not be as conspiratorial as 'deep state' theories claim, but it is certainly not a drama of high-minded principle.

There were some true public servants among those who gave testimony, and the most impressive was Kurt Volker. But most of the official witnesses were unimpressive, inauthentic schemers who do not serve the public. Too many betrayed weaknesses of personal ambition, status obsession, and intellectual vanity. These temptations can lead officials astray when they only mix among themselves. They can be damning when officials tell themselves legends, such as these defiant bureaucrats are heroes of a Resistance. Witnesses revealed much of this toxic personalisation of integrity. They fused conviction and presumption. They believed in the high-mindedness of their views, and scorned the low-rent nature of dirty politicians. Nowhere was this temptation disclosed more clearly than in Dr Fiona Hill's testimony. During the hearings 'it became clear to her', the unelected Dr Hill, that she and colleagues in the Resistance were pursuing the national interest, whereas the elected populist President, and his small loyal team, were merely pursuing a 'domestic political errand'.

I was struck by the contempt of several of the witnesses. Alex Vindman, who clearly was considered by many of his former work colleagues to lack judgement, bristled at the elevated member of Congress who did not use Colonel Vindman's correct title when questioning. There was the ever smirking David Holmes, who could not sustain his calm in response to the simplest questions. There was the always patronising Dr Hill who assumed her role was not to give evidence about alleged crimes, but to teach the congressional members how to conduct foreign policy by her standards. There was the remarkable moment of vanity from Lt-Colonel Vindman, when he reported, despite his high-minded concern with the ethical behaviour of President Trump, that he was offered three times the role of Defence Minister of Ukraine. He clearly felt he was entitled to the job, and his flush of pride when he talked about it showed his lack of judgement. This boast may be the closest any witness at this hearing came to presenting evidence of bribery.

The most aggressive advocate of the career service view was Dr Fiona Hill, and perhaps it is right that her motives and ethos be subjected to the most severe testing. The fact is she is not a career civil servant, not at all. She was dropped in as a political appointee from the Brookings Institution, and lasted not very long. She was an anti-Russia zealot who showed little discernment. Memorably, within a week of the election of President Trump, she published an opinion piece that implied that Trump came to power with the assistance of Putin. She made the following remarkable comparison:

> The U.S. election came hot on the heels of the 99th anniversary of the Russian revolution (November 7, 1917) —the result was the *contemporary American version of a Bolshevik revolution. Donald Trump rode a wave of popular anger against the establishment, promising to bring down the old guard and seize the White House* [my emphasis]. Like the Bolsheviks, his campaign was big on slogans and short on content. Maybe it takes a "Bolshevik" to know one—or rather, someone who knows what a Bolshevik, a revolutionary, thinks like. And among the handful of people who seemed to call this electoral outcome was Russian President Vladimir Putin. The reasons why are instructive.[93]

Let me read that back so it is clear, and let us remember this text was written by someone with a PhD in Russian history. Fiona Hill just said that Trump seized the White House in the same way as the Bolsheviks seized power in 1917. The only problem was there was no

---

[93] Fiona Hill, "Order From Chaos – Putin And The Kremlin Are Experts At Reading The Popular Mood. And They Were Watching America," 11 November 2016, Brookings Blog.

election in October 1917, and the Bolsheviks later closed down the elected Russian chamber with guns and guards when it was clear that they had only minority support. *Vive la resistance?* Yet this coal-miner's testimony was repeated unquestionably in the media with the borrowed authority of an impartial, expert public servant.

In fact, she plainly is not. She is another example of the penetration of patronage and partisanship into the ethos of governing. She has made a career out of her expertise and her biases. But she has not humbly served people of differing views. The same point might be made about the 'whistleblower', who reportedly has had a baby career as an 'intelligence analyst', that is full of leaking, questionable dealings and partisan operations. He does not practise the ordinary virtues of governing well. He plays cowardly games with political operatives, who have no deep knowledge or experience of institutions that truly matter.

I have one last observation about the dilemmas of the declining American state that have been exposed by the impeachment hearings. While the long difficult retrenchment of the American Empire proceeds, its foreign policy establishment will need to disentangle itself from a thousand private attachments, in places all around the world. It will need to cut these ties, even though its bureaucracy holds them near and dear. This will be made difficult by the conflicting ideas and values, and by the slow detachment from the foreign loyalties that have been nurtured by local elites and dual loyalty Americans. Americans with Eastern European heritage especially have built wealthy networks to fight wars in the lands they have left. They have built and led institutions committed to analysis and supremacy over one enemy or another. Donald Trump's historical significance will surely be that he is the first to initiate some retrenchment of American Empire, and he has encountered terrific resistance, perhaps even plots and conspiracies, to remove him because of this very purpose. For comparison, the British Empire formed through multiple entanglements of local interests and political pressures. So too the American Empire will only be able to untangle its overextended network if it overcomes these local and emigre pressures to deploy weapons, to intervene in domestic issues, to advance the interests of American business, to overlook corruption, prejudice and misconduct, and so on.[94]

The impeachment hearings may damage the Democrats and their co-conspirators, if serious action arises from the Inspector General and Durham reports. But the greatest damage will be from another unintended backfire of the hearings. The hearings have failed to impeach a President, and instead impeached the institutions of the American republic and the American Empire. If these issues are exposed in the Senate trial and through the criminal investigations of Justice Department officials, the real constitutional crisis may begin.

Notes on my reading in 2019

From The Burning Archive December 2019.

The year's reading has been among my least studious. The troubles of the year have robbed me of time and concentration to read deeply and widely, and there has been less discovery of new topics or rediscovery of old masters than in recent years. Yet still if I document my reading I may discover curiosities about my self.

Following the impeachment hearings and my own investigation of the bizarre political mirage of the Russia Gate and Ukraine (non)scandals, I read Lee Smith, *The plot against the President: the true story of how Congressman Devin Nunes uncovered the biggest political scandal in US history*. For years I have largely avoided reading anything about US politics and Donald Trump. The endless,

---

[94] John Darwin, *Unfinished Empire: The Global Expansion of Britain* (2013).

Political Disorder

breathless reporting on the the imminent fall of the immoral Donald Trump by the biased commentariat, which had lost its bearings on objectivity, only made me want to turn away. I always had a concern about the shrill, absurd talk about Russia as an enemy, and was deeply sceptical that Russian interference explained the defeat of Hilary Clinton, rather than excused her mistakes. After all, I predicted Donald Trump's victory six months out from the election. That post also predicted that Trump would 'bring to white heat a burning political system'. It did not foresee a paper coup by the permanent political class in collusion with police, intelligence agencies and a degraded news media. Yet Smith makes a strong case that a coup is exactly what happened. A close reading of the Inspector-General's report on FISA abuse bears out the case that, far more than the latest impeachment charade, this conspiracy of intertwined elites who had their power threatened is the true scandal of our democratic republics in distress.

Ian Kershaw, *Roller Coaster: Europe 1950-2017* gave a compelling account of the events and changes of this time and region. There are ups and downs, and Kershaw never pretends his narrative to the brink of our time is one coherent journey. Reading this book while the British Parliament became a quagmire for Brexit was an education. Kershaw makes clear how long the British have been reluctant to cede power to Europe, and the protracted difficulties of the European project. Boris Johnson's ultimate victory for Brexit would be no surprise to a reader of *Roller Coaster*, even though Kershaw's own judgement is that Brexit is a recipe to make his country poorer and less secure. Kershaw ends his account with our new age of insecurity, and the difficulties that Europe faces in responding to these insecurities. Yet. for me, the abiding sensation of this book are the flashbacks it evoked of fragmentary memories of my childhood and young adulthood, which have shaped my outlook on the world. Margaret Thatcher makes an appearance as do many others I have known through the spectacle of news, through their texts and their actions. Willy Brandt, Vaclav Havel, Gorbachev, Lech Walesa, and many more minor figures. I relived the inconclusive roller coaster of my own life through this book.

13 Ways of Looking at a Bureaucrat

Felipe Fernández-Armesto published *Out of our Minds: what we think and how we came to think it*, and I read about a quarter of it. This book or essay reprised many ideas of his recent books on change, imagination and deep history. His statement that imagination is central to human thought and history is the most redeeming message that I can take at this troubled time.

Richard Haas, *A world in disarray: American foreign policy and the crisis of the old order* sets out the official world view of the American foreign policy elite. I made my way through 18 per cent of this book on my kindle. I also watched the accompanying broadcast documentary with its teaching notes by Haas. I read Haas because I was curious about foreign policy 'realism' and the multi-polar threat to the American empire. I remain unconvinced by the liberal globalists and their delusion of a world order. They really should read *After Tamerlane*. And I have been surprised by the sense spoken by Steven K Bannon, and other critics of the American empire.

The same interest led me to John Mearsheimer, *Great Delusion: Liberal Dreams and International Realities*. It was a compelling, if surprisingly theoretical, book. But he made the observation that "Perhaps the greatest cost of liberal hegemony… [is] the damage it does to the American political and social fabric. Individual rights and the rules of law will not fare well in a country addicted to fighting wars." This statement is surely a coda to the great hoaxes of Russia Gate and the Ukraine impeachment, and all the fabricated hysteria about the enemy Russia that has been launched by the war factions of the US Democrats and the deep state.

I enjoyed Douglas Murray, *The Madness of Crowds: Gender, Race and Identity*. It is an essay of blessed disdain for the insanity of identity politics and intersectionality. This mimetic radicalism has poisoned the institutions that I work in, but Murray's intelligent, empathetic scepticism has helped inoculate me against this poison.

During the year, I completed reading Kevin Rudd, *The PM Years*,

Political Disorder

which I had begun last year, but dropped because of its sheer tedium. I resumed reading because I wanted to talk with Terry Moran about Rudd, but that wish I have since abandoned. Rudd makes a case that his rival, Gillard, was a very bad Prime Minister, a leader who had no ideas, but only political instincts of the most venal kind. Rudd failed, however, to convince this reader that he himself was a capable Prime Minister. One day in the future, an historian should work their way through the many memoirs of Rudd's Cabinet. They will need to proceed cautiously because there are tangled briars and bitter berries. But they might emerge to write an account of the disaster of the Rudd-Gillard-Rudd Governments, and what they really meant for our governing institutions. I have sketched a prose-poem fragment, 'Frankenstein's Children', but cannot devote any more time to the bitterness of this failed republic.

On reflection, my reading this year was too dominated by politics. There have been exceptions. I reread the first two books of the *Song of Fire and Ice* series, after the disappointment of the closing TV narrative of *Game of Thrones*. I started reading Andrei Bely *Petersburg*, when in St Petersburg. I read some of Pessoa's *The Book of Disquiet* when in Lisbon, and a new translation of Kafka's *The Castle* on the way to Prague. But deep culture this year has been pushed aside by distressed republics, dark sisterhoods and deep states. There were fragments: some stories by Borges; a chapter or two of *The Name of the Rose*, after watching the new television drama of the book; the start of *Sagaland;* grand histories such as Slezkine, *The House of Government: a sage of the Russian Revolution,* and Dalrymple, *The Anarchy*, his history of the East India Company; poems; poetics; travel notes; a few essays that squealed dismay at the world.

Next year I want to find a better way of reading, to take me to deeper, more satisfying places. Less politics. More culture. Less diagnosis, and more remedies.

13 Ways of Looking at a Bureaucrat

Six asides on the USA 2020 election

(From *The Burning Archive* 22 November 2020.)

This long post contained my reflections on the strange 2020 election in America. There are six reflections. *One*. The folly of forecasts: my confession. *Two*. The Presidency is determined not by broadcast anchors, but by Constitutional procedure. *Three*. The pending legitimacy crisis. *Four*. Our deformed, barren political society. *Five*. The post-democratic society. *Six*. Heaven is high and the emperor is far away.

I composed this post over two days after the election, and made some updates and corrections afterwards. In editing the essay for publication, I have chosen largely to leave in the final text any errors of misinterpretation that were essential to my thinking at the time. I chose not to tidy up my thinking for the sake of appearances. I chose not to airbrush my errors out of history. Instead, I present this document of a mind at work in the chaos of political disorder. Its insights and its errors are equally instructive to an unknown reader.

One. The folly of forecasts: my confession. My prediction of the result of the USA election turned out to be part right, part wrong, and part yet to be decided.

I predicted Trump would defy the polls and win. This prediction was part right and part to be decided. The polls and data pseudo-scientists, like 538's Nate Silver, were marvellously or malignantly wrong. 2020 has been a bad year for modellers, forecasters and statisticians, now known as data dudes. There was no blue wave. There was rather a strange red wave with a deep under-current. Driven by a tempest, this wave has brought to shore all the struggling, surviving sailors of a capsized, altered conservative ship – a Republican Senate maybe (just), a more Republican House, more Republican state

Political Disorder

legislatures, the end of calls to pack the Supreme Court. But the undercurrent of distaste for Trump's character and the rip of information warfare by Big Media and Big Tech may have drowned the Republican Captain.

We don't know yet whether that captain, who waves desperately in the waters, will drown or will make it to shore. Whether Trump or Biden has won will need to be determined by electoral, legal and constitutional procedure, institutions and actors. No media 'decision desk' makes that call. No celebrity journalist or statistician decides that.

But it does seem likely now that either Biden (most likely) or Trump will only win, at least on the first electoral count, by a whisker and after litigation. And certainly in my updated prediction, 'The Fall of the American Brezhnev', following the shocking revelations of the 'laptop from hell', I over-estimated the anticipated fade of Biden's support.

I also did not pay attention to the minor but arguably decisive Libertarian candidate, Jo Jorgensen, who received about 1 to 1.5 per cent of the vote. If 70 per cent of his vote had gone to Trump, the following states would be clearly in Trump's camp: Arizona, Georgia, Pennsylvania, Wisconsin. Perhaps the never Trump republican vote was decisive after all?

But still there were things I did get right – even far away as an antipodean observer, who tries to see the whole playing field, not just watch one team's champion, and who is not interested in shouting 'Boooo!' at Punch during the pantomime. What was my reasoning on 30 August?

> The riots will alienate suburban voters. Black Lives Matter will scare off Latino, Indian and Asian American voters. Enough Black voters will despise the chains of condescension imposed by the DNC elite. The travesty of the Democratic party presenting a candidate too far past

his prime, who has too many questions about his character and the corruption of family Biden, will dismay independent voters. The pandemic will wane, and treatments will appear as salvation. And the deceit of the liberal media establishment will trap them again in their own illusions. Biden's polls are already failing, if they can even be relied upon. I suspect they will spiral down, even in the storm of events – domestic terror and international instability – we are likely to steer through in the months to November.

There is clearly a realignment and a cultural reassembly going on in America, and perhaps also in my own remote society in the South Pacific. It is a motile kaleidoscope. It is time for forecasters and the commentariat to stop performing for the cameras, to cease their premature proclamations on the unknown, and to open their lying eyes.

Two. The Presidency is determined not by broadcast anchors, but by Constitutional procedure. The Claremont Institute and Texas Public Policy Foundation foresaw most accurately, in its *79 Days Report,* the chaotic battlefield we are glimpsing through the fog of information war. A group of Constitutional scholars and other experts imagined what could happen, given the unusual conditions, divided opinions and institutional weaknesses that underlay this election.

> Due to the political stoking of fears of contracting COVID-19, a massive push has been made, mostly by the left, to encourage voting by mail. This significantly alters the calculus on Election Day and completely upends the post-election period. Most states and local election officials aren't prepared to process, validate, and count large number of mail-in ballots. In five swing states (totalling 68 Electoral College votes)—Georgia, Iowa, Michigan, Pennsylvania, and Wisconsin—no mail-in ballots may be counted before Election Day (Nevada's legislature changed election law to allow early mail-in ballot counting in August). Since reports indicate a far greater interest in

voting by mail for Democrats than Republicans, it's likely that President Trump will be winning these states by large margins on Election Day, only to see that margin shrink in the days and weeks after Election Day.[95]

Whether there were in fact frauds or other irregularities will need to be determined, but the systemic weaknesses of America's electoral administration have clearly set up a test of the Republic's constitution. There are widespread reports of irregularities of large numbers of votes, and a recent Supreme Court decision on 6 or 7 November required separate counting of late ballots in Pennsylvania. I respect the views of conservative blogger, Rod Dreher, who writes of his own guilt in succumbing to a belief cascade about weapons of mass destruction and the Iraq war:

> Do I believe vote fraud might have occurred in this election? Of course it might have. Where we have solid reason to suspect it, we should dispatch a phalanx of Republican lawyers to challenge it in court. But Donald Trump is exactly the kind of man who would make reckless, inflammatory allegations — and has done so. I have walked this walk before, and it leads nowhere good. Let's be patient, and let the lawyers do their work.[96]

But one can hardly expect Trump to go down without testing the results in the court of disputed returns. After all, his opponent of 2016, Hilary Clinton, still considers that election outcome 'stolen', despite never testing that claim in the courts and despite that result being clearer, cleaner and more quickly apparent on the night. Trump's willingness to fight and to disrupt the norms of the gridlocked Washington system made him popular and got him elected in the first place. Then his opponents, from all points along the spectrum, spent three or more years denouncing his legitimacy and seeking his impeachment. The denunciations were made on the basis of

---

[95] Claremont Institute and Texas Public Policy Foundation, *79 Days Report* (2020), p. 1.
[96] Rod Dreher, 'Disintegration Nation', Rod Dreher Blog (6 November 2020) at *American Conservative*.

misinformation they created, the RussiaGate hoax. The impeachment was initiated by an investigation of irregular conduct they were party to, UkraineGate. Now they claim Trump is destroying democracy by asking the courts to check that election law has been complied with. As Joe Biden might say, 'C'mon Man!'

One scenario the *79 Days Report* gamed out is precisely the circumstance we face.

> An ambiguous result, with several states' final election results delayed and subject to intense court fights resulting in a struggle right up to the Jan. 6 joint session of Congress where the Electors' ballots are unsealed. Uncertainty could extend even beyond this as decisions for both the presidency and vice presidency are battled out in Congress and before the U.S. Supreme Court.[97]

The report made seven predictions on the political struggle arising from this scenario. First, the winner would not be known on election night. True. Second, the report predicted many mail-in ballots may be hard to check "as systems have not been prepared to process the ballots and count them while tremendous pressure will be brought to bear to bypass safeguards against fraud and produce results." True, though we are in the fog of claim and counter-claim right now. Third, the American legal system would be 'up to the task' of adjudicating disputes. Too early to tell. Fourth, unrest will occur, and flames will be fanned by media, loss of trust, foreign powers, and the efforts of Big Tech and the media to shape and suppress the news. True, if not yet acute. Fifth, risks of 'international adventurism by the PRC and Russia'. Doubtful so far. Almost certainly a Russophobic phantasm about Russia; maybe something to watch for China. Sixth, critically: "If the contest doesn't produce a majority (50% +1) of the votes of seated Electors by Jan. 6, there are clearly established Constitutional procedures to determine a victor." Yet to be seen, but this seems a likely possibility. People need to await the outcomes of recounts and

---

[97] *79 Days Report,* p. 2.

courts of disputed returns. Seventh and finally, there are two large uncertainties at the late stage of a contested election that may sorely test the American Constitution and Republic. These difficult dramas will be profoundly difficult, and are worth quoting at length.

> Each house determines the final election results of its membership. This means that the Democratic majority in the U.S. House might decide not to seat duly elected Republican Members so as to prevent the Republicans from holding a 26-seat majority in the state delegations in the event that state delegations, each with one vote per state, are used to determine the President in the event that no candidate has the needed absolute majority of seated Electors' votes. Given that the majority's power to determine the membership of the body, House or Senate, is absolute, the sole check on the use of this absolute political power is the potentially dire consequences of its abuse.
>
> Should the results be undetermined through Jan. 20, Inauguration Day, the Succession Act would suggest that the Speaker of the House would become President. Should the results be undetermined through Jan. 20, Inauguration Day, the Succession Act would suggest that the Speaker of the House would become acting President until one is determined and, if the House cannot decide, then elevating the Vice President, even if selected out of the Senate.

In short, we should all stop expecting an answer tomorrow morning. We should all wake up to the severity of the test of the American republic. It is feasible that the US Constitution, institutions and actors may not withstand the test without many casualties. This may end up being the most contested election since 1876, and may be a new phase of the political civil war that began with Trump's nomination.

In August I wrote, posing a difficult question,

> Have the Democratic political elite truly espoused the Devil's totalitarian creed that was articulated by Hilary Clinton when she claimed that Biden "should not concede under any circumstances?" Perhaps the prediction in 2020 may be that Trump will win, and the American republic may fail.

Again I was half-wrong (Trump will win), and half-right (the American republic will fail).

Three. The pending legitimacy crisis. And if the American Republic does fail, how might it fail? And if the 'indispensable' republic does fail, what will be the consequences of this failure? Will this republic in distress, which was once the 'leader of the free world' and the fountainhead of democracy, become to democracy worldwide like a rotting head is to a spoiled and corrupted fish? Is this gloom catastrophic thinking? Are we not heading back to norms and normality? Are we not ridding our homes of that bright, bad, orange glare that blinded *Libertas* in the darkness? Let us pencil in some *chiaroscuro*. Dark thoughts first, then some glimmers of light.

How might the American Republic fail? Well, for starters, just maybe some electoral fraud or malfeasance might have happened. It is certainly not proven, but history, even very recent history, tells us it cannot be discounted. There is plenty of smelly fish at this market. What if a court finds substance in one or other claim? Suddenly, Washington has a problem.

Then, evidence of electoral interference might appear. After all, for the last four years, many people blamed a few cheap Russian-funded Facebook memes for rigging the last election. These claims were enough for political actors in politics and the media to withhold legitimacy from Trump. They licensed an army of officials and hacks to pursue the McCarthyite RussiaGate hoax, all the way down its spiral of hysterical nonsense.[98] Is electoral interference by technology

---

[98] Jeff Gerth, 'The press versus the president' *Columbia Journalism Review*, January 2023, and the Durham Report have since commented.

companies so unimaginable? After all, back in 2015, when the press had not yet become deranged by Trump, journalists then reported that Google's search algorithm could shift the voting preferences of undecided voters by more than 20 percent on average, and up to 80 percent in some voter groups. Yet virtually no one would be aware that they were being manipulated. If such manipulation was possible in 2015, what might be the effects of the brazen audacity of Big Tech in 2020? Is that evidence supporting arguments challenging the legitimacy of the President and the election result? In 2020 it was not Vladimir Putin who swung the election with cheap digital ads. It may have been Big Tech firms themselves that interfered in the election. They suppressed news. They banned the paper founded by Alexander Hamilton. They blocked countless elected, celebrity and ordinary voices. They used Facebook and Twitter as censors, like a modern day Union of Soviet Writers.

It may be that any discovered claims of fraud or irregular procedures or interference may prove minor, inconsequential mistakes. But, what if evidence emerges in coming days that proves these mistakes to be systemic, deliberate and decisive? Today, many journalists and political actors mock Trump for his allegation that the Democrat machine – with Big Money, Big Media, Big Tech – is 'stealing the election'. Such an allegation is a shameful, shambolic stain on democracy, they say. But what if evidence emerges that it is true? Surely, there is a *prima facie* case at least to investigate. Will they bite their tongues and freeze their minds? Will they repeat their mockery of Trump when he claimed that 'they spied on my campaign'? Will journalists similarly fail to correct their specious first draft of history if and when Trump's claim becomes a documented archived fact? It seems the media and mainstream politics, left, right and centre, want only one reading of this confusing situation. They want all doubts and suspicions about the American political system just to go away. But, if they all decide to live in lies, to put our signs calling on Democrats of America to Unite, then their republic will fail.

13 Ways of Looking at a Bureaucrat

It is possible, therefore, the stress of this contested election may overwhelm the legal system, the constitutional order, and the frail actors who perform there. They may need to make their way calmly through the procedures, outlined in the *79 Days Report*. But the American Republic has rarely tested these dispute resolution procedures. They were devised in the 18th and 19th century. The 24/7 world of relentless high-tech information warfare may exhaust them. Both actors and order may break, and the Republic may fail.

Recriminations within the parties may undermine the capacity of the political actors to follow the constitutional process or to navigate the tensions of this new political equilibrium. Already, we are seeing disappointments with the results for the Democratic Party leading to distractions and recriminations, such as Ocasio-Cortez's 'hit list of Trump sycophants'. Already, Trump's son and other loyalists have lashed out, and threatened Republicans who might go soft on conceding.

Order may breakdown. Unrest may descend into violence and then into open conflict. In mid-2020 my darkest fears were cultural revolution, induced insurrection, colour revolution, wild dissent, acts of extremism or just unsafe streets. They could all lead to the failure of the Republic.

On the other hand, there are other views I respect that there may be a silver lining in the crisis. Niall Ferguson and H.R. McMaster are relieved that there is a weakened Presidency without Trump's erratic disruption. They are reassured there is a divided government, curbed by a cautious Republican Senate, and made timid by a chastened woke Left. All this caution was mandated by a large, increased voter turnout. To their minds, in the cozy think tanks of America, this immobility might be the best of all possible outcomes.

But it is a starting position, and not an outcome. I doubt the gerontocracy that rules America can really navigate this damaged ship of state through the stormy waters and difficult reefs to come. Joe

Political Disorder

Biden is 78, and has had a 47 year track record of dithering, glad-handling, and misjudgement. His opponents allege misconduct, and point to signs of cognitive decline. He demonstrated no capacity to persuade throughout the election campaign. He has a penchant for getting tired and flustered when challenged or posed difficult questions. He claims to be a unifier; but a few car honks outside his rally provoke him to act like Bad Grandpa yelling at the neighbouring chumps to get off his lawn. On the porch with him are 80 year-old Nancy Pelosi and 78 year-old Mitch McConnell.

How will they respond if China moves into Taiwan in the week before Christmas? As Niall Ferguson wrote in 'Joe Biden could end up being a wartime President', the conflict over access to superconductors from Taiwan for Huawei (and the 5G network) is an existential threat for China and the USA, and could readily provoke military escalation. Despite all the rhetoric of peace and domestic rebuilding, Democrats have a tradition of rushing into endless wars. So we may see the clash of Empires in the middle of a messy, contested American Presidential handover. And this handover is more akin to the Bourbon Restoration. It is the return of a dynasty that has forgotten nothing and learned nothing. The Emperor of the American Imperial War Faction is being returned to the throne, but with shaky hands and wandering mind. As Ferguson wrote that he could readily imagine Jo Biden inadvertently, and with good intentions and noble rhetoric, stumbling from Cold War II into World War III.

If the shaky, stained hands of this Bourbon Restoration are forced to steer a rickety Republic in a war with its rising imperial rival, China, which many American citizens appear to believe compromised their President-elect, then that American Republic may fail.

What will be the consequences of this failure? In August 2020, I wondered if the unrest in America would lead to civil war, fragmentation or collapse. The republic might also endure, muddle through, or even be renewed. There seems no realistic prospect of

13 Ways of Looking at a Bureaucrat

Creepy Joe Biden singin' some political healin'.

All the over-excited people, who are delighted that Trump is finally done, ought to stop a moment, and listen to the phrases of the people who suspect that an election, a democracy, a republic, a way of life has been stolen from them in the darkness of the morning of Wednesday 4 November. I have heard the phrase "the stab in the back". Compliant republicans, who urge Trump to go quietly, are called the "surrender caucus." People say they have been "red-pilled" by Trump and will not go back to "Vulture capitalism." Others believe the two-party system has failed. Some believe the left-right or red-blue paradigm has collapsed.

Elections have consequences. True, but only if the governing actors and institutions are capable of executing matters of consequence. Rigged elections – or even more so, colour revolution elections – have deeper, more troubling consequences, regardless of the over-estimated manipulative capabilities of political operatives. The consequences of the crisis or failure of the republic can also be imagined through a short thought experiment.

First, what will Trump do next if Biden becomes President? He will fight all the way, but, if the legal and court battles go against him, he will exit to a potentially more potent role of dissident leader. He could easily step aside and assume a non-congressional, non-executive role as Leader of the Opposition. After all, he has some claim to a real charismatic phenomenon of the MAGA movement. With his talent for media and celebrity, his provocative mythopoetic truth-telling, and the chance to recruit a new circle of loyal insiders, Trump could make life very difficult for the stumbling, gerontocrat, Joe Biden. Veteran journalist Peter Lavelle has raised this possibility.

Second, what will the Democrat factions do next if Biden becomes President, but then is soon replaced by Harris? This succession may occur because of debility, incompetence or allegations of misconduct. But then Harris, and the weak, fractured Democrat Party might

Political Disorder

implode. In the bankrupt gridlock of vetocracy, soft left authoritarianism and oligarchic collusion will slug it out. It is plausible that Biden may win by a small, disputed margin, without control of the Senate or the Supreme Court, and a diminished House majority. The party of the new President is already fighting among themselves, and and display no ideas, no persuasive capability, and far too many debts to Wall Street, Silicon Valley, the intelligence agencies and the legacy media.

The glimmer of hope I see is that a new crop of leaders, more artful disrupters than Trump, may emerge across the political spectrum,such as Andrew Yang, Tulsi Gabbard, Ted Cruz, Josh Hawley or even Tucker Carlson. But they must find a way to defeat the Blob that is spreading all over the ruins of the Republic.

How will this failure affect the rest of the world? Let's face it America looks like a disaster to the rest of the world. The beacon of democracy in the world has been snuffed out, and replaced with a sputtering corporatist oligarchy. Old Corruption has defeated the new Andrew Jackson, and spurned its own American Tradition, or, so it seems, before the courts review the evidence. The other Half of the World cannot believe why the Wicked Half of America voted for Trump, he who must not be praised.

The possibly temporary defeat of Trump has inspired many progressive cheerleaders around the world with a brief *schadenfreude*. But how will they respond when the new Democratic administration, beclouded with false dreams, is mugged by reality in the forms of imperial decline, institutional gridlock and legitimacy crisis? What if they cannot deliver? What if their failure springs from the same source as Trump's? How will they respond if the Supreme Court of the Grand Old Republic ultimately judges that the so-called Democratic Party in the "Leader of the Free World," has a case to answer that they collaborated with Big Tech and Big Media to perpetrate, as the Trump camp claims, the largest election rigging in the history of democracy?

Will they recant? Will they apologise? Will they admit they have let democracy die in the darkness of their self-deceit?

Four. Our deformed, barren political society. And if Trump is no longer President, then all the ills of political system can no longer be blamed on Trump. For four years now, in America and through viral spread around the world, all the ills of our deformed, barren political society have been personified in one metonymic myth, Donald Trump.

Victor Davis Hanson compared Trump to chemotherapy. It makes you sick, but cures a cancer. The challenge for our political societies now is, can we face up to the remaining cancer?

Five. We have entered the post-democratic society. Long ago, in the 1970's, Vaclav Havel, in his essay, "The Power of the Powerless," warned Western liberal democracies that their way of being was not so different to that experienced by the unfree citizens of totalitarian Eastern Europe.

> In highly simplified terms, it could be said that the post-totalitarian system has been built on foundations laid by the historical encounter between dictatorship and the consumer society. Is it not true that the far-reaching adaptability to living a lie and the effortless spread of social auto-totality have some connection with the general unwillingness of consumption-oriented people to sacrifice some material certainties for the sake of their own spiritual and moral integrity? With their willingness to surrender higher values when faced with the trivializing temptations of modern civilization? With their vulnerability to the attractions of mass indifference? And in the end, is not the grayness and the emptiness of life in the post-totalitarian system only an insulated caricature of modern life in general? And do we not in fact stand (although in the external measures of civilization, we are far behind) as a kind of warning to the West, revealing to its own latent tendencies?[99]

---

[99] Vaclav Havel, 'The Power Of The Powerless' (1978), *Living in Truth*.

Political Disorder

Do the events of this remarkable year and this contested election not raise that warning to an insistent air-raid alarm? When Twitter and Big Tech censor the President of the United States on election night, have we not entered a post-democratic society? The spasm of hysteric denunciation of Trump as Hitler Reborn, ready to administer cyanide to democracy in his barricaded bunker, is a pure case of transference.

Six. Heaven is high and the emperor is far away. The old Chinese proverb is, "Heaven is high, and the emperor is far away." The Russians have a similar saying. до бога высоко, до царя далеко, God is high, and the Tsar is far away.

The last twelve months have been a journey of discovery for me about American politics. Before last year I had rarely paid much attention to American politics and history. The 2020 election is the first I have ever followed closely. This late curiosity has been conscious, but quite confronting. I am writing these thoughts alone. I stand with no crowd. I am politically homeless, disillusioned, tormented by dire prophecies.

I am attracted to the vision of the community of dissidents who step away from an oppressive, soft totalitarian society that Rod Dreher articulated in *Live not by lies: a manual of Christian dissidents*. I see myself as a dissident, but not a Christian. I have a very peculiar faith in the infinite conversation. This community of faith is the company of cold skulls. So, this dissident finds refuge in the renunciation of the political world. I find shelter in the remote ruins of the vast decaying empire of our culture and political society. In those remote ruins the task of maintaining sanity in an insane world requires redirection of attention, away from the belief cascades of Big Media and Big Tech, and away from the sickened Dowager Empire of America. But most of all it requires a regathering of affirmative ideas and affiliations. Where will I find them?

13 Ways of Looking at a Bureaucrat

The Time of Troubles to come in America

(From *The Burning Archive* 22 November 2020.)

> "There always is this fallacious belief: 'It would not be the same here; here such things are impossible.' Alas, all the evil of the twentieth century is possible everywhere on earth." (Aleksander Solzhenitsyn)

The events of the 2020 USA election confirmed Solzhenitsyn's insight. America stands on the brink of collapse into an oligarchy. The Newspeakers of democracy have made a Mephistophelean bargain. They exchanged their will for power for the rule of law. They calculated they could make Trump the sacrificial victim, and in the frenzy of the blood rites conceal the degradation of their restoration. But the crowd and the victim stood against the illusion, and the rite did not go as rehearsed. It got messy. The fraud of the high priests was revealed. Beneath their dress robes, they carried fake ballots.

The American Republic has been exposed as a theatre state. The theatre is enacted in the legacy media, and the spectacle is framed rigidly by Big Tech. The spectacle evokes all the great myths of the American Republic: the greatest democracy, the wisest founders, the greatest lovers of freedom, the home of the brave, the unifier-in-chief. But the fourth wall has collapsed. The audience can now see the technical operators behind stage. They can see these technicians scrambling to hide their cocked-up manipulations. They see the old actors, reading badly from the auto-cue. They see the oligarchs tamper with the production. The audience now must decide: do we walk out of the show? If we do, what form of government does that leave us with?

What happens next is difficult to predict and terrible to imagine. If the allegations of systematic election fraud are substantiated, you

Political Disorder

would imagine the cultural elites would be scandalised by this most inconvenient truth, and the political elites ashamed of their cowardice and corruption. How could a party and leadership class, who claim to act for democracy, decency and truth, support such alleged conduct? How could they obstruct investigation of irregularities, if they authentically lived in the truth? But these same elites have slinked away from justice for the RussiaGate hoax, that involved a tacit alliance of the same Newspeakers of Democracy, Big Media and the shadow security state to sabotage a democratically elected President. These elites say nothing about this betrayal of the Republic. There is no retraction, no apology. They just continue the media lines. They shout down any calls to investigate irregularities. They force the failing theatre state to go on with the show.

If significant election fraud is demonstrated, two political scenarios seem likely. Both suggest a time of troubles for the American Empire, and all its allied city-states around the world, including my democratically challenged province of the Great Southern Land.

The first scenario is that Biden prevails at first, with the backing of oligarchs and the mercenary merchant elite. The plans of the "Transition Integrity Project" succeed. They 'bombard the headquarters' of the courts by repeating their Big Lie loud enough. They ratchet up the threats to officials, the courts and Republican doubters, who may question the legality and constitutionality of the transition. They increase the appeals to the military to intervene and to guarantee the transition. The courts may baulk at overturning results. The state legislatures may give in, and certify results despite unaudited counts. The media will fan the hysteria of Trump's norm-breaking threat to democracy, and Big Tech will twist the screws of censorship harder. The electoral college will fall into line, and then Biden will be inaugurated as a stained, illegitimate President. But one-third or more of the country will dissent. They will face a decision. Do they live in the truth or comply with the fraud? Do they choose exit, voice or loyalty? So will begin a long war of the oligarchs and the new *nomenklatura* against the people to enforce the restoration of this *ancien regime*. Soft left totalitarianism will become brutal in America. There will be organised opposition, but it will face an overwhelming full-court press in the newly revealed post-democratic society.

The second scenario is that, against the odds, Trump prevails. A court or state legislature may overturn an illegally conducted election. Or, after an inconclusive Electoral College, the House of Representatives, in state counts that favour the Republicans, votes for Trump to be President in a contingent election. This is the procedure set out in the Constitution. This is exactly the scenario described by Steve Bannon and by the *79 days report* of the Claremont Institute and Texas Public Policy Institute. But for this result to be secured, there will need to be a clear strike against Biden and the Democrats that undermines their legal claim to have sought election by free and fair rules. Supporters of the ruling group would see it as assertion of republican virtue against majoritarian illusion. But that republican virtue will be opposed by the Furies of the Oligarchs. If Trump prevails, he will hold a deeply insecure position against a ruthlessly determined and well-resourced enemy. The same post-democratic full-court press will constrain the constitutional government of America.

Either way, a time of troubles is coming for America. The Time of Troubles or Smuta (Смутное время) is the period of political crisis, civil war and invasion in Russia between 1598 and 1613. The Rurik dynasty died out, with the death of Fyodor, likely intellectually disabled and incompetent. In its wake, competing claims to authority fought for fifteen years. Boris Godunov became Tsar. Pretenders claimed to be the surviving son of Ivan the Terrible, the true heir of the old dynasty. These pretenders even gained the throne. Poland and Sweden occupied almost all of European Russia. The state was almost extinguished. In the end, the Romanov dynasty rebuilt a new Holy Mother Russia, an alliance of autocracy and Orthodox faith. It did so in part through the actions of the volunteer army activated by Prince Dmitry Pozharsky and Kuzma Minin, who are commemorated outside St. Basil's Church

Political Disorder

in Red Square, Moscow.

America's fate will not be Russia's. Its time of troubles will see a different kind of war, new claims to authority, new pretenders, new heroes. But all unhappy families are unhappy after their own fashion. And so too, all disintegrating empires crumble in their own unique pattern.

Doom, disaster and decay

(In episode 5 of *The Burning Archive* podcast (May 2021), I went full-on pessimist to discuss Doom, disaster and decay. I took a quick tour of Niall Ferguson analysis of the politics of catastrophe and Francis Fukuyama's ideas on political decay, and what they tell us about the responses of governments around the world to the pandemic. And the podcast asked what can we do to hold back the decline of governing institutions?)

Welcome to *The Burning Archive*, the podcast where the past is never dead, the past is not even past and where, by thinking about the past, we try to live better in the present.

In this episode of *The Burning Archive* I am talking about doom, disaster and decay. Full on pessimism, but maybe not. And it's not just any doom, disaster or decay, but political decay and how it is discussed in Neil Ferguson's recent book, *Doom: the Politics of Catastrophe*. So the question for today's podcast is how well do our political institutions cope with huge disasters such as the coronavirus pandemic? And does the response to the pandemic or other examples of disaster suggest that our political institutions are in decay?

I want to approach this question by looking at the historian Neil Ferguson's recent book, *Doom: The Politics of Catastrophe*. This history of catastrophes and responses to disasters focuses on the coronavirus pandemic. It compares this crisis to other major pandemics and catastrophic events in history. In some ways, Neil Ferguson asks the question whether the worst disease exposed by the pandemic is not coronavirus itself, but the chronic disease and decay of our political institutions. He even points the finger a little bit, not so much at the leaders of governments, but middle level bureaucracies, specifically public health.

I am Jeff Rich. I am a writer, historian and a very minor government official. Let me add, especially for this podcast, since we are talking about political topics, that my podcast is entirely separate from my official duties and do not reflect the views of the organisations that I work for or indeed even comments on the direct experiences of working on those organisations. This podcast is quite separate from my official role. It is very much just following my curiosity about history and culture, and how they are unfolding in the real world today.

So doom, disaster and decay. This is the first of a second trilogy of three episodes of the podcast on my four themes. Briefly, to recap, especially for new listeners, those four themes are political decay, which we are talking about today, imperial rivalry, which the last three episodes of the podcast were about, social fragmentation, and cultural decay. My plan at this point is to do a trilogy on each of those four topics and see how the podcast evolves from there.

Let me just add, of course, I am quite politically neutral. None of these comments are in any way commentary on current political events, and merely reflect my personal views.

So what is the meaning of this theme of political decay? Broadly, it means that the quality of political institutions, the quality of government, if you like, seems to be getting worse. These institutions are less able to cope with challenges. Some fundamental dimensions of those institutions, and the culture that underlies them, are not as robust as they used to be. Of course, I do not want to talk about the

Political Disorder

good old days and and vague nostalgia about some previous regime or leader who had some miraculous qualities of political leadership. Everyone, all political leaders or governments are flawed, I guess. But I do believe that over the last 30 or 40 years, there has been a significant decay in political institutions in our modern liberal democratic societies. That is evident in a number of ways, which we will get to over time in the podcast. It does not mean we are not better off. In many ways, we are. Steven Pinker and Hans Rosling have shown how, for good or ill, despite a lot of gnashing of teeth, our world does seem to be getting better. We are living longer. We are better educated, or at least accumulate more years of formal education. We are wealthier, and less prone to sickness. But there is this nagging doubt about how well our democracies are performing. Now, government, of course, is a people business, and perfection is not possible. So these are all relative, qualitative judgements. But I think I am not just being a grumpy old man when I say that the performances of political institutions seem to be getting worse.

The reason I wanted to start off this theme with Neil Ferguson's book, *Doom: The Politics of Catastrophe* is because he offers a tangible comparison, which we all know something about, of the response of political institutions to catastrophic challenges. He compares how leaders responded to the 2020 pandemic to a very similar pandemic challenge in earlier times. Ferguson has written on this theme before including in *Degeneration: Why Institutions Decay*. But *Doom: The Politics of Catastrophe* only came out a week or two ago. You can read the book, obviously, but you can also catch Neil Ferguson talking about it on on multiple podcasts, including the Hoover Institution podcast, *Goodfellas,* or on some YouTube interviews. If you prefer to absorb the ideas that way, you absolutely can.

In any form, the comparison Ferguson makes is between the 1957 influenza pandemic and the 2020 coronavirus pandemic. It turns out that the 2020 coronavirus pandemic is not really a 'once in a century unprecedented event,' as some people say. It is certainly nothing like

13 Ways of Looking at a Bureaucrat

the 1918 Spanish flu pandemic, which killed somewhere between 50 and 100 million people around the world, when population was much smaller, and the world was still dealing with a world war. The 2020 pandemic is closer to the 1957 flu that affected many countries around the world. The 1957 Asian flu had similar impacts as a disease to the 2020 coronavirus pandemic, in scale of impact, prevalence of disease, rates of infection and mortality.

Yet the response to the 1957 flu was dramatically different. In 1957, in America the President was Dwight Eisenhower, who was a former general from the American Army, one of the major generals of the Second World War. He might have led the Normandy invasion of France to expel Germany from France. He subsequently became President, when America was a newly ascendant empire. In 1957 we are about a year after the Suez crisis, which led to the rapid collapse of British world influence and empire. America and the West had newly prosperous societies, but really had only just got penicillin and other now mainstream medicines. Yet its response to the pandemic appears, in Ferguson's account, to have been vastly more effective and less flummoxed than the response of many governments around the world in 2020. Apparently, in 1957, the American institutions were even able quite quickly to develop a vaccine. There were not lockdowns. There were not many of the extreme, economic reactions that led to major impacts on income and economic activity. There was not the general, social panic, best symbolised by the great toilet paper panics of 2020.

Neil Ferguson attributes at least part of this different response to the quality of government, of political institutions, of competence of government. There were difference in social attitudes and the entrepreneurial nature of the medical bureaucracy in 1957. But the largest difference, for Ferguson, between 2020 and 1957 was in the competence of government. It appears to have diminished, even while the size of government has expanded in the past six decades.

Now, there is a link here to my earlier episodes on imperial rivalry

Political Disorder

and decline. Neil Ferguson makes clear that we need to think about the nature of political, by which I mean broadly governmental, public policy decision making, when we look at responses to natural disasters or responses to public health disasters like the coronavirus pandemic. It is often the political decision making that creates the disastrous social and economic consequences of a natural event, as much as the event itself. This principle is, documented, for example, to some degree in Amartya Sen's work on famines. The consequences of famine are not really caused by the weather or poor agricultural practices. They result from decision making on prices and the distributions of food. Sen argued essentially that all famines are humanly made events. Ferguson takes a similar approach to public health disasters or other catastrophes. They are political disasters, not just in the narrow sense of decisions made by leaders of government or elected officials, but in the broader sense of poor decision making and poor functioning of the political system. This is why his book is so relevant to the theme of political decay, because political decay is not so much about leader X or Y being not as good as they used to be. or not as good as leader X or Y from another political party. It is really about the functioning of the overall institutions and culture of the political system, and if there is poor political decision making, it can have a big impact.

It also plays into the theme of imperial rivalry and imperial decline. So Ferguson writes in *Doom* that "empires are the most complex of all political units that humans have constructed, precisely because they seek to exert power over very large areas and diverse cultures. It is not surprising then to find that they exhibit many of the characteristics of other complex adaptive systems, including the tendency for apparent stability to give way quite suddenly to disorder." Neil Ferguson gives two examples of imperial decline, the Western Roman Empire (roughly 300-400 AD) and the Ming Dynasty in China, (about 1600 AD). Both empires transitioned from equipoise, or stable equilibrium, to anarchy in little more than a decade, and with devastating consequences. So, Ferguson summarizes, of "all the forms catastrophe can take, the death agony of an empire may be the most difficult to fathom, precisely because it is the most complex." This thought leads to the question, is the coronavirus pandemic part of the death agony of the American empire?

So political decay matters a lot to us. If empires collapse, no one within that empire has a great time for a while. Death agonies are not exciting things to observe or to participate in. If the systems by which our human social problems are governed become unstable, there can be devastating and sudden consequences. We should be worried that there are signs of political decay everywhere.

What is my overall hypothesis or definition on political decay? By political decay, I mean a weakening in the quality, competence, and capability of both governing institutions and political actors. My hypothesis is that over the last 50 years, approximately from the 1970's, there has been a decline in the capability of and quality of our political institutions. Paradoxically, this decline has happened at the same time as growing professionalisation of those political institutions. We have more and more political marketing professionals, spin doctors, and career political advisers, but less and less high quality government. One example, detached from my immediate circumstances working in one of the Australian governments, is the 2020 American election. In 1957, America faced a mild influenza pandemic led by a person who had led that country through World War II, who had conducted military campaigns, and who had decades of experience dealing with difficult situations. In 2020, what do we have? We see a choice between Donald Trump and Joe Biden. We see the American political system hyper-activated in terms of its news media coverage, and yet barely able to organise a coherent, credible election count. I understand there are 12,000 or 1,200, I cannot immediately recall, organisations involved in the administration of a United States election. And how well do these organisations deploy the people involved? The personnel, skills and thought these myriad, ill-coordinated organisations can bring to bear to all the problems and dilemmas they face are just less and less capable. There are many other examples, but my hypothesis is that the capabilities of many institutions are incrementally weakened. The parliaments become a little bit less focused on deliberative assembly and open, meaningful debate. The political spin doctors become more and more cynical about spreading messages. The news media gets less and less focused on independent reporting, and more and more focused on presenting their celebrity journalists in the media. The bureaucracy becomes less and less merit-based, and less and less competent to do its job. The associated professions of politics, the lobby groups and advocacy organisations, become more and more focused on their issue alone, and less and less focused on a general public interest. All of thisse wearing down of competence and capability, of culture and institutions contributes to a disordered network of political institutions. That chaotic network is vulnerable to the sudden transition from equipoise to anarchy that Neil Ferguson talks about. All these little deficits, or little examples of decay and under-performance, add up to a much bigger, unmanageable problem.

Now, I am not just making up this idea of political decay. I have drawn the idea from the work of Francis Fukuyama, and in particular, from his two volume, *Political Order and Political Decay*, which is a global history of political institutions. He sets this history against an anthropological theory of the key behaviours in politics, and key conditions on the functioning of politics in human society. It describes the early Chinese development of bureaucracy, and many eras. Its second volume is largely related to the 19th and 20th century worlds. Now, Francis Fukuyama is, to some degree, a very famous American intellectual, who is most famous for the frequently misunderstood hypothesis that the end of the Cold War in 1989 marked the end of history. He wrote a book, originally an essay, called *The End of History and the Last Man*. It is frequently misunderstood as hypothesising that history had come to an end with liberal democracy. To some degree, he did suggest that, but more subtly he argued that institutions of contemporary liberal democracy best satisfy the human drive for universal recognition. So the end of history did not mean ambition,

13 Ways of Looking at a Bureaucrat

fame and glory would not still drive people in society and politics. As a bit of a historical curiosity, back in 1989, Fukuyama actually referred to none other than Donald Trump. In an extraordinary piece of prophecy, perhaps, he referred to Donald Trump. Here, in the book, he says,

> For are there not reservoirs of idealism that cannot be exhausted, indeed, that are not even touched, if one becomes a developer like Donald Trump, or a mountain climber like Reinhold Meissner, or a politician like George Bush? Difficult as it is in many ways to be these individuals, and for all the recognition they receive, their lives are not the most difficult, and the causes they serve are not the most serious or the most just. And as long as they are not, the horizon of human possibilities that they define will not be ultimately satisfying for the most thymotic natures.[100]

Now, thymotic natures referred to the drive for honour and pride. Fukuyama speculated a little bit further on from the cited passage that there will there be people who, like Donald Trump, will climb to the top of political institutions to demonstrate their honour and prestige to the world. That is an aside, I guess, but a curious aside.

Now, Francis Fukuyama has endured a couple of decades of mockery for his idea of the end of history. *Political Order and Political Decay* responds, to some degree, to that mockery, and recants at least some youthful follies. It is a less optimistic portrait of the character of liberal democratic institutions. In particular, he has focused a lot in recent years on the idea of political decay, especially with ongoing problems in the American political system. Here is a short clip of Fukuyama.

> The really hard part is getting to actually a modern state that can deliver services, provide security, and is regarded as legitimate. And that's really the overweening failure, I think, in both of those places in the area where we didn't really understand how to do things. I'll get to the case of

---

[100] Fukuyama, *End of History*, p. 328.

developed democracies because I think that there's also a big problem there, beginning with my own country, the United States. So there's no question that we've got a state and rule of law and democratic accountability, but I would say that we are subject to something I've described as political decay. Because an impersonal government that is well run and effective is a vulnerable thing because elites in the country are constantly trying to recapture it and re-patrimonialize it. And furthermore, I think countries are subject to institutional rigidity, that we create a set of institutions for a certain set of circumstances, and then when the circumstances change, we don't adapt mentally, we don't rebuild the institutions, and as a result we're stuck with things that are quite ineffective. And I think that's really what's happened in the United States.[101]

So Fukuyama presents this more dynamic picture of history, where political institutions develop, but there are these other forces that work against the broader aspirations of the system. Indeed, political decay comes from the inability of institutions to adapt to changing circumstances, specifically the rise of new social groups and their political demands. For example, the European and aristocratic elite at the time of World War I was not really capable of accommodating properly the demands of the more prosperous working class and other social groups that are emerging at the start of the 20th century. But yet, they maintained their grand illusions about their society. Underneath it all, decay was happening, and then the disaster of World War I happened, in which many aristocratic officers made disastrous, inept decisions, with devastating consequences for people.

When we talk about institutions, they can be understood as organisations, but also as stable, recurring patterns of behaviour. So there are institutions of the justice system, the institutions of law and order, and some people even describe the family as an institution. The parliament as an assembly and the conventions of parliament are both examples of institutions. Fukuyama argues that, "we [humans] are

---

[101] Fukuyama, via @RSAorg YouTube.

instinctively conformist and look around at our fellows for guidelines to our own behaviour." So institutions are made and reinforced by our desire to be like other people, to follow the herd, let's say, or to belong to the group or tribe. When in Rome, be like the Romans. This marriage of affirming instinct with adaptive institutions is a good thing because it makes for successful social cooperation. When in Rome, do as the Romans; and then you will get all the benefits of what the Romans do.

Successful social cooperation is essentially what the task of government is. Cooperation emerges from the virtuous cycle between an adaptive institution that looks around at its environment and changes appropriately in response. The virtuous cycle reinforces people's feelings when they do as other people. It makes following directions into a positive, constructive thing for those who both give and receive otherwise unwelcome orders. Social cooperation is essential to respond to the challenges of government, whether to manage a pandemic or a war or any other major challenge that political institutions might face. When the positive reinforcement does not work well, social cooperation tends to break down. Responses to challenges fail, and that is the risk of political decay.

Now, Fukuyama also argued that three main sources cause political decay. First, there is a misfit of mental models. The governing ideas do not align or are too far removed from reality. To return to the example of the aristocratic European elites of World War One, there is a great film by the French director Jean Renoir called *La Grande Illusion*, which is almost like the perfect symbol of this misfit of mental models. The film portrays the social and mental worlds of the aristocratic French or German officers of World War One, and how they tried to maintain the mental models of the 19th century aristocracy amongst the slaughterhouse trenches of World War One. There was this clash of mental models between the kind of societies they thought they were governing, and the actual people they faced in the daily realities of governing. On this source of decay, misfit of mental models, we can probably say there is a bit of that going on, since the world becomes more perplexing to us. It is not behaving in the way we have grown accustomed to expect. The second cause of political decay is the behaviour of elites and insiders, and specifically the phenomenon of insider capture. Elites find their way to the top of political institutions. They may have other interests involved, and then they slowly turn those political institutions to serve those other interests. They seek to prosper as leaders of their institutions and to entrench their advantages, but slowly forget or neglect the mission or purpose of the institution, as it was initially conceived, separate from their interests and their command. Fukuyama describes the third driver of political decay as 're-patrimonialisation'. He means that political institutions move away from objective, liberal democratic principles of justice, and turn more to do favours for the people who lead the institution. Those favours may be deeply corrupt, like money for family and mates, or softly corrupt, like advantages for the people who support the leaders. Soft corruption could be called clientelistic, and describes the simple reciprocity of 'you scratch my back and I'll scratch yours'. Government provides some money to this interest group or that service or that good cause, and the people of the group, the service, the cause and all their followers will support or vote for the government in turn.

All three factors of political decay - misfit of mental models, insider capture and re-patrimonialisation – are observable in polities today. We can all see examples, without labouring the point. Fukuyama intentionally casts them as broad sociological patterns of behaviour that cross time and cross cultures. Liberal democracy is only a fairly incomplete curb on any of those drivers, and hence Fukuyama has a more pessimistic view as an older man of the prospects for the end of history. However, Fukuyama also makes the point that discussions of political decay can be cast as moral judgments, just as with 'civilizational decline', to hearken back to the earlier episodes on grand narratives of decline and fall. Fukuyama is trying to describe political decay using language from political science or sociology. He is identifying a social force that is driven by fundamental social behaviour, which clashes against the institutions that people have built up to defend against those patterns of behaviour. There are two particular processes that Fukuyama focuses on here. One is called kinship affiliation and one is called reciprocal altruism.

Kinship affiliation is, well, looking after one's family, or more broadly understood, looking after one's mates, looking after people like us, looking after people from our party, our supporters, or however it goes. It is not something to be ashamed of, necessarily. It is just a very natural thing. One looks after one's children, and one wants the best for them. But it is a kind of human instinct, let's say, that needs to be controlled within political institutions because, taken to its natural extension, you get family dynasties, monarchies, clans and that sort of thing. We know that even modern political institutions have family dynasties, and leaders can show soft-heartedness perhaps towards political children. Let us just think about Joe Biden and Hunter Biden, for example. So it is a very strong tendency, that many political institutions have to put guardrails around to protect against political decay. If there is a strong feeling that the institution is run by the one family or run by the one group or run by a single set of ideas, and no one from outside of those circles can influence society, then that drives discontent. It drives conflict, and undermines legitimacy.

The second process is reciprocal altruism, summarised as 'you scratch my back, I scratch yours'. You do this for me, I do this for you. In anthropological terms, it is gift exchange, and is at the heart of human culture. There are many simple examples. I make dinner for you, and we will be friends. You shout me a drink this time, and I'll shout you a drink next time. Reciprocal altruism is just the thing that we do. We seek symmetry in our exchanges with other people, and we do not want to be used. We want to be part of things, and exchanging favours helps us belong. But then, if you transplant that instinctive social behaviour into a political institution, or complex network of institutions like a liberal democracy, you have a problem. You can not just go around saying, 'Oh well, because he recommended people vote for me, let's give him this grant of money.' Or you can not just say, 'That guy helped me out early in my career, and therefore I am going to help him out now regardless of the merits of other candidates for the job.' Reciprocal altruism is this normal human behaviour, and drives political behaviour, to some degree, because politics is a people business. Politics or government is about making people feel that they are involved in and connected with important members of the group. But within large, complex, formal, legally accountable, openly democratic, and heavily scrutinised political institutions, there need to be guardrails around this social behaviour. These curbs on social drives prevent reciprocal altruism from undermining fairness, efficiency, and the missions of organisations, as distinct from the missions of the people within the organisation.

With these interacting processes, Fukuyama presents a complex picture of political decay. He describes an ecosystem where we human drives of social behaviour (kinship affiliation, reciprocal altruism) are placed within the most complex forms of social cooperation that humans have devised, that is, governments and their political institutions. Those drives are a threat to those institutions, and yet they also sustain them. The high arts of social cooperation cannot work without those drives. On the other hand, those institutions are undermined unless there are strong sets of institutions and cultures that actually guide those social drives in the correct way.

Now all of that can sound a bit abstract and complicated, but let me try to bring it back now to Neil Ferguson and *Doom*. In *Doom*, Neil Ferguson points out an awkward fact about the responses of different countries to the coronavirus pandemic. Taiwan and South Korea did exceptionally well with a strategy of contact tracing, isolation, empowering digital monitoring of people, and managing borders very effectively. They are also relatively small, easily governed, effectively island states. South Korea is not an island, but it is at the bottom of a peninsula below the hermit empire in North Korea. Those countries have done remarkably well compared to the United States and

England, or at least until now. They have had on average less than 25 new confirmed cases per day, since the start of the outbreak. As I speak, there has been a rapid climb to over 300 cases on the 22nd of May. So that's quite sad. And perhaps that will shoot down Neil Ferguson's argument. The different performance on coronavirus in different countries might turn out to be caused by sheer, physical facts and biology, rather than quality of government. But for this discussion, the main point is that the United States and the United Kingdom have not done too well. So Ferguson asks,

> who was to blame for the fact that the two biggest English speaking countries handled the first wave of COVID-19 so much worse than their Asian and European peers? For most journalists, the answer was blindingly obvious. The two populist leaders, Boris Johnson and Donald Trump, neither can be said to have handled the crisis ably, to put it mildly. But to turn the story of COVID-19 into a morality play, the populists' nemesis is to miss the more profound systemic and societal failure that occurred in a way that future historians will surely see as facile.[102]

As Ferguson goes on to say, it was not the Prime Minister who worked out how to respond to a deadly pandemic. Certainly some political leadership is needed to get through a crisis, but the response to a pandemic is very much reliant on the quality of the public health bureaucracy: the chief medical officer, the leading academic experts, the key modellers, the experts on the various committees, the officials who organise all manner of things, such as tests, regulations, funding for services, vaccine approvals, and information campaigns. In Ferguson's story, first these experts and officials dithered; then they panicked; and then, in their panic, they imposed blunt, overreactive responses that were not terribly effective, were perhaps too much, too late, and were the cause of dramatic, unwanted impacts.

Now we could have a whole extra podcast around the coronavirus, but the real relevance for here, is that the quality of those governing

---

[102] Ferguson, *Doom*.

institutions, such as the public health bureaucracy, was found wanting at this crucial time. It was their moment in the sun, and they blew it. At least, in many countries and in the international organisations, the outcomes of their social coordination were poor. They did many things well, but other things poorly. Some of those poorly done things point to systemic failures, to use Ferguson's word, or to political decay, to use my word.

It is no small thing to have problems of systemic failure, or political decay, in the public health bureaucracy. Health is not a minor add-on to government. It is totally at the core of what governments have done for centuries. Public health has been at the heart of government longer than most Western public health practitioners generally acknowledge. Public health specialists tends to trace their own history, the origin story of public health, back to John Snow in 19th century London. Snow identified the source of a cholera outbreak, an infected tap, by analysis of some good statistics. But public health has been an aspect of governing institutions long before this orthodox public health approach. It has long been at the heart of organising collective responses to social challenges. So it is quite troubling that our political health institutions, in their interaction with public health, have been sorely tested, if not totally failed. The pandemic and *Doom* exposed real weaknesses in how they go about things. I do not want particularly to focus alone on public health, because of speech code restrictions. But the problems of systemic failure, or political decay, are apparent in other areas. For example, in Australia, the Banking Royal Commission highlighted systemic weaknesses of the regulators in government, and, by extension, the political direction of those regulatory institutions, such as the Australian Securities and Investments Commission. They failed to control and monitor the banks adequately, and failed to do the simpler job of enforcing the law.

So political decay has real world consequences. There are signs of it everywhere, and it will be a constant theme of this podcast. Now really what I've tried to do today is just introduce the idea of political decay and to wrap it up in a little bit of a topical story related to Neil Ferguson's book about *Doom*. Political decay, parliamentary institutions, democracy, and the quality of government are quite abstract concepts that can be really hard to put your finger on. But there are serious consequences if we let those institutions weaken to the extent that they cannot do the demanding job of social coordination that we ask them to do in a crisis.

Over the next two episodes in this little trilogy, I am going to focus on two bulwarks against political decay. They are good institutions, strong institutions, and the other bulwark against decay is, if you like, culture or let's call it the ordinary virtues. So institutions describe more formal arrangements. They are often legal, well-established arrangements that structure what we do in our societies, the rules of a bureaucracy, and how bureaucracy or other political organisations form themselves as coherent actors in society. The other bulwark is culture. Culture can be described as what is in the hearts and minds of the people in those institutions. What ideas and symbols are used by the leaders, and by the ordinary, middle and lower officials, lowly under-castellan officials such as myself? How do those ideas and symbols shape how all those officials can practice the ordinary virtues of governing well?

So that is what the next two episodes on political decay will cover. And that is the end of the podcast number five, *Doom, Disaster and Decay*. I hope you have enjoyed it, and I hope it has not been too abstract. I should just reiterate again, that I am talking about my own personal views. I am not making any commentary on any particular government or anything like that. So no controversy there. And until next week, that's all from me, Jeff Rich. And thanks for listening to The Burning Archive, the podcast where the past isn't dead. The past is not even past. And by thinking about the past, we learn how to act better in the present.

Political Disorder

13 Ways of Looking at a Bureaucrat

Chapter Ten   On the institutions of government

On the institutions of government

On metaphors and machinery of government

The metaphors we use about the world define the way we see the world. Sometimes the metaphors are all we really know of the world. How else can you describe your love but as a red, red rose, or as a summer's day? Metaphors define how bureaucrats, citizens and politicians perceive and act on government. Perhaps government itself is figurative language. Is there any essence at all to this strange being that unfolds, iterates and flowers like a Julia set? Is there any real way to turn this verb, 'to govern', into a noun? But there are many common metaphors of government. The Leviathan. The criminal gang. The country club. The personification into a tyrant or a fool. A network. A body, with its head, its heart, its limbs and its stomach. More recently metaphors have proliferated: cathedral, pyramid, matrix, and maze. But one of the oldest metaphors of government is the machine.

Among bureaucrats the metaphor of government as a machine or as machinery has a strange mesmeric power among those who claim a Schmittian power of decision. The metaphor of machinery is loved by consultants, designers and political leaders who seek to engineer the political soul. They believe they have discovered the secret manual to drive this machinery to produce whatever outcome they dream on. To make decisions on the machinery of government is perceived by the elites to be their ultimate power.

Within government the term, 'machinery of government', refers to the occasional decisions of political leaders to restructure, relabel, rename, realign, reform, reestablish, or even retrench government organisations. It can include decisions on: the assignment of Ministerial responsibilities, the shape, size, number and mission of Government Departments; the functioning of that humble cog, the committee, in turning the many wheels of government processes; the allocation of personnel to political and bureaucratic leadership roles;

the balance of legislative, regulatory and executive heads of power; the symbolic priority of issues, as reflected in titles for Ministers and names for organisations; and even sometimes that most sought-after secret of the government maze, the strategic purpose of the government itself.

Machinery of government decisions are best made rarely, and are usually tightly held by the most trusted, senior decision-makers of the government. They are, in general, the prerogative of the political leader, in the case of Victoria where I worked, the Premier, as advised by the head of the Department of Premier and Cabinet. They should reflect long-term perspectives and stable priorities. As a former head of the Public Service Board once said to me, these decisions are extraordinarily expensive to implement, and should be carefully considered. His caution reflected experience with the overuse of machinery of government decisions, especially in Victoria in the 1980s, when it became a kind of furtive fiddling. More often than not, these days, major decisions on machinery of government are driven by crisis, political messaging, and the viral effects of letting too many leaders, advisers and bureaucrats into the circle of prestige that decides these matters.

Machinery of government decisions express the ultimate arbitrary power of decision. Today, this organisation exists. Tomorrow, it will not. Today, you work for this purpose. Tomorrow, I order you to serve that purpose. This attribute of the machinery of government is, in fact, a metaphor, and perhaps a cloudy metaphor. The decision to change the machinery of government, one velvet morning, does not change much at all about a government organisation. It does not change most of the people, the habits, the customs, the stories, the culture, the constraints, the laws, the resources, the client relationships, the community connections, and the entrenched difficulties. But it gives leaders an announcement, and a reassuring cloak of decisiveness. It also gives the bureaucrats who advise on these decisive announcements a certain prestige, as if they have drunk from the

On the institutions of government

magic spring of power itself.

Consequently, when governments drift and decay, as they always do, machinery of government decisions become more common, and the circle who claim to advise on them expands. This deflation of the the machinery of government finds linguistic expression. In the last decade of my career in the public service, I observed the increased, widespread use of a new term for machinery of government decisions. Machinery of government was dismantled into its acronym, M-O-G. When governments made decisions on administrative arrangements or organisational boundaries, they no longer reorganised the machinery of government. They 'mogged it'. In the first twenty years of my career, I never heard this term, even though I wrote the advice to Premiers on the structure and machinery of government. In the latter years of my career, I found the term ubiquitous. Minor officials faced with some recurrent problem, driven in part by their own failures, such as juvenile justice institutions, would claim that the obvious solution to their dilemmas was to tell the government to 'mog it.' It was never clear to me whether these minor officials were aware of the meaning of 'mog it' within the game, *World of Warcraft*, that I played at night for consolation. But they appeared to me to be engaged in the same magical game of dress-ups.

I was irritated by this use of the term 'mog'. It appeared to me as casual tough guy talk by officials who had illusions of omnipotence, or 'delusions of adequacy' as a football commentator used to say. Looking back today after my retirement, I think this talk was driven by social mimesis and the desire to be in the prestigious circle of sovereign decision-makers. It also reflected a strain of Utopian thought among managers that imagined institutions and cultures to be plastic, reshaped every season by the latest fashionable ideas of progress. I recoiled from this usage out of a desire for recognition out of my own experience and expertise. I believed I had had the rare privilege of authoring advice on the structure of government, not once but twice, under governments with different political beliefs. These courtiers, consultants and vulgar hacks knew nothing, asked me nothing, and stamped all over the arcane knowledge that I had preciously kept secret. I did not want to admit that I had fallen under a spell. I only freed myself from these illusions, this mirage of prestige, during my crisis of faith in my life as a bureaucrat from 2015. Then I lost belief that the machinery of government was real or even the supreme bureaucratic fiction. I came to see it one of the new symbolic rituals of power.

During my career, I advised on actual machinery of government decisions by government and bureaucratic leaders three times. In 1994 and 1995, I advised the Liberal Government (Premier Kennett) on the department structures that would be implemented after the 1996 election. In 2002, I advised the Labor Government (Premier Bracks) on the reorganisation of departments and Ministerial portfolios. I no longer have access to any of the briefings to the Premiers that I wrote for those machinery of government decisions. I recall some of the decisions, and the arguments. I recall some of the conversations, but my memories are too fragmentary at this point to serve as an interesting memoir. I recall also that, as with any piece of advice in government, the ideas, concepts and proposals emerged from shared discussion, promptings and ideation. It did not all come from my own head, and was a workable compromise generated by the principal players, the heads of the Department and a handful of key bureaucratic and political leaders. But the advice I provided in 2002 had many more of my own ideas, as you would expect with maturation and experience.

The third occasion on which I advised on machinery of government was, however, quite different. On both previous occasions, I provided my advice as an employee of the Department of Premier and Cabinet. In 2014, amid my great disappointment and disillusionment with the way of governing in Victoria, I offered advice, as a private citizen, to the then former Premier, Mr Bracks. In 2014 Mr Bracks secretly headed a small 'Transition to Government' team that advised the then Opposition Leader, Mr Andrews, on preparations to form government

On the institutions of government

after the November 2014 election.

But when I initiated contact with Mr Bracks I did not know that. I remembered him as the Premier I had advised directly in 2002. I even had briefly worked in his private office in 2002, although I had a dismal time on an impossible mission on behalf of the then Secretary of the Department, Mr Terry Moran. Still, Mr Bracks had sent me a short thank you note that redeemed some of the troubles. I also had spoken to Mr Bracks when he was himself a public servant, if a political appointment in the early 1990s, before the fall of the Kirner Government. I recalled his victory speech in 1999, which he declared a victory for decency in Victoria. It was decency, democracy and good government that I wanted to restore. I still believed then that I had some power to restore these virtues, given my unique experience. I had not yet given up hope of being removed from the blacklist, real or imagined, that excluded me from the ruling group of courtiers and consultocrats who dominated the public service.

So I made a desperate plea to Steve Bracks, based on conflicting emotions. It was a gamble with my career, driven by an urge to have my reflections on the republic in distress recognised by someone who really mattered. It was not a planned move. I spoke with no-one about it, and had no real expectation of success. But in late 2013 or early 2014 I wrote to Mr Bracks, whose email I got from the internet, with a short memo I titled, 'Ideas for Victorian Labor – Transition to Government Plan'.

*

'Ideas for Victorian Labor – Transition to Government Plan'.

Victorian Labor is now on the brink of a great political opportunity. The Government is drifting, if not panicking. People say, "This is how the world ends, not with a bang but a whimper." But this Government has been all whimper, from beginning to end. I have no insider political intelligence and only see the public polls and the tone of the public discussion of politics. But Labor's recent transport policy is a bold, successful step. It may well be a bridge to Government. Victorian Labor's election to government now seems likely, more likely than Baillieu's election in 2010. A fresh opportunity of power is within its grasp.

But to make the most of this opportunity the Opposition needs to prepare and then to deliver a better way of governing. Good policies, good politics, good campaigning, good candidates and a good election are not enough. The Opposition needs to begin to establish its authority as a good government. It can begin to do this now, as it has with its transport plan. This is especially important after the federal fiasco in recent years.

I do not pretend to help with the political tasks of getting elected, nor with party politics, but I believe I can help you govern well. I assume Mr Andrews has begun to plan for this, and would have his own clear ideas. I think I have unique qualities that can help develop those ideas, with attention to the essential relationship between a new Government and the public service.

Three observations:

1. *The senior public service is part of the problem.* The drift of the current Victorian Government is not only the fault of the Liberal-National parties and their leaders. It is in part the fault of the bureaucracy, and especially the bad judgment, misdirection and wheel-spinning by the Departments of Premier and Cabinet and Treasury and Finance. Evidence? - the Vertigan Review, the "Better Services Implementation Taskforce" and the empty-headed Cabinet processes of the Government. These two Departments are, in my judgment, the two worst performing departments in Victoria. But they are not alone. There are far too many senior executives in the Government who court advisers and consultants, and do not serve the public. They are lost in a bubble of consultants, advisers, and executive status symbols, and have lost touch with ordinary life. You need to be prepared for your

On the institutions of government

Government - your Cabinet, not its political advisers - to redefine their goals from day one of its term, and to take action early to redirect the senior bureaucracy and to mobilise the institutions below them.

2. *Modern Labor's style of Government is part of the problem.* The implications for a new Victorian Labor Government of the dismal failures of the Rudd/Gillard Governments need to be faced honestly. Putting aside debates about legacies, their way of governing was a failure. Within a couple of years, a government with a supreme mandate was reduced to a tragi-comic soap opera that had no authority. This was a failure of personnel, institutions, culture and processes, not only leaders and messaging. You need to be prepared to protect a new government from recruiting too many of the failed advisers, ideas and methods of the Rudd/Gillard era, or indeed merely restoring a revanchist Bracks/Brumby Government. This is especially so since Victoria may be the only Labor Government honey pot in the country.

3. *Mr Andrews can do better.* Victoria is not alone in suffering from ineffective governance. The problem has been simply and compellingly put in a recent book by Stein Ringen, *Nation of Devils: democratic leadership and the problem of obedience*. It diagnoses the widespread loss of confidence in the very idea of governments. That loss of confidence cannot be restored by nagging the public on productivity or toadying up to business, or being bedazzled by the latest nonsense from consultancy firms, stocked with ex-public servants who no longer serve the public. It requires a redirection of government attention to its core purposes - discerning the public good and mobilising all social groups to deliver it. I sense the same intention in Daniel Andrews' words on what he wants to accomplish in government. I welcome his belief that "politics could be a force for change and that governments could make real change for the better." Ringen's book provides sensible and practical advice on how to do it. The shadow Cabinet can prepare by reading this book, and applying its lessons. If a whole book seems too much, just read the final chapter

13 Ways of Looking at a Bureaucrat

"Good Government."

I have now worked in Victorian Government under Premiers Cain, Kirner, Kennett, Bracks, Brumby, Baillieu and Napthine. It breaks my heart to see the decay of these institutions to which I have given most of my professional life. I despair when I see all the new courtiers who fill executive officer roles, accomplish nothing, fumble most things, obfuscate tirelessly with abstract drivel, and confuse ideas with a powerpoint slide.

For most of my career I have worked part-time to look after my family. Now, the life I have led has left me no patrons among our senior public servants. I am not an insider in Labor's world either, and have no wish to be partisan or to cultivate insider networks or to earn favour within party circles. But nor do I wish to see my hopes for better government die on the vine. Labor also needs to step away from party autarky, and return to traditions John Cain practised of employing leaders from other walks of life, not just political operatives.

So I have taken a risk, and approached you directly with this proposal. I would like the next ten to fifteen years - likely the last years of my career in the public service - to be a period of restoring public faith in what good government can accomplish. They could be years of a very successful Andrews Labor Government. A successful Andrews Government could preserve and advance the idea of good government itself. It could be the nursery of a different kind of national government.

There is inspiration surely in what was achieved in the first seven years of the Cain Government. Cabinet process. Bringing public servants and statutory authorities under proper political democratic control. Plain English legislation with clearly stated objectives. Consistent annual reporting rules. Major social policy reforms including fundamental changes in child welfare, housing, schooling, disability and health. Extensive law reform. Southbank. The TAC. Workcover. VicHealth. Nieuwenhuysen's review of licensing laws. And

On the institutions of government

more. Mistakes were made too, but there was much, much more good.

Today, Victorian Government has grown tired, overweight and lost again, like the Victorian Government that Cain took over. This is not just a matter of which political party is in charge. It is the end of a cycle of a way of governing. The slow death of this way of governing creates an opportunity to lead public life back to its true spirit.

***

To my astonishment, I received a reply. I met with Mr Bracks during which I suppose he screened me in some way. He asked me about my rank, and I felt nervous, a little ashamed at my blacklisting within the bureaucracy, and the discrepancy between this act of recognition by the decent Mr Bracks and the far from civil servants of power within the bureaucracy today. He said he would ask some people about me, but there may be a way I might be able to contribute. A month or two later I was invited to a second meeting with Mr Bracks and the other members of the 'Transition to Government' team. This team comprised Mr John Lenders, Mr Mark Madden, and Rod Glover. Mr Lenders would subsequently be connected with the 'Red Shirts' scandal in Victoria, that was subject of a number of integrity investigations. After this meeting, which I attended on a day of leave, with no phone on my person, I sensed already that I had been drawn into another mirage in the maze of power. I would not be let this close again to the inner circle of power. Mark Madden, a long-term career Ministerial adviser, was tasked with being my handler. Madden and I met one more time about the task that I was assigned, to write a paper on the structure of government.

I wrote this paper on weekends and evenings. It reflected the reading I had done on the problems of political disorder, and the organisation of government. It reflected my rage at the treason of the clerks, that I saw in the decay of the bureaucracy. I sometimes expressed my resentment at my mistreatment and exclusion from opportunities to realise my abilities within the bureaucracy. I submitted the paper that had grown to approximately 20 pages in July 2014, and waited for feedback.

This was my last throw. I received a brief email from Mark Madden that said the paper was helpful and interesting, and some proposals would be fed into the process. Other proposals would be ignored for 'constitutional' or political reasons. For the next four months, until the election in November 2014, I was on tenterhooks. I was afraid I would be caught out and my actions treated as illegal, even though I was careful to keep boundaries around my very minor, unrelated current public service role. I also hoped, or imagined, that I might be called upon in case the Opposition won the election. I followed up with Mark Madden a couple of times, and each time felt more distance. Still I hopefully reminded him of my contact details ahead of the election date, vaguely thinking I might at last benefit from, rather than be excluded from, political patronage.

The election came, and the Labor Party won. There was, however, no call for me. Snippets of news broke out about Mr Bracks' secret transition team, but I kept the secret. Still no call. Then, news of a dramatic change in the structure of government was announced. It did not reflect my paper or principles. A new Secretary of the Department of Premier and Cabinet was brought in, as well as loyal deputies. Still no call. Madden stopped responding to my messages. I felt betrayed and deceived. At the moment when I felt I had almost found the monster at the centre of the labyrinth, the floor collapsed underneath me. My world of dreams about bureaucracy and the virtuous use of power also collapsed. I fell into another maze, the maze of the psyche. But, at least, this lower maze of the underworld had a way out.

The rest of the story is this book. But let me preserve here at least some fragments from the text that I wrote in 2014 when I still believed that an ordinary bureaucrat, with his heart in the right place, could still change the course of his country. This secret private paper that may offer perspective into the life of a bureaucrat.

On the institutions of government

Structure of government paper

(The text that follows is most of the paper on the 'Structure of Government' that I submitted to Mr Steve Bracks, via Mr Mark Madden in July 2014. It was done as a voluntary initiative with no reward, no recognition, no contract and no conflict with my employment, as described in 'Metaphors and Machinery of Government'. It betrays no confidences. None were given to me.)

Overview - approach of this paper

Three papers are being prepared on transition planning: policy and programs, logistics, and this paper on structure of government. The paper sets out proposals to make significant reforms to Victorian government institutions and culture, and a model for Ministers, public servants and advisers to deliver results for people.

The transition plan should not preempt the decision-making that is best done in government, nor make the task of governing more difficult. The transition planning should discuss how an Andrews Government will govern; the role and initial key decisions on Cabinet, machinery of government and advisers, and a game plan for winning over the public service and key external leaders to this approach.

The approach to these issues needs to be worked through in a series of discussions, and owned by the prospective Premier and Shadow Cabinet. This paper outlines proposals as a starting point to frame that discussion. The paper does not aim to put fully developed structure of government proposals. Machinery of government changes can be costly, are often ineffectual, and ought to be tested by expert advice and political judgement. Organising government is complex, and some organisational changes do not need to be rushed.

This paper then presents initial, rather than final, proposals, with the expectation of significant modification. In particular, this paper anticipates that some decisions ought not be made finally until after a prospective Government is formed, and discussions held with the most senior Ministers and public servants who will implement changes.

Background research has been kept to a minimum and can be expanded in discussion. The ideas in the paper are drawn from the experience of the team, international research on transitions to government and machinery of government published by the UK Institute of Government, and the advice on how governments can establish authority and get things done set out in Stein Ringen's *A nation of devils: democratic leadership and the problem of obedience* (2013).

2. Problem or Situation

In brief, the quality of government and democracy has deteriorated, reflecting the wearing out of a model for governing born in the 1980s. This deterioration underlies poor performance of governments of both sides of politics in recent years. Structure of government changes need to strengthen public trust that governments work well. They need to put people first.

Governments are failing because a way of governing, which worked well from the early 80s, has degenerated into bad habits, poor ideas, weak institutions, and democratic disaffection.

Enduring results for people and political success will only come from adapting and inventing ways of governing that suit the times, serve well-defined public purposes, and redirect elites.

Governing well is the prime skill of enduring political leadership. However political leaders come to power, their fortunes rest on how well they institutionalise good government.

Governments have a 6-12 months window to institutionalise a successful way of governing. If they fail to do that well, their political fortunes sink. Both Rudd/Gillard and Baillieu/Napthine failed to do so.

On the institutions of government

The jury is still out on the Abbott Government. They aspired to do so, but appear to have become mesmerised by svengalis of the right. In recent Victorian history, Cain, Kennett and Bracks have succeeded.

There are some set ways of doing things in government, but many of these methods can be changed or given a new inflection. They also can decay over time. Modern Labor's way of government was born in the late 1970s and early 1980s with Wran, Cain and Hawke. But the model and the talent pool to staff the model has decayed, and has infected other institutions of government. The ways of doing things have drifted, and public institutions have lost their way.

Clarity of purpose and persuasive normative leadership can restore a better way of governing. In Ringen's terms this means discerning the public good and mobilising institutions. The election of an Andrews Government is an opportunity to restore confidence that politics and government can make real change for the better for most of the public.

The task of transition to government is to be ready to mobilise and to reshape the institutions of government to deliver clear political objectives. This requires a clear discernment of the public good and intuitions of realistic opportunities for change. It also requires establishing a culture of governing well. This culture should be shared among the Ministry, the parliament, the bureaucracy, ministerial staff, and key external advisers to government. Not all things can be planned for, but the game plan can help adapt to alternative situations as they arise.

A very substantial remobilisation of public interest institutions is necessary. This will require something of a cultural revolution in the leadership of the bureaucracy, but not a night of the long knives. From day one it should be clear this is not a business as usual government, nor one lost in the past or the polls. The idea is not to map out all changes to government institutions, but a strategy to mobilise the good people within them towards different ends and different values.

To accomplish this task will require some clear principles to guide how the Government (understood as the members of the Ministry) will govern, changes to the structure of government to mobilise these institutions towards a small number of top priorities, and skilful choreography of the transition process to quickly stamp the authority of the Government on public service and other elites.

3. Principles

This section sets out some basic behavioural rules that can provide some key principles - a common culture or brand essence - to guide the actions of all key players in a new government.

Australian Governments are failing because their models of governing have let people down. Their decisions, manner and words lost people's trust. Rudd, Gillard, Baillieu, Napthine, Abbott, and perhaps Brumby illustrate this. Blair and Obama are international failures. They have become victims of their own games of manipulating the punters.

In their own time and ways, Hawke, Cain, Kennett and Bracks were models of success. International examples such as Havel, Mandela, or Deng Xiaoping, show just how much change is possible if political leaders reshape the institutions of governing at their disposal. It shows it is possible to restore confidence that politics and government can make real change for the better

Ringen, *Nation of Devils* is a brilliant account of how governments - understood as the 20 or so Ministers of the Government - can do this. A new government can govern authoritatively in this way, but to do so it needs to let go of some institutional habits, and define its own.

Planning for transition to Government should consider the model of government that will mobilise, first, the Cabinet, and then others, towards well-chosen public goals. Others might describe this as brand essence - it should be captured in a simply understood phrase that can

On the institutions of government

galvanise people to act in a common spirit despite the inevitable differences of purpose, values and interests.

Putting people first may be that phrase. It describes not only an outcome but a way of acting.

It expresses essentially democratic values - giving people the society they want. While Labor values rally the party in Opposition, it is democratic values that need to be rally people to the purposes of government.

Underneath that phrase should be some simple behavioural rules that can provide some key principles - a common culture or brand essence - to guide the actions of all key players in a new government.

The shadow Cabinet may best articulate these basic principles of conduct of the Government, and then set up major processes and reviews in government to develop these core principles further. For example, the Scottish National Party Government in 2007 entered government with a clear philosophy of using a small number (20) key outcomes to drive policy changes, and a smaller Ministry, more tightly aligned with departments, and with Cabinet and Assistant Ministers. It subsequently used a major review of public institutions - the Christie Commission - to flesh out its governing philosophy.

This paper suggests a starting point for that discussion with three core guiding principles that develop the idea of "putting people first."

Governing well is a people business. Structures are important, but not as important as mobilising people to do things they do not at first want to do. This idea underpins Stein Ringen's analysis of how governments get things done and establish their authority. It underpins his advice that as much as possible Governments - in the sense of the 20 or so Ministers of the Government - should rely on signals, not commands, and on authority, not fear. His advice to new leaders of Governments is to work normatively. From day one, your job is to win over the hearts and minds of the people and institutions who work for you and are really the people who do things - collect the taxes, deliver the services, apply the rules to change behaviour. If anyone starts acting like Kevin Rudd, show them the door.

A "four pillars" statement of purpose can help pull people towards your goals. It will not persuade all senior officials, stakeholders, and the public, but it is a launching pad for setting a few clear priorities, and deprioritising many more activities. Steve Bracks' four pillars is an example of how this worked, especially within the Cabinet. The policy and programs paper can define the "four pillars" but this paper suggests four core elements: better social services (health, education, social care, safety); infrastructure that meets people's long-term needs; laws and rules that reflect Victorians' fairness, diversity and compassion; and a stronger democracy.

Victorians deserve a better democracy. Political news panellists and econocrats endlessly lecture the public about economic reform. They claim the "political class" has failed because it does not bully people enough into supporting technocratic solutions. This behaviour only worsens the authority of governments. They weaken the trust of the community that, in the end, democracy is for the people.

The trust problem is not a problem of community attitudes. It is a reasonable assessment of poor performance by elites in making society work better for ordinary people. Misreading this problem is especially deadly for state governments. Strengthening local democracy is especially important for state governments since they are judged on the services, infrastructure and community values they deliver, not GDP growth or productivity.

Much of the early advice to the Government will likely proceed from all sorts of false assumptions about what must be done, according to the exigencies of management reform, economic reform, "the markets," new public management, ratings agencies, emulating the private sector, and so on. While sensible advice should not be ignored, the structure of government should be guided by democratic

On the institutions of government

principles, not unexamined edicts of economic reform.

It will take some time to apply a new approach, and reverse the weakening of Government authority and public institutions that has been the unfortunate side effect of economic reform. It will require gentle persuasion, relentlessly applied; but in the end stronger democratic public institutions, good government processes, open policy-making, and arguments based on public reason and moral judgement will give back Victorians the democracy they built and deserve.

4. Structure of Government Proposals

This section sets out specific and connected proposals for changes to the organisation of government, ordered by institutional and cultural changes for the three main actors - the Ministry, the public service and advisers.

Ministry - The organisation of the Ministry should strengthen democratic leadership through an inner Cabinet with matched assistant Ministers, simplified portfolios, reforms to how Ministers drive policies, budgets, decision-making and performance, a new committee system for both Cabinet and Parliament, and mobilising higher standards of advice, public argument, and public service.

Public service - Immediate changes to organisation of government should focus on mobilising government, not risky machinery of government changes that often disappoint. Changes to the public service should reinforce the way of governing by sharing power with Secretaries; rebuilding a strong policy centre with a Central Research Office and Cabinet Office; shifting responsibility for budgets to delivery departments away from Treasury; creating a State Governing Council that oversees major white paper reviews of public institutions, public budgeting and scrutiny, and democratic reform. They should include selected methods adapted from overseas models such as the British Government's structural reform four year (term) plans

Advisers - Ministerial officers should establish a blended office model composed of fewer political staff, senior Departmental staff and lead expert advisers. Staff should be accountable to the Premier, supported by a panel that oversees performance. Their conduct should be controlled by culture, not codes, and facilitate team approaches between Ministers and senior Department officers.

4.1 Ministry and Parliament

The paper proposes a smaller, tiered and simplified Ministry structure, and new committee arrangements to direct public institutions and to engage the Parliament and the public.

Most of the proposals will be put sparsely with little explanation, but one pivotal proposal requires some discussion given its importance for managing the people of the Government.

This paper proposes that the Ministry be reduced in size, and be divided into an inner and outer Cabinet. Each Cabinet Minister's portfolio would match a Department, except the Cabinet Secretary or Special Minister of State who would be a Cabinet Minister without portfolio assisting the Premier.

This is clearly a decision that affects expectations of Ministerial appointments and caucus votes, but it has wide precedents. One innovation of the Hawke Government was to establish an inner Cabinet (initially of 12), and, consequently, designate clear lead or coordinating Ministers to match its reorganised super-departments. The Commonwealth Government has since continued the practice. Most Ministries around the world are divided similarly into inner and outer Cabinets. Yet Victoria has never followed the practice. There have been various informal and formal means of recognising a batting order, but no publicly acknowledged difference in power and status among Ministers. All Ministers are equal formally, but not in truth. However, the public, the caucus, and the Ministry are grown up enough to handle the truth. Similarly, the size of Victoria's Cabinet has drifted upwards over the years and over the life of governments.

Establishing an inner Cabinet of smaller size will need to be well executed and supported by MPs. However, it could have large benefits for the patterns, structures and routines of decision-making. It will moderate the learning curve for new, less experienced Ministers. It will assist lead Ministers assert control over the bureaucracy and Ministerial staff appointments. It will establish clear lines of sight for both the public and political leadership between policy decisions and implementation. In itself it would be a signal of a determination to govern well and efficiently. Large, unwieldy Cabinets quickly make poor, expensive decisions. Shaping a Cabinet and Ministry, of course, is a political task, not a management task. However, a clear structural proposal enables any compromises to be built around core principles.

This paper makes 12 proposals for the design of the Cabinet, the Ministry, the organisation of their business and relationship with Parliament and the bureaucracy

4.1.1 Number of Ministers. The size of the Ministry will be reduced from 23 to 20.

4.1.2 Division of Ministry into Cabinet and Ministry. A group of 11 Ministers will form the Cabinet. A group of 9 Assistant Ministers will form the outer Ministry. The full Ministry will meet regularly, and Assistant Ministers will participate in Cabinet Committees.

4.1.3 Portfolios. Portfolio names are simple, plain language. They represent basic public goods (e.g. education), rather than sectional interests or stakeholder groups. The portfolio names match the proposed organisation of Departments. No Minister will have portfolios across more than one Department. There will be no more than three Ministers for each Department. Assistant Ministers assist in the portfolio of Cabinet Ministers. Specific responsibilities will be assigned through both the administrative arrangement orders and discussions between Ministers and the Premier.

4.1.4 Cabinet Secretary or Special Minister for State role. One Cabinet Minister will perform the role of Cabinet Secretary and Special Minister of State with few administrative responsibilities, but assisting the Premier with Cabinet policy processes, public engagement, government and political reform, and coordinating cross-portfolio action.

4.1.5 Parliamentary Secretaries. There will be 9 Parliamentary Secretaries (2 or 3 less than now). Parliamentary Secretaries will work with Cabinet and Assistant Ministers as the political team for each portfolio. Parliamentary Secretaries will chair caucus policy committees and Parliamentary Committees. Their role will be better defined.

4.1.6 Assignment of portfolios. The assignment of portfolios will need to balance diverse representation of interests within the Cabinet and the Outer Ministry. Assignment of Cabinet Ministers to portfolios should primarily be determined by the major political priorities and challenges of the portfolio, not administrative demands of Departments. It is desirable for a reasonable number of Cabinet Ministers to hold similar portfolios to those they hold as Shadow Ministers to smooth the transition and to maximise the benefits of their established relationships. Portfolios should reflect the Minister's administrative and political responsibility, and should not be specially tailored to special interests of the individual, interest groups or pet policies.

4.1.8 Cabinet Committee structure. The creation of an inner Cabinet of 11 will create conditions for more focused discussion and integrated decision-making at Cabinet. It ought to obviate the need for a strategic policy cabinet committee, since the Cabinet ought to perform that role. Cabinet Committees will be organised by function, rather than policy domain. Five Cabinet Committees are proposed:

- *Public Issues* - This Committee would discuss conduct of the Government's public communications and debates, parliamentary business, public engagement, communications campaigns, and initial problem defining responses to emerging policy and political issues in the community.

- *Performance* - This Committee would drive effective delivery of Government policies and commitments, act on any major organisational issues impeding performance or service delivery, and scrutinise Departmental performance on a quarterly basis.

- *Long-term projects* - This Committee would drive the delivery on time and on budget of both major capital projects, long-term plans (more than 4 years) especially for assets and infrastructure, and complex change projects requiring coordination of services and infrastructure.

- *Appointments* - This Committee would review all appointments, and streamline Cabinet level consideration of appointments.

- *Finance* - This Committee would set the budget process, determine the budget, set productivity goals for public spending, scrutinise the financial results of Departments, and drive reforms to the financial management framework.

Temporary Special Purpose Committees may be formed in a small number of cases to act on cross-portfolio issues or for emergency management. However, the Cabinet Secretary/Special Minister for State will facilitate this happening without formal committees as a key part of his or her role.

Each Cabinet Committee will comprise both Cabinet Ministers and Assistant Ministers. Each Cabinet Committee will be chaired by the Premier or by a designated Deputy Chair. Cabinet Committee Chairs form the core leadership group of the Government.

All Cabinet Committees will be serviced by the Cabinet Office - not, as has emerged as practice recently, by other Departments. The Cabinet Office should actively broker higher quality submissions, decisions and results, and not be a post office box as currently.

An alternative Committee structure to consider is to establish essentially three committees for economic, social and environmental policy. This approach is long established, and would work. However, this approach suffers with issues of integration across policy domains, and tends to focus Ministerial time on starting things, not following through to results and sustaining public arguments. The proposed committee structure aims for more integration across policy domains, and clarifying the decision-making role Ministers are performing with each Committee. These changes aim to improve the authority of political leadership, and the quality of Cabinet and Ministerial discussion and decision-making.

4.1.7 Cabinet and Ministry decision-making approach. As a broad rule, Cabinet will meet fortnightly (not weekly) on Monday or Tuesday mornings, with Cabinet Committees meeting on alternate Mondays. This procedure is to require more discipline with compliance with procedural rules for consideration of Cabinet papers (eg 5/10 day rule), and to make Cabinet Committees more frequent and business-like. Cabinet will operate as a collegiate, collective decision-making group. The Premier should not seek to develop a chief executive style of Government. Cabinet Committees ought to consider and debate detailed matters of submissions prior to their presentation to Cabinet. They should work as forums for Ministers, not audiences for officials.

4.1.9 Cabinet Submissions, forms, rules and initial 6 month plan. The Premier should prepare for discussion with Secretaries of Departments a foreshadowed 6 months agenda for Cabinet. In the first two weeks of Government this agenda should be settled through discussion, and focus in particular on major budget, legislative and policy review decisions of the government. No submissions to Cabinet or Cabinet Committees signed by officials will be accepted. This has

On the institutions of government

become common practice for Cabinet Committees, and reflects confusion about accountability. The performance committee of Cabinet will function partly as a corporate governance board for the performance of Secretaries. There will be a need to limit attendance of officials at Cabinet Committee meetings, and ensure there is more consistent practice between Departments. In general, only Secretaries and Deputy-Secretaries (including from DPC and DTF) will attend Cabinet Committees.

The Secretary DPC should be asked prior to the election to prepare as part of the incoming Government a revised and simplified template for Cabinet submissions The Government ought to establish an expert group to prepare a plan for both immediate and 6 to 12 month changes to the form, rules and expected content of Cabinet submissions. It will take time to diffuse better practices in preparation of Cabinet submissions. Each Secretary should be directed to focus effort on preparing high quality submissions on a limited forward agenda of major decisions in the first six months.

4.1.10 Parliamentary Committees. Parliamentary Committees could be changed in a similar way to Cabinet Committees. For example, the Public Accounts and Estimates Committee could develop as a Parliamentary parallel to the Performance Committee of Cabinet. It should be empowered to question officials in a similar way to the Senate Estimates Committee, and to focus on performance of public institutions. In addition, the Premier could establish a group of backbench MPs, including some members of Parliamentary Committees, to form a Premier's policy committee. They would work with officials and provide a forum to develop talent and to shape new ideas.

4.1.11 Relationship between ministers and department heads. As a general rule, Ministers should govern through their Secretaries and not through their advisers or Ministerial office. They should see their role as defining the public goods that the Departments are serving and working normatively with Departments. They should share power with Secretaries, rather than seek to prove themselves against Departments (this was one of the Baillieu Government's mistakes). However, the trade off for that is that Secretaries should be more publicly accountable, and be expected to be more open in public about the challenges and issues involved in key decisions. More should be expected of them.

4.2 Departments, agencies and public institutions. The paper proposes modest changes to Departments that clarify their purpose, improve the centre and quality of government, and ensures Treasury is "on tap, but not on top." It proposes more far-reaching cultural change to government processes to be achieved through four-year structural reform plans for Departments and major reviews of public accountability and institutions.

The structure of the Victorian bureaucracy today still bears the hallmarks of structural and cultural changes introduced in the 80s and 90s. John Cain introduced for the first time in Victoria disciplined, well-structured Cabinet processes and program budgeting, and subjected the sprawling public corporations and commissions to more disciplined political and public control. Jeff Kennett redesigned 27 Departments into 13, and then down to 8, and redefined the relationship between political and administrative executives. Alan Stockdale sold off the corporations, and rewrote the government management framework around outputs, market testing and purchaser/provider splits. Fundamentally, those changes remain, with adjustments in response to issues and events over time.

Since 2000, many changes to administrative structures have been more driven by ideas from particular policy domains, rather than ideas about how to organise government. As a result, things have got messy, cluttered and confused. Outputs, business plans and the budget papers have become obscure, meaningless red tape. The administrative executives of Departments lack vision, purpose and deep knowledge of issues. They are courtiers to a baffled court. There is a whole-of-government strategy for everything, and real priorities set for nothing. Commissioners spring up everywhere as a popular way to work around poor performance by departments. Chronic failures are allowed to drift on, with no institution responsible for directing change in performance, but countless monitoring reports being produced. These reports pass the parcel of "risk" onto the institutions that Departments supervise, but do not diagnose their own failures. This problem is at its worst in the "central agencies." Treasury runs the government, but on the basis of ideas from bitter warriors of the 90s (such as the Vertigan review or Commission of Audit), and reforming impulses have degenerated into bureaucratic routines that are every bit as pointless and unproductive as the old Treasury rules of the 1970s. Premier and Cabinet has presided over a degeneration of Cabinet process. It has walked too far into the desert without water, by competing with Treasury for influence in the budget process and with the Commonwealth for national policy agendas. It offers Departments all assistance short of real help, and provides no intellectual or policy leadership.

These problems arise from related problems of personnel, structure and culture. The central agencies have become a bureaucratic court, and too many courtiers, ex-advisers and consultants have been rushed through DPC and DTF to preside over public institutions. The strategic centre is powerful but without authority, and is overly focused on budgets, rather than policy, performance and public engagement. The culture and routines of government are dominated by layers upon layers of past management reform ideas, budget bids, "managing risk," and the procedures of "new public management." As the OECD has observed, Australia has gone further with new public management than nearly any developed country, and so experienced more of its benefits, but also more of its negative consequences.

The OECD, countries including Sweden, Finland, New Zealand and the UK, and the British think tank, the Institute of Government are giving increasing attention to how to reorganise both structures and processes at the centre of government to overcome these problems. The proposals in this paper are drawn from some of these models and ideas, and focus on better core policy processes, public engagement (David Cameron promised to "turn government on its head" and "make it accountable to the people, not to Treasury bureaucrats") and concentration on performance.

They also reflect research that machinery of government changes often disappoint, and caution should be exercised in deciding on them. It is true that a new Premier has an opportunity and power to make major changes. Recent work on machinery of government changes, however, stresses the issues to consider carefully before making major mergers or splits of departments.

The proposals for change in this paper, then, focus on both structure and culture. The structural changes are largely in the centre and limit the scale and range of organisational battles in the first year of the government. The cultural changes shift core government practices such as Cabinet decision-making, policy, research, budgets and public engagement. The structural changes aim to make the top layer of government clear, simple and clearly related to basic public goods that mean things for people, such as education. The cultural changes reshape the centre of government around a new "operating model" that aims to mobilise political and bureaucratic talent at all levels of public institutions.

However, early structural change also asserts a new Government's authority over the public service. This paper proposes that authority is best established through a strong, swift political strike against the rotting fish heads at the top of the public service, the central agencies, while Ministers secure strong support within their Departments and stakeholder groups to implement policy priorities in line Departments.

In particular, the habits of Treasury need to be decisively challenged, but in a way that assures both economic observers and

On the institutions of government

commentators of the Government's determination to spend money prudently and to maintain robust fiscal rules. It needs to be done in a way that does not paralyse the Government's first budget, and supports Secretaries of line Departments to deliver key priorities. In brief, this paper proposes redistributing power, authority and resources away from Treasury to stronger line departments and a rebuilt Premier's Department, to be renamed Government and Citizens. It proposes rebuilding that Department through a new, clear focus on people, policy and performance. However, careful consideration ought to be given to the political tactics for implementing these changes in the first weeks of the Government.

A key device is required to drive changes in Departments that deliver structural reform, accountability, public engagement and policy priorities of the Cabinet. The proposed device is a structural reform plan, linked to the new performance committee of Cabinet, and the performance and research teams in the Department of Government and Citizens (former DPC). This idea is borrowed from the UK Cameron Government, and reforms in NZ and other countries to steer policy less through budgets. The research team would also form the nucleus of more capable central staff who can drive the early policy implementation and major policy reviews of the Government.

4.2.1 Establish a nine Department structure. Nine Departments are proposed. the structure largely reflects current structures in social policy departments but with more significant changes to economic departments and central agencies. Names of Departments express in simple terms their core purpose or public good they serve. These departments are: Government and Citizens; Finance; Cities, Regions, Transport; Environment; Justice and Safety; Health; Social Care; Education and Culture; and Jobs and Wealth.

4.2.2 Transfer functions between Departments. Changes in functions of Departments largely reflect changes to central agencies and to economic departments. Government performance functions are moved from current DTF to new Government and Citizens. Some DTF economic policy and infrastructure assessment functions are moved to Jobs and Wealth and Cities, Regions and Transport. Primary Industries moves to form a single core economic development department. Arts largely moves from DPC to Education and Culture, although another option is to assign arts to Jobs and Wealth. Public engagement offices - such as office of multicultural affairs or youth - stay or move to Government and Citizens, but in a newly configured public engagement division.

Proposed changes are relatively small, with the exception of the transfer of arts and primary industries. In some cases, new names of Departments signal priorities, values and redirections of departments. So, DHS changes to Social Care. Names reflect core public goods, and aim to be short and clear. References to particular population groups in Department names are avoided.

4.2.3. Prepare structural reform plans for Department, with most immediate change in the centre. The Shadow Cabinet should use the pre-election period to prepare structural reform plans for each of the nine proposed Departments. These plans should be modelled on the structural reform plans used by the UK Cameron Government, but more focused on setting directions, rather than committing to milestones. They should identify the top five priorities, policy reviews, milestones and impact measures over the term.

These plans should reflect public commitments but be kept confidential and be more targeted to their key audience, the senior public service. On transition to government they should be provided to Secretaries, along with any priorities for immediate policy, budget or legislative changes, and Secretaries directed to develop these reform plans into a 4 year, full-term plan for each Department in the first six months for inclusion in the first budget.

The structural reform plans should set up a phased process to investigate and resolve particular concerns, organisational or "line-of-sight" issues in Departments. They should limit disruption and focus policy development and review in the first six months. Immediate structural changes should focus on rebuilding a strategic centre to focus on people, policy and performance.

4.2.4. Change name of DPC to Government and Citizens (DGC) and rebuild government policy, performance and public engagement processes around newly organised senior teams. It is proposed to reorganise the Department of Premier and Cabinet as a Department of Government and Citizens with the following top level structure. - Cabinet Office, Performance Team, Central Policy Research Team, Public Engagement Team and Leader Support or Public Institutions. The newly organised Department will drive the changes to the Government's operating model. The model would be developed from ideas put forward in New Zealand's 2006 central agency review, and the UK's Institute of Government reports *Shaping Up* and *Centre Forward* reports.

7. Force major change and staff and budget savings on DTF/Finance early. To rebalance and rebuild the centre will need a ruthless strike against Treasury. Its name will change to Finance, to focus it on core financial management, revenue and more credible analysis of government productivity. This paper proposes that as part of the initial machinery of government changes, the Government transfer most roles, executives and staff from DTF to line departments and a small number to help form the nucleus of the Performance Division in DGC. Some of its economic capability should be transferred to the economic development and infrastructure departments. Treasury should no longer always brief on Cabinet papers, and Cabinet Office can enforce rules about submissions with financial consequences. The head of Treasury should be offered the compensating challenge of rebuilding an effective budget process. This process should abide by strict fiscal rules, learn from advice from other countries and the OECD, move away from output budgeting and the new public management, and align with the new Government's policy priorities and philosophy of government. An external audit (point 10 below) of the Finance's administration of the Government's first budget process should identify recommendations for improvements.

8. Focus the economic and infrastructure departments on timely delivery of major capital projects. The Opposition has made important commitments to establish an independent public authority, Infrastructure Victoria, fundamentally important transport commitments, and a jobs and growth plan. The proposed Cities, Transport and Regions Department is a simpler reincarnation of the current planning department and would, with Infrastructure Victoria and supervision by the Long Term Projects Committee of Cabinet, drive delivery of the city, regional and statewide infrastructure. State Development (renamed Jobs and Wealth) would merge with Primary Industries to bring together policies that promote jobs and wealth-creating industries. The biggest challenge for this Department is to define an economic strategy for the State, to suit reduced economic influence of the State Government and the imminent end of the era of corporate welfare and investment attraction. New thinking is needed, but this is best delivered through an existing Department and not a private sector board.

9 Reorient performance, people and policy in the key social policy departments through strong political leadership and selective major "White Paper" policy reviews. Few changes are proposed for the core social policy departments. There are minor transfers of functions related to the "offices of," and name changes. Health is unchanged. Safety is added to Justice reflecting this central objective. Human Services is changed to Social Care to express a more truly people first spirit. Education becomes Education [Science] and Culture, reflecting the addition of arts [and science]. The name signals a redirection to fundamental educational values, away from its current preoccupation with "market design." All of these Departments work with each other (and associated authorities such as Victoria Police) on a daily and constant basis. Their problems in recent years do not arise from how boundaries are drawn between them, so much as from too little attention to real performance for people, and too much attention, people and resources spent on committees and waffle. They should be redirected through the structural reform plan process, new policy goals and highly selective and major White Paper style policy reviews. In health and education, policy directions at the Commonwealth level will be fundamental, and major policy reviews may be best delayed till the back half of the term, while Ministers and Department heads focus on improving performance. Justice will need to be redirected away from the current punitive law and order approach, but will respond well to these ideas. Both Justice and Human Services will be profoundly affected by the Family Violence Royal Commission, and indeed the Royal Commission into Institutional Child Sexual Abuse. Redirecting the Department of Human Service's senior leadership from its current attachment to "transformative system change" (rather than, more simply, better care for people) will be a major challenge of political leadership.

10 Establish a public budgeting and accountability review. To rebuild the centre, the Government should establish an audit of the efficiency and effectiveness of Treasury and Finance's budget process, performance in revenue projections, reallocation of expenditure, and validity of its advice on productivity and savings measures. This is a health check or performance review on a core government institution. In addition, a major White Paper process should be established to redesign Victoria's appropriations and budget, budget papers, annual reporting, output and financial management frameworks. This review should aim to deliver more open government, more effective government, better spending decisions, and executive government more capable of intelligent scrutiny by the Parliament and the public. It will free Ministers and the bureaucracy from the morass of output, budget corporate planning and other reporting rules that distract from meeting public goals, performance and good corporate governance. This review could potentially be conducted by a panel including a former Treasurer, an auditor-general, and an international expert.

11 Establish a public institutions review. There has been a proliferation of Commissioners, and similar independent, investigation and monitoring agencies. In addition there are some long standing authorities that need to have their ongoing role challenged. But the growth in these organisations reflects wishes to appoint particular experts, to entrench certain methods or perspectives (eg Victorian Competition and Efficiency Commission, Red Tape Commissioner), and to provide a comforting gesture that a performance issue is being addressed because someone is writing reports on it. In addition, the core public scrutiny agencies, such as the Auditor-General, have suffered mission creep, especially in relation to performance reviews because they rightly perceive no-one else is doing this job. As a result, public institutions of scrutiny become fragmented, and benefit the adamant individuals who make their way to these leadership roles, more so than the quality of government or and popular trust in democracy. The Government should establish a White Paper process, potentially with Parliamentary involvement, that will assess all Commissions, agencies, advisory groups and governance arrangements for public institutions, and make recommendations for simplification and change. In addition, the Government should immediately abolish or not reappoint, a small number of agencies or commissions in its first 100 days. A list of candidates for abolition should be developed before the election.

12 Establish a Victorian Government Advisory Council. Finally, a number of countries, including the UK, have established Department Boards to strengthen the public accountability of administrative Departments and to assist Ministers steer them. These Boards have not fully worked out as planned. This paper proposes that the new Government begins with a simpler model of an advisory committee. It proposes an interim step to establish an advisory council that will oversee the major reforms to the centre of government and public institutions. This experiment could test the feasibility of Department Boards. A Victorian Government and Citizens Advisory Council would comprise 7 to 10 distinguished members (e.g. ex-Premier, business, education, welfare, health leaders). Alternatively, it could be set up as a Democratic Reform Commission, and oversee set of major reviews (steered by the Advisory Council) on public institutions, public scrutiny, the public service, Parliament and public engagement. More radically, this Council could be used to lead responses to the Commonwealth Government's White Paper on Federalism into a new direction that is preparing Victoria for a federal republic with more fundamental redesign of national political institutions than tax arrangements and a partial bureaucratic deal on roles and responsibilities.

4.3 *Ministerial support and advisers* - The paper proposes a blended office model of Ministerial support with more senior Departmental staff, expert advisers and disciplined political staff. There has been extensive discussion of Ministerial advisers in Australia and other OECD countries in recent years. Some of this discussion has highlighted real flaws with how Ministerial staff have operated in Victoria and Australia. It is generally recognised that political Ministerial offices in Victoria and Australia are larger than many other OECD countries. The rule that advisers should not direct public servants is honoured more in the breach than the observance. In any case, there are deeper problems. In particular, the social influences exercised by advisers and ex-advisers in institutions lead the public service to tell people what they want to hear. Social pressures lead the public servants to think that black is white, if they are told to think so. Solutions to these problems need to work with the grain of the culture of the people who work in and with Ministerial offices. Codes and other formal procedural rules will not work for that reason. Rather proposals need to focus on culture and capability, and to ensure a better team of people, talent and culture serve Ministers' needs.

5. *Sequence and Strategy.* Finally, the paper raises some considerations of timing and strategy, premised on the assumption that care will need to be taken with how to shock, manoeuvre, and then mobilise leading figures working for the government over three

transition timelines - the first 100 days, the first budget (six months) and the first anniversary.

Recent Australian governments have been obedient to the 100 day myth producing glossy brochures or emblematic statements in time for this milestone. Most of the media and the public just yawn. This paper suggests five periods to consider, including the pre-election period as an opportunity to send signals and to explore relationships. However, the first 100 days is a crucial time for the Government to establish authority, and to use the early legitimacy of a newly elected government to reset working styles and priorities within the senior bureaucracy. It is a crucial time for Ministers to mobilise people behind them. While much of this action takes place away from public view, the bureaucracy is acutely attentive to the theatre of how early messages, acts and gestures are performed in these early days. So, this paper argues that there should be some planning of the small group political tactics of decisions on Secretaries, briefing books, early Cabinet meetings, early communication between Ministers and Departments, and delivery of a very small number of real priorities in that first period.

These tactics should, in phases, unfreeze, push and consolidate the senior public service towards your goals, and then use the internal theatre and communications of government to mobilise the broader public service, beyond those senior officials who are close to Ministers.

In truth, there is a very brief and limited opportunity to make a mark in the first few weeks before the Government before people psychologically turn away from politics over Christmas and summer. It is best to take time - say a week - over the immediate transition, and ensure all key Ministers have a short rest. Key Ministers should immediately and visibly get prepared for emergencies. The budget process will need to be reset, and Treasury's ideologues brought to heel, and a few key matters should get rolling (eg Family Violence Royal Commission). The first week (straight after the election) of

On the institutions of government

engagements between Secretaries, the Premier and key Ministers-elect ought to be planned in advance as part of the shock, mobilise and consolidate strategy, and focus on changes to structure and culture of government. For example you might invite all Secretaries as a group to brief you and two or three senior Ministers on key priorities and to hear yours (structural reform plans) in the first day or so after the election, and arrange one-on-one meetings with each of them later in that week - as Narendra Modi did after his recent election in India.

It is better to focus the effort of Ministers on winning over the people in their Departments, rather than lording it over them or finding fault in small things. Expect mistakes - everyone will be tired and anxious. Charm and persuasion will go further than bully tactics in securing a handful of critical early decisions to reshape budgets, reorienting Departments around the structural reform plans, and beginning crucial priorities. It may be better to use the earliest sitting of Parliament to discuss important issues - such as bringing the structure of government changes to Parliament for an affirmative vote - rather than bring hasty symbolic legislation. This is the time to establish a distinct and enduring "look and feel" of the government in how you do things, as much as what you do.

Finally, putting people first means making the relationship between Ministers, advisers and public servants work effectively. This is a people business. Purnell and Lewis, *Leading a Government Department - the first 100 days* provided practical advice for both Ministers and Department Secretaries in working together for the first 100 days of a new Government. This short document may be a useful guide for any preparatory work or inductions for Ministers.

Postscript 2023

Very few, if any, of these proposals were implemented, and certainly not with any later referral to me. I do not even know how many people other than Mark Madden and myself read the document. I publish it here as a rare historical document, now detached from its specific proposals and situation. It offers one rare way to look at a bureaucrat, and some insight into how this rare bureaucrat looked at the institutions of government.

Treasury's Red Book - seven reflections

(From *The Happy Pessimist* 29 September 2010.)

The Commonwealth Treasury has released its briefing to the incoming government, following "numerous" FOI requests and public curiosity. The briefing is provided in full with some parts blacked out, or, in the legal language, the redacted versions. More on the blacked out bits shortly. The release of this document is surprising, and I have several reflections on reading most of the document over the last two days. In an earlier post, I had some strong views about the Independents' requests for both the red and blue books. The release of these documents reinforce these views.

1. We are all better informed for the release of this document. Perhaps this is indicative of what could be possible with more open and publicly expressed bureaucratic policy advice. However, there comes a time when these documents become difficult to write, and harder to read, if they are intended from the outset for the general reader, not the decision-maker.

2. A fun dinner party game among policy wonks will be guessing what is in the blacked out bits. Some are more serious than others. Some may be guessed to relate to security matters if related to investment or defence. Others seem weak attempts to conceal disclosure of possibly inappropriate commentary on Opposition

policies. All the next steps on implementing the agreement with Wilkie on gambling are blacked out, presumably since they may relate to legal advice on the powers to act. Others relate to brewing conflicts with the states on tax revenues. And others are still more intriguing; such as the slabs of text blacked out in the otherwise bland section on service delivery. Could this relate to an enabling infrastructure to implement a shift from in-person to electronic transactions, and would this make more sense of Julia Gillard role as PM overseeing digital productivity?

3. The irregular verb of "structural adjustment". Bernard in *Yes, Minister* used to make fun of the occasional hypocrisies in policy judgements marked by the use of the irregular verb conjugations. One example in Treasury's briefing, though not without some intellectual respectability, is 'structural adjustment'. So, I make a policy judgement; you express concerns; and they are "manifestations of the costs of structural adjustment, both perceived and actual."

4. Other documents that allow us to compare Treasury's view to other Departments would inform us still further. Have similar requests been made for the Department of Prime Minister and Cabinet briefing, and will it be revealed? Traditionally, the Prime Minister's briefing is better on cross-cutting policies, and not just the economic mantra. For this Government, in particular, the Department of Prime Minister and Cabinet's views on health, education or skills, and broadband would inform the nation well.

5. There is some gentle chiding from Treasury expressed in central banker language that might inform some directions for the Government. There are delicately worded admonitions, or perhaps stern encouragement on the 'deficit exit strategy', population targets, losing the thread of tax reform, carbon pricing, health reform, an over-crowded reform agenda, especially for COAG, the costs of the Broadband Network, and more. My favourite rebuke appears on page 12, unusually bolded, with a section blacked out. The Government response to the NBN implementation study warrants "very careful

consideration [blacked out section - maybe independently of the NBN/Minister?]."

6. The tension of the debate on parliamentary conventions shows. Page 3 states that the Charter of Budget Honesty has not 'stood the test of time'. The release of the document includes strong advice not to release the blue book. The advice noted the Opposition Leader's strong concern about release, if for the different reason that it contravened Westminster conventions.

7. The document makes clear how many hard decisions face PM Julia Gillard, and how hazardous the road over the next three years will be. These hazards deserve some further attention in a later post.

Behavioural Anecdotes Team

(From *The Burning Archive* 1 May 2016.)

One of the more puzzling cases of British export success is the spread of successive generations of bad ideas on public management and government. This niche export industry has been especially successful in former British colonies like Victoria, where bedazzled political leaders and officials rub shoulders with confidants of Number 10, never stopping to question the merit of importing ideas out of context and unsuited to local affiliations. It is puzzling since the results of these ideas have been consistently poor, rather like London weather, or, perhaps more to the point, quite consistent with the poor functioning of government in the precariously United Kingdom.

Nor does political affiliation seem to matter much to the sway of the Brits. I have now sat through underwhelming presentations of quasi-political bureaucrats from the regimes of Thatcher, Major, Blair,

On the institutions of government

Brown and Cameron. All these bureaucrats on tour enriched their summer holiday with a few jejune talks on the latest management fad in Westminster.

Despite sometimes elegant charm and the charisma of nearness to our colonial ancestral home, none of these fads have achieved much at all. The analyses of Christopher Hood and Patrick Dunleavy are clear: these changes have on the whole worsened productivity, muddied responsibility to the public, failed to meet their professed goals, and hosted the parasites of new governance, especially well-marketed and ill-conceived consultants, that have damaged the institutions and culture of government.

The latest in this series of fairs, which advertise the trade secrets of failing governments, is the Behavioural Insights Team (BIT), conveniently known as an acronym, BIT, with a hint of literary computer science. Also known as the 'Nudge Unit', this unit claims to apply "very empirical" insights from behavioural science to policy and government. It is led by Dr David Halpern, who once was a psychologist. I presume, from the depth of his discussions of mental health, Halpern was only ever a research psychologist, perhaps in Skinner's tradition. Still, Halpern claims an intellectual lease from Thaler, Sunstein and Kahnemann (who he referred to as 'Danny', when promoting this intimacy in his public talks). But his real power comes from once being an adviser to Tony Blair, and he still displays his spiritual relics from the great mesmeriser.

Halpern has learned the same skill of endearing, simple explanations of complex bodies of thought. The trademark idea of his Behavioural Insights Team is distilled into an anagram, EAST, that stands for easy, attractive, social and timely. These are the qualities, so behavioural science tells BIT, that governments should design into their policies and the "decision architecture" (using Thaler and Sunstein's rather clumsier language) that will lead people to making better choices. There is an admirable skill in BIT's presentation of ideas, which draws largely from the oral-visual tradition of management consulting, and there are a list of achievements of clever nudges that appear to have made a few decisions, at least, easy, attractive, social and timely.

But there is also an uneasy feeling that BIT accomplishes much less than it claims. It likes to claim it applies randomised controlled trials to policy making; but this claim is more a co-option of the charisma of medical research to vastly different social policy experiments. It likes to point to the immediate effects of its nudges; but rarely examines whether these effects endure beyond the short term horizon or a single round of the social game into which they are intervening. There is too a nagging quality to the issues they intervene in and the impacts they have. It makes a virtue of small and easy changes. These claims however are largely grounded in mystic convictions about butterfly wings disturbing sub-optimal equilibrium. On examination, most of the successes claimed by BIT simply do not seem to be that important or consequential. They are small changes in letters, which a direct marketing consultant could have proposed; reordering of appointments; or changes in 'default options', the order of the menu, if you prefer. The larger messier questions of governing are avoided because, one suspects, BIT's methods are not that useful for the things that matter. BIT's representatives tell a story about folding a sheet of paper one hundred times, so making the flimsy object as strong as steel. This magic trick supports their claim that our common sense cognition has limits. It sounds like a toothpaste ad, not advice to serious people. When considering profound difficulties of conflicting values and interests, tired anecdotes do not add up to much at all.

Despite, or even perhaps because of, this imperfect track record, the Behavioural Insights Team has, however, taken to a whole new level the British tradition of exporting its nicely dressed, bad ideas of government. The team has been spun off from the Cabinet Office in the UK, and is now owned by its employees and operates as a 'public sector mutual'. The Behavioural Insights Team has turned itself into a private mutual company that sells its anecdotes to the rest of the world. Dr Halpern has sold the name to a number of governments in the old colonies of Australia, and to the Bloomberg foundation in America. He has just completed a two-year 'thinker in residency' in Australia, during which his main project appears to have been a widely ridiculed citizen's jury on obesity. No-one seems to ask, why is the UK Cabinet Office so ready to do without the expertise of this ground-breaking team? Why did it feel capable of governing while Dr Halpern and his innovative team were absent on a multi-year book tour around the world. Presumably, the UK Prime Minister felt he could do without the advice. Perhaps that made things easier, more attractive, simpler and more timely for the Cabinet? And maybe PM Cameron found, after a while, that dull anecdotes were not substitutes for real insights. So, he dispensed with the Behavioural Anecdotes Team in a fashionably nonsensical way, that at least would help pay the bills for advice on the issues that really mattered.

Post-script 2023. Unfortunately in this case, history occurred first as farce and secondly as tragedy. Behaviour Insights Teams achieved peak power during the COVID pandemic. The unethical conduct of these behaviouralists during the Great Seclusion has been dissected by Laura Dodsworth in her book, *A State of Fear: How the UK Government weaponised fear during the COVID-19 pandemic* (2021).

13 Ways of Looking at a Bureaucrat

The collapsing new buildings of government

(From *The Burning Archive* 29 April 2018.)

> "In truth, the problem of declining trust in political institutions, is better conceived as the collapse of authority of the new *nomenklatura* in liberal democracies. And that, I hypothesise, has its roots in the disintegration of the civic cultures that these elites attempt to govern."
> *The Burning Archive* (22 April 2018)

My apologies for quoting from my own posts; but it seemed the simplest way to connect today's post to last week's and its promise to explore the cultural roots of the collapse of political authority in liberal democracies. I find myself too enfeebled this morning to write in fluid prose and extended argument. The problems I point to in this concluding paragraph trouble me deeply. I dwell and labour among these difficulties each day at work. In response I have committed myself to a purpose: to write in my own voice on the ordinary virtues of governing well.

I write this testimony with the burden of sad prophecy. I can have no hope of seeing large scale transformations of the institutions I work in or the broader society. I do not have the will, the temperament or the skills to direct changes in the world. I am no schemer. I am no powerful insider. I am rather an outcast who has embraced his exile, and made of its suffering an idea to teach to my tormentors. I do not seek to change the world, but I turn instead to cultivate my own garden, and make of myself a more virtuous life. All I can hope for is to put my own garden in order, to know and to hold close to my true heritage (in tryst it will not be reft from me), and to give these words of self-transformation – for I too am full of weaknesses, temptation, folly

On the institutions of government

and mistakes – to the infinite conversation that will succeed beyond me. Instead of a mini-essay, let me stammer some notes on my theme.

1. The Collapse of Authority. The collapse of trust is the common way to see problems of democratic disobedience. But there is little substantial evidence to show that trust has declined in liberal democracies or even that trust is a problem for democracies.[103]

Elites blame their inability to command authority on the declining trust of the public. The public's doubts about the performance of elites are more accurate judgements. Elites should look to their own failures to explain the disobedience of the public: they are not able to exercise power rightfully, with clear purpose, to make reluctant others serve a worthwhile purpose.

Former Australian Prime Minister, John Howard once said of the then Prime Minister, Julia Gillard, that her government had a problem with authority: "It has neither ideals, or an idea of where it wants to take the country, and it is this lack of direction that is disabling [Julia Gillard], as well as, of course, her lack of authority." What he said of this government is true more broadly of modern governments. Their authority has collapsed.

Trust is a problem of commerce. Without trust, buyers are too wary of sellers. The problem of politics, the essence of governing, is authority. Without authority, citizens do not obey the state.

Authority is an unusual attribute. It is a quality that the powerful seek, and that only those who are reluctant at first to follow them are able to grant. Authority rests in culture and institutions, not individuals. Individual political leaders only borrow the authority of the institutions and cultures which they scramble their way to the top of. Without a strong culture and institutions, these individual political leaders are feckless pseudo-celebrities, confected products of political

---

[103] Tom van der Meer, "Political Trust and the 'Crisis of Democracy,'" *Oxford Research Encyclopedia of Politics*, January 25, 2017.

marketing machines – the 'real Julia,' as the former Australian Prime Minister Gillard's advisers once mislabelled her – that we know today. However, skilled and professional they seem to be, however hard they work at 'retail politics', they lack the character that is the product of culture, and the authority that is the product of institutions.

2. *The New Nomenklatura.* The *nomenklatura* was the name given to register of the party officials and bureaucrats who ruled the East European communist states. It became a term to describe this new class in the supposedly classless society. They were a caste apart whose careers were dependent on patron-client relationships that controlled government appointments, and on submission to empty slogans of orthodoxy.

The political institutions of Western liberal democracies are increasingly subjected to a new *nomenklatura*. It is a new class that is more open than the Soviet system, and composed of some competing factions: Labor vs Liberal, Democrat vs Republican, red vs blue. It is not identical to the old Soviet system; many of its characteristics are only imaginable in our society of infomercials.

But modern democracy has some essential similarities to the communist system. It spawns through patron-client relationships, fostered by appointments within governments, parties, and the para-political institutions of think tanks, lobbyists, interest groups, advocacy groups and consulting firms. It encloses the minds of the network members in orthodoxies that insulate them from the *lebenswelt* of ordinary people. It is a cultural world dominated by talking points and gesture politics that rarely breaks through to making substantial change in people's social conditions. It deforms political institutions by cultivating the loyalty to the network and the skill at positioning the individual within the network, rather than educating citizens and rulers alike in civic virtues.

The new *nomenklatura* is the product of the growing professionalisation of politics over the last 50 years. Political

On the institutions of government

leadership is now a subsidiary to the game of political marketing.[104]

It is also the product of the rising dominance in society since the early 1970s of the the merchant caste, to use David Priestland's characterisation.[105] The careers of the new *nomenklatura* are not restricted, like Soviet predecessors, to appointments within parties and governments. Their careers flourish through affiliated business leaders, philanthropists and communications firms, who celebrate the creative energies of the private sector, rather than the institutional cultures of government. They bring the same cast of mind, political marketing, to government, and view the institutions of government as arenas in which they perform, like parasitic celebrities. They do not treat these institutions as bearers of traditions in which we are born, live and die.

3. The Disintegration of Civic Culture. Zygmunt Bauman, the great cultural sociologist, wrote of the liquid modernity of our times. He also once observed that more British young people had voted in Big Brother evictions than had voted in the British general elections. Is there a better example of the degradation of civic culture, without which a virtuous state is difficult to enact? Bauman speculated that in modern societies equality, democracy and self-determination were at risk because society had become so fragmented. Society was no longer the joint product of collective effort and the organised form of people with common. It was merely a platform or a container of goods and services from which competing individuals grabbed the best they could get. He imagined our liquid, modern society as unpiloted airplane. Its passengers and inexpert crew, we former citizens of democracy, were afraid, ignorant, impotent and unable to assume responsibility.

Bauman went on on to argue that, over the last fifty years, power, or the ability to do things, has become separated from politics, the

---

[104] Yee-Fui Ng, Senate Occasional Lecture, 21 July 2017, Parliament of Australia. Rune Karlsen and Jo Saglie, "Party Bureaucrats, Independent Professionals, or Politicians? A Study of Party Employees," *West European Politics* 40 (6) 2017, pp. 1331–51.
[105] Priestland, David. *Merchant, Soldier, Sage: A New History of Power*

ability to choose together which things to do. The state has withered in affluence. The state has been crowded out by the proliferation of identities consequent of cultural fragmentation. The state is overwhelmed. It overflows with the projects of its captors. It is overtaken by viruses and parasites. The state no longer has the inner strength of civic culture that enables resistance to its enemies.

The disintegration of civic culture is part of the malaise of identity politics as diagnosed by Jordan B. Peterson. But the warning bells on civic culture have been ringing deeply for a long time. Robert Nisbet, the American sociologist, rang the bells in the 1970s. In *The Twilight of Authority* (1975), he wrote how democracy is not immune from decay. This intimation of mortality was not known by the American founding fathers. They imagined themselves exceptional and immune from the erosion and decay that had been experienced by all other states. They imagined themselves freed from the tragic daemon that the classical Greek authors saw in the story of all political communities. But Nisbet perceived new doubts in the American state, revealed by the tawdriness of modern society and politics. There was too much individualism, too much hedonism and too much equality. Power in America, a term which Nisbet used as a metonym for civilisation itself, destroyed hierarchy and native social bonds.

This decay in the political order led to vulnerabilities in the culture. Nisbet saw his society wracked by cultural decay. The moral order had become empty for large numbers of people. Society had become an arid desert. Human loyalties, uprooted from soils of custom, tumbled across the landscape. The striving of individuals was no longer heroic, industrious or aimed at achievement. It merely expressed ego in endless virtual performances. The attention of the best that has ever been written, Arnold's maxim of culture, fell away. Minds focused on the petty, not the noble. They obsessed about the personal, not the communal. They conceived the subjective, not the objective. Most people had come to believe values were degraded and culture was corrupt. They were estranged from community and communion. Five

On the institutions of government

decades later, Nisbet's twilight has fallen into deep night.

4. The Burden of Sad Prophecy. Cassandra should not fool herself. But neither should we forget the truth of the laments of the past. In *fin-de-siècle* Europe the strange prophet, Max Nordau wrote, in *Degeneration* (1892):

> In our time, the more highly developed minds have been visited with vague forebodings of a Dusk of Nations, in which the sunlight and the starlight are gradually fading, and the human race with all its institutions and achievements is dying out amidst a dying world.

And even longer ago, Gregory of Tours (539-594 C.E.) wrote in the *History of the Franks* this dark vision. "With liberal culture on the wane," the saint wrote "there were many deeds being done both good and evil." Kings grew more cruel. The church was attacked by heretics, and his version of the true faith found some devout worshippers, but left most cold. Traitors and corrupt stole the riches of the church. Yet no writers spoke out, no "grammarian skilled in the dialectic art could be found to describe these matters either in prose or verse." Sixth century social media was full of doom-scrolling and laments. People cried out, Gregory wrote, "Woe to our day, since the pursuit of letters has perished from among us and no one can be found among the people who can set forth the deeds of the present on the written page."

In response Gregory took up the task of the lonely historian and the sad prophet's burden.

> Hearing continually these complaints and others like them I [have undertaken] to commemorate the past, order that it may come to the knowledge of the future; and although my speech is rude, I have been unable to be silent as to the struggles between the wicked and the upright; and I have been especially encouraged because, to my surprise, it has often been said by men of our day, that few understand the learned words of the rhetorician but many the rude language of the common people.

13 Ways of Looking at a Bureaucrat

Life is delay, to transform Salisbury's adage. The sad prophet's burden is to know this.

Bureaucratic Utopianism

(From *The Burning Archive* 17 June 2018.)

Bureaucracy is not meant to be Utopian. After all, is not bureaucracy the home of the conformist, the cynical realist, the domesticator of conflict, the administrator of dreams, the banal practitioner of evil? Karl Mannheim wrote, in *Ideology and Utopia*, 'The fundamental tendency of all bureaucratic thought is to turn all problems of politics into administration." The officials are limited in imagination and bow to the current order of things. They "attempt to hide all problems of politics under the cover of administration." In other words, bureaucrats play it safe.

Bureaucracy is rule-bound, conservative, a force for stability, and no place for dreamers. So the story goes, at least as it is told in the traveller tales of academics and writers. Bureaucratic Utopianism is an oxymoron. If only this were true.

Most political theorists are unsympathetic tourists of government. They are not insiders. They do not try even to be participant observers. I, who am an insider and a participant observer, see different phenomena to most political theorists. I see officials who dream of Utopia and have broken the chains of this bureaucratic oxymoron.

I see it when officials and consultants talk endlessly about about the 'future state' – to describe how they want to change the world, even with the most mundane and practical of projects.

On the institutions of government

I see it in the training programs in which young bureaucrats are introduced to the 'competencies' required of the new twenty-first century bureaucrats. In these workshops, young officials are seduced into a kind of religiosity, obsessed with innovation, by posting sticky notes to A2 pieces of paper under the heading of 'Ideal State'. Through this ritual, they join the faith that believes they, acting as One Government, can control human destiny, and fulfil all social fantasies.

I see it in talk of 'reform readiness', 'bold thinking', and 'ambitious plans'. The zeal persists even when these plans are expressed in vacuous abstractions, such as "a shift to more personalised, evidence-informed and integrated services that are well-connected to informal community networks and supports."

I see it in the growing fondness for grandiose claims of the power of government to change social facts. Utopians urge governments to set outcome targets that are not anchored in any reality or sense of history: end family violence, halve the suicide rate, zero road deaths, and zero avoidable harm from the practice of medicine. The Utopians scheme to prevent human frailties from ever happening again.

I see it in the revenge against reality practised by forms of social constructivism, and fluid gender politics. The Utopians dream that the constraints of culture, history and biology can be wished away by a suitably bold, radical and ambitious reform plan.

Utopian thought has always had its advocates. Amid the ruins of our political culture, it is no surprise that it is resurgent. Some like, Russell Jacoby, seek to distance the Utopians from their many failures, and close associations with the dictatorship of ideas.[106] He distanced himself from traditions of blueprint Utopians, but held hopes for a schismatic alternative, which he called "iconoclastic utopianism". Jacoby embraced this apocalyptic longing for better that can "shake the world off its hinges." He avowed this creed of the "disruptors," who

---

[106] Russell Jacoby, *Picture Imperfect: Utopian Thought for an Anti-Utopian Age* (2005).

want to tear the whole place down. He did not pause to think: how will we all survive the ruin?

Other writers seek resurgence of practical Utopias, such as Rutger Bregman's *Utopia for Realists,* which advocates the universal basic income. These Utopians harness their dreams to social movements, practical ideas for change, and innovative practices. They make the most of their ideals, in times of rupture, disruption and ceaseless change.

It is this latter style of Utopian who succeeds in today's degraded bureaucracies. These Utopians are courtiers who promise disruption, and claim to be the enemy of the institution in which they operate. They play successfully to one of Robert Conquest's three laws of politics. Conquest theorised that the simplest way to explain the behaviour of any bureaucratic organisation is to assume that it is controlled by a cabal of its enemies. This cabal of Utopian courtiers thrives on the chaos of change. They prosper on the fantasy of better outcomes, which are outside of their control. They envision 'future states,' but never answer for the messy present.

We should always remind ourselves of one lesson of time. This kind of thought and action has a long and tragic history. It seeks to obliterate the conflict, competition and compromise, which, on reflection, prove to be the dignified, necessary, terrible beauty of human societies. The road to Utopia is laid out in clean lines and marked all along the route by many sacrificial deaths. As Roger Scruton reminded us in *The Uses of Pessimism,* the Utopian fallacy proposes that the ideal is immune to refutation. It can never be disproved, but nor can it ever be denied. To deny the hope and ambition of the 'future state, would be to submit the dream to reality. Doubters will be dismissed as haters and timid bureaucrats, who lack all vision. The Utopia then functions as "an abstract condemnation of everything around us." More darkly still, it justifies the true believers in taking full control of the levers of power.

On the institutions of government

This temper sits ill with the conservative disposition and the ordinary virtues of governing well. Those virtues require the bureaucrat to live with the difficult world, as it really is. Virtuous bureaucrats do not raid institutions to claim the loot of the future. They draw prudently on the resources of institutions and cultures. They take care of our shared heritage. They manage social conflicts, mistakes and our misunderstandings of each other, if inevitably imperfectly.

Bureaucratic Utopians share this attribute with all Utopias. They enact revenge against reality. As Scruton wrote:

> The ideal remains forever on the horizon of our experience, unsullied and untried, casting judgement on all that is actual, like a sun that cannot be looked at but which creates a dark side to everything on which it shines.

I do not honour the values celebrated by bureaucratic Utopians: bold thinking, innovation, disruption, design thinking, and all the total dreams of systems, change, and outcomes. I celebrate instead the ordinary virtues of governing well. Those who govern well do not dream of future states, but keep a modest awareness of the limits of government, the delicacy of human culture, and the frailty of all social institutions. These bureaucrats talk to strangers, compromise with others, and believe the best approaches to social problems are discovered, not designed.

In *The Uses of Pessimism*, Scruton made a fundamental attack on Utopias of all kinds. He wrote:

> The solution to human conflicts is discovered case by case, and embodied thereafter in precedents, customs and laws. The solution does not exist as a plan, a scheme, or a utopia. It is the residue of myriad agreements and negotiations, preserved in customs and laws.... And it is precisely this deposit, in customs and institutions, that the Utopian sets out to destroy.

Truly, bureaucracy, and we who work in all variants of

13 Ways of Looking at a Bureaucrat

bureaucracy, are not meant to be Utopian. Coincidentally – a word that tricks chance into being fate – I was reading this week Maria Popova's account of a celebration of not knowing by the Polish poet, Wisława Szymborska. In her Nobel Prize acceptance speech, she spoke of the humility of not knowing in many fields. In any profession, not merely writing, Szymborska said that inspiration comes from accepting we do not have the solutions.

> Inspiration is not the exclusive privilege of poets or artists generally. There is, has been, and will always be a certain group of people whom inspiration visits. It's made up of all those who've consciously chosen their calling and do their job with love and imagination. It may include doctors, teachers, gardeners — and I could list a hundred more professions. Their work becomes one continuous adventure as long as they manage to keep discovering new challenges in it. Difficulties and setbacks never quell their curiosity. A swarm of new questions emerges from every problem they solve. Whatever inspiration is, it's born from a continuous 'I don't know.'

Szymborska celebrates this 'I don't know' as a virtue of literature and life. It is also one of the ordinary virtues of my workaday profession, the bureaucrat, they who govern. It is certainly an antidote to bureaucratic Utopianism.

So, the coincidence came when Popova cited Szymborska's gentle pillory of the certainty of Utopians in both its deadly and comical forms. In 'Utopia' Szymborska wrote how Utopians live beside a Lake of Deep Conviction and a Tower of Unshakeable Confidence, where they see the Essence of Things. But despite their omniscience, they are unhappy. They can never sit still. They must always leave for some future state, and not plunge into unfathomable life.

On the institutions of government

The failure of institutions in the pandemic crisis

(From *The Burning Archive* 6 August 2020.)

Yuval Levin argued that the institutions of contemporary society, which he equates with America, have become degraded. We have lost trust in these institutions because, simply, they have become less trustworthy. Their performance has been sapped by a perversion of purpose in these institutions.

Institutions work well when they are forges for the character of those who come to belong in them. Then, the institution allows ordinary people to achieve extraordinary things, such as winning wars, making laws, dispensing justice, raising children to be solid citizens, preserving both freedom and order, protecting the frail heritage of our dead ancestors from the ravages of forgetting, and shielding life from the furies of the future. A soldier becomes part of an army; a street fight is transformed into a victorious battle. But for this alchemy of character to occur, the individual needs to accept the constraints, the heritage, the norms and the gifts of the institution, which exceeds him or her as an individual. Then the institution is formative of virtue. From such little platoons, good men and women are formed to resist the evils and tragedies of the world.

But institutions have stopped being formative, Yuval Levin contended. Changes in incentives and in culture have led people within institutions to resist being moulded in these forges. In the world of social media, service economy and 24/7 news, everyone wants to break the mould, be made of stars, be the guest on the panel show, not the follower in the trenches. Institutions have lost their way: they no longer discipline their members' characters through convention, tradition and order; they have become platforms to promote the brands of the individuals who occupy, but do not belong to them.

This deformation of institutions from formative to performative is seen in many types of organisations. For example, parliamentary institutions (the Congress in Levin's nation, the Australian and Victorian Parliaments in mine) become platforms to get Youtube clips and campaign highlights. They do not work as assemblies of lawmakers who deliberate on the critical issues, scrutinise the executive, and debate the merits and pitfalls of legislation. Read *Hansard* from any day of the Victorian Parliament (if it ever sits), and you will see the pathetic spectacle that parliamentary democracy has become. The same perversion of purpose, twisted from disciplined character to shallow performance, is seen in education, arts, the media, bureaucracy, business, philanthropy, social services, and even, disastrously so during this pandemic in Victoria, in health.

Because institutions became isolated from their past, their immune systems weakened. Parasitic viruses of 'innovation' and 'leadership' colonised them. Everyone wants to be a leader. No one wants to learn their craft. The fastest route to be recognised as a leader is to drop into institutions from above, like a paratrooper. Do things new. Don't do things well. And, most of all, sell your brand. This philosophy has led to institutions being overwhelmed by the new *nomenklatura* of our society. The same philosophy underwrites the catastrophic failure across so many institutions over the last twenty years, including the tragic cluster of failures in government, health, universities and the media that has unfolded during the pandemic crisis.

Sadly, this cluster of failures has occurred in the institutions I have worked in for the last thirty years. Truly, the Victorian Government's response to the coronavirus pandemic is the worst failure I have witnessed in government institutions in my entire public service career. I now live under government house arrest, in a deep lockdown and within a cruel curfew; under orders not made lawfully by a Parliament, but arbitrarily, without public justification or reasoning;

by a Chief Health Officer who is in command of nothing but his daily media performances. In the words of the Chief Health Officer himself, the latest episode of draconian interventions are structured as performance. They seek to send a message of 'shock and awe', directed by a government against its very own population, not to build habits, institutions and immunity with which people can resist the virus.

What is the treatment against this virus of institutional decay? Levin argued to restore an ethic of institution building, including the family. He recalled de Tocqueville's observation of nineteenth century America, that wherever three Americans are gathered, one will be elected Treasurer. I can think of no better cure, even if the manner of institutional building today will take new form.

A similar argument is made more extensively in the final chapter of Patrick J. Dineen's *Why Liberalism Failed*. He first explained the paradox of cultivating an organic culture amidst today's 'anticulture'. This anticulture of modern liberalism has created a flattened cultural wasteland. It is hostile to its competitors, even though they offer the biodiversity that would reverse the desertification of culture. But that restorative culture cannot be planned. It cannot not be engineered like the soul of artificial intelligence. It must grow from scattered seeds, from the bottom up. It is certain that some seeds will be barren, and all the plants will eventually die. But over time, in a way that cannot be planned or predicted, the DNA of the survivor culture will pass itself on to subsequent generations.

The unfavourable environment to culture provoked the post-liberal Dineen to imagine a conscious effort to rebuild this organic culture, even though the intentional design of a culture goes against the grain of culture itself. Where should such effort to rebuild the culture occur? Dineen proposed practices to sustain cultures in communities, households and civic life. We must found new schools of our culture for our republics, and, in the discipline of their education in character, find our way to true, ancient liberty.

13 Ways of Looking at a Bureaucrat

The true history of the bureaucracy gang

(In episode 6 of *The Burning Archive* podcast (released on 4 June 2021), I discussed the history of the bureaucracy in the UK, USA and Germany, and its relationship to political decay. Is the bureaucracy to blame for our republics in distress?)

Welcome to *The Burning Archive*, the podcast where the past is never dead, the past is not even past, and where, by thinking about the past, we try to live better in the present.

In this episode of *The Burning Archive* I am talking about one decaying political institution I know very well, the bureaucracy, civil service or public service. And I ask, is the bureaucracy to blame for our republics in distress, and can it act as a bulwark against political decay? So bureaucracy and political decay, and what is the true history of the bureaucracy game? That is the topic of today's episode of *The Burning Archive*.

I am Jeff Rich, I am a writer, historian and a very minor government official. Let me add this podcast is my own creative conceptual work, and not related to my official role. Let me just give a shout out to everyone who, like me, is living in Victoria and in lockdown, again. Hopefully, we'll survive this, and for those of you who might be listening to the podcast in weeks, years past, going back over old episodes, yes indeed, we are still in the midst of a coronavirus pandemic, and, for one reason or another, we have been locked down in Melbourne. So very tight rules, but fortunately no rules against podcasting.

Today we're talking about the second of our topics under the little mini-theme of political decay. Last time we talked about the general concept of political decay, and today we're talking about one of the institutions that is caught up in this trend of political decay. It is an

On the institutions of government

institution about which we rarely hear an authentic, unfiltered voice from the inside. You hear a lot of people speaking for or about the bureaucracy. They speak generally in not very favourable terms. But very few speak honestly from their own, let's say, lived experience of being a bureaucrat. Now that is what I'm going to do today, or at least I'm going to offer an insider's *historical* perspective on the institution of bureaucracy. What is its place in our political order? What current trends influence the institution? How do they illustrate the broad theme of political decay that I have been talking about in this podcast.

Last week I introduced the theme of political decay and the work of Francis Fukuyama on political order and political decay. I discussed Fukuyama's idea of political decay, and how it relates to political institutions and political culture. It might be worth mentioning here, since we are talking about the topic of political decay, that the artwork for my podcast, which is also featured on my blog, is a painting by Joseph Turner, 'The Burning of the Houses of Parliament'. It represents a catastrophic fire in the Palace of Westminster in London in October 1834 that destroyed parts of the Parliament buildings. It is a symbol of a set of political institutions facing a grim future, and also the opportunity for renewal, which fire does provide.

So last week I explained how Fukuyama had, in his work *Political Order and Political Decay*, presented this tension between basic behaviours of human sociability or basic human social behaviours. Examples are looking after your own kin and doing favours for others in exchange for favours they do for you so. Fukuyama used the terms *kinship affiliation* and *reciprocal altruism*. Kinship affiliation can be broadened out from direct blood relatives to include people similar in kind, however you might define that. So there is a tension between those basic drives of human sociability and the formal impartial rules of a capable political state. That tension really is the underlying sociological, even perhaps cultural-biological, process that underlies the process of political decay. It underlies how political systems oscillate between stable regimes of political order, and states of

13 Ways of Looking at a Bureaucrat

disorder, even if the swings are slow. When systems fall into disorder, they require rebuilding and reconstitution in different ways.

This tension is shown in how politics and governments use patronage, which, of course, is a very important political phenomenon of kinship affiliation and reciprocal affiliation. There is a tension between patronage, as a fundamental tool of politics, and the institution of a professional impartial public service. Of course, the whole concept of a politically neutral professional public service is at the heart of a well-functioning government, especially a well-functioning democratic government. It is really crucial to its role, and yet the whole issue of political appointments ('jobs for the boys', 'jobs for mates') wears away at that.

The tension between having a professional impartial merit-based public service, where there are not political appointments, favourites or cliques, is at the heart of a well-functioning political system. But to maintain that kind of institution requires political systems constantly to work against that basic human drive of sociability. Impartiality grates with the drive to look after your own and to do favours for others in exchange for the favours they do for you. Consequently, a professional impartial public service, when established as a good quality institution, needs to have guardrails against the very natural social behaviours that go on within any culture.

In Francis Fukuyama's story of the development of political order, the development of a professionalised public service or a strong capable bureaucracy really plays a quite central role. It is unusual, given most accounts of politics do not focus on the central role of the bureaucracy. But Fukuyama provides a central role to the development of a strong bureaucracy, a strong, capable, professional, independent, impartial bureaucracy. He does not use the exact term of 'independent', but I will get back to that. A strong capable bureaucracy is totally fundamental to his story. Indeed, he commented that the big historical mystery that has to be solved is not, why does political

On the institutions of government

patronage exist? It is, rather, why did modern political systems come to outlaw patronage and to replace basic sociability drives with impartial codes and impersonal organisation? Now, 'impersonal' might seem a negative term, and in some ways it is. But Fukuyama uses this term to mean that an organisation functions by clear and objective rules that are fair or neutral to all, rather than being driven by kinship affiliation and favours.

If, as Fukuyama says, it is a quite an achievement to create bureaucratic institutions that resist those processes of affiliation and altruism, then it is not a surprise that we are always putting our finger in the dyke to hold back political decay and 'politicisation' of bureaucracy. It is actually a social achievement that is hard to create, and easy to break down. So, it is not surprising that we continually over time, with peaks and troughs, discuss concerns with political appointments to the public service: 'jobs for the boys', 'jobs for the girls', jobs that are 'not based on merit' or real achievements, appointments that made, in fact, to secure and consolidate the party in power.

It is not a particularly political thing to say that the process of political decay affects the bureaucracy. It is more a general principle drawn out from Fukuyama's description of political order and political decay. This fundamental institution, the public service, is subjected to these same processes, that strain against instinctive sociability. It goes through this same dynamic. Its institutions cycle through phases when they form strong objective rules for behaviour, and phases when those guardrails are worn away and broken down. Sometimes, leaders of institutions jump over whole Chesterton fences. There are phases of elite capture, when a close knit gang at the top are sociable to themselves alone. There are phases when officials, high and low, reconstitute rules in response to competition and other social changes.

Although capable bureaucracy is a social achievement that is hard to create and easy to break down, it is important to note that, when it does break down, its loss threatens the stability of political order. So, it is not a trivial thing to find that one's state institutions are not working effectively as impersonal organisations, but rather becoming 'repatrimonialized', to use Fukuyama's term that described how leaders use patronage system to control government institutions.

Here it might be worth just saying that Fukuyama's concept of political order has a three-legged foundation. So for him political order, or a well-functioning political system, has three fundamental elements. One is this capable state. Another is the rule of law. In well-ordered polities there is not just fickle monarchical decisions or tyrannical decisions, but there is a rule of law that governs how disputes within the society are resolved. The third leg is accountability. Mechanisms of accountability include parliament, even if it does burn down every now and then, as in Joseph Turner's painting that I referred to at the start of the show, his depiction of the fire in the Palace of Westminster in 1834. A parliament is a crucial form of democratic accountability that supports political orders. The people who make big political decisions or coordinate social actions have some sort of accountability to those who are affected by those institutions. This accountability can take many forms, and Fukuyama uses sociological, neutral terms to apply his analysis to political orders.

The third crucial leg is the capable state. Fukuyama's *Political Order and Political Decay* really focuses on state capacity, in contrast to strong American libertarian or neo-liberal traditions. His argument contrasts to the elite or econocratic thinking of the last 30 years that very much overvalues markets over governments. Fukuyama argued that you can not just have law. You can not just have accountability mechanisms, scrutiny and so on. You actually need a government, a state, that can do things, and that can do them effectively and well. Its capacity to do things is fundamental to the authority, legitimacy and stability, that is required in political order. So what matters is not primarily the size of government. What matters is not big government versus small government, or questions of whether government has a

On the institutions of government

role in this industry or that industry. What matters most is the effectiveness of government, rather than its size.

In a way, Francis Fukuyama is putting a view that is shared by a sociologist who has ventured into the world of politics and political order, Stein Ringen. He is a Norwegian sociologist, who largely writes in English, and he wrote a book called *A Nation of Devils*. The title is a fantastic description of government. It describes the democratic problem of maintaining authority with an uppity citizenry. Like many others, Fukuyama and Ringen observe in opinion polls and surveys the loss of trust in democracy, loss of faith in democracy, and loss of confidence in the performance of democracies. But they argue these losses are not caused by fickle citizens, but largely by failing performance by governments and elites.

These losses also relate to the theme of political decay. In speaking of my theme of political decay, I am not commenting on whether I like who is in government or who is the leader now. It is more a commentary on this declining sense of trust, declining sense of authority, declining sense of legitimacy and declining sense of performance by government elites. These declines create their own dilemmas. If there is less confidence that your society is being governed well and governed in a rightful sort of way, there is a kind of vicious circle of declining trust and authority.

For Fukuyama, then, a critical institution to a well-functioning state is the bureaucracy. Importantly, he made the point that the bureaucracy is not just one single organisation. It is a collection of government organisations or institutions, a networked collection of government organisations and institutions. How well those institutions function is fundamental to state capacity or the capable state. It keeps standing one of the three legs of a stable political order. Fukuyama wrote that governments are collections of complex organisations. How well they perform depends on how they are organised, and the human and material resources at their disposal.

13 Ways of Looking at a Bureaucrat

Certainly, from an insider's point of view, without talking specifics, government is a very complicated network of organisations. Most of what you see reported in the media, and even a lot of academic commentary, on how governments function is very shallow in its understanding. This commentary often just calls the political horse race. There are a couple of celebrity political figures, who set the course and whose news conferences one follows constantly, and it is all just one big show. From the inside perspective, from the experience of someone who has lived in this habitat for thirty years, government looks like a very complicated ecosystem of these different institutions. They all have their own patterns, lives and ways of organisation. None work perfectly. None interact together perfectly as well.

But to work well as a complex political network of organisations, the bureaucracy needs to establish a balanced arrangement between these two design principles. Establishing balance is difficult, however, because there is significant tension between these principles that spills out into the organisations.

The first principle is what is often referred to as the principal-agent dilemma. If bureaucracies are to be politically and democratically accountable, they cannot set their own agenda entirely by themselves. They need to do things that someone, who has a mandate, authority or democratic accountability, wants them to do. That person or persons is the 'principal'. Let us call them the Minister or the Premier or the Government, the elected officials. The 'agents' are the actual bureaucrats in the institution. This dilemma is commonly referred to as an economic problem. How does the principal get the agent to do what they want them to do? How does the principal do this when they have limited information? How do they do this when they are just one person or a small band of people who are trying to coerce a large group of agents, the big bad bureaucracy, which has thousands of people (who are all lazy, wear cardigans, and work from home), to do what they are meant to do?

On the institutions of government

So that is the principal-agent dilemma, which is fundamental. There is a lot of discussion of this dilemma. There have been a lot of interventions over the years to make sure the bureaucracy works well with the principal-agent dilemma. Governments have implemented, for example, reforms to establish clear missions, to have business plans and to establish performance objectives for senior bureaucrats or even Ministers with Premiers. The whole system of Westminster parliamentary accountability deals with this dilemma. The Minister will tell the bureaucrats what to do, not the other way around. So there are an awful lot of systems around that.

What is interesting about Fukuyama's discussion is that he puts a lot of emphasis on the other design principle of making the institution work well, which is relative autonomy. So, an institution will not be effective if it is really just acting as a cat's paw for another's ideas. It needs to be able to, if you like, come up with its own ideas, turn them into reality, and make them work. There is clearly a tension between the principles of principal-agent and relative autonomy. You could compare it to the tensions in a family, when children grow up and become adults. You want the bureaucracy to be the loyal child to the parent of the Minister. But, at another level, you actually want the bureaucracy to be the grown-up independent adults, who make their own decisions. So trying to get those two design principles to work effectively together is a real, fundamental dilemma.

This dilemma returns us to the tension between patronage and state capacity. If you are a political agent (a Minister, Premier or Cabinet), you can assert control of the bureaucracy through two broad strategies. You can appoint your own, who you know will do what you want. Or, you can try persuasive influence over established people, who will change their position to agree to do what you want. If you assert control the first way, you undermine the relative autonomy and effectiveness of the institution. If you assert control the second way, you maintain the relative autonomy of the institution but at the risk of not persuading people to do what you want. The choice of strategy is made more complex by the fact that no political principal is ever completely happy with how a bureaucracy is performing. There is always reason to restrict the relative autonomy of any bureaucracy. Nor is any political principal the perfect persuader. Sometimes, the Premier loses the argument, and so there are always reasons to appoint people you do not have to argue with.

So you see this dilemma with bureaucracy over the history of government. How do you get the bureaucracy to do the things you want it to do? Number one is, well, we will just appoint our own people to run it and then we will run it, as we like, through our proxies. The other way is to win over the hearts and minds of the people in the institution. Then principals might even take on board some ideas of the existing bureaucracy about how they can most effectively help the principals to achieve their goals.

This tension is fundamental to how bureaucracies are managed, and indeed to the history of bureaucracies. It is fundamental to the whole institution of a merit-based, impartial, public service that is capable, and, in some ways, independent or relatively autonomous. In my view, one piece of evidence that our polities are in political decay, is the falling away over the last 30 or 40 years of a merit-based, impartial public service, that is capable and independent. I will not say a lot about this now, because I am still a serving public servant and do not want to infringe any speech code rules, but that is my view of the governments that I am aware of, and probably broadly within Western or Anglophone, liberal democratic societies.

This view is also actually one of Fukuyama's key points. It is one reason he feels that we are in this process of political decay. The way in which Fukuyama tells the story is through the forest service in America. The forest service was established in the late 19th century or maybe early 20th century in America. It became an incredibly capable and effective institution in terms of managing the the forests of America, both preventing fires, distributing the timber, and protecting

On the institutions of government

the nature in the forest, the animals, trees and all that stuff. But Fukuyama really tells the story of how it has become much much less effective, and, in some ways, has lost its way as an institution in recent years.

Without going into all the details, I am sure listeners can probably think of their own cases of major bureaucratic institutions, that have featured in press stories, wherever they might live in recent years. Your cases similarly may have not performed so well. I do not really want to get into any particulars of any current institutions that may have not performed their mission well; or have been seen to have followed influential leaders; or pursued 'creeping assumptions' (a term used in the Victorian inquiry into failures of management of hotel quarantine during the pandemic) that they they thought were the right thing to do. These institutions have done what people wanted them to do. They have not acted, in Fukuyama's terms as a 'relatively autonomous' institution that has a strong sense of its own identity, mission, purpose and systems for ensuring the right sort of talent rises to the top. People can find examples within their own experience of those kind of institutions.

Since I am a serving public servant, I am not free to talk so much about the present, but I am going to present a historical perspective. I will relay Fukuyama's story of how a merit-based, professional, impartial, capable bureaucracy has developed in three different countries. The three countries are the United States, Britain, and Germany. In each case, bureaucracy developed in relationship to other democratic institutions. The sequence of that development was really instrumental to the extent to which those bureaucracies were subjected to these processes of patronage and political decay.

It is useful to look back at these stories because, in my experience, people in the bureaucracy, often very senior people in the bureaucracy, do not know enough about the history of their institutions. They often know little history of their specific local institution nor the broader

13 Ways of Looking at a Bureaucrat

history of political institutions that is outlined in Fukuyama's work. They tend to operate in response to very immediate pressures around them, bobble around in the turbulence, and operate with these very perfunctory understandings. They might tell the story something like this, "Oh well, you know, there was a Northcote-Trevelyan report in the 19th century that established a merit-based system and the merit principle has been fundamental to bureaucracy ever since."

We all operate within the Westminster system; but often our understanding of those institutions, rules and cultures, what they are really about and what they are really capable of, is limited to much more recent, immediate experiences. The management of the principal-agent dilemma is managed by a habit of just satisfying the minister's most recent request. This 'responsiveness' removes an immediate problem for leaders, but has longer term consequences for the pattern of behaviour. Fukuyama's story then is a pretty valuable corrective to these simplified understandings of bureaucracy.

His story begins with perhaps the earliest cases of the formation of a highly professionalised bureaucracy in Europe, and that is Germany. In other parts of his book he discusses other traditions of government and forms of merit-based bureaucracy in China, India, Persia and other countries many years before. But for our purposes we are zeroing in the discussion on this formative century or so between the mid-19th century and mid-20th century, which fashioned the political institutions that we still live with today. So Germany has this tradition or institution called the *Rechtsstaat,* which refers to a constitutional state in which the exercise of governmental power is constrained by the law, and more broadly to a well-organised legally based system of public law and bureaucracy. It is established in the late 18th century, when the German state's principalities, including especially Prussia, are run autocratically. They are not democracies at this point. They are not parliamentary democracies, but autocracies that have a strong institutional bureaucracy with a foundation in law. This *Rechtsstaat* provides forms of accountability, rule of law, and a capable state. It

On the institutions of government

provides Fukuyama's three-legged foundation of a sensible political order. Fukuyama highlighted how Germany had a long history of this highly capable state, with a strong institutional bureaucracy, and with a strong system of public law. It was rooted in the traditions of Holy Roman Empire and, to some extent, the Napoleonic Code, which came with the expansion of the French Empire across Europe in the early 19th century. These developments all happened prior to the extension of the democratic franchise.

Fukuyama made the point that a key driver in the dynamic of political decay in institutions of the state is the sequence of development. When and how did the state develop? When and how did each of the three foundations (accountability, rule of law and state capacity) get established? How does capable state relate to rule of law and to democratic accountability? In Germany's case there is a strong well-developed bureaucracy that is established before mass party systems get off the ground and before a widespread democratic franchise. The widened franchise brings with it the tendency to enlarge patronage systems so that political leaders can reward political supporters. Fukuyama noted that the capability of German state institutions went through lots of changes but fundamentally survived multiple regimes. Some regimes and events tested the state to breaking point: the two World Wars, the Weimar Republic, Nazi Germany, and post-war reconstruction. But throughout those strains, Fukuyama argued, the bureaucracy retained an *esprit de corps* and political support for its autonomy. This German bureaucracy of *Rechtsstaat* is the very model and conceptual basis for Max Weber's famous definition of one form of political authority, the legal-rational form. So that is story number one. In Germany, a strong system of bureaucracy that values public law, merit, capability and effectiveness gets established. It adapts to different political regimes, but, because of its relative autonomy, it maintains a relationship with political actors or the political elite, that supports its autonomy. Its effectiveness is vital to being a well-functioning institution. It does not succumb to being a place where lots of supporters of the current regime are appointed.

The second case is the USA, and it is at the other extreme of the spectrum. In the USA, the democratic franchise comes a lot earlier, in the early 19th century. With the wider franchise, there came an extensive system of party-based appointments to government posts, which is generally known as the 'spoils system'. Even today, when the President gets elected, a huge draft of appointments are made. They are often party appointments. They are often people who have displayed personal loyalty to the leader. These appointments include Cabinet Ministers of the state, who unlike Australia are not directly elected, and many posts in the bureaucracy. They are direct appointees of the President, although some posts need to be endorsed by Congress. This creates a large patronage system. In the 19th century, even minor positions were party-based appointments, including clerical roles in post offices and similar kind of work.

This spoils system created an extensive system of patronage and 'clientelism', which is a word Fukuyama uses. In some ways, this system is positive. Those people are being helped out by those appointments; but they are, if you like, clients of the party. In response to the system, there is, through the late 19th and early 20th centuries, a long, difficult process of reforms to public administration. Woodrow Wilson, later President of the United States, is associated with these reforms, and the very concept of public administration is, to some degree, an outgrowth of that. Reforms are slowly implemented, but never wholly successful. To this day, America remains a state of 'courts and parties'. This commonly used term describes the system of two oligarchic parties that have power to make many political appointments to courts, and, through the enormous spoil system, to the bureaucracy. All of this means that the institutions of bureaucracy are more subjected to patronage and political decay, and more exposed to the behaviour of kinship affiliation and reciprocal altruism. As a result of the spoils system, bureaucratic institutions just do not have the same relative autonomy. Political leaders control these institutions by appointing proxies, rather than through rightful persuasion.

On the institutions of government

The final example is Britain. In a way, this national case study is most familiar to Australia. We have our kinship with Westminster traditions. The Australian bureaucracies have internalised as their own histories the Westminster mental model of how an independent public service was formed. So what happened in the UK was really quite interesting. We should recall that the German states, especially Prussia, had a highly effective bureaucracy by the early 19th century. By contrast, Fukuyama wrote, Britain began the 19th century with an unreformed and patronage-ridden civil service. It began to clean up its bureaucracy in the middle decades of the century. Those changes laid the foundations for a modern civil service. One has to really understand that in the 19th century, England is really run by an aristocracy. The exclusive dominance of the aristocracy has been challenged by the industrial and commercial middle class, but throughout Britain there is this tight aristocracy. You can read in the *Palliser* novels of Anthony Trollope a brilliant depiction of the social patterns of these political elites in 19th century Britain. Indeed, Trollope himself was actually a bureaucrat in the post office, and his novels are brilliant pieces of observation from within the bureaucracy. He showed how all these aristocrats, who had tightly knit connections, ran patronage systems. Nonetheless, this elite aspired to the ideas of liberal reform that were associated with a 'merit-based' bureaucracy.

The big changes began in the 1850s with the Northcote-Trevelyan report, which is frequently referred to in dumbed-down managerialist interpretations of the history of the bureaucracy. These simplistic accounts claim the idea of a merit-based bureaucracy, including competitive selection by exams, came into being with this report. These simplified versions of history do not acknowledge how the report was specific to Britain, or how they adapted practices from the Indian civil service. Nor do they clarify how Northcote and Trevelyan were responding to an institutional problem that Fukuyama described. Britain did not have a capable bureaucracy like Prussia. It had a collection of well-connected office holders of questionable competence and often non-existent training. There was no real way to climb to the top of the the institution, if you like, without that patronage. Moreover, the people who wrote the famous report, Northcote and Trevelyan, were themselves, in fact, highly connected aristocrats. They owed positions and influence to that same elite patronage system. Yet they also tried to rebuild the institution in some ways, if without totally surrendering aristocratic control.

Again, in part, the Northcote-Trevelyan civil service reforms were provoked by the failures of that bureaucratic system that were evident in military and other incompetence during the Crimean war in the 1850s. The reforms were in part a response to imperial failures in that war. However, it took another 20 years before the ideas that were set out in the Northcote-Trevelyan report were actually implemented by British Governments. It took a series of Prime Ministers, Gladstone, Disraeli and others, but it was ultimately done. Again these reforms were largely done in England before the most significant extension of the democratic franchise. They were done before the really strong formation of political parties, which would later operate different American-style patronage or clientelistic systems in Britain. Those electoral reforms did not really happen until the 1870s or 1880s, or later with the emergence of highly organised political parties. It was during those 20 years or so, after the 1850s Crimean War to the early 1880s, that the civil service was slowly rebuilt.

There were, of course, many later reforms to the public service. But, in some fundamental ways, the basic institutions and ideas of Westminster bureaucracy were formed in this period. Again, it is decisive that these reforms were done a little bit free of the forces of popular patronage and clientelism, that were associated with the extension the democratic franchise in America. This context was fundamental to the creation of a strong institution that had some relative autonomy and some genuine capability as well.

Now, the story of the development of the public service or bureaucracy in Australia and Victoria is different again. I will not fully sketch this history. Our bureaucracies have obviously been strongly shaped, as ex-British colonies, by the British experience, culturally, legally and institutionally. They have taken on many aspects of that experience, but also had some different characteristics that are important to note. The state in mid-19th century Australia had, in some ways, a much larger role in society than the British state at home. It had extensive roles to settle areas, to distribute land, to build all the infrastructure, and to set up all the the institutions of the newly established colonial society. It did these functions, certainly in Victoria, at broadly the same time as the extension of the democratic franchise, wider and earlier than in Britain. But these states were limited in another way. Until 1900, they were still colonies. After the federalist movement and 1900, these relatively strong government institutions expand further. Social observers commented on the large state experiments in Australia and New Zealand, such as electricity, water, gas and fuel, and transport corporations.

This large role for the state influenced the history of bureaucracy in Australia. It had some broad similarities to the English story, but also definite differences. I only want to sketch the history of the last 30 to 40 years, without getting too direct about current organisations, given my role as a current public servant. But over the last 30 to 40 years, I have observed significant change in society and political systems that have created new pressures on the institution of bureaucracy, and made it more difficult to hold back the strong forces of political patronage. The role of the private sector has grown through contracts, commercial arrangements and partnerships with private sector organisations. The professionalisation of political parties has occurred. There has been a professionalisation of politics. Numbers of professional political advisers have increased significantly. The phenomenon of 'spin doctors' or political marketing has become much more pronounced. There are overlapping networks between political professionals and media journalists. Many journalists have become political advisers and political advisers have become journalists. They move in and out of roles as communications professionals or political advisers or, in some cases, bureaucrats, including in very senior roles. As well, there has been a conscious effort over time to improve the responsiveness of the bureaucracy to political direction. Political control of the bureaucracy is necessary, of course, but the efforts to increase responsiveness to political direction have upset the balance between responsiveness of agents to principals and relative autonomy of agents.

The growing demand for responsiveness and the growing forces of political patronage have probably undermined the capability and relative autonomy of the bureaucracy in Australia. As a result, Australian bureaucracies have come to operate in a spoils system, much closer to the American model of courts, parties and spoils. Australia has certainly moved further from the German system of a strong relatively autonomous institutions that have a strong *esprit de corps* and a fundamental sense of being rooted in public law. We have taken our own detour through a new form of clientelism. These trends have had a big impact on institutions losing relative autonomy. Leaders of institutions are more prone to follow 'creeping assumptions,' rather than to strike out in clear strong directions.

This is, I think, the true history of the bureaucracy gang. It is a story of political decay. I can only comment from my own experience, but I suspect similar patterns have occurred in other countries. Ultimately, how these patterns play out in other countries is an empirical question that I cannot answer. I can only share my honest observation from three decades of experience in these institutions. What I see around me is a less capable state, that is served by less relatively autonomous institutions, and that is more prone to those political processes that Fukuyama described as fundamental to political. So I think it is a good little case study of my theme of political decay. Of course, those institutions could be rebuilt around a strong sense of *Rechtsstaat,* fundamental purpose and relative autonomy. But that is a job to be done, I guess, rather than something that is happening now. Hopefully that will happen.

On the institutions of government

So that is where I end the podcast for this week. Next week I am going to speak perhaps on somewhat safer ground. I hope some of the slightly indirect ways in which I've had to express things, given that I am a current public servant, has not been too annoying this time. Hopefully, I have not said anything too spicy. Next week I will talk on the third topic of political decay, the issue of culture. Institutions can be a bulwark of against political decay if they are strong relatively autonomous institutions. They can use their sense of *Rechtsstaat* and purpose to resist processes that degrade their capability. But there is also a sense in which culture can resist decay. Culture can be a form of regeneration against this pattern of political decay. Culture is the spirit in people's hearts and minds, the ideas that they hold dear, and the virtues that they practice. Next week, I want to talk about what you can call the 'ordinary virtues of governing well', and how they are a source of hope to deal with this structural process of political decay. We are all wrestling with that process of decay, which is closely linked to other themes of the podcast. So you have been listening to the *Burning Archive* podcast where the past is never dead the past is not even past and we're by thinking about the past we learn or try to live better in the present.

Politicisation of the public service

In 2022 I made a submission to the Victorian Ombudsman Inquiry into the Politicisation of the Public Service. I made this submission while still employed as a public servant, if a very, very minor government official. It was an act not without some risk.

The inquiry was established among numerous political scandals involving the alleged misuse of government funds (by politicians from the party elected to power in 2014) for electioneering. These scandals led to a motion in the Upper House of the Victorian Parliament that urged the Ombudsman to investigate a host of issues related to corruption, including the politicisation of the public service. One member of Parliament who supported this motion quipped that the Victorian public service resembled a Labor Party branch meeting.

I called the Ombudsman's office a few days after this motion and privately supported to her staff the proposal to investigate the politicisation of the public service. A month or two later, the Ombudsman quietly announced that she would conduct an inquiry. I called the submission inquiry line, and spoke to the inquiry staff about the issues for me, in making a submission as a current public servant. I had broad, long experience of the issues being investigated, and yet I was concerned that sharing my knowledge would lead to retribution against me. One issue was whether to seek protected disclosure status of any revelations of confidential information in the public interest. This status would secure legal protection against retribution. Another issue was whether to provide specific evidence or documents that I had access to.

While I weighed up these issues, I decided to accept an 'early retirement package', or redundancy from the public service. I decided to proceed with my submission to the Ombudsman, but not to seek specific legal protections nor provide specific documents or evidence. I made my submission as general observations on the institution. They were reflections on how the public service had changed, based on my knowledge of specific decisions, history, and careful observation and broad study over 30 or more years. I pointed the inquiry to issues that it could investigate further, including through any legal powers to order the production of documents.

So I made this submission, and decided to live in truth. I remained discreet, however, and told no one but my family about it. I called the Inquiry staff a few months later, to clarify if the Ombudsman's report would come out before the Victorian election in November 2022, and before my departure, or dishonourable discharge, from the public

On the institutions of government

service after a career of 33 years and a thousand sorrows. The report did not come out. At the time of publication of this book, the inquiry still has not reported. The Ombudsman staff have told me a report is intended for later in 2023. I confirmed with them that I could publish this submission without impacting their investigation. It is after all my intellectual property. For this wider readership without investigatory responsibilities, I have removed most individual names. My hopes had that this Ombudsman Inquiry might fix the problems I described in this submission have not yet died in the darkness. Here is the submission. For small reasons, I hope it might find a corner of light in your imagination.

POLITICISATION OF THE PUBLIC SERVICE - SUBMISSION

Dear Ombudsman,

I have served as an apolitical public servant for 33 years since 1990. I have maintained this service through periods of governments of both major political parties. However, I will be taking early retirement later this year in part because of the discouragement created by the widespread politicisation of the Victorian Public Service.

I am making this submission from a sense of public duty. I feel obliged to give this testimony of a well-informed observer, who has been a direct witness of this process of politicisation and its damaging effects on the quality of our governing institutions.

Over my career I have worked across multiple departments, including two periods in the Department of Premier and Cabinet in the 1990s and 2000s. For the last sixteen years I have worked in the Department of Health and its predecessors. I have worked directly with Secretaries, Ministers, Premiers, ex-Premiers, scores of ministerial advisers, hundreds of executive officers, and many more non-executive public servants. I have also worked with all arms of government - police, judiciary, independent officers, parliamentarians, and the administrative executive in all its aspects - decision-makers, decision-implementers, policy-makers, investigators, regulators, financial managers, contract managers, and service deliverers.

I have myself sat on many selection committees and performed executive officer roles. I have known the direct pressures of balancing responsiveness to the political executive with the duties of an impartial public service, including during critical periods such as transitions of government (1992, 1999, 2010 and 2014) and the extended caretaker period of 1999.

I am also an historian of Victoria, and a student of literature on political institutions, including the role of bureaucracy in what Francis Fukuyama calls political order and political decay. I have no partisan affiliation, and believe I can offer some insights to your inquiry.

There are five main points I submit to the inquiry. First, there is widespread politicisation of public service executive appointments. Second, this politicisation is institutionalised, including through the use of consultancies, adviser roles, and think tank and NGO appointments. Third, the politicisation has affected the culture of the whole public service. Fourth, it has had on balance a negative impact on the quality of government and democracy. Fifth, reform needs to address long term causes and the institutional nature of the problem, preferably through a broad major public inquiry.

I have identified some cases in my submission that you may wish to investigate. I have also made brief suggestions for reforms to these problems, although I have not assessed them in depth. However, I believe the best result from your inquiry would be a broad ranging public inquiry into the public service and institutions of government. Such a public dialogue would be able to develop robust and lasting reforms. I wish your inquiry well as a first step towards such reforms.

Overview

There is *widespread politicisation* of Public Service executive appointments. In Victoria today, it is more likely that a Public Service executive will be a former adviser to an ALP Minister than a career public servant.

The practice has *become institutionalised*, creating in effect a cadre of executive officers and consultants who are politically aligned and personally loyal. This cadre is recruited, in effect, separately from the career public service, and then advanced through political patronage.

This politicisation has *broken down the politically impartial culture in the whole public service, including non-executive positions.* There is now a dominant culture of supporting the government through the political and election cycle, advocacy of progressive political causes in the workplace, and 'doing what the MO/PPO (Minister's Office and Premier's Private Office) want'. This culture has supplanted traditions of balanced judgement of alternative views in the public interest.

The politicisation has brought benefits for some groups. It has opened channels of advice to the government by consultancy firms and non-government organisations. Over several decades, it has increased the responsiveness of the administrative executive to the political executive. But in the context of diminished parliamentary and public scrutiny, *politicisation has undermined relative autonomy of the bureaucracy, and so contributed to failures in the Victorian Government over the last decade.*

Reforms to politicisation need to deal with the specific issues of executive appointments within a broader institutional framework, and *devise a better balance between the political and administrative executive, public law and informal codes, and parliamentary and executive institutions of democracy in Victoria.*

Widespread Politicisation

There is widespread politicisation of Victorian Public service appointments. Anecdotally, it appears more likely that an executive will be a former ALP adviser or affiliated consultant than a career public servant.

This is my impression, and the only evidence I can test it with is my personal knowledge of the backgrounds of many executives over my 33 years in the Victorian Government. However, the extent of political appointments is an empirical question that could be tested. For example, the Ombudsman or a later, larger public inquiry could undertake a forensic audit of executive appointments in one or more departments over the last five or more years to make an assessment. Key candidates to examine in my experience would be the Department of Premier and Cabinet, Department of Health, Department of Families, Fairness and Housing, and the Department of Justice and Community Safety. From my personal knowledge, however, I can provide a very long list of politically affiliated executives in my and other Departments. Many of these people are capable and committed servants of the public. However, they are not markedly more capable and committed than the career public servants whose careers they block.

The sheer number of people drawn from one politically affiliated source has an impact on perceptions of the public service in the Parliament, among stakeholders and within the service itself. It deters many career public servants from putting themselves forward for executive roles. As it is said, quantity has a quality all of its own.

The preponderance of politically affiliated executives also raises doubts about the true propriety or genuine application of the merit-principle in many appointments in today's public service. Again, I cannot make definite judgements without examining the detailed processes, paperwork and relative judgements of individual appointments. However, there have been numerous appointments in recent years that have raised questions in my mind.

For example, the current head of DPC was appointed within a few weeks of the resignation of Mr Chris Eccles, after his embarrassment during the Coate Inquiry. This individual has a background as a journalist, a political adviser, a basketball coach (following loss of political office) and then a communications executive in government. Yet he is nominally the head of the Victorian public service in the same role performed by George Brouwer, Terry Moran or Elizabeth Proust. His appointment creates a standard for all to follow.

I would also point out the role of several former senior political advisers of the current Premier and state or federal ALP political leaders to highly sensitive public service executive positions. There are also several former staffers to the current Premier who are in senior executive positions in the Department of Health.

In one case, a senior political adviser was appointed to a role as Director of Long-Term Strategy in the then Department of Health and Human Services in mid-2017. The role was created in a restructure, but the job was advertised prior to the restructure being announced and finalised. In this role the executive was primarily responsible for preparing advice for the incoming governments, including developing policy proposals ahead of the 2018 election. The political adviser's previous role had been as the Policy Director in the political office of the current Premier, both in Government and in Opposition. The person is a highly effective executive. However, on the surface, there may be questions about a clear separation of this person's political and public service roles, and whether the public service role contributed directly to the ALP's re-election campaign.

Finally, the Age reported on 18 June 2022 on the case of mass executive sacking and hiring in 2018-19 in the Department of Justice and Community Safety, following the appointment of Ms Rebecca Falkingham (a former adviser to Labor Minister, Mary Delahunty). 'Shock and awe' incidents like these have a chilling impact on the public service and frame the norms of the institution. I perceived these events at the time as a clean-out of the Justice Department that followed a similar pattern to processes undertaken in the Department of Health and Human Services Department from 2015.

Institutional Character of Politicisation

There are so many politicised executive appointments in Victoria now that the practice could be considered institutionalised or systemic. It is more than just a problem of individual cases of poor practice or abuse. The practice has accelerated since 2014, but has longer term roots and broader institutional drivers. It is also linked to career paths, institutions and businesses outside the public service. In effect, Victoria now operates a covert US style 'spoils system', rather than a professional civil service.

Over decades, a loyal cadre has been put in place by networks of direct political patronage. These directly politicised appointments radiate out into wider and wider networks of patron-client relationships. Many executives who are not clearly associated with political parties are, on closer examination, loyal to primary or secondary patrons within the network.

The cadre is largely not made of career public servants, but political advisers for state and federal politicians, journalists and communications advisers, consultants from strategy firms (e.g. KPMG, Boston Consulting Group) or nominally independent, but in fact politically affiliated, NGOs or think-tanks, such as the Grattan Institute. Some individuals may point to brief periods of public service in their careers. On the whole, however, they have pursued careers through a system of loyalty, patronage and favours that promotes different behaviours and values to those expected of true career public servants.

This network includes close relationships, and exchange of favours, between political executive, political advisers, public service communications executives, the media and the commentariat. These networks increasingly are moving through senior public service roles, and affecting the quality of public discussion of policy issues.

On the institutions of government

This pattern of recruitment accelerated after 2000, and included a number of significant cases in the early to mid-2000s. For example, Mr Terry Moran brought into top-level roles in the Department of Premier and Cabinet: Mr David Fredericks (an ALP political adviser), Mr Greg Hywood (a journalist and media executive) and Mr George Pappas (a strategy consultant from the Boston Consulting Group). It was not significantly checked during the Baillieu/Napthine Government, and has expanded significantly since. Each appointment year by year pushed harder against the fence established by apolitical conventions, until, after 2014, the fence was overrun. Now there are no normative or practical barriers to the practice. It is just the way of doing government in Victoria.

The long term roots of the politicisation of the public service lie in the over-emphasis of the principle of responsiveness to the political executive in public sector reforms over the last fifty years. Responsiveness was a cure to overly powerful and badly coordinated departments and statutory authorities when these reforms began in the years after the Bland Report (1976) and during the Cain Government (1982-1991). It merged with managerialism and market reforms through the 1990s and 2000s during a time when parliamentary and public scrutiny of state politics waned. But today the political executive has captured bureaucratic institutions and controls them through this loyal cadre who are not brought up in traditions of a professional and sufficiently autonomous public service. This cadre increasingly leads the public service to support the government's political aims rather than to serve the public interest.

For this reason, I think it is important to devise solutions to the politicisation of the public service through a broader comparative framework than the Westminster system. The problem of politicisation goes to the heart of well-functioning political institutions, that can execute common purposes, operate within a framework of law, and respond to a democratic assembly. A good public service should balance all three of these principles: responsiveness to a democratic mandate, conduct within the rule of law, and relative autonomy and capability of the executive (both political and administrative). Francis Fukuyama (*Political Order and Political Decay*, 2014) expands on these issues.

Given the complexity of these issues, I will not discuss them in full in this submission. I consider a broad ranging inquiry into Victoria's public service and institutions of government is necessary. The recent work of Stein Ringen (*How Democracies Live*, 2022) offers proposals and insights that may inform any recommendation by the Ombudsman for such an inquiry.

Politicised Culture of the whole Public Service

Politicisation of executive appointments has not only had an impact on individual careers and the institutional systems of the public service. It has had a pervasive impact on the professional culture of the whole public service, including non-executive staff. People mimic their leaders in social institutions, and the models of success displayed too often in the VPS are of partisan or social media followership, not independent judgement.

There is a widespread culture of framing issues with the question of "What does the MO/PPO want?" This question displaces reasoned argument from evidence, tested by experts from inside and outside the public service. This culture is promoted by the pervasive pattern of public service executives reporting, in practice, to ministerial advisers.

In some cases, politically affiliated communications consultants also meet regularly with the Minister's offices and play a role as an outposted political adviser within a mixed team of consultants and public servants. For example, during the consultation process on the Melbourne supervised injecting room, the government engaged one former chief of staff to an ALP Minister to work as a communications consultant on the process. Another former ALP adviser and strategy consultant was employed, indirectly through state government

On the institutions of government

funding, by a community health organisation as part of the consultation process. This person was also mentioned during testimony before the Independent Broad-Based Anti-Corruption Commission. This consultation process was led by Mr Ken Lay, the Lieutenant-Governor and former Chief Commissioner of Police, who by convention the public would assume to be strictly apolitical.

There is a widespread culture of open partisan political identifications in the public service, and of speaking disrespectfully of Opposition politicians or some stakeholder groups, including when formulating replies to correspondence or freedom of information requests or parliamentary responses. There are routine promotions or advocacy of specific progressive causes, which are subject to political debate. There is a general breakdown in administrative law principles and a constant muddying of decisions with political factors. People will say "We're not being political, but...." They then proceed to be political. This problem has heightened in the Department of Health over the last two years due to the extended powers granted by the public health emergency.

These changes have undermined the professional ethos of the whole public service. They do not create a climate when the merits of policy proposals and the public interest can be dispassionately discussed by the public service. They do not create an environment that supports open discussion of differing points of view on matters of public importance. They promote a culture of loyal followership.

Such a culture must also undermine confidence of the alternative government that the public service will effectively implement its policies, if elected. If a significant body of the Parliament has doubts about the professionalism and impartiality of the public service, that is a catastrophic failure of the public service, and, in particular, of its senior leadership. In my career, I have worked through four transitions of government. In my view, the Victorian public service today has never been less ready to serve an alternative government, should

Victorians vote differently, or to consider fairly all community opinions.

Impact

The institutionalisation of a covert spoils system and the loss of a professional public service ethos have led to a loss of confidence in the public service's ability and commitment to serve the whole community. This loss of confidence among elected representatives from multiple parties (including ALP or ex-ALP members) led to the Upper House motion that prompted this inquiry. Indeed, the loss of confidence in the public service to serve the whole community is perhaps the most significant impact of the widespread politicisation of executive appointments. The simple fact that the Upper House of Parliament should have voted to investigate such an issue should be seen as a sign of critical distress for the public service.

There have certainly been benefits from the recruitment of many of these executives and some changes in culture and systems in the public service. It has opened channels of advice to the government by consultancy firms and non-government organisations. Over several decades, it has increased the responsiveness of the administrative executive to the political executive. Other submissions can document the successes since I will focus on the often concealed failures.

The politicisation of the public service has had a negative impact across a wide range of functions of Victorian Government, and contributed to significant failures in public administration over the last decade. It has been one among many causes of failures, across the board, in areas including: poorly conducted consultations, wasteful spending on consultants, poor legislation, badly designed policies, high-handed decision-making, and indeed all aspects of Victorian Government. Since I am still a serving public servant, I am not going into detail about or to document specific failures.

However, the perfect storm of these failures was the Crisis Council

On the institutions of government

of Cabinet system implemented during the COVID pandemic. Several executives referred to earlier in this submission played central roles in this process. The way in which so many heads of Department and senior executives gave evidence before the Coate Inquiry, in my opinion and that of trusted colleagues, brought shame on the public service.

The Ombudsman may wish to compare the findings of the Coate Inquiry with the way in which Mr Chris Eccles, the then Secretary, Department of Premier and Cabinet, described the public service in June 2020 in an interview with IPAA on "Leading Victoria from Crisis to Recovery". His excitement about the "public purpose sector" and new ways of decision making during the COVID crisis turned into excuses and memory lapses during his appearance at the Coate Inquiry.

The contribution of politicisation to the many failures of public administration in Victoria over the last twenty years is difficult to disentangle from other causes. However, if the foundations of institutions and culture are rotten, can the house stand?

Reforms

Finally, I would like to make some brief suggestions on reforms that might restore the public service in Victoria as a professional, capable and trusted institution of democracy.

First, and most importantly, I believe we need a broad ranging public inquiry to recommend major reforms to the public service and our wider political institutions. This inquiry could look at a broader range of issues than the current Ombudsman investigation. It should develop solutions grounded in our own factual circumstances and history, rather than repeat pieties about the Westminster system.

Second, I propose Victoria develop a stronger tradition of public law to guide bureaucrats. Public servants should feel accountable to clear legal principles and to the Parliament, and not simply be "supportive of the government of the day." Any code of conduct should reflect these principles.

Third, there should be decisive changes to the law, process and practice of executive appointments. These changes should rebalance the institutions, including through radical proposals such as: making the Governor, not the Premier, the employer of Secretaries; abolishing the executive service and establishing a single hierarchy of public service positions; reestablishing a powerful central function (like the old Public Service Board) to oversight executive or senior appointments and standards.

Fourth, there should be limitations placed on the employment in public service roles of former advisers, lobbyists, journalists and strategy consultants. Similarly, restrictions should be placed on executive public servants leaving the service to take up consultancy roles that rely on government contracts.

Fifth, there should be open government reforms to recreate a culture of public dialogue between public service officials, parliamentarians and the public. These reforms could include processes for Parliamentary inquiries, making all cabinet documents open to the public after a short period (e.g. 3-6 months) with minimal security exemptions, changes in freedom of information practices, and removing public comment restrictions on public servants. Keeping public advice secret breeds a culture of courtiership, not a discipline of open inquiry into public concerns.

There may also be a need for more openness in the dealings between political advisers, communications advisers and media organisations. Such openness may make clearer to the public the extent of planting and manipulation of news stories. It may lead the public over time to place higher value on quality sources of information from genuine public institutions.

We need to rebuild the culture and institutions of our public

On the institutions of government

service as one essential part of a better democracy. The Ombudsman's investigation will shine a light on this crucial issue. It has given me some hope that repair of the public service is not beyond reach.

Thank you for considering my submission.

13 Ways of Looking at a Bureaucrat

Chapter Eleven   Beware of Staring into the Abyss

Governing through disasters

(From *The Happy Pessimist,* 7 March 2011.)

Disaster has been the sign of our times. This last year especially, public imagination has encountered the tragic, the shocking and the devastating. The Queensland floods gave us the appalling stories of children wrenched from each other's arms as a wall of water devastated whole towns. The heroic escape of the miners in Chile was tragically reprised as sheer impotence, before an underground explosion that killed completely and instantly. We have seen Victorian floods which taunt with their slow endurance, and leave their victims feeling stranded and forgotten. A major city is turned into sludge and thousands are displaced from their homes, leaving open the question of can they ever rebuild this town? Then, Libya descends - or might I say ascends? - into a civil war of liberation, still marked by shocking murders by the ruling regime. We have seen leaders, such as Anna Bligh, overcome their flaws and redeem their image through service in the simple act of giving information in a crisis. We have seen Aunt Julia (Prime Minister Gillard) pilloried for her stiff detachment during the floods crisis, only to reveal at last a choking voice of stifled feeling when she described the flood's cruelty in marking one child for death and one child for survival.

There are many people working in governments in these states who must be in need of respite. For example, there are police officers who have mobilised emergency responses for one earthquake, then one cruelly indifferent mine explosion, then one more earthquake, that defeated all search and rescue teams. Yet respite does not come for the governing.

I can only imagine that this task of governing through disasters will become more common. In some respects, it returns the state to its most elementary function of protector and organiser of safety. It may, however, crowd out some of the functions people yearn to see performed by states. Those people aspire for the state to express a community's values, to confront difficult challenges, and to lead through transformations. But those missions of protection demand authentic helpers, not prophets. The people, who are all victims sooner or later, respond to enablers, not wreckers. They reward those who project a trace of authentic lived experience, and not the gossips of the political world.

The tragedy of the modern university

From The Burning Archive 13 July 2018.

Jordan Peterson has proposed the creation of an alternative to the modern university that offers free or low-cost education, rooted in the true traditions of the liberal humanities, stripped of their post-modern 'indoctrination cults'.[107]

I support this venture. I agree with Peterson's criticisms of the ideological possession of the shouty professors, who are read by no-one and who despise all appreciative reading. His book, 12 *Rules for Life: an antidote for chaos*, is truly wonderful, and is a powerful diagnosis of the cultural malaise affecting the university and much of contemporary intellectual life.

Peterson is also not the only proponent of such a revival of traditions of liberal education, and the creation of an alternative to the

---

[107] *The Varsity*. "Professor Jordan Peterson Wants to Create Online University," September 18, 2017.

modern hieratic screamers of heresy. Roger Scruton has written of the incurable corruption of the modern university, and his own experience of an alternative in the celebration of free association, culture and speech in the Czech dissident movement.[108] A.C. Grayling has set up an alternative College for the Humanities in London, and advocated a freeing of the rules to permit more such institutions to emerge. Yet Grayling's experiment relies on high fees, whereas Peterson is advocating a kind of return to the citizen of letters, if I may adapt the idea of the citizen scientist.

This idea perhaps will find fertile soil. We do live in the best educated societies that have ever lived, and with conditions in which anyone, including this blogger, can live a life of the mind and produce works of high culture without the need for a guardian class of professors and publishers. Such conditions can promote a true appreciative inquiry, rather than support institutional social climbers, who are more committed to their prestige than to learning.

But I do not think Peterson or Scruton or Grayling have captured the full tragedy of the modern university, which plays itself out across more disciplines than the humanities. The university has broken its own way of life through its expansion over the last fifty years. It has become a vast feral city in which its citizens can no longer rely on the university to fulfil its fundamental social, moral purpose, which is, in Scruton's words, to hand on "a store of knowledge and the culture that makes sense of it."

I feel I have been a witness to this slowly unfolding tragedy, through my experiences of government. I have worked directly with people like Mark Burford, Peter Noonan and Terry Moran who were at the heart of education reforms since the 1980s, especially the mass expansion and concurrent corporatisation of the university through the Dawkins reforms. I remember an occasion when Terry Moran mocked Dame Leonie Kramer's opposition to these reforms and her

---

[108] Roger Scruton, "The End of the University." *First Things*, April 2015.

conservative defence of the humanities as an archaic world view. Moran joined the earlier generations of the ideologically possessed who sought to turn literary analysis into intellectual Molotov cocktails, not the gentle appreciation of the infinite conversation practised by Kramer. In retrospect, however, Dame Leonie was unexpectedly right. Liberal humanities have declined. Universities are infected with administration. University teaching has declined. The competition for overseas student revenue, tenure and prestige in the little fishbowls of academia has crowded out any careful attention to the educational needs of students.

My children, who study at these degraded institutions, report first hand to me the cheapening of the experience across a range of disciplines. We all now need to live with the broken institutions these reforms have wrecked. Back before these reforms, Michael Oakeshott wrote about the fundamental mistake of all these reforms. They turned an association that preserved culture into an enterprise that served utilitarian ends. Oakeshott wrote, "A University is not a machine for achieving a particular purpose or producing a particular result; it is a manner of human activity." Universities might not today articulate their mission in this way, but they know in their bones and their sandstone feet the lost knowledge of how to be a university. When Oakeshott wrote the university still carried its precious living tradition on proud, broad shoulders. Oakeshott spoke to those who bore that living tradition when he wrote, "This knowledge is not a gift of nature; it is a knowledge of a tradition, it has to be acquired." He could, however, sense the risk in the air: "it is always mixed up with error and ignorance, and it may even be lost."[109] Lost it was. The living tradition fell from the shoulders some time in the 1980s or 1990s, and has been dragged through the mud and the dust for the last three decades.

The great unrecognised tragedy of modern government is that the zeal of reformers, the crowds of willing students and the surge of new money led to the loss of those living traditions that had been

---
[109] Michael Oakeshott *The Voice of Liberal Learning (1989)*, pp.106-7.

maintained successfully for centuries, with less resources and fewer people, by their host institution, the university.

The hope is that these living traditions survive, and may yet find a home in a newly invented institution outside of the ruins of the feral city. Best wishes Jordan Peterson.

On suicide

(From *The Burning Archive* 17 April 2016.)

Over the last month or two I have been writing a government policy statement on suicide. Here is an interesting conundrum: how do you write about a topic that has such deep, rich veins of emotion, and use the favoured managerial babble of today's governments? How do you write with care for the traditions of thought and symbols that a learned person surely knows, while being forced to obtain the approval of the courtiers who astonish only in their ignorance? How do you write deeply on life and death issues, while running the gauntlet of these minds inflated by hot air who carelessly declare 'cases for changes' and float big ideas like helium balloons? How can you write inspired by the voices in your head of Donne and Durkheim, Ajax and Judas, Mishima and Plath, and many, many more, and still get a text approved by people whose cultural repertoire fits on a PowerPoint slide?

It seems to go one of three ways. The first way is to adopt an impenetrable armour of managerial pseudo-science. In this approach, suicide is a problem to be solved, and not a freedom to be wondered about. The problem is solved with all the illusions of technique with which these managers seek to govern the unruly world of human emotion. Despair is countered by 'systems approaches'. Uncertainty is banished with targets, and the suicide is again buried outside the courtyard of modern counting. The suicide must be banished because we will only be satisfied when there are zero suicides. So, suicide resumes its status as the gravest sin against the theology of policy. The researchers support the theology by confections of models and evidence, in which they stir fictional numbers with heady assumptions. These researchers rename themselves 'chief scientists', and engage in old-fashioned rivalry about the competing ideas. The unpredictability of suicide becomes a threat, and statistics that do not tell the right story are suppressed.

The second way is to clothe old ideas in corny sentiment. Suicide is preventable because, well, it is just wrong to think any other way. If we can aim for zero road deaths, even when they are increasing, why not also for suicide? Lived experience excuses the most mawkish of sentiments, and muddled thinking stalks moral urgency. If everyone just works together, 'at a local level', and does everything they can, and all at the same time, well, then, we can do this. Do what? Make this troubling phenomenon go away.

The third way is to speak of a balance of ambition and complexity. All the richness of traditions of thought, symbolism and events is gestured to by the word, complexity. Even if the author cannot release the magic that lies within that code-word, it sits within the policy text on suicide like an alchemist's stone. The knowing readers, even if they are not those readers who approve the text, will understand what is meant by the use of this word. They will hear in it Donne's words: "no man can take away my soul... I have the power to lay it down." But this complexity cannot paralyse us in thought, that enemy of the modern bureaucrat. Action rushes in, at once, and still we must seek to express a governing ambition to change these outcomes. A more tragic view of life is incorporated into the text, but the sea of troubles is finally nobly opposed. Here then all the targets, systems, interventions and the rational nomenclature of modern government dress themselves like a new Don Quixote, who despite knowing his folly, still marches on those windmills. Despite the impotence of the effort, the nobility of the aim rings truly that bell that tolls for us all.

Whatever the final result of these policy texts on suicide then, they will have little impact on the outcomes that the modern bureaucrat measures so dear. Suicide rates fluctuate year to year in response to ideas, events and passions that disobey the wills of ministers and the forensic techniques of coroners. They change remarkably over time for reasons that are hard to fathom, but that dwell in the chaos of cultural change, or so argues Marzio Barbagli in the magisterial, yet compassionate *Farewell to the World: a history of suicide* (2015). He looks over centuries, not a line graph with three annual data points. He looks at literature, not only systematic literature reviews. He finds an explanation for the variation in suicides in different times, places and social groups. It is not the decrees and media releases of Ministers and managers. It is not the latest fashion of the mental health grandees. It is, instead, something we once called, culture. The chaos of suicide is bounded by the formation, breakdown and refashioning of that culture. Barbagli defines that culture as a set of rules and beliefs, symbols and meanings, cognitive schemas and classification systems. The resources of that culture, in Barbagli's words "help people variously to resist or to impel them to take their own lives." I secretly write into the policy document that culture, whenever I whisper the code-word, complexity.

Postscript 2023

In my journal, 'The Year of Governing Dangerously', I made a note on the misuse of suicide in government policy. In late 2021 the annual Australian statistics on suicide were published. I noted the numbers: 2017, 682; 2018, 703; 2019, 721; 2020, 713. I recalled the farcical, theatrical goal of 'halving the suicide rate' in the 2016/17 Victorian Government Suicide Prevention Framework. I thought it was absurd, and reflected nothing but inflated claims by grant-seekers and postures by politicians. It was the perfect example of the madness of the parasitic virtual reality state. Even the misfortune and tragedy of suicide becomes a token of performed, meaningless gestures that have no effect on reality. These gestures are the essence of the modern virtual reality state. These mistakes have no consequences in the post-democratic world. Later, in my last month or so as a public servant, the team who were preparing the next suicide plan, as recommended by the Mental Health Royal Commission, spoke to me about my experiences. The same traps of appearances were at play. Never trust governments who claim to save lives.

Mental illness and government failure

When I joined the public service in 1990 there was one field I wanted to work in, mental health, or responses to mental illness. I have written in *From the Burning Archive* of my long personal and cultural connection to mental illness. My mother had bipolar disorder, and I first walked into a psychiatric hospital in the mid-1970s. I long wondered if I would suffer the same fate, which, since it is with varying colours and intensity only the human fate, of course, I did. But my personal experience of madness led me, as a university student and historian, to Michel Foucault and his ground-breaking, *History of Madness*. These deep experiences on the threshold of adulthood shaped the life of my mind for decades. I tacked between alternating winds of Foucault's poetic vision of the transgression of madness, my own doubts and despair about my personal diagnosis, and my unending curiosity about the re-imagined lived experience of the dead, even the maddened dead and mind-doctors of many forgotten cultures. Yet madness and mental illness also steered the course of my bureaucratic mind for the three decades of my career. I was always worried that my sanity was fragile, and that I could not endure the strains of executive office. I always felt distinct, chaotic and poetic as I was, from the humdrum, standard, orderly and earthly ambitions of my mentors and colleagues. I always suspected that my mark of the possessed would lead to my exclusion from polite, political society. Even my gracious mentor, Terry Moran, would sometimes signal to me that I was too 'unworldly' ever to be seriously considered for a serious job. My distinctive experience also defined for me the career objective that I silently pursued for decades in the public service, to improve the mental health of society.

In the year I began as a Victorian public servant, there appeared to be a new opportunity to make a difference to the experience of fools like me or my mother. Then Australian Human Rights Commissioner, Brian Burdekin (1986-94) conducted a major, ground-breaking inquiry into the infringement of the human rights of people with mental illness. The inquiry was launched in mid-1990, the year I began as an administrative trainee, and this career induction program offered the young public servant three placements in three departments over twelve months. One placement on offer was to work in the then Office of Psychiatric Services, coincidentally with a man, Trevor Fleming, whom I played cricket with. The placement contributed to coordinating the Victorian response to this ground-breaking Burdekin inquiry, and I pleaded, weakly since my powers of negotiation were limp at this time, with the organisers of the trainee program to place me here, where I wanted to make a difference. But they ignored my pleas, and shunted me into two dull, painful placements in industry assistance and workforce planning.

Burdekin's inquiry challenged the state bureaucrats, politicians, health practitioners and social workers who presided over the Victorian Government's failed response to people with mental illness. The Burdekin 1993 report, and earlier public hearings created a strong moral argument that governments had to do better for people with mental illness. The inquiry and hearings exposed the widespread violation of human rights of people with mental illness, including in compulsory and ill-conceived treatments in state psychiatric hospitals, such as those I had visited since the mid-1970s. He set out an agenda for least-restrictive treatment, improved public understanding of mental illness, greater attention to recovery for people with mental illness, better laws to control mental health practitioners and to protect people with mental illness, and an expanded role for the national government. Burdekin, in particular, challenged the role of the states, that dominated the delivery of mental health services. In turn, Burdekin was privately and publicly criticised by those bureaucrats, including chiefly Dr John Paterson, who had reformed the failing child welfare department, tasked with responsibility for intellectual disability services from the mid 1980s) with the help of coterie of new public managerial zealots, such as the former head of the Children's Protection Society and later Victorian Royal Commissioner into Mental Health, ex-social worker turned social justice bureaucrat, Penny Armytage. From 1992, Paterson had taken charge of a newly integrated Department of Health and Community Services. He fended off Burdekin with savage, private criticisms of his naivete and humanistic inattention to the 'real world' of economics and resource allocation. But Paterson's quality was such that he also bravely tried to establish an alternative realistic vision of how to deliver better mental health services.

But like so many government reforms of mental illness, these aspirations capsized. Why do governments keep failing people with mental illness? Why do grand plans for mental health reform make some politicians popular, some reformers rich, but leave too many people with mental illness alone on the streets or abandoned to despair?

Mental illness tends to be closeted away as a special topic in government. It is sensitive and difficult, and the problems are so great that governments are often given credit merely for making an effort. People who work in or have a passion for the issue can be sensitive to criticism of how governments are performing since any effort to improve things can be considered positive, and any criticism of that performance may lead to governments giving up on the effort.

But the performance of governments on mental illness rest on broader foundations of the political order. For example, there is a rarely discussed but intimate link between the growth of rights-based advocacy or progressive identity politics and the experience of mental illness. The ideas of the radical French thinker and historian of mental illness, Michel Foucault, profoundly influenced what we now know as identity politics. It made political issues of personal experiences, such as madness, gender and sexuality. The anti-psychiatry movement was central to 1960s cultural radicalism, and one of several motives for the slogan that the personal is political. This political movement extended human rights protections to people with mental illness, and similar movements have blossomed in other fields. In some ways, the political system is still adapting to this disorder of identity politics.

The performance of governments on mental illness is also adapting to the profound changes in the real social experience of mental illness and treatment since the 1960s. It is one of several profound transformations in real social conditions all around the world, which governments are still seeking to understand and to respond to, such as population aging, mass higher education, abundance, the replacement of physical labour by largely symbolic and interpersonal work, and the explosion of travel, communications and digital or virtual experiences. The real experiences of mental illness has changed profoundly over the last sixty years with the availability of psychotropic medications, lithium, the SSRIs, the development of psychological treatments, and the expansion of professional, peer and carer support for people with mental illness. Some experts, such as psychiatrist and philosopher, Iain McGilchrist, even argue that the culture and biological experience of the mind and mental illness have changed in western societies because of left hemisphere brain dominance. There have certainly been changes in our cultural ideas of madness. We accept, perceive, recognise, display and interpret mental illness differently today. It is no longer hidden away in asylums and prisons.

13 Ways of Looking at a Bureaucrat

So governments have not had it easy. But if the test of a good society is how it treats its most vulnerable, then should not government's performance on mental health be a key test of the functioning of democracy? In my view democratic governments keep failing people with mental illness. Shouldn't we be curious about why?

Of course, there are shades of grey and signs of progress. In Australia, for example, the widespread availability of psychological services through the Medicare system has improved people's actual lives. Curiously, many mental health "reformers" still fight and resent this program. I think a verdict of failure is, however, justified by the overall record. Let me share what this eyewitness of failure saw over 30 years.

In my experience, mental health was a policy field where governments too often made grandiose announcements of their commitment to reform, but did not persist with the problem to change people's experience on the ground. This gap between symbolism and reality has grown over the last 30 years with increased community concern with mental health. Public awareness and interest has grown, but so too has the value of using mental health as a political symbol. Joining the political spectacle, unfortunately, does not secure real practical concern and compassionate support for people. Rather than work patiently on methods of care, institutions and support networks for people with mental illness, governments have rushed to proclaim symbols of justice. As a result, there have been catastrophic failures in mental health.

For 33 years I worked as a government official on many issues directly connected with mental health. I met many of the leading characters, visited institutions, inspected services, and conversed with interest groups. I read government reports, archival documents and cabinet submissions. For a while, I worked on the Victorian Government response to the Royal Commission into Institutional Responses to Child Sexual Abuse, and researched the history of the

Beware of Staring into the Abyss

health department, especially its mental health components and care for children. I developed a good understanding of the public and archival history of Victorian mental health services. I can share my impressions of government failure without disclosing any confidential information. It is not court testimony, but rather glimpses of a rarely reported perspective on government failure on mental health.

In the 1880s Victoria held its real first royal commission into mental health in Victoria. This Royal Commission recommended many changes to improve institutions, care and people's experience, but it ran aground on a catastrophic economic depression in the 1890s, which led 50 years of hard times for Victoria. During this time Victorian mental health institutions became shockingly under-resourced. In the 1950s and 1960s, Cunningham Dax and Alan Stoller rebuilt this system from scratch, on the basis of a community mental health model that by the 1960s they presented to the World Health Organisation as a model for the world. But the 1970s saw a new wave of economic hardship and fiscal tightening, a growing role for the Commonwealth Government in health and social policy, and a first wave of the profound social changes prompted by the affluent society, new demographics, post-modern culture and changes in the experience of mental illness. In particular institutions of all kinds premised on older models of society and care were closing down – disability institutions, congregate child care, and, of course, mental health hospitals. Their closure offered a windfall to governments, who owned the real estate, but no dividend for the patients sent out to be cared for "in the community". Within government institutions the old caste of sages and professionals were being challenged by a new breed of managers. Their clash over resources and control occurred in mental health as in so many other fields. This battle of ideas and values was occurring in the Victorian Public Service when I joined in 1990.

I remember seeing some of the responses of senior Victorian government bureaucrats to the early 1990s Burdekin Human Rights Commission inquiry into the rights and experiences of people with

13 Ways of Looking at a Bureaucrat

mental illness. Some new public sector managers dismissed the groundbreaking report as the cloudy vision of lawyers, human rights advocates and professional rent-seekers. They attempted, to their credit, to create a counter vision based in managerial ideas of social justice. I visited the large psychiatric hospitals, and the big intellectual disability institutions while they were being closed down for sale. At one point, these institutions were the largest public sector employers. By the 1990s the unions were perhaps more concerned to protect their members, rather than to look after the interests of people with mental illness. Governments were perhaps more obsessed with paying off debt by the sale of these institutions, rather establishing better services in their place. These institutions emptied through the 60s, 70s and 80s when new medications and treatments enabled new models of supervision. But their closure failed to transform care for the better. I saw many alcohol and drug policies, the Penington inquiry on illegal drugs in the late 1990s, and the early formation of Beyond Blue. In the mid-2000s I sat helpless in meetings while mental health was yoked to the "human capital agenda." This abstraction sought to make mental health attractive to economists and Treasury officials. But it turned the complexities of mental illness into simple formulas for productivity and workforce participation. I saw the whole era of the construction of Headspace and Patrick McGorry's brave reforms for youth mental health; but they also ran aground in turbulent bureaucratic, institutional and disciplinary waters. I saw a well-meaning but overly complicated policy from the mid-2000s, *Mental Health Matters* march into a quagmire of bureaucratic nonsense. I witnessed the birth two mental health acts, with all the complex legal and human rights issues of compulsory treatment. I personally wrote, developed and led several whole-of-government strategies on alcohol and drugs. I was frustrated with the persistent failure by many in government, in the community, and in the mental health and drugs sectors to accept addiction as core to mental health policy and services. I saw welfare reforms that were conveniently obsessed with getting people on disability benefits a job to solve their mental health problems, rather than consider what was really going on in their minds. I saw convenient arguments that providing housing first will solve the problems of mental illness. Those arguments were advanced by housing bureaucrats and housing non-government organisations. I saw a new Victorian government in 2014 promise to develop a 10-year mental health plan; tick it off its list of commitments; but deliver nothing in it. I saw a government produce a suicide prevention plan with the grandiose target to reduce the suicide rate by 50 percent; but sadly the suicide rate has not budged since. I saw the government play with coercive approaches to people with complex needs, or combinations of mental illness and violence, even though all the best advice was that those coercive approaches would not work. I saw a constant failure to respond to the well-documented need to increase resources for mental health services. It was always easier to pass the buck to another level of government, and to spin the fantasy that Victoria's low per capita expenditure on mental health was proof our bureaucrats' exceptional quality and competence. In fact it just cloaked tight-fisted decisions by officials and Ministers. I too many inquiries from the Productivity Commissions and many panels of experts, which lost their way obsessing about system changes, rather than real practical improvements in care.

But the worst failure was the Victorian Royal Commission on Mental Health. This inquiry was chaired by Penny Armytage, a former social worker, head of the Children's Protection Society in the 1980s, and later a senior bureaucrat in child protection, state welfare services and the justice system. She was the head of the Department of Justice before becoming a consultant and a widely used board and committee appointee. No inquiry should be treated as a sacred cow so let me just briefly sketch why I describe it as a failure. Of course, I may be wrong. The Commission was promised cynically in 2018 by the very same government that had delivered a wet squib of a 10-year mental health plan in 2015. The Government wanted another talisman of its prowess as social reformers. Key personnel were favourites and people associated with the governing party or its key ministers. Some commissioners frankly had passed their prime. Its public hearings were indulgences of bureaucrats who spoke from the televised dock about 'systems reform' and rehashed old complaints about the mental health system. The Commission's inquiry process did not justify the expensive and coercive investigatory powers of a royal commission. Its first report undermined its credibility by proposing new tax measures, outside the commissioner's expertise if known to be favoured by the Government. This initial report also included various funding proposals that seemed to me to be closely linked to interests of key Commissioners and advisers. Its second report was a tiresome meandering consultant's document. Its recommendations were implemented with more politicised appointments. There were also many well-meaning, but poorly directed, people who collapsed under the weight of the grand rhetoric, excessive documentation and cloudy reform visions of the Royal Commission. They lost track of practical priorities to get things done. As often occurs in government, various interest groups took first place to feed from the trough of the new funding stream. Implementation was delayed and confused. Reformers were startled by impatient Utopian managers, not guided by the simple virtues of humility, kindness, compassion and persistence. Many loyal servants tried to do the right thing, but found it difficult to admit that the Royal Commission's new bible was impractical and flawed. Then, came the pandemic. It cramped the effectiveness of all fields of government, but delivered a particular shock to the mental health of the community. Victoria pursued zealous Zero COVID policies, and neglected the mental issue impacts of those policies. For these reasons, I judge the Victorian mental health royal commission a failure. It failed people with mental illness, their carers, families and fellow citizens. It became a spectacle for politics, not a foundation for better experiences for people with mental illness. It became another example of government failure in mental health and democracy.

The real question is not why this individual Commission failed, but why do governments persistently fail in mental health? After all, one Royal Commission, no matter how talented, cannot make up for the failure of a whole network of institutions, people and ideas.

Beware of Staring into the Abyss

One common explanation for this failure is offered in the mental health world. Many leaders in this sector argue that mental health is uniquely badly treated in the health system and in government policy. They advocate parity of esteem between mental health and physical health. They claim that mental health is Cinderella, the unloved stepchild of government policy. I disagree. I do not think mental health is the Cinderella of government policy. In fact, it has enjoyed privileges in recent times because it ranks as a top issue of concern for many people. As a result governments want to be seen to be trying to 'do something' about mental health. Some key advisers have enjoyed very special relationships with governments, but I do not think those relationships ultimately have led to enough positive change for people with mental illness.

Another hypothesis is that there may be an incompatibility between the style of thinking required to deal with messy mental illness and the preferred mode of the leaders, reformers and executives who you find at the top of managerial and political organisations. I do think, in part, some failures of governments in mental health are caused by the preference of the manipulative, managerial mind to create visions dominated by left hemisphere thinking, to use Ian McGilchrist's terms from the *Master and the Emissary*. This mode of thinking does not marry well with the chaotic, messy experience of mental illness. Mental illness generates uncontrollable ups and downs, for people with mental illness, for carers and for the services that seek to help. It is all a bit unmanageable.

However, these specific aspects of mental health are not the primary reason that governments fail in this sensitive field. Governments fail in mental health in the same way that they fail in other realms of policy. Mental illness is not a tragic exception to policy reform, but a variation of democratic government failure. These governments promise much, and deliver too little, too late. In the contemporary political spectacle, democratic governments have to reinvent their 'brands' continually. Visions of progress, firsts, groundbreaking policies, big initiatives, major announcements are planned meticulously. Delivery of these results is neglected. Announcements can sell the new brands into a consumer market, and mental health, like all policy fields, has been sucked into that vacuum. Democratic governments have difficulty putting reasonable boundaries around their aims. They do not set modest, achievable goals anchored in practical concerns for others, especially when those concerns from the enigmatic human experience of mental illness or madness. Governments tend to build systems in the sky, and do not pay enough attention to the troubled person who stands before them.

I however, have long been inspired by a kinder, gentler, more patient attitude towards politics. The great Czech playwright, Vaclav Havel, wrote in his essay, "Politics and Conscience," that he favoured

> politics as one of the ways of seeking and achieving meaningful lives of protecting them and serving them. I favour politics as practical morality as service to the truth as essentially human and humanly measured care for our fellow humans It is, I presume an approach which in this world is extremely impractical, and difficult to apply in daily life. Still i know no better alternative.[110]

If governments brought that attitude to mental health reform, we would have many fewer reforms, and much better mental health. But to do so, governments and reformers need to let go of the "unscrupulous optimism," described by Roger Scruton in *The Uses of Pessimism*. They need to stop believing they are "system managers" who can design single, complete solutions to human dilemmas. They need to stop setting targets to eliminate problems forever. These mindsets destroy the institutions that enable us to negotiate with difference, to resolve conflicts peacefully, and to find compromises one step at a time through consensual processes of dialogue with strangers. Governments and reformers need to restore a culture of tolerance for imperfection, and forsake multiyear plans for Utopia. Mental illness,

---

[110] Havel, *Living in Truth*, p. 155.

and the madness of all our minds are the ultimate reminders of social imperfection. They remind us that plans for Zero COVID, Zero harm, Zero suicide, Zero road deaths or any kind of Year Zero all ultimately fail.

Over the last 30 years I have witnessed the people who work in governments forget, indeed spurn, this culture of tolerance for imperfection. Instead, politics has increasingly become a spectacle of progress in some virtual reality. Governments eliminate harms or make nations great again. They level up, and speak to their citizens as NPCs. They seek to dissolve all difficulties by simply changing the word we use to point to them. This attitude is fundamentally why governments keep failing people with mental illness. Our political culture has grown uncomfortable with imperfection, and obsessed with virtual reality spectacles. We need to abandon the spectacle, and instead offer, as Vaclav Havel said, humanly measured care for our fellow humans. How we do that - in our imperfect democracies that govern imperfect societies performing in imperfect cultures - is the great ethical challenge of our time.

13 Ways of Looking at a Bureaucrat

Chapter Twelve   Towards Life After Democracy

Towards Life After Democracy

Cultural fragmentation and authority collapse

(From *The Burning Archive* 22 April 2018.)

During the week I was discussing with a young colleague at work the preparation of a briefing. I offered some simple guidance and encouragement: the briefing did not need to be long, but the words ought to be carefully selected, and focused on what was most important. 'After all,' I said, 'brevity is the soul of wit.'

To my surprise, my 20-something colleague, who studied journalism and international relations at university, said he liked that phrase, but had not heard it before. Taken aback, I confirmed with him that he was serious, and, in truth, he had never heard this advice spoken by Polonius.

This incident was a minor example of the impoverishment of the cultural commons today. How can it be that two university educated people from the same city, although not the same generation, do not share knowledge of this basic cultural reference, Shakespeare's evergreen advice to every writer?

The cultural commons is being impoverished by fragmentation, which in turn is generated by the profusion of wealth, self-expression, image-making and identity-formation in our post-modern societies. Our garden is overrun with the sprawling higgledy-piggledy plants that more and more of us have planted. We can no longer see the shape of the garden's beds, and the more precious heritage plants are smothered in foliage and deprived of light.

Fragmentation of the culture is not wholly a bad thing. Cracks of freedom open up. New voices emerge. Terrible new beauties are born. The art of living is rethought and remade. Like the breaking up of

Pangea, new continents, new ecosystems of cultural forms, drift apart and forget the times when they shared a common identity. The fundamental processes of differentiation and development take hold, and, within the broken continents of a once shared culture, new dramas are performed in old theatres.

It may be a nostalgic fancy to imagine that our cultures could ever be bounded by a single book of common prayer. One book is not enough for a population that is more highly educated than ever before, and that has more time, freedom and widely available means to produce, share and consume cultural artefacts. No-one in these conditions can stand against the forces of continental drift. These historical forces of divergence and re-convergence around new poles are very strong and very deep. Felipe Fernández-Armesto has argued that these antagonist cultural forces have long fought their subterranean battle through the deep history of the world. He made these arguments at the peak of political enthusiasm for globalization, and spotted the discontents coming in with the tides. Fernández-Armesto pointed to the long, deep history of divergence in human cultures which turned, around 1492, towards a history of convergence for another 500 years. Yet beneath the superficial unity of a world brought together in the name of Western culture, new dreams of differentiation were emerging: "If recent history has a lesson, it is that whenever a big state is nestled, smaller-scale identities and political aspirations incubate under its shell until eventually they poke their beaks through the cracks and take flight."[111]

Liberal globalization is the latest dream of a universal culture. I have never been too excited by this last all-American dream, but remain anchored in an earlier European ambition. I am a member of those dying generations who imagined a reforging of myth, tradition and culture through the 20th century practice of modernist *bildung*. I can see that this dream of a shared culture is impossible in today's conditions. There is too much to read. There are too many human

---
[111] *Millenium* (1995), p. 704.

possibilities to explore. There are too many ideas to encircle, without a constriction on freedom, within a single story, however grand the narrative. The institutions of education have been overrun by commerce and new philistines. The great words are repeated incessantly by fewer of us; we few seek the company of cold skulls, not the frisson of the pumped up dance floor. Cultural communities proliferate online, yet share no embodied customs: no church in which we stand to hear the common prayer; no university in which we practise *bildung*, rather than vocational learning. The besieged city has lost its theatre, which stands in broken, neglected ruins. Yet still, strange flowers grow among the ruins, and throughout the city small groups come together to create the rituals of new cults. Perhaps these new cults and strange flowers will sustain the generations to come? I recognise the reality of these conditions, and still I mourn what we have lost. To echo Ezra Pound, I can only put my faith in the love of my true heritage, and trust that what I lovest well shall not be reft from me.

One thing we have lost amid our cultural fragmentation is a civic culture of governing. I encounter this disordered culture most days in my day job as a government bureaucrat. Our political communities have been shattered. We are riven by identity politics and hyper-partisanship. We fight culture wars and proclaim fluid fissured identities that separate us from traditions of civil dialogue. We have lost the art of talking to strangers, and working across the aisle. Government has become a theatre of activists, spin-doctors, marketers of political brands, social innovators, and a new mercenary class of political *condottiere* and consultocrats. This new class has colonised the institutions of government, and suborned once strong autonomous institutions to the fractious, factionalised, fickle, impatient, self-absorbed purposes of this new *nomenklatura*. The new class has stripped the institutions of a virtuous republic of its autonomous traditions of value and serious purpose.

The ascendancy of this new *nomenklatura* – which one day I will find a better name for – is only possible in the conditions created by the breakdown of civic culture and cultural fragmentation. They are the bandits who emerge when the city lies in ruins. It is the common complaint of these bandits that the people are fickle, have "expectations" that cannot be delivered, and lack trust. For example, the OECD reports, "Trust in government is deteriorating in many OECD countries. Lack of trust compromises the willingness of citizens and business to respond to public policies and contribute to a sustainable economic recovery."[112] Foolish citizens and silly business! Why do they not respond to public policies in the ways desired by the new *nomenklatura*?

In truth, the problem of declining trust in political institutions, is better conceived as the collapse of authority of the new *nomenklatura* in liberal democracies. I hypothesise that collapse is impelled by the disintegration of the civic cultures that these elites attempt to govern.

The post-democratic society is here

(From *The Burning Archive*, 11 April 2021.)

We, who live in the mythical states of the West, do cherish our status as democracies. We like to celebrate the freedom and the dignity which that designation of our political institutions grants us as citizens. We like to denigrate the benighted societies ruled by the 'new breed of autocrats', Putin, Xi Jinping, Erdogan, Orban and, in some minds, even Trump, who must surely have been the most impotent autocrat of all time. We are too easily lulled into trances by lazy talk from the 'Leader of the Free World', the Pretender President Joe Biden, about 'inflection

---

[112] OECD, *Building Trust to Reinforce Democracy: Main Findings from the 2021 OECD Survey on Drivers of Trust in Public Institutions* (2022).

points' in the fate of the world, where we must choose whether our best way forward is 'autocracy', or the soul of America, democracy.[113] Democracy is conjugated by Americans as an irregular verb. We are free, and they are slaves.

But when I look at the actual conditions of our political institutions, their culture and actors, especially in the wake of the Great Seclusion of 2020, the response of our governing elites to the SARS-COV-2 pandemic, then I see a different drama. In the great coliseum of the city, there is a theatrical combat of democracy with autocracy, but this performance is stage managed by manipulative politicians and celebrity journalists. Outside the walls of this circus, in the great feral city of our distressed republics, I see a post-democratic society growing wild over the ruins of democracy.

I see political institutions that have become empty husks of their great traditions: parliaments, filled with time-serving hacks who are unable to conduct meaningful debate; political parties, adrift on the social tides, and suborned to empty marketing machines; bureaucracies, ravaged by political mercenaries and consultants, and starved of dignified purpose; universities, converted into student shops, and stripped of humane ideals; courts, conceited with their power to rule, and too timid to defend the most powerful resource of the powerless; the fourth estate or media, dazed by its own dim celebrity, and confused by reading as truth the talking points rolling down the teleprompter; civil society, leashed to government and oligarchical patronage, and no longer enlisting ordinary people in little platoons; the citizenry, free enough to live outside politics, and intimidated enough to live within lies.

This is the rough beast slouching towards Bethlehem in this new century. It is not the threat of the 'new autocrats' or the 'new populists'. Putin, Xi Jinping and the others are not autocrats. Such an idea is pure

---

[113] Remarks by President Biden at the 2021 Virtual Munich Security Conference, 19 February 2021.

misinformation, a tired reworking of 1950's American Cold War propaganda. Donald Trump was never an 'existential threat' to American democracy. He saw it was dead, and fantasised he could make it great again. Along the way, he called out many of the oligarchs, hoaxers and deep state operatives who prowled around the cadaver. Perhaps the 'new autocrats' and 'new populists' arrived at a post-democratic society first. At least, they rule without the illusion that America = global freedom = democracy = good government = the end of history. Perhaps we should see their struggle as akin to ours: how to fashion a decent republic in a post-democratic society? A dangerous thought, but in our conditions we must dare to think dangerously.

Democracy as a concept cannot save us from the difficulties, injustices and failures of this new set of political institutions. We would do well to break the spell of democracy, as the English political theorist, John Dunn, has urged us to do. In *Breaking Democracy's Spell*, he asked why the word *democracy* held so much political authority? His response was to say that democracy offer its citizens a fair trade. They allowed government to exercise power over their lives and choices, but without sacrificing personal dignity or voluntarily jeopardising individual or family interests.

Can we say still that this formula of 'democracy' still keeps our personal dignity safe? Can we still say that, after more than a year of masks, lockdowns, seclusions, Big Tech censorship, Big Media collusion, oligarchical Great Resets, arrests of dissenters, celebration of some protesters and designation of others as 'domestic terrorists' or 'conspiracy theorists'?

The post-democratic society has arrived. We need to turn away from the old priests and performers who mutter grand concepts of democracy in weakened rites that only initiate another circus performance in the decaying coliseum. We need to find some new way in the feral cities of our distressed republics. There is no easy recourse to live well among friends and strangers in a political community, not when that society of strangers are no longer entranced by democracy. And yet, we have survived through democracy's fall, and we cannot rule out the prospect that we may tomorrow find our way to some new decent polity. If we do we may discover the path, close to home, in our own dignity, ordinary virtue and decision to live in truth.

Our barren, deformed political society

(From *The Burning Archive*, 27 November 2020.)

If, and when, Trump is no longer President, all the ills of the political system can no longer be blamed on Trump.

For four years now – in America but also through viral spread around the world – all the ills of our deformed, barren political society have been personified in a metonymic myth: Donald Trump.

Victor David Hanson has said in a way that Trump is chemotherapy. It makes you sick, but cures a cancer. The challenge for our political societies now is: will we face up to the remaining cancer?

Ben Shapiro says Trump is not the killer of American politics, but the coroner. He declared the body politic dead, and correctly diagnosed the cause of its death. Perhaps this is the role of the insurgent populist; to highlight the emperor has no clothes, and to leave to successors the task of redressing the royals.

However, I think reports of the death of our body politics are exaggerated. It is more accurate to say our republics, not just in America but all liberal democratic states, are gravely ill. All sorts of parasitic pathogens inhabit the body, but require that the host live on. As Trump found, the swamp monsters may be diseased and deformed, but they are not dead. They do fight back. Thus while a populist might expose the failures of the elite, the populist outsider cannot nourish the culture and institutions that might replenish the great dying forests of our polities.

Elsewhere on this blog I have written on the failure of our institutions in the pandemic crisis. That post sprang from Yuval Levin's account of the decay of institutions, and Patrick Dineen's reflections on the cultural wasteland of modern liberalism. There, I sketched some signs of the barren, deformed political society through which we roam as do refugees through a ruined city: Parliaments full of empty posturing, and stripped of purposeful deliberation; a viral urge by everyone to be a 'leader'; institutions overwhelmed by the new *nomenklatura* of our society.

Dineen is worth returning to as a launch-pad for a description of our diseased political society. He argued the success of liberalism has brought with it the injuries of affluence. The system tries to patch and cover the wounds, but limps on. There are rolling blackouts in electoral politics, administration and markets. A trust and legitimacy crisis rises within democracy. But so many problems stack up that there is a deeply felt sense of uncontrolled crisis and apocalyptic liberal fears that history had returned, and never really did end.

America's electoral and political system, and its institutions of mass communications, recently imposed a blackout on news adverse to the Democratic Presidential candidate. It is the latest episode in the crisis of legitimacy. It is exposing the yawning chasm between ideal and real that is leading to the breakdown of order. It is an event that one attorney said threatens to be of 'biblical' grandeur in exposing the 'corruption' of the American elite and the decay of its political system. Whether those claim can be sustained is not at all certain. But the disputes on the election have exposed America's gimcrack electoral system and partisan justice system. It may yet reveal the most astonishing defrauding of democracy by elites in the recent history of our republics. Future historians of American collapse may write of the fury and misperception in the *Affair of the Dominion Machines* in the same way that historians of the French Revolution have written of the *Affair of the Diamond Necklace*. The claims that Marie Antoinette acted to defraud the French Crown to acquire a precious necklace were not justified, but the social myths accelerated disillusionment with the Bourbon dynasty.

But we should not only fret about America, nor tut-tut about Trump. The barren fields of our local political society can be seen in our own political institutions in Australia, in Victoria, in this locked down city. Parliaments no longer debate, deliberate or investigate in ways that honour the past practice of their greatest practitioners. Which Parliamentarian or Congressperson of today will deliver speeches that will be be read 100, 200 or more years from now, as are those of Edmund Burke?

Parliaments are filled with functionaries from modern political parties, which have become exhausted husks of political marketing machines. These political parties do not function as organic associations, which generate ideas, an ethos, or democratic political movements. They are not even Leninist cadres of dedicated political revolutionaries, mobilising an army ready to besiege society. They can barely be described, as Maurice Duverger did, as mass political parties. Parties in the first 70 years of the 20th century had strong, organic connections with significant sections of the society. But today these parties have even descended to a lower circle of hell than Michels' iron law of oligarchy. They have become mere machines for factional warlords, obedient operatives and insurgent media identities to engage in electoral manipulation. The electoral frauds allegedly perpetrated by the Democratic Party of the USA may not have occurred, but its leading operatives boast without shame of the very latest models of manipulation of information, elections and voters.

The manipulation occurs partly through a strange form of

prophecy, conducted with evermore unreliable opinion polls. These polls seduce their practitioners into the illusion that they conduct science, or they predict with mathematical rigour. Their recent performance, however, reveals what a degraded augury they have become. Perhaps the rite of reading out the headline numbers of the latest poll has become its own form of political weapon. They are the symbol of the empty husk of politics as marketing to the punters. They degrade the *polis* to a betting market.

The core institutions of political government are diseased. They no longer bear fruit of imaginative compromises to civil conflicts. This degradation would not have happened without rot in the para-political institutions of the culture. The professions have become both venal and ideologically possessed. The governing crisis of lockdowns would not have happened without the distorted ideological culture of 'public health' spreading like the virus of language in the medical professions and their para-professions of medical, social research. The news media have spun the lie to themselves, a diseased delusion, that it is they, journalists before cameras, who hold power to account. But the professional standards they apply only promote the self-regarding mini-celebrity of journalists, not any reasonable standard of truthful reporting of public debate that could support self-government. In the nineteenth century, Thomas Carlyle gave journalists the dignity of the term 'fourth estate' when he wrote, "Burke said there were Three Estates in Parliament; but, in the Reporters' Gallery yonder, there sat a Fourth Estate more important far than they all."[114] Two centuries later, after *1984*, *Brave New World* and the Twitter Files, the Fourth Estate has become a Fifth Column at the service of the New Oligarchs.

We are in a bad state. Things could readily get worse. America may spiral into a constitutional crisis or collapse into institutional inertia. My own minor province of the outer Empire has become a demoralised republic, frozen by fear, run by a deeply unimpressive, inauthentic clique, and masked in empty gestures of virtue. There are times I am

---

[114] Carlyle, *On Heroes and Hero Worship*.

tempted to give in to despair.

Now more than ever I turn to Vaclav Havel to renew the small garden I tend among the ruins of this barren political society. Havel described two cultures in 'post-totalitarian' societies. He saw similarities between the social claustrophobia in 1970s Eastern European states, and the consumption addicted societies of the West. In both kinds of societies there were two cultures; the first, a sterile culture approved by those with power and status; the second, an authentic culture that lived in truth, even when it struggled to be seen. The first culture grows "what is permitted, subsidised or at least tolerated, an area that naturally tends to attract more of those who, for reasons of advantage, are willing to compromise their truth."[115] We see this culture every day in our political actors, posturing professionals, media and anti-journalist B-grade celebrities, and 'thought leaders' of every brand.

But there is also a second culture that springs from autonomous free humanity. The second culture is "an area constituted through self-help, which is the refuge, voluntary or enforced, of those who refuse all compromise (regardless of how overtly 'political' or 'non-political' their work is." Courage will take me on that path of the second culture, even as I watch the first culture crumble all around me.

How democracies really die

(From *The Burning Archive,* 11 May 2020.)

I found by chance on my bookshelf yesterday the 2018 jeremiad by two Harvard University professors. These American academics profess

---

[115] Havel, "Six Asides about culture," *Living in Truth (1986)*, p. 132.

disciplines of government and the 'science of government', no less! Steven Levitsky and Daniel Ziblatt profess both historical science and prophecy in their book of revelations, *How Democracies Die: What History Reveals about our Future.* This book created a small sensation when first published. The prophets' visions came in the year of darkness, 2017, when the ruling castes of our distressed republics panicked about their imminent displacement, after the combined shocks of Brexit, new 'illiberal democrats', like Victor Orban, and, of course, Donald Trump. I bought it, read it quickly, and discarded it in disappointment into a dusty corner of my bookshelf. In this case, disappointment was truly a teacher of wisdom. More so than the professors, the history of a disappointment revealed the future.

How Democracies Die claimed that Donald Trump's first year in office showed his 'authoritarian instincts'. The professors marked down the freshman President because he merely conformed to, or even plagiarised, the model of the new authoritarians, those illiberal democrats these academics had discerned in Fujimori, Chavez and Erdogan. The first year report card highlighted how Trump, that scythe that cut down the institutions of democracy, did so through lies, displays of disrespect for the media, attacks on his opponents and the judicial system, a lack of forbearance, attempts to sideline key players, like CNN or the 'resistance' within his own government, and a plague of antidemocratic initiatives, of which the most prominent were the firing of James Comey, Director of the FBI, and Trump's resentment of the Michael Flynn investigation, the Mueller probe and the whole RussiaGate theatre.

This President, Trump, had said in his Inaugural Address, "We will no longer accept politicians who are all talk and no action – constantly complaining but never doing anything about it. The time for empty talk is over. Now arrives the hour of action." But, like patronising academics, Levitsky and Ziblatt assessed that the President Trump was inferior to such fine democratic orators, as Clinton and Barack Obama, practitioners of American liberal sanctimony. President Trump was "more talk than action." After one year in office, President Trump, despite being the face that launched a thousand *faux* scholarly tomes, had failed, the professors of the science of government concluded, to end democracy.

> [He] repeatedly scraped up against the guardrails, like a reckless driver, but he did not break through them. Despite clear causes for concern, little actual backsliding occurred in 2017. We did not cross the line into authoritarianism.[116]

I wondered what these defenders of democratic norms make of all the other crashes into the guardrails of democracy in America: the culmination of the rolling series of revelations about the RussiaGate hoax; the misconduct of the FBI and CIA; the prosecutory harassment of General Michael Flynn; and an apparent coup in the shadows orchestrated by the law enforcement and intelligence agencies alongside scions of the Democratic Party of the United States. After all, some observers saw these events as a *coup d'etat* within a modern democratic state . I thought they might be shamed into silence. I thought they might be remorseful. I thought they might have with contrition corrected some of their prior claims about James Comey.

But, no. Sadly, and disturbingly for the health of democracy, no. Professor Ziblatt, who has now widened his professions, well beyond professor in the 'science of government', and lays claim to being a legal scholar, even an armchair judge, tweeted about the withdrawal of the outrageously unfair prosecution of Michael Flynn: "Capture the referees. Then use them as a shield to protect yourself and your friends and a weapon to persecute your opponents. I read that somewhere.... And let's remember: he pleaded guilty."[117] This little piece of self-promotion was made on the back of gross injustice. It responded to a news report that the errant prosecutor leading the case had withdrawn the case. The Professor chose to ignore the publication of documents,

---

[116] Levitsky And Zablitt, *How Democracies Die* (2018), p. 187.
[117] Ziblatt tweet, since deleted.

which taken as a whole, strongly suggested the Flynn case was a set-up from the get-go.

But let's be clear here. Many academics, media celebrities, politicians, lawyers, all sorts of figures in the culture and the general public have perversely taken the wrong side of this contemporary Dreyfus Case. They have become deranged in their distaste for Donald Trump, and his mob of 'deplorables', 'populists', and 'alt-right nutters'. They were maddened that democracies could make choices different to their own. In the frenzy of their Lear-like rage, they sabotaged their own institutions, ethos and principles. They became the cheer-leaders for the real, antidemocratic actions of progressives in 2016, 2017 and beyond. This is how democracies truly die.

I also read James Comey, *A Higher Loyalty*, the autobiography of the former Director of the FBI. I found it enigmatic and puzzling. I always found his declared reaction to his elected President odd. Trump, reportedly, had simply asked for the loyalty of service to a new President. Comey appeared to actively misinterpret Trump's whispered greeting. Comey even confessed unwittingly in his book that he was "preoccupied about keeping a healthy distance from Trump." In fact, this preoccupation turned to unhealthy obsession. Before long, Comey was organising an unmerited investigation through a conspiracy of questionable legality. His book may be an attempt to build his profile, and to trade off his resistance to Trump. One really wonders if, one day, scholars will produce a critical edition that compares the claims in *A Higher Loyalty* to the now heavily documented evidence of Comey's mistakes and misstatements.

At the end of his book, Comey made a grand pronouncement that reads, after so many revelations of misdeeds and political bias by the FBI, with distressing dramatic irony:

> Whatever your politics, it is wrong to dismiss the damage to the norms and traditions that have guided the presidency and our public life for decades or, in many

cases, since the republic was founded. It is also wrong to stand idly by, or worse to stay silent when you know better, while a president brazenly seeks to undermine public confidence in law enforcement institutions that were established to keep our leaders in check. Every organization has its flaws, but the career prosecutors and agents at the Justice Department and the FBI are there for a reason – to rise above partisanship and do what's right for the country, regardless of their own political views. Without these checks on our leaders, without those institutions vigorously standing against abuses of power, our country cannot sustain itself as a functioning democracy.[118]

It is regrettably much worse for a functioning democracy, Mr Comey, when the spies, cops and guys with the guns get to decide who should lead and how. Pompously, Comey claimed his book would help those "living among the flames who are thinking about what comes next" to pursue ethical leadership. In truth, he has shown himself to be a Lucifer who challenged God, and found himself condemned as a fallen angel to eternal torment in the flames.

Democracy's discontents

(From *The Burning Archive,* 15 November 2016.)

Election nights are rites of reunification. The divisions of a society spew out over weeks, with licensed vitriol and contemptuous sneers permitted for all, and then, while the consequences of the strife are tallied, the champions of right and wrong bicker about predictions, polls, and the latest certainties they have received by rumour. Then,

---
[118] Comey, *A Higher Loyalty* (2018), p. 276.

sometime around midnight, one standard is lowered, with speeches that humbly, gracefully admit weakness. Another banner is raised. It is pledged to unity. It rallies the people to service to those greater things that bind us as one nation, whichever nation we should be. The standard is raised, but the grandeur of the victor is dimmed. The winner expresses humility before the enormity of the challenges that lie before us.

These rites have been troubled in recent years, as if, as in Kafka's fable, some leopards have broken into the temple grounds to change the meaning of the rite forever. Clever hierophants appear on every panel show. They had started with confidence in the belief that intense study of the manipulative arts had granted them a sacred authority to interpret the runes cast by the voters. But now they appear dazed and confused. The ceremony was not meant to go this way. George Stephanopolous, to pick one of these arcane priests at random, spoke like a bullying catechist on the night of the 2016 USA Presidential election. "What do these people who voted for Trump want?" he said. Left unspoken was his real grievance. Why do they not understand it cannot be done?

The gracious speech of harmony is forgotten. The victor's magical words, which forgive and honour the animal that has just been killed, are today read like a mumbled, unstressed prayer. The prayer has lost its power. It no longer heals the wounds of bitter words of recrimination. In 2016, Trump was gracious as victor. So, too was Obama as past victor. But not the crowd-shy Clinton, who chose to send out her chief fundraiser at 2 am to tell everyone to go home. Beneath a glass ceiling that was not touched, the operatives pretended, and danced a little longer, rather than face the music of the humiliating rite. But despite the performance of the ceremony, in its improvised and broken forms, the church members have drifted away in bitter and drifting factions. The prayers for unity no longer ring true.

America appears to be descending into democratic dissension, and elites everywhere are checking their domestic security, while fudging the record on their predictions. Trump's victory was a surprise, and the many instant interpretations that are springing up everywhere to explain a 50-50 vote in a two-horse race are as reliable as all the wrong predictions based on careful analysis of ground games, private polling, big data, demographic profiling, identity politics and all the other runic nonsense.

Perhaps no one should be surprised. After all, one candidate had spent 30 years telling idealistic challengers to the professional political class that there was no alternative to pragmatic realities. This candidate, Clinton, opposed the television demagogue. Trump had brought people to a frenzy with his talk of real change, big dreams, long walls and drained swamps, and always emphasised his rhetoric with the reassuring *sotto voce* affirmation, "We're going to do this, we're going to win big." Against this wave of popular sentiment, Clinton insisted on another dynastic President repeating the Washington Consensus. She told the public that she would merely administer more pallid meals with no flavour, no choice, no change in the rations for those off Wall Street. In response, enough of the people decided, we will try the other guy.

But now the other guy faces his own kind of legitimacy crisis. Improvised street demonstrations do not usually mean much, but perhaps this time it is the protests that are the leopards breaking into the temple. What will become of democracy's rites if voters and the elected can spurn the results of an election, within hours of its declaration, and refuse the pleas of the vanquished champions to offer the new President, an 'open mind' (Obama), whatever that is? Has democracy's spell been broken, and all its high priests been expelled by the people from their riotous city?

I am grateful that I do not live in America, and expect troubled times for America in coming years. A crisis in American democracy, however, is not a crisis in every other nation's. But if democracy's spell is broken here, can it last anywhere?

My thoughts over the last week have turned away from poetry and towards these ruminations of a forsaken Cassandra. But to break democracy's spell is not wholly a bad thing. If this mesmeric concept weakens its grip, then can we not find other language, ideas and rites to work out together the ordinary virtues of governing well?

So my thoughts have turned to the difficult English intellectual historian, John Dunn. He argued democracy has been much more effective as "paradigm for deauthorising incumbent power than for authorising it."[119] Whether through street demonstrations, the ballot box or the tattle press, democracy is better at stripping authority away. It tears the place down better than it builds things up. It smashes icons, more than it raises banners of unity. Its professed election night rite fails. The people do not join together in service of a single authority. So, Dunn wrote:

> What it cannot ever do with comparable conclusiveness is authorise particular holders of power, and what it can virtually never do is authorise particular state decisions unless the parameters of these are luminously clear in themselves and can be put in that form to a demos genuinely equipped to understand them. It is especially implausible to see iterative mass suffrage elections, even under conditions of uncoerced participation, and unconstrained and effectively equalised opportunity for the citizens to communicate and inform themselves as yet unmet in any modern state, as authorising the particular decisions their victors proceed to make.

This condition makes democracies a constant insurrection of the ambitious against the established. The contestants for power in today's political order suppress this revolt. They seek to mute this conflict by making democracies "sedative and uninformative" through modern manipulative marketing-politics. Democracy has fallen into a

---

[119] *Breaking democracy's spell*, 2014.

perfunctory checkbox every few years. Trump's celebrity TV candidature was an insurrection against this sedative regime of the politicos.

John Dunn helps us break the spell of democracy. Reading his difficult sentences helps us to avoid misty sentiment about democracy, or hysterical nonsense about Trump being our century's Hitler. His book encourages us rather to look at the kaleidoscope of 'our democracy' and see arrangements of multiple political orders. Dunn wrote:

> I have argued that we need to learn to understand democracy very differently: to see it more clearly, hear it with less self-congratulatory ears, recognize more accurately where its real potency comes from, and face up to the limits of its capacity to direct our political purposes. To do so, we need now to take in the historical process that has inserted democracy so prominently into the way we see and feel politics and struggle to understand it. More hazardously and ambitiously, I argue that our cumulative failure to do any of these things gravely aggravates many of the worst dangers that now menace us as a species. We need to find a way out of the maze democracy has become for us and face the awesome decisions that lie ahead as directly and lucidly as we can.

Some of those decisions, he intimated gloomily, may now be beyond human control. America's decline, I feel sure, is now beyond any President's control. But are democracies' discontents also boiling beyond our control? I fear yes, but counsel not despair, but a return to cherishing ordinary virtues in distressing times.

Letter from Melbourne, mirror to the post-democratic world

(From *The Burning Archive,* 14 September 2021.)

This long letter comes from the locked down city of Melbourne. I explore between its lines what had led to the recent international disgrace of Australia's reputation. It is an essay. All statements are provisional, uncertain attempts to make sense of two troubling questions facing us today. Are we losing our democracies? Have the public health responses to COVID accelerated our loss?

1. *"Australia has fallen"*

Australia's weird and W.E.I.R.D. (Western, educated, industrialized, rich and democratic) authoritarian response to coronavirus has been making global headlines. As COVID-Zero has deranged the minds of our elites, the world's perceptions of my country have flipped dramatically.

We were once some faraway place for a sun-drenched holiday, but are now the largest prison on earth, visible from space. We were once home to an extraordinary crop of Hollywood favoured actors, but are now a talent agency of chief health officers, who, dizzy with fame, earnestly tell their docile populations not to talk to each other, not to catch balls kicked into the crowd at football games, and to believe, contrary to their own facts, that the virus has intelligence and wicked intent, and that the masses are sick until proven healthy (just assume you have the virus even though less than 0.1 per cent of those tested actually do). And then they spoke, if in a bit of a funk, of the 'New World Order' they were bringing into being.

We were once the loyal, laughing, outer province of the Anglo-

Towards Life After Democracy

American empire of democracy, but some American media present us variously as a fascist or communist state, an over-ripe Weimar Germany that has fallen to the Nazis, complete with quarantine camps for the infected or unvaccinated, or a slave state in Communist China's Belt and Road Rim that is testing its master's social credit scheme.

There has been no shortage of absurd statements and chilling actions to justify this change of perception. Many are perfect for satire, comedy and ridicule, even if they are outlier events, which ordinary people in this besieged city shrug off with muted grumbles. A caged poet like me writes to no one about *ketman* and Czeslaw Milosz. We have seen dogs being shot, people told to drink beer through masks, and someone, who sneezed in a lift, being hunted down like a fugitive.

More menacingly, we have seen protesters, including children, being shot with pepper spray and rubber bullets. At the iconic corner of Flinders Street station, Melbourne's dull postcard gateway to its bluestone grid of shops, black-armoured riot police-soldiers faced off at protesters who called for an end to lockdowns and the arbitrary rules of our new COVID-safe tyranny. One police officer taunted the protesters, 'Come at me, you pussy.' Another shot a pelt of pepper spray, but the panic in his face was visible because he had untidily pulled his obedience mask down to his chin. The police later enlisted an hysterical, complicit media to denounce the protesters as enemies of the people. When the protesters responded by publishing the names of the miscreant police officers, the police state made use of its emergency powers, and arrested the dissidents.

While these events occurred, the local servants of the social media oligarchs briefly allowed to trend the hashtag, #AustraliahasFallen. It captured a mood among a small marginalised group in the population who had the courage to refuse to live in the lie. Australia had indeed fallen. The truth is Australia had descended into something other than democracy. This descent was steepest in my state of Victoria, home of the secret ballot and cradle of liberal democracy in the nineteenth

13 Ways of Looking at a Bureaucrat

century.

All sorts of public health orders were declared, but the reasons and the evidence supporting these regulations never released. For heaven's sake, children's playgrounds were closed, and then worse still, those rules were enforced by signs, barriers and petty tyrants. Why? The Chief Health Officer had noticed, or had informants report to HQ, some 'non-compliant behaviour'. Parliaments have been shut down on the basis of letters from minor officials. Seeming authoritarianism has been cheered on by journalists who audition for a starring role in a post-totalitarian theatre-state. Totalitarianism dehumanises by forbidding questions, and regrettably Australia's media have been the strongest secret police to enforce that prohibition.

The hashtag, #AustraliahasFallen, was a cry for help to the outer world, that our new masters in the Great Southern Land had forbidden us to travel to. Like subjects of Eastern European communist states, we sent out to America, Europe and, ironically, Russia, coded dissident messages in our new *samizdat* with the hope we could free Australia from tyranny. Oh, to be in Copenhagen today.

When the messages were first noticed, including by major TV hosts like Tucker Carlson, sighs of relief came from the locked down, isolated and quarantined dissidents of Australia. This recognition gave succour to the silenced, courage to the ostracised, and purpose to the persecuted. Laughter, mockery and sarcasm had survived. They were the residual powers of the powerless. When we, chroniclers of a besieged city, saw Tucker Carlson mock our local authorities, we heard Zbigniew Herbert's words, from "Mr Cogito on Upright Attitudes", where in a besieged city a weak man realises not much is left to him but the choice of an attitude or a final word before the end.

But after a while, the stories began to grate. Just as complacent, Americans in the 1970s and 1980s never really understood the dissidents of Eastern Europe on their own terms, so these contemporary media figures did not bother to learn what was really happening in Australia. They did not ask, what were our real concerns, or what was our real experience? Ignorant of the historical situation, they spouted off with their narcissistic cultural obsessions. In one case, a respected conservative outlet, *The Federalist*, set an intern to write a piece that claimed that Australia's democratic self-defeat was due to giving up our guns.[120] WTF? Australia's tough gun laws were introduced by a conservative Prime Minister in 1996, twenty-five years ago. No one in Australia thinks that American gun rights make any sense at all.

Both Big Media, like Fox, and independent media, like Tim Pool, repeated silly stories. Neither ever bothered to ask about the facts. They just traded cartoon card misunderstandings, counters of self-obsession. Our enslavement was exploited for news entertainment, whether on news media or social media. Our democratic catastrophe became yet another ephemeral piece of clickbait.

It is doing more harm than good. Each time it happens, the local authorities and their media servants jump on the distortions as examples of fake news and extremism. The authorities manipulate the news, with the American entertainment media's support, to present the Australian dissidents and protesters as conspiracy theorists, far-right nut-jobs, Made-in-America Trump-obsessed ideologues, or cruel libertarians who are inspired by Ayn Rand's madder moments. They are given permission not to report the simpler truth; that these dissidents are Australians who want to live in truth, freedom and civil society, not in a medical tyranny of COVID-safe practices. As Australians used to say when playing two-up: come in, spinner.

Some people have objected. Claire Lehmann from *Quillette* commented on the distortions presented in the global media in a tweet that said: "the vast majority of people tweeting about Australia don't actually care about us, but are instead using impressions of what is

---

[120] 'Pursuing 'COVID Zero' Has Turned Australia Into An Authoritarian State,' *The Federalist*, 9 September 2021.

going on here to further their own domestic culture war interests."[121]

But the international criticism provoked in many people a more defensive response. One ABC Broadcaster, a leading member of our new virtual Union of Soviet Writers, Josh Szeps, set out to defend the covidocratic regime. While he recognised that Australia was having a 'viral moment', his handlers insisted he set out 'essential context for American followers and interested Aussies'. Szeps made the fallen Australian democracy sound like a progressive COVID Zero heaven.[122] Other commentators can make the corrections, especially to the misreading of our blight as a deviation from American institutions and ideas. I would still like to thank the media of the world for drawing attention to the situation in Australia.

Things are very serious here indeed, especially in the state in which I serve as a lowly under-castellan, Victoria. There is a mental health crisis. We have endured a state of emergency since March 2020. It reminds me of the Eastern European communist states that I studied in my youth. The authorities of this state pretend to lead, and we pretend to follow. Normal rules of government decision making have not applied – like Cabinet processes, cost-benefit assessment, regulatory or social impact assessments, consultation with the affected, or open deliberation on alternatives in public forums. We have pursued a progressive, bureaucratic and medical utopia of COVID Zero. We have paid a stunning cost for this impossible dream. It is something that should never happen again, and hopefully, at the right time in the right way by the right people, this disaster will be deeply investigated and reflected on. In the meantime, Gigi Foster's book, *The Great COVID Panic: what happened, why and what to do next* can give us insight and a start towards a better way.

I have made comment on the pandemic situation on this blog before in posts on 'Public Health Rules, OK?', 'From here to immunity:

---

[121] twitter.com/clairlemon/status/1434712745442643970 Account since deleted.
[122] twitter.com/joshzepps/status/1434692531892076548

charting COVID from pandemic to endemic', 'The failure of institutions in the pandemic crisis', 'Dr Cogito endures Melbourne's fifth lockdown', and 'Cease the endless war against the virus'. I have also briefly written on the concept of post-democracy in 'The post-democratic society is here'. But these earlier posts referred to the global pandemic situation, and made only limited specific references to my own polity. Dear reader, please understand that when I write these words, this polity in which I dwell is trapped in a state of emergency that suspends the normal rules and conventions of civil, open society. I am constrained in what I can say, but determined to live in truth, even if that may be written between the lines. Even saying what I have done may be considered dangerous. If I am prosecuted or disappeared or ostracised or otherwise punished, the regime will have revealed its teeth to me.

2. *Australia is a mirror to the post-democratic world*

The world needs to understand, however, two essential points about our situation in Melbourne: what is happening in Australia is not over, and it is not only about Australia.

I would invite the world not to indulge in panic porn, which spreads the very virus that has disabled our democracies. Rather, dear outside, once-free world, please view Australia as a mirror to the world, a mirror to your own situation. There you see, reflected in surgical light, the common suffering of our post-democratic societies. There you see, the flaws of your own republics in distress. We, citizens abandoned in the Southern Ocean, are not waving. We are drowning. A few brave lifesavers are ringing a bell of rescue. But ask not for whom the bell tolls. It tolls for thee.

What are the features of this post-democratic world? It is, I confess, an imperfect term. It gestures to that which comes after, but does not define what this new political order is. The term emerged from the 1990's and Blairite New Brittania in a book by Colin Crouch, which provoked some academic debate. In 2021 Crouch discussed his idea of post-democracy, how the crises of recent years, especially crises of populism, had intensified the trend away from democratic systems.[123] In his earlier work, Crouch wrote:

> A post-democratic society is one that continues to have and to use all the institutions of democracy, but in which they increasingly become a formal shell. The energy and innovative drive pass away from the democratic arena and into small circles of a politico-economic elite.[124]

Crouch identified four essential features of post-democracy. First, democratic forms persist without meaning or real effect. There are elections and other institutional forms, but they meet the letter, not the spirit, of the law. Second, all the major forms of democracy or political institutions are hollowed out. Eliot's 'hollow men' has become a term to describe the actors of the post-democratic political order. Hollow actors prevail in democratic assemblies, law making, executive action and elections. Public deliberation and debate among informed citizens is stripped down into set-piece panel shows. The protections of liberties and minority rights, especially freedom of conscience and speech, are hollow. The 'separation of powers' operates in name only. In theory, this democratic form ensures the legal-rational state apparatus is subordinated to the democratic assembly, scrutinised by an impartial judicial system, and enlivened by a responsible political executive. But the shell is hollow. The rule of law, in which all powers are constrained by public law, open scrutiny and social conventions, fades to grey. Third, political actors are disconnected from the lifeworld of ordinary people. As a result, the relationship between political operatives and the 'punters' is characterised increasingly by manipulation. Fourth, the elite is corrupt, in a broad ethical sense. Political elites have lost clear separation from private interests, and damaged their integrity. They have lost focus on the public good, the

---

[123] Webinar with Prof. Colin Crouch, "Post-Democracy After the Crises," VUZF University, 14 April 2021, YouTube.
[124] Colin Crouch, *Coping with Post-Democracy* (2000).

republic. In Crouch's analysis, this entanglement of public and private focuses very much on relationships between politicians and business leaders. His prime examples are privatisation, deregulation and the dominant neo-liberal economic policies of the last 40 years. But in the post-democracy of the 2020's, this entanglement, without brown paper-bag corruption, affects other elites. All manner of experts, media commentators, high-profile journalists, university thought leaders, consultants, community celebrities and entertainers are paid to lend their brand to government and political advertising campaigns.

In the era of COVID, this soft corruption of the experts has been exposed in medicine and science, which were formerly institutions that claimed to be pure exponents of just truth. John Ioannidis recently published an important article, 'How the pandemic is changing the norms of science', that explored the disastrous impact on democratic public health of this blind enthronement of 'following the science'.

> Politics had a deleterious influence on pandemic science. Anything any apolitical scientist said or wrote could be weaponized for political agendas. Tying public health interventions like masks and vaccines to a faction, political or otherwise, satisfies those devoted to that faction, but infuriates the opposing faction. This process undermines the wider adoption required for such interventions to be effective. Politics dressed up as public health not only injured science. It also shot down participatory public health where people are empowered, rather than obligated and humiliated.[125]

Public health leaders have created a public health disaster by obligating and humiliating the people who they could have empowered. This disaster may take years to recover from. It is an essential feature of the democratic malaise that we are suffering from. But this malaise is not unique to COVID. It reflects a more general way of doing things in the post-democratic political order, including in the idea multiplex

---

[125] John Ioannidis, 'How The Pandemic Is Changing The Norms Of Science,' *Tablet Magazine*, 9 September 2021.

of research and science.

Crouch's analysis of post-democracy has strengths, but needs to be extended. It especially needs to be extended to reflect the culture, institutions and actors that have revealed themselves as the real enemies of democracy during the pandemic. I would add three features of post-democracy to those described by Crouch.

The first additional attribute I would define is that post-democracy operates a media/theatre state. The great anthropologist, Clifford Geertz, coined the term 'theatre state' to describe Bali in the 19th century.[126] In the theatre state, Geertz wrote, 'Pomp served power, not pomp power.' The theatre state is governed by rituals and symbols, rather than by force. It aims not for tyranny, conquest, or effective administration, but rather spectacle. In our emerging media/theatre states, the spectacle is performed on TV, radio and digital media, not on stage or in dance. But the spectacle still becomes a new form of pomp, which other authors, Baudrillard and the situationists, anticipated with the terms 'hyperreality' and 'simulacrum'. In the post-democratic society, the realities of power and authority can not be discovered outside the entangled worlds of political media spin. Politics becomes simulation. The real and the imaginary have been absorbed into the symbol. Politics becomes a symbolic performance of a chosen narrative. For example, the response to COVID was the perfect melodrama in which the caring state and responsible media kept us all safe from evil viruses and the enemies within.

The second attribute of post-democracy that I would add to Crouch's analysis is that post-democracy is characterised by degraded institutions. In the media/theatre state, simulacra of the state replace real public institutions that can moderate the culture and behaviour of citizens. The behaviour of power serving pomp infects all public institutions, not just the mainstream media. All institutions are raided

---

[126] Clifford Geertz, *Negara: the Theatre State in Nineteenth-Century Bali* (1981).

by parasitic performers. As Yuval Levin argued, performance dominates all institutions, where purpose once ruled. The degeneration into performance distorts the functions of these institutions. They are twisted to serve the individuals who claim control of them, and no longer cultivate individuals who serve deeper purposes. In Levin's view, all institutions, from Congress to courts to classes to culture, have become platforms for the performance of a personal brand. They no longer function as cloistered schools in a virtuous life.

So much more could be written on this topic, and I have previously commented on the topic in my podcast episode six, 'The true history of the bureaucracy gang', and episode seven, 'The ordinary virtues of governing well'. But let me just quote Levin, without endorsing his typically insular belief in American exceptionalism, on the destructive force of institutional leaders who perform in social media:

> The argument of the book is about the importance of institutions as the formative structures of our social lives and therefore of ourselves. Social media, when seen through that lens, and as it now presents itself, is just a profoundly destructive force. It disintermediates: it pulls people out of institutions that are fundamentally mediative institutions, puts people on platforms by themselves, and asks them to participate, basically passively, in acts of affirmation and peer pressure. It just puts on the table some vague, shallow notion and says to everybody, "Thumbs up or thumbs down." That's just an awful way to mediate our social existence as a society. And the more of that social life that we channel through social media, the worse we become.[127]

The third additional feature of post-democracy is that cultural and social fragmentation degrades the sense of belonging to an 'imagined community', coterminous with the state. As Benedict Anderson

---

[127] Yuval Levin, 'Our Post-Pandemic Institutions: A Conversation With Yuval Levin' 3 May 2021, and *A Time to Build: From Family and Community to Congress and the Campus, How Recommitting to Our Institutions Can Revive the American Dream* (2021).

famously wrote, nation states were formed not just by government institutions, but by the 'imagined community' of a nation. These communities or identities were imagined in newspapers, discussion clubs, mass media and other cultural practices. These national communities were imagined in a time of shared headlines, common narratives and newspapers of record. But today's culture has been shattered by time-shifted streaming, filter bubbles, and the attention economy. With no common cultural platform, our societies have fragmented.

We have not yet discovered how virtuous republics can serve these fragmented societies. Again, I could say more, but will keep it elliptical here in this already over-long post that may yet endanger me. I have addressed this topic in previous posts, 'Cultural fragmentation and the collapse of authority in Western democracies', and in my podcast, such as episode 12, 'Towards the Society of Islands'.

These are fragmentary ideas of an essayist, who is condemned to live outside the walls of privileged institutions. A more disciplined scholar might bring all these fragments together into a more comprehensive picture of post-democracy. But I think it is clear enough, this far into the pandemic, that the last ten years of teeth gnashing about the threats to democracy have been deadly distractions. They have been distractions whether they conceive the threat as neo-liberalism, Donald Trump or the elites. This post-democratic virus has infected us all, because we live, as we do, in compromised bodies, without the vaccine of strong institutions. Democracy is not threatened by a particular ideology or political movement. Populism is not the problem. Nor is progressive millenarianism, even with its recently fashionable revolutionary overtones. Our society is not post-democratic because one or other set of political ideas that we do not like have prevailed in the latest opinion poll. It is not post-democratic because anti-democratic forces have gathered strength. These political phenotypes have dwelt in thriving democracies for a long time. They are long-standing impulses, that have been at times destructive, at times creative. The problem today is these ideas, movements, ideologies and anti-democratic forces are no longer moderated by shared responsible institutions. The house of democracy has fallen.

As a result, the parasitic elite feeds off the dying body of politics. Democracy has become government of the elites, for the elites, by the elites. It merely imposes a few light obligations on those leaders who are convinced they are the elect. The people watch the spectacle, as if it were the sports of the *Hunger Games*. But the spectacle has little effect on their reality; unless they choose to ascend into the imagined community of the media/theatre state, and become cheering fans in a virtual stadium; unless they transform themselves from citizens into covidizens.

3. COVID, post-democracy and the rise of the covidizen

We cannot understand the course of the last years (2020 and 2021) unless we start with the assumption that COVID attacked already weakened, if not dying, democracies. COVID infected a weakened, immune-compromised body politics. It incited existing inflammations and infections, such as decadent elites, rampant technocracy, hollow institutions, miscreant universities, a poisoned public sphere, millenarian progressivism, and resentful populism.

It entered post-democracy through the vulnerable sites of this broken system. The normal checks and balances had already stopped working. The traditions of institutional moderation were no longer taught. Government by *diktat* was already a preferred option. Then COVID enthroned it. The coronation was based on public health advice, which followed the science. But the real power behind the throne was fear; fear, driven by manipulative strategies which were dressed up for respectability as 'behavioural insights'.

As Laura Dodsworth has shown, the use of fear against the citizenry, and the unethical application of behavioural science by political leaders, bureaucrats, consultants and researchers, drove the response to the pandemic in many parts of the world.[128] Fear helped to create the phenomenon of the covidizen. But to understand the extreme path taken by Australia, it is necessary to understand two contextual conditions. These conditions were the particular way in which the disease spread in our island continent, and the power of public health ideas and institutions in our political history. Both of these contextual conditions exacerbated our vulnerability to the post-democratic virus.

The timing and nature of the COVID spread in our island continent affected our response, especially as the world's media obliterated differences between countries and contexts. Australia is an island nation. Its borders presented a high sea wall against the early waves of the pandemic. This natural advantage allowed for early apparent success, when Europe and America burned, but it trapped our leaders, officials, media, epidemiologists and zealots in a gambler's curse. The 'first wave' never really came to our shores, just like the 1918 Spanish Influenza pandemic came later to Australia. The advocates of COVID Zero, however, misunderstood this random physical event in the circulation of a microscopic RNA virus around the globe. They mistook the weak ripple of COVID against our sea wall for an outcome that was determined by their actions and their policies. They attributed the early success in resisting the first wave, not to the nature of the wave, but the way in which they chose policies that 'go hard and go fast'. This attribution mistake created an illusion of control. They committed a cognitive fallacy, an attribution error, which an ethical 'behavioural insights' team would have warned them off. They attributed an event outside their control to their agency. The suffered the gambler's curse. The gamblers in our governments have been losing money on this same bet ever since.

There was one other contingent factor that I think was important

---

[128] Laura Dodsworth, *A State of Fear: How the UK government weaponised fear during the Covid-19 pandemic* (2021).

to the way COVID put Australian democracy in a death-grip. This factor influenced the political dynamics of the federation and the psychological state of the citizenry. COVID came to our shores just weeks after the extraordinary fires of the summer of 2019/2020. These fires captured global attention. They were deeply shocking and eerie as my own city was darkened by great clouds of smoke. The fires provided an opening for a new melodrama of the media-theatre state. Everyday on the news, on public broadcasts, the local response to the emergency dominated. State Premiers were the star actors. They control emergency services, disaster response and emergency legislation. They controlled the flow of information, emotion and narrative. They were given the perfect stage to perform every day as community saviours. But the Federal Government had no real role in responding to emergencies. They were stranded, and impotent, and were soon painted by the Premiers as uncaring, remote, impotent and out-of-touch with the sense of urgency on the ground. Almost to script, the Prime Minister happened to be enjoying a brief Pacific Island holiday with his family when the fires broke out. The pantomime raged on.

Then, the pandemic immediately followed the great fires. It channelled the same forces of social psychology. Leaders in politics and public health became reassuring or frightening 'risk communicators'. They ascended beyond political choices to the special zone of 'keeping us all safe'. The fires and then the pandemic converted Australian political news coverage into a rolling emergency, used for the purposes of the media-theatre state. And in this rolling emergency the state leaders had an advantage in reality not just optics. In the Australian federation, the State leaders primarily control the institutions and legislation of disaster response, police, public health and emergency services. Armed with both theatre and reality, the State Premiers pitted themselves against the national leader. They sought the crown of the Great Protector.

The institutions of public health also proved susceptible to the strain in progressive ideology of millenarianism.[129] This strain fuelled the COVID zero fallacy. I have hinted at how these ideas worked in public health. I will not explore it in detail here because it is not safe for me to say more.

But this fuel fanned flames that were burning all around the world, not only in Australia. They activated the authoritarian instinct that dwells in progressive minds. More than that, they energised a desire to mobilise around a new imagined community. In a recent episode of The *Rest is History* podcast the Silicon Valley entrepreneur, Marc Andreesen commented that digital media has created new potential to mobilise dispirited communities.[130] In ways, recent extremes in politics reflect this longing to belong. Most powerfully, however, the pandemic provided our media-theatre state, politicians, media and social media with a rare opportunity to join with the rest of the community, and to mobilise people into a sacred, life-and-death struggle.

They came together as an imagined, unavowable community, not as citizens. They came together as *covidizens*. They took to heart the endless banal pleas that we can be more together by staying further apart. They watched the daily press conferences, and pronounced on Twitter on the case numbers. Their certainty was never matched by the quality of their analysis. They followed the pronouncements of epidemiologists and media doctors. They turned themselves into data scientists and conversed about R numbers and delta variants. They stood outside their homes to clap the NHS in the United Kingdom. They posted 'vaccies' of themselves getting the shots. They dutifully banned their own children from visiting their homes. They denounced 'covidiots', who reported breaches of COVID-safe rules, and who sheltered in secure places. They religiously practised the new rites of social distancing.

There will come a time when this imagined community will fade

---

[129] On progressive millenarianism, Yuri Slezkine, *The House of Government: A Saga of the Russian Revolution* (2017).
[130] *Rest is History*, Episode 94 (September 2021), 'Silicon Valley Part 2'.

and dissolve. Then, the spectacle of the pandemic will no longer carry on. Our post-democratic states will then face new questions. Was the pandemic an unique circumstance? Was this the only crisis that the authorities can use to mobilise this community? Or will a new cause be found? Will *covidizens* be reawakened and marched to new unwittingly authoritarian drums? Will our weak civil institutions ever recover sufficiently to resist the next wave of communitarian infection?

4. *The broken mirror of democracy.*

The collapse of democracy in Australia has been frightening, but leaves us all with a difficult task. Australia is a warning to the world because we show the 'free world' its fate. We, in the outer reaches of the empire of democracy, know that American leaders wake each morning, stand before the indispensable mirror, and ask, 'Mirror, mirror on the wall, who is the finest democracy of all?'

The whole free world should know that we, Australians, once did that too. We once preened ourselves, spellbound, before the mirror of democracy, and listed our democratic achievements. Home of the secret ballot. A record of no substantial civil violence. No coups engineered by technocrats nor generals. One of the oldest continuous democracies in the world. But Australians can no longer perform that vanity ritual. Nor do ordinary Australians ever look enviously at America as the beacon of democracy. We see rather a failed state on that distant, deforested hill.

There is an old superstition that to break a mirror will bring many years of bad luck. The spell of democracy is broken. The mirror on the wall is shattered. We need to learn to see our political world, our social institutions, our cultural freedoms as they really are. We should no longer trap ourselves in the spell of this mesmerising tradition.

As John Dunn, *eminence grise* of political theory, has written, democracy is a formula for imagining subjection to the power and will of others without sacrificing personal dignity or interests. But in the dying generations of Western democracy, after the pandemic, who can say that they have not sacrificed their personal dignity in subjection to the will of zealots in these last few years? Do you sacrifice your dignity when you walk around a lake, with your face concealed behind a useless mask that only advertises your obedience to the public health rules? Who can say they have not voluntarily jeopardised individual or family interests when they cannot attend the death of a parent? The funeral of a friend? When you cannot open your business despite the supermarket, full of people, operating a mile down the road? Truly, COVID has broken the spell of democracy.

John Dunn also wrote that the spell of democracy is not capable of handling the great collective problems of human societies today. This failure of self-government is an intellectual embarrassment, a political threat, and may become a biological disaster. Dunn was thinking of climate change; but he may also have predicted the pandemic, which may have been initiated by the grandiose misadventures of American funded research to control pandemics by manipulating coronaviruses, in a Wuhan lab. Dunn wrote that modern professionalised, commoditised politics had stripped the democratic public from nearly all overt public decisions. Society is left with a shell of:

> unremittingly pseudo-democratic authorisation of the entire structure of of covert or inadvertent decision and non-decision within which those overt decisions nest. In this setting, the predication of democracy has become overwhelmingly sedative and disinformative.

Dunn's book was published in 2014. In 2020, the mask fell from this pseudo-democracy. In the decade ahead, the world will need to learn how to deal with the reality so exposed. What comes next? I do not know. All I can see is a bounded patch of ethical concern for the others who share this place and this virtual reality state with me. We may not any longer be a democracy, but we still need to act ethically in the governments that we share, even if we, the people, do not control them. Politics is practical ethical action for others and for strangers, as

Vaclav Havel wrote. It is not ideals. It is not vision. It is not freedom. It is not limited to democracy. It is much more than safety. It is time to leave behind the zeal of the *covidizens*.

Talleyrand once described the critical quality of a good diplomat as 'an absence of zeal'. The same might be said of good governments. It is certainly true of public health officials. It is surely time to oblige these officials to curb their zeal, and to strip them of their rank. By allowing other cultures and other leaders into the service of greater public institutions, those ruined remnants of our once democratic institutions, we might craft a more virtuous way of public life.

13 Ways of Looking at a Bureaucrat

Chapter Thirteen   On Leaving the Maze of Power

On Leaving the Maze of Power

I have wandered now for over 30 years in this strange maze of power. Did I find the Minotaur at the centre of this maze? Will I end my days here, unsatisfied and defeated? Will I die inside this maze? Has the Minotaur, that I believed I had hunted, in fact stalked me for these three decades, and will it spring out from some hidden niche now that this human prey is exhausted, disoriented and at the final border of his mind?

In the last five years of my government career, I had asked myself many times, loyalty, voice or exit? Hirschman's dilemma came to my mind more frequently, more urgently as I grew old, and with more despair. I had failed to govern the drunken commons. My testimony on childhood sexual abuse was ignored, and only gave me vicarious trauma. My last attempts to reach out to a decent political leader to implement ordinary virtues in government ended in silence and humiliation. I had endured one whole year as a bureaucrat in the time of terror. I had come to believe that I would never be accepted in the organisation that I had come to know as the Department of Hell and Human Suffering (my darker name for the Department of Health and Human Services). I looked on helplessly as the government was infected by a totalitarian virus during the Plague Years. I had seen my best work praised, but left unrewarded. I had been shunned and disparaged. I believed, with some reasons, I had been blacklisted. I had stared into the abyss for too long. It was time for me to learn to stop hunting monsters in government. It was time for Orpheus to leave the Department of Hell and Human Suffering, and not look back. I chose exit.

My last year in government was difficult. I began a journal, *The year of governing dangerously*, but I did not maintain it. It was a project of heroism. It expressed hope that the reality of modern institutions of government could be other than they were. I oscillated between hope that there was someone out there who would listen to me, and black despair. I still clung to a personal narrative that I could extract revenge, or, in more noble terms, that I could persuade the great and good of the world to deliver justice. I still, if fitfully and in a fading cadence, dreamed that there was a good Minotaur somewhere in this maze. If I could speak to an honourable politician or an honest ombudsman or a true investigative journalist then the truth would still live in this state. I could let these paragons of virtue know what I had seen. They could give me more time, and keep my belief in virtuous government today going a little longer. Finally, I imagined there would be someone who would listen to how I had suffered. I could show the world, at last, how at least one ordinary bureaucrat, with his heart in the right place, had not succumbed to the new monstrous post-democratic state. I struggled in the rips and the tides, but I never drowned. I still clung to my dying belief that a new virtuous tribune of the people would declare the truth, and democracy would be saved. Then my faith in power would be restored.

I imagined myself like Roy in *Bladerunner*, going to meet my maker at Tyrone Corporation, and demanding my faults be rectified so that I would have more time. Violence I refused, but still at times I sought an intellectual revenge. I would expose the treason of the clerks. I reviewed the documents in my possession or within my direct access that showed the treason, betrayal, cowardice and dishonesty that so deranged me. I thought if I released these documents to honest media or purposeful politicians, then surely someone would listen. But I couldn't find them. I couldn't find them. There were specific issues that troubled me most. The lies about the safe injecting room, and the failure of ethics of the behavioural insights teams troubled me. But the greatest burden was the vast fiasco of the the COVID zero fantasy, and its catastrophic consequences.

But I realised after a time that these obsessions were merely poisonous vapours spread by the dark powers that had created this maze of power. I could not change how power worked in the state. I could not change it from the inside, that was the path of loyalty. I could not change it by speaking out with the sponsorship of a powerful outsider or critic, that was the path of loyalty. I had to leave.

On Leaving the Maze of Power

So I began to imagine myself again as Roy from *Bladerunner*, but not when he confronted his maker, but after the final hand-to-hand combat with Deckard (the Harrison Ford character). On top of the ruined building in a dystopian Los Angeles, Roy speaks as a defeated but honoured combatant to the Bladerunner who will share his fate before too long. Bleeding and broken, decorated by pouring rain, Roy speaks with straightened back of all that he has seen and done.

> I've seen things you people wouldn't believe. Attack ships on fire off the shoulder of Orion. I watched C-beams glitter in the dark near the Tannhäuser Gate. All those moments will be lost in time, like tears in rain. Time to die.

It was time for me to leave. It was time for me to die in the underworld maze of power, and go to some new sprung field. It was time to renounce ambition, renounce power and renounce political life. And, as in Herbert's poem, I realised the only power left to me, this broken victim, besieged in an inescapable maze, was to choose a final word.

I let go of the struggle. I accepted my status as an abandoned outcast. There were consequences. I was bullied and given odd jobs, well beneath my ability. I filled holes, served functions, played roles, facilitated outcomes, stuck to bad structures, and nodded silently at grandiose strategic plans. I worked diligently, but with no conviction. No one wanted my real ideas. No one really wanted to engage with my skills. No one wanted to govern seriously with virtue. Occasionally, I would feel the old bureaucratic fire within. I had a short burst of belief in the honour of my dying profession when I worked on the outcomes framework of the department, that is the way in which it measured its effects on the real world. I approached it with intellectual seriousness. But before long I discovered that some overpaid consultants, who were friends of the Secretary, wanted to roll out their patented techniques and dumb ideas. These fights were no longer mine, however, and I prepared to leave.

13 Ways of Looking at a Bureaucrat

I was working on a health technology statement when the information about the redundancy packages came out. I had been anticipating these redundancy packages for some time because the finances of the government were so bad. It was only a question of time when they would want to push out the older bureaucrats, so they could make room in the salary budget for a new stream of patronage. I believed these financial problems would only get worse so these redundancy packages would likely be the best deal on offer. In any case, I could no longer psychologically endure the ostracism, the corruption, the politicisation and the degradation of the institution that I had reluctantly given three decades of my life to. If I had any belief that an election result might displace the ruling party from power, I might have acted differently. But that is the old illusion of the maze talking. In truth, I had lost faith in our democracy and the virtual reality state. I had been lured by false hope too many times before.

I began to prepare myself for a life as an independent author, who was no longer a minor government official. I had launched my Burning Archive podcast in April 2021, and published my book of poetry in June 2021. I began to assemble my writings into the book that became, *From the Burning Archive: Selected Essays and Fragments*, which I released a few weeks after my final departure. I began to plan and assemble the writing on government that became this book. I worked through various financial, career and personal issues. But the deepest difficulty was to shed the illusions of power. I had no fantasy that I was leaving with a sense of accomplishment, honour, or pride. Power had degraded me. It had abandoned and betrayed me. It left me to bleed out among my fallen comrades, while the mercenary, incompetent officers fled the scene. I knew that I was just one more body count in the collateral damage of the endless wars of power.

My departure carried no weight. It had no impact, and so I began to practise detachment. I found that the maze I had struggled in for so long began to dissipate. At first, it was like a glitching computer game. Then, ultimately the mists dissolved completely. I realised those high

On Leaving the Maze of Power

walls, small cells and long walkways were mists made in my mind.

My last bosses acted as if they took an interest, some with more sincerity than others. They were all younger and less experienced than me; but they were also more politically connected or deluded than me. One boss, who had formerly been a political adviser, put me in touch with his friend who worked at the School of Government. Unknown to the young boss, I had helped to found this School twenty years before. This ex-adviser even suggested that I contact various Labor party politicians. I politely told him that was all a bit political for me. He then suggested I give a fireside chat about what the next generation should learn. To whom, I asked? Well to him, of course. It was all a piece of incompetently executed flattery with the aim of misdirection.

I abandoned all plans of being a whistle-blower. I had even come to question whether some of the watchdogs were really lapdogs for the regime. I let go of any plans to hold onto evidence of misdoing. I had abandoned my journal of the year of living dangerously. I let go of all my documents and records. I still reviewed my files and many of my emails to reflect on my experiences. I looked back at all those tears in rain. I thought I might keep some emails and main briefings as a kind of a record of my "intellectual property", as a journal of my long difficult journey through the maze. But in the last two months, I let go even of these thoughts to archive these personal work documents. I deleted all emails, but those that were formal public records. I stopped holding on to any Cabinet-in-confidence emails, in the false belief that any email sent to me could be consequential enough to retain. I deleted all my draft documents, and let go of all my records. I only kept a few public domain documents, such as the media stories on the report on assisted reproductive treatment, which I was proud of. I shed thirty-three years of tracks and fingerprints in this maze.

My last days in government were simple and lonely. On paper, government staff were working three days a week in the office. In practice, it was more like one, and many people still hid behind masks

13 Ways of Looking at a Bureaucrat

and Teams screens. I put effort into a writing course in which I shared much that I had learnt in my greatest skill of my 30 year career, and perhaps my only true vocation. I let go of all attachments.

My farewell event was attended by maybe a dozen people, of whom a handful were dear to me. No senior leadership attended. None let me know they would not. None even said goodbye. My Director, who was a good man in a bad culture, had messaged me just before lunch to ask if there was a summary of my career that I could send him so he could prepare a farewell speech. I had deleted all my personal files and resumes, and scrubbed my entire existence in the department from the electronic records available to me by this time. So I let him know there was a summary on my Linkedin page. As we chatted at the farewell event, he got Linkedin up on his phone, and, as we stood shoulder to shoulder, he consulted my public lies about a successful career in government, to frame his farewell speech. The disregard, blatant or blundering though it was, did not blind me. By contrast, I had spent considerable time thinking about my farewell speech, even if I was to be reduced to preaching to the birds. I had considered speeches of vindication, of revenge, of spite, of declaration, and of defiance. I had considered performing Roy's final words from *Bladerunner*, since now it was my time to die. But I chose in the end a speech of gratitude and release. I spoke of three things over the three decades of my career that I was grateful for, and three good things I had done. It was a simple mindfulness exercise applied to my life as a bureaucrat. I was happy with my final speech written in government. I received a modest gift voucher as a farewell; gold watches on retirement are no more. But it did not trouble me. The maze had dissipated, and I could see the open field in the distance, and how easy it was to leave the underworld.

My farewell was held three days before I was to leave. It had been scheduled on a Wednesday afternoon because all staff of the unit were attending a 'policy skills' training workshop over the last two days of my final week. I thought I would attend the school of government training, if only to see if this was something I could offer as a post-bureaucratic career. I knew the trainer from 20 years before, when I had worked on arts policy with Terry Moran. I had even applied to be her successor in her role then; yet another role that I was never seriously considered for; yet another illusion that I could slay the Minotaur in the maze, if only I could find it. I arrived late on the first day, and said hello to my former colleague. I let her know, before the whole group, that I was leaving. I doubt any of the organisers and executives knew that I had known her. The training proved to be too trite for me, though entertaining and energetic. I left at midday. I walked through the city and went to the paperback and Hill of Content bookshops, where I picked up one or two history books and classics. Then I took myself home. That afternoon I joined the afternoon quiz, which had been established as an organisational ritual by some former colleagues and staff of mine. Their final question was, "Who is the author of *Gathering Flowers of the Mind*?" The true virtues are found in the ordinary places.

The next day I went into the office, for the last time ever, to hand in my security pass, phone and laptop. I did not bother going to the policy training workshop. I said farewell to the serving ladies and managers of the cafes at which I had bought morning coffee in Madame Brussels Lane for so many years. I sat in a desolate sun-glared corner, near to a desk I had once occupied on the ninth floor, and did some final acts of expurgation. I answered one or two messages from people who wished me well, though they could not make my farewell. I waited to see if any senior leader would have the grace to send a message to me. But I did not waste much time on this last false hope. There was no farewell notice. No graceful message of good wishes came. There was not even a trite email of thanks. I walked the floor that my Division occupied to see if there were old colleagues to say a last goodbye to. But they were all strangers. How could I know that death had undone so many? I thought that I might walk the other floors of the building to farewell any remaining old colleagues, since I remembered how touched I was once thirty years before when Terry Moran had done that. But the emptiness of the floor discouraged me.

13 Ways of Looking at a Bureaucrat

I changed my plan, and decided to leave a message of blessing on a whiteboard. I considered the whiteboard where I had taught my writing class, but it was exposed. I found another whiteboard in a 'creative space area' that acted as a passageway between desks and the bathrooms. There, I wrote the stanza from Pound's *Pisan Cantos* that I had adopted as a kind of prayer of ostracism. Pound himself wrote this poem when incarcerated for treason in a cage at the US Army base outside Pisa. I wrote without any explanation on the barren whiteboard, among diagrams and watchwords, "What thou lovest well remains the rest is dross." I wrote in imperfect blue ink on the whiteboard, among calculations and strategies, "What thou lov'st well shall not be reft from thee." I wrote, with no plan and no objective, on the crowded, useless whiteboard, "What thou lov'st well is thy true heritage." I attributed Ezra Pound, but did not write down my own name on this lost whiteboard. I do not know if my message on the whiteboard survived the day. I do not know if it was ever read by anyone. I do not know if it was wiped off by some laughing clown within the hour that I had left. These words, however, were the last I was ever to write in government.

Then, by 11.30 AM, I had had enough. I took my technology to the ground floor kiosk, and severed the final digital connection to thirty-three years of work. I handed in my security pass, and thanked the staff for all their guardianship over the years. I turned around and began to leave. At that moment, a young executive, who was connected politically to the very top of the Victorian Government, flashed by. The executive greeted me with the usual bubbly, smiling haste, and bustled on to the next node of power. I had named this person in my submission to the Ombudsman on the politicisation of the public service. This person was the last I would ever speak to the Victorian Government. I walked through the revolving doors one last time. I took a photograph of myself outside the doors, and messaged my family that as this public servant left his career, he said, don't look back.

I had exhausted all thirteen ways of looking at a bureaucrat. I had

On Leaving the Maze of Power

found my way out of the maze of power. I had discovered that my own mind had imprisoned me in this poisoned maze for thirty-three years. Now it was time to discover what healthy illusions my mind could create. Now it was time to discover thirteen ways of looking at an author.

www.ingramcontent.com/pod-product-compliance
Lightning Source LLC
Chambersburg PA
CBHW071951290426
44109CB00018B/1989